WOMEN AGAINST CENSORSHIP

ESSAYS BY

VARDA BURSTYN
JUNE CALLWOOD
SARA DIAMOND
LISA DUGGAN
ANNA GRONAU
NAN HUNTER
LYNN KING
MYRNA KOSTASH
THELMA McCORMACK
ANN SNITOW
LISA STEELE
MARIANA VALVERDE
CAROLE S. VANCE
LORNA WEIR

WOMEN

AGAINST

CENSORSHIP

EDITED BY

VARDA BURSTYN

DOUGLAS & McINTYRE

VANCOUVER & TORONTO

Douglas & McIntyre Ltd.
1615 Venables Street
Vancouver, British Columbia V5L 2H1

Canadian Cataloguing in Publication Data

Main entry under title:

Women against censorship

ISBN 0-88894-455-1.

1. Pornography – Social aspects.   2.
Censorship.   3. Feminism.   I. Burstyn,
Varda.   II. Callwood, June.

HQ471.W65 1985   363.4'7   C85-098057-7

Designed by Michael Solomon
Printed and bound in Canada

Table of Contents

Acknowledgments

This book is the product of a remarkable effort on the part of all of its contributors. Each one put aside pressing commitments to prepare articles, working under extremely difficult time constraints, and I want to thank them very much. Special thanks go to Lynn King, Lisa Steele and Ann Snitow, who at several points provided crucial moral and practical support, without which this volume would not have achieved its present form. In addition, I want to thank Patsy Aldana and Susan Ditta for constant encouragement and insight. To Gad Horowitz I owe an especially large debt for over a decade of exemplary inspiration. From Robin Wood I have learned much about imagery and the politics of culture. To Lynn Cunningham, whose skillful and tireless editing brought the book together, profuse thanks. Thanks too to Kelly Mitchell for much help and to Joanne Harris for valuable feedback. I want also gratefully to acknowledge the support of the Explorations Program of the Canada Council, and the people at CBC's *Ideas* for the opportunity to research and work through many important issues. Finally I want to express my appreciation to David Fujiwara, who helped me to live through the demanding process of producing this collection.

V.B.

Introduction

No one who reads newspapers, watches television or talks about politics with others can doubt that sex is embattled territory today.

In 1984 hardly a week went by in Canada without a major media story about struggle on one of its many fronts. The year was marked by the cross-country travels of the Special Committee on Pornography and Prostitution (the Fraser committee) and the hundreds of briefs presented to it by all kinds of interest groups; by the trial of those accused of firebombing Red Hot Video, a Vancouver porn outlet; by the passing of municipal bylaws restricting the display of pornography and, in one case, their overturning by a provincial supreme court; by the declaration of the Ontario Board of Censors as unconstitutional by the provincial appeal court; by the new expansion of the board's powers, notwithstanding the legal opinion, by the Ontario government; by the censoring of progressive artists' work in Toronto and Vancouver; by the trial of Doctors Henry Morgentaler, Leslie Smoling and Robert Scott, physicians at a Toronto abortion clinic, for conspiring to procure an abortion, their sensational acquittal by a jury and the decision to appeal the acquittal; by an injunction against Vancouver prostitutes, forbidding them to work in the west end of Vancouver, forcing them into the gritty skid row districts of that city; by a similar injunction at this writing being considered in Halifax; by mass arrests of gay men in Montreal bars and baths; by the extraordinary entrapment of gay men in Orillia, Ontario; by the Alberta government's attempts to eliminate sex education; by the report of the Badgley Commission on Sexual Offences against Children and Youth; by trials of sexually explicit material — both commercial and artistic — in a series of courts; and, as the year drew to its close, by the country-wide banning of the December issue of *Penthouse* magazine — containing bondage photos of women — by the Canadian government and the charging of several of its distributors by the Ontario attorney-general.

In the U.S. the New Right's ongoing crusade against abortion, homosexuality and pornography gained new momentum with the reelection of Ronald Reagan. The intention to launch a new president's commission on pornography has been declared, apparently designed to discredit the controversial and liberal findings of the last commission, which reported in 1970. Congressional committees on sexual abuse and child pornography have been created. In addition, an emerging alliance of feminists, neoconservatives and members of the Moral Majority have launched new initiatives to suppress pornography in ways meant to circumvent the reluctance demonstrated by the American courts to censor this kind of material. These initiatives, discussed at length in this volume, are the prelude to a new and very dangerous stage in the battle over sexuality.

Two aspects of the current preoccupation with sexual issues are especially notable. First, while skirmishes and battles occur on all questions, pornography has taken centre stage politically. Second, the protagonists in this fight over pornography are not simply the old contestants — social conservatives and the Catholic and fundamentalist churches. What is new is that many feminists — traditionally supporters of sex education, contraception, abortion and sexual preference rights — have also taken up the fight in the name of women's liberation. Consequently, a new array of concerns is being debated, ranging from the sanctity of procreative sex and men's authority in society to women's right to sexual autonomy and freedom from misogynist violence. As a result, the issue of pornography has now become a focal point around which important political negotiations are taking place. Both the symbolic and the more practical aspects of these issues have major implications for the health of the women's movement as a whole, and, by extension, for the well-being of our entire society.

The women's movement is itself in conflict over explicit sexual material, especially that large and mixed body of material we lump together under the single term "pornography." Most media have conveyed the impression that all feminists have a uniform assessment of pornography and uniformly advocate its censorship. In fact there is no consensus on either of these points. The multifaceted evaluations of the content, meaning and function of pornography in this volume alone attest to the diversity of feminist opinion about this material. And with respect to strategy — especially censorship — many feminists reject this direction and believe that women must instead direct their analysis and action toward dealing with problems of sexist imagery and violence against women.

The essays in this book bear witness to this current within feminism. They are in a real sense documents of struggle — partisan, passionate, committed. They are not academic pieces, but chronicles of real events and experiences by women involved in the processes they describe. The contributors hope that they can serve as a resource for others involved in or concerned about the direction our society is taking on sexual issues. We hope, too, that the deep concern that women and those concerned with women's rights feel about sex and sexual depictions is affirmed in these pages and that the suggestions for action contained here are useful in working to make positive change.

Because social policy with respect to pornography has been developing so quickly, we opted to get this book together quickly so that its ideas could begin to circulate, rather than to refine each argument and cover all bases until it was perfect — and obsolete. The articles range in length and subject matter, providing both compact summaries of arguments and experiences and longer, more detailed considerations of issues that have been largely ignored in media discussions, and are only now becoming well known even among concerned and well-informed feminists. We have ourselves come to understand how complicated the combination of cultural, economic, political and strategic factors involved in this issue really is. From the overwhelming number of requests that many of us are getting to speak and write these days, we also know that people want to take the time to work through these issues so they can arrive at considered and careful positions.

For many of us working around the issues of pornography and censorship, sorting out our ideas has been like putting together a difficult puzzle: only when all — or at least most — of the pieces are in place does the whole picture become clear. The articles in this collection are like those pieces, and, inevitably, along the edges where they meet, they cover similar ground. Each one both stands on its own and constitutes part of a whole linked by a set of common themes. We hope that from the first article — a call for reconsideration of current strategies — to the last — a set of proposals for alternatives to censorship — the record of our thoughts on the issues and the stakes in this fight will convince many others that difficulties and contradictions notwithstanding, for women freedom lies not in accepting censorship, but in repudiating it.

— Varda Burstyn

Political Precedents and Moral Crusades: Women, Sex and the State

Varda Burstyn

As a Jewish child born in Israel in 1948, I have always been aware of the power the past wields over the present. I grew up in the intense debates following World War II, in the shadow of the Holocaust. And in more recent decades, along with millions of other distressed Jews, in Israel and all over the world, I have watched the lengthening shadows of armed aggression and expansion cast by Israeli regimes that have themselves become oppressors. Despite some of the most noble intentions ever articulated in the project of nation building — intentions to build a society that could be a living alternative to coercion and repression — something very serious has gone wrong. In trying to come to grips with the causes of this painful reality, I have come to understand that political sophistication is not a luxury but an absolute necessity if even the best of intentions are not to wind up as inadvertent instruments of oppression.

Especially for movements of the disenfranchised and powerless, such political sophistication is intimately bound up with an understanding of the dynamics of power in political life. And that kind of understanding is virtually impossible without some awareness of what history itself has to teach us. History is not a dead and immaterial backdrop, but a living force, embodied in major social movements and institutions. Because it is dynamic, it carries us forward with powerful momentum, presenting us with tasks and conundrums that arise out of its own development. More like a vast river than a smooth road, history contains streams and currents, whirlpools and eddies that often seize us and carry us to points very different from our intended destinations. If we are to have a chance of charting a clear and independent course within that flow, of making our own living history, we must predict the motion of these currents.

In this article, I want to discuss the political questions at stake in the pornography controversy by placing present debates and political directions within their historical context. First I'll describe — the map is crude, but I think the main contours are visible — what major trends are at work in the relationship of men and women to each other in society. I think it is virtually impossible to understand the degree of mobilization and anxiety around the existence of sexual pictures without understanding what kinds of contradictions and conflicts they have come — consciously and unconsciously — to represent. I also want to refresh our own memories of the respective traditions of the present protagonists in the political arena so we can better understand where we are all travelling in the broad river of history, and what can happen when the currents of different streams meet. I then want to look at what is wrong with the political thrust of the procensorship/legal reform/social control strategy that has been growing out of some feminist sectors; and, finally, in the context of our present economic and political situation to identify alternatives.

If one dates the beginning of the second wave of feminism to 1963, when Betty Friedan published *The Feminine Mystique*, then contemporary feminism has existed as a social and political force for just over 20 years. In comparison with the 70-year span of the first wave, we are still young, only now approaching our political adulthood. Like the present wave, the first began with many small groups in major urban centres in America and Europe. By the turn of the century, it had grown to massive proportions in many countries, bringing to public meetings, rallies, professional associations, educational institutions and trade unions the themes and challenges of women asserting their right to equality.

From its zenith in the early part of this century, however, the first wave crashed upon the shoals of pre- and post-World War I political society, its waters diverging and dividing, until nothing was left of the mass movement of women who had been mobilized for three generations. Many women's organizations — the YWCA, a number of professional associations, women's auxiliaries in political parties and trade unions — remained in place But though feminists continued to work within them, these groups were no longer actively out to improve the lot of women and gain equality with men. Feminism would not raise its head openly again until the 1960s.

But rise it did, for the women's movement is as inevitable a product of the modern conditions of women's lives as bread is a product of flour, water, yeast and heat. Although relations between men and women are never entirely static, although sexual life is never fixed, it is still true that during some periods gender relations are more stable than they are in others. Historians differ on how far back the roots of modern change date, but there is a consensus among most that by about 150 years ago, Western societies had irreversibly moved into a period of massive upheaval. This change holds out the possibility of a new and different social arrangement between men and women so qualitative that the term "world-historical" has been used to describe it.

Historians and political scientists have applied this term to other times, but not often. For the most part it has been reserved for the period many millenia ago when men as a group extended and consolidated economic, social and political control over women, becoming the dominant gender class in many important cultures. That lengthy epoch, measured in thousands of years, culminated in the full-fledged system of economic and gender class heirarchy we today call classical patriarchal civilization. Of all the ancient patriarchal societies, the cultures of Jerusalem, Athens and Rome have most influenced Europe and North America, providing the major foundation stones for what we have come to call Western tradition. Based in the economics and politics of trade, conquest, plunder and slavery, these were imperial cultures. At their centre, power was concentrated in the hands of the men of the ruling families, and it is their institutions — from the Jewish rabbinate to Greek democracy — that have had the greatest impact on our own ideas of politics, religion, science and art.

There were many important differences among these three societies, and the religion that their intersection produced — Christianity — differed in important ways from its sources. Nevertheless, they did share a fundamental social organizing principle that gave shape and unity to their economic and political life: the power of men over women and children, the supremacy of the senior males of the ruling-class families, the law of the patriarchs and patricians. From the Greeks' Zeus to Christianity's God the Father, divinity itself came to be described in the image of the powerful ruling men of these societies. The patriarch ruled over wife, children, slaves and peasants, commanded soldiers and laborers in conquest and consolidation. He and his brothers formed the powerful priestly cadres of their societies, and comprised their assemblies and senates. The laboring father, though unable to command the work of other men, nevertheless shared with his ruling-class counterpart authority over the women and children of his own social class and, as a soldier, over other women as well.

Athens, Jerusalem and Rome all eventually collapsed economically and militarily. But their cultural values lived on in both religious (the two Testaments of the Bible, later the Koran) and secular texts (Greek philosophy, Latin arts) and influenced, directly and indirectly, a vast array of cultures. Feudalism in Christian Europe and the later heroic masculinism of the Renaissance are the traditions most directly connected to the dominant culture in North America. In many critical respects, the differences between these societies are more important than their similarities, and making simple equations between them on all matters would be wrong. But in terms of gender relations, they all developed as variations on the basic theme of patriarchal agrarianism and culture, and it would be equally wrong to deny this commonality. So ubiquitous and so profound has the inequality between the sexes been that to most of the best minds produced by these cultures, this imbalance has seemed natural, predetermined and eternal.

What a shock, what a sense of chaos and disorder people felt when patriarchal forms of social organization were openly challenged in the nineteenth century. Urbanization and industrialization, the twin motors of modern society, functioned at different rhythms from country to country. But wherever they were at work, they destroyed the patriarchal kinship systems of obligation and fealty in which women had had different and fewer social rights than men, but in which social responsibility for children was accommodated by extended family ties and communal lifeways. City life uprooted and scattered working families and required them to fend for themselves, increasingly with only the strained nuclear unit as economic and emotional resource. Although women had to work for wages to survive in the cities, their pay was a fraction of men's, and even this was usually appropriated by the men of their families. On the one hand utterly dependent on men for subsistence, on the other denied the accountability of previous kinship arrangements, working-class women were dreadfully oppressed by the conditions of urban life.

Concurrently, middle- and upper-class women found that as the scope of the household-based economy shrank and economic, educational and professional fields expanded, their exclusion from this growing public realm narrowed their life possibilities intolerably. Though they brought capital and property to their marriages, they had no access to or control of them and were forced to become absolutely dependent on the men of their families. Told that they exemplified morality and goodness, they were nevertheless denied the most elementary political rights. Legally infantilized, economically shackled, bored by their confinement, frustrated by their forced inactivity, cruelly bound by a rigid double standard of sexual life, many were also profoundly angered by the dreadful conditions of their working-class sisters. These were the conditions that underlay the rise of the first wave of feminism in the mid-1800s .

During our own century, the falling value of the wage has meant that ever larger numbers of women have had to work outside the home to sustain a standard of living that was previously attainable by the families of skilled workers and professionals on a single income. But in addition to this, especially over the last 30 years, even the nuclear unit itself has been coming apart. Large numbers of women — one in every six Canadian families is headed by a sole-support woman — have to rear children on economic resources equalling less than 60 percent of men's. These are the realities that have given rise to the second wave of feminism — our own. Women have had to fight for equal social rights with men out of the need to survive: the majority of women have realized that to achieve more than subsistence today requires at least the same rights that men have.

Women have been concerned about economic issues not simply as adults who have to make their way in society, but as those responsible for children. Women's biological and social connection to children has meant that no issues have been more explosive in this transitional period than those associated with sexuality. In pre-industrial patriarchal society, women did not have legal or, in most cases, even de facto rights over their procreative and erotic capacities. Both were put at the disposal of their affiliated men, in exchange — at least in theory — for certain forms of protection and support. Laws that made women's adultery and abortion serious crimes, indeed all double standards with respect to sexual behavior, were initially products of classical patriarchal relations. In the absence of fertility control (prohibited by law to women, and enforced through the witchhunts whose targets were midwives and healers), women were unable to sustain themselves and their children outside the nexus of the household economy, which was based on the patriarchal division of labor. Women made do as best they could and passed on to their daughters an awareness of the rules they too would have to follow in order to survive in a man's world. Far from being timeless and universal, they reflected two imperatives: men's control over women's bodies, the keystone to other forms of control and subordination; and women's attempt within an unequal arrangement to get from men the most in terms of protection and accountability.

Thus, it is only logical that the terrain of women's bodies, both in terms of childbearing and erotic pleasure, should become intensely politicized by all sides in the growing social upheaval and conflict over gender relations in the nineteenth century. Without the accountability of kinship and community, with the devastating effects of migration on family life, with sexual depredations of masters being common for those in domestic service, working-class women were cast by the hundreds of thousands into appalling poverty, the terrors of single motherhood and, for a great many, into prostitution, disease and early death. Middle-class women, able to see the horrors of the life of working-class women, and terrified in their own right of the ravages of venereal disease, moved to rigidify sexual morality in an attempt to strengthen the ties of accountability written into the marriage contract. Many feminists further demanded that women be given the education and means to prevent pregnancy, terminate unwanted pregnancies and hold men accountable for their own sexual activity with women.

Although the nineteenth-century women's movement inevitably grew out of the conditions of industrial society, feminism's claims and demands were resisted in determined, systematic and carefully organized ways by very powerful social forces. In some cases, the resistance reflected a direct economic advantage: equal pay for women was, and continues to be, a threat to what is known as the super-profitability of women's labor. In other cases, the resistance had more to do with gender privilege and even gender panic. For many men sensed that sexual autonomy and reproductive rights for women, especially if combined with economic equality, would erode women's dependence on, and therefore servility to, them. Those women who also resisted feminism (and this pattern still holds today) were women who benefited from the buffer against the world that affluent husbands provided, women for whom working in a wage ghetto seemed infinitely — and understandably — worse than being able to stay home and raise children.

The resistance to women's demands for equality came from all segments of masculine society: from industrialists, professionals, politicians, educators, even from many trade union leaders. But as the old patriarchal institutions fell away and as the organized churches lost much of their direct power, other institutions with the moral and physical force to maintain men's still-dominant position were needed to orchestrate and manipulate the tensions of gender up-heaval to safeguard men's power and privilege. The institutions that fulfilled this need, that grew increasingly more aggressive in regu-lating gender and sexual life, were those that are best described under the general rubric of the "state."

The Legacy of the First Wave

The political landscape of the nineteenth and early twentieth cen-turies was deeply marked by long, intense struggles around issues of sexuality and the development of a variety of distinct positions and approaches by the different camps involved. Then, as now, certain questions came to occupy public awareness and to symbolize and affect other related issues. Like our present debates, nineteenth-century controversies about birth control, prostitution, homosex-uality and even pornography were also general discussions about gender relations, social responsibility and the appropriate role of the state in these matters.

The history of these debates, the social movements that launched them and the outcome of their struggles has only recently been uncovered. But though the excavation is still in its early stages, it is already clear that there are several key experiences in the first feminist movement that provide invaluable lessons. With the clarity of hindsight, we can now see that many of the early feminists made a number of major errors in their campaigns on sexual issues, errors that hurt the women's movement as a whole and undermined its ability to fight for women on other fronts. A brief summary of these lessons cannot but oversimplify the complexity of previous events, because the first wave of feminism, like the present one, was comprised of many different currents, with different analyses and priorities. However, as is increasingly true today, some were perceived as representative of feminism as a whole, and this perception corresponded with their very great influence in the women's movement and beyond it. It is to their politics that I am speaking here.

The work of feminist historian Judith Walkowitz illuminates perhaps the most instructive single case: the campaign around the Contagious Diseases Acts passed by British Parliament in 1866 and 1869. These required prostitutes to register with police authorities and undergo biweekly examinations for venereal disease. The Contagious Diseases Acts were sold to the public as a necessary measure for the health of the population, threatened, according to Parliament, by the spectre of VD epidemics. In reality, as a whole generation of feminists realized when the implications of the acts became clear, they had virtually nothing to do with bringing venereal disease under control. Rather, they served to scapegoat prostitutes and control women.

The acts did this in a number of ways. First, they cemented the already prevalent tendency to blame and punish women prostitutes for the spread of venereal disease, ignoring the much larger number of men who were the clients of prostitutes. Second, both symbolically and in the most concrete and sexually charged of terms, they asserted the right of men as a group, through the power of the state, to invade and control the bodies of women who were not the "property" of husbands or fathers. Third, they served to isolate and stigmatize women who worked as prostitutes out of dire need either occasionally or full-time, almost eliminating their chances of having an acceptable family or community life. By so clearly marking them, the legislation tended to turn other women against even the most occasional prostitute, and made it much more difficult for women to move out of prostitution if better opportunities presented themselves.

For all these reasons, in 1871, a group of British feminists joined the campaign for repeal of the Contagious Diseases Acts that had been launched by a group of men in 1869. Led by Josephine Butler and a dedicated core of experienced feminists, they worked tirelessly for 16 years, participating in a broader coalition. The leadership of the feminist component always opposed the acts on the grounds that they violated women's rights to bodily integrity and control. But despite this insistence, toward the end of the long campaign, many of the rank and file activists of the feminist component were coopted by the other current in the coalition: the forces who organized under the banner of "Social Purity."

Made up of religious groups and secular organizations whose leaderships were male dominated and traditionalist in their sexual politics, these groups also fought for repeal. But their concerns and political agenda were different from the feminists' in several crucial respects. To the social purists, the Contagious Diseases Acts were unacceptable because by acknowledging and regulating prostitution they were sanctioning "female vice" and "male licentiousness." The social purists rejected the proposition that women had a right to control their own bodies, sexually or otherwise; nor did they think that people in general had the right to seek sexual satisfaction outside religiously sanctioned patriarchal marriage. For them prostitutes were "fallen women" who were to be either uplifted or repudiated.

Because so many feminists came from the same social background as the social purists, because it was still economically impossible for middle-class women to reject marriage itself as the only safe framework for adult women's lives, and because many were justifiably concerned with the problems of venereal disease, many shared or accepted important elements of the social purists' beliefs about sex, prostitution and marriage. Indeed, it was this agreement that created the bridge between the feminists and the social purists in the 1870s and 1880s — an alliance that led to the ultimate cooption of the legitimacy and energy of the broad women's movement into support for a whole new set of legal measures that were passed by Parliament in 1886 in the wake of the successful repeal of the legislation itself.

As the campaign for repeal gathered momentum and moved toward success in the late 1870s and early '80s, social purists and many feminists agitated for a series of measures that would use the state — through the courts and jails, and the developing social welfare agencies and school system — to enforce their views of acceptable sexual behavior. They won stricter restrictions on prostitution, which further victimized women; the raising of the age of consent from 12 to 16, which became a means of controlling working-class girls; harsher restrictions on same-sex practices ostensibly to "protect" women and children, but in fact a means of persecuting people who engaged in sexual activity with members of their own gender; laws that denied women welfare and other social provisions for "cohabiting" with a man; laws that denied jobs to women — ex-prostitutes — with criminal records; and extremely harsh sanctions against abortion. "Female chastity" — no sex except under conditions of marriage and procreation (and, for feminists, with the added proviso that only if women were willing) — became the standard by which all other sexual practices were judged.

Women's poverty — and the systematic discrimination and economic stratification that caused it — was left untouched by these reforms. Great numbers of poor and working women were still forced to resort to prostitution to survive. In a number of ways, sexual fear and ignorance were reinforced, with many women activists actually working against birth control because it threatened feminine chastity and masculine fidelity. Unwed or unwanted pregnancy remained a nightmare for women of all classes, but particularly for working-class women, who had no access to educational and contraceptive materials, nor to skilled, expensive abortionists. The rates of disease and death associated with their attempts to terminate pregnancies were very high. In other words, although laws that tried to regulate sexuality were put in place and agencies for social welfare and control expanded, the causes of women's economic and sexual exploitation remained basically unchanged. It is true that during these years women made some gains in education (the opening up of some places in universities and professions) and legal status. But relative to the kind of change required to end women's sexual victimization, these were easy and cheap. And even these were meaningful for only a small minority of women.

According to the recent historical work of Carol Lee Bacchi, while the specific campaigns were different, the pattern of feminist-social purist collaboration was even more pronounced in Canada than in Britain or the U.S. According to her, only a tiny fraction women's suffrage leaders were feminist first and foremost; most saw votes for women more as a tactic to hasten the implementation of temperance and social purity — key goals of the larger Reform Movement in which they worked — than as means to hasten equality for women, though this formed part of their program. Like many of their counterparts in the U.S. and Britain, they saw their mission as bringing into public life the skills and qualities of maternalism.

On the one hand, as wives and daughters, these reformers were part of the governing class in society and they were used to the idea of political action and social regulation. On the other, having been virtually excluded from the political process, and hence never having had the opportunity to be representatives of their gender, they were politically naive. Both their orientation to governing and their naivete were evident in their unqualified advocacy of regulatory legislation that imposed their own standard of sexual behavior. This approach hardly differed from that of men with power — indeed it was modelled on it. With hindsight we can now see how flawed it was.

During the 40-odd years of the Reform, Suffrage and Social Purity movements in Britain, Canada and the U.S., many middle-class women did finally emerge in public and professional life as "specialists" in extending the "maternal qualities" of women into politics and government bureaucracy. Their struggles validated the idea that the state and society were responsible for the weak and disabled; that women's needs and problems merited special attention; and that women had a place in public life as politicians and professionals. But the cost of these victories, won as they were through collaboration with and accommodation of powerful non- and antifeminist forces, was high. The majority of women continued to be excluded in meaningful terms from public life and the political process. Working-class women continued to be exploited, immigrant women to be sweated and discarded. For these women the only other option was the life of the "public woman" — the prostitute — constantly harassed, stigmatized and assaulted. Surveillance and persecution of all those who lived outside the standards of heterosexual marriage so punctiliously enshrined in law increased. And the idea that the state should intervene in sexual life became accepted and stamped with women's approval.

A minority of women gained access to parts of government and state bureaucracies, or founded social agencies that eventually became dependent on public funding, so opening the door for other women. But ultimately, through bitter compromise or willing collaboration, they did this by sanctioning a code of behavior and means of social control that reinforced economic stratification and men's dominance in society. Paid relatively well compared to the men of their own class, and qualitatively far beyond what working-class women earned, it was not surprising that these women reformers should see the state as a benign and appropriate tool for social intervention. They did not see the danger in the way that the goals and values of the non- and antifeminist social reformers resonated with those of the powerful and privileged men who already controlled the state apparatus and other institutions that shaped the political process. But it was these values that ultimately outweighed the suffragists' and the feminists', that came to inform the expansion of the state and the political outlook of a critical stratum of women activists — who increasingly parted company with less privileged women activists.

This was a complex and extended process, and it contributed much to the dissipation of the first wave of feminism.

The Inheritance Comes to Life

The experience of the early feminists has bequeathed to us a number of bitter lessons. First among them is that alliances with non- and antifeminist forces are dangerous, even when there is apparent agreement on goals. Whether it is repeal of the Contagious Diseases Acts or censorship of pornography, when the motivation behind the similar demands of different social forces are so much at variance, feminists will not be the ones to determine the way these reforms will be carried out.

In part what shapes state implementation is the relative weight of the forces that make up a coalition around specific issues. When women are widely mobilized to fight for their needs, distinctly defined, government response always reflects their concerns, at least rhetorically. But when campaigns demand policy that cannot easily be coopted through rhetoric and that threatens the status quo, another, more decisive factor comes into play. This is an alignment between interests in the male-dominated state already in place and the non- and antifeminist components of social coalitions. That alignment is very powerful. It prevented, for example, the addition of the Equal Rights Amendment to the U.S. Constitution, despite overwhelming popular support. It continues to deny a woman's right to choose abortion in Canada, though the majority of Canadians endorse it.

Unfortunately — and this is the second lesson — state institutions are not empty vessels into which any group in society can pour content and meaning. They are part of a larger apparatus with an inbuilt bias toward protecting the status quo, which for now and for a long time yet to come is a sexist one. And, by extension, heterosexist as well — for a look at this problem, see page 99. The logic of state processes invariably favors political agendas and methods that reinforce capitalist and patriarchal social relations and the powerful place of state structures within them, although many progressive individuals, feminists now included, work in the public sector. This does not mean that women should not demand that government go to work for us and that public resources not be used to better our lives. But it does mean that we must be extremely selective about the kind of power that we confer on the state in our name, identifying and avoiding all measures that could be used against us.

The third lesson has to do with what kinds of social and political methods are useful and appropriate to bring about positive change. We can't do needlework with a sledge hammer; we cannot use the controlling, punitive and top-down structures of the state to mend and reweave the delicate fabric of sexual life. This point is so important that it merits an article to itself, and the last chapter of this volume is devoted to it. But it is vital to register here that feminists must clearly distinguish between using public resources to help people become sexually and socially responsible and self-determining and using the state to try to control and punish any deviation from one dictated sexual norm.

With these points in mind, then, I want to look at who's who in the current fight around pornography, for we need to be very clear on what agendas are represented by the different protagonists. The danger, as our history proves, is that we may begin with very good intentions and end up with very bad results.

On the one hand, then, we have a major current of conservative forces, symbolized most vividly in Canada by the politically ambitious Mary Brown, head of the Ontario Board of Censors. For these people, the censorship/legal reform/social control strategy is comfortable, traditional and necessary. They are philosophically close to the American Moral Majority and New Right, and lately have been growing in confidence and political ambition. Representative of their increasing strength in Canada is the recent series of attacks on liberal and profeminist artists; relentless prosecutions of gay publications; attempts to remove works of literature from libraries and school curricula; new initiatives against prostitutes; general calls for greater censorship; agitation against sex education; and, in Ontario, efforts to censor videotapes of movies designed for home viewing, previously a private and sacrosanct sphere. (The minority that makes up the extreme political right is an exception to the move toward repression by political conservatives. This group opposes almost all government intervention in business, and so rejects censorship of pornography, in effect supporting the pornography industry's virtual monopoly over depiction of sexuality.)

The philosophy underlying the conservative evaluation of sexually explicit material is rooted firmly in a harsh interpretation of biblical ideas, an interpretation that defines sexuality in the first instance as a *problem*: a dangerous, corrupting force that must be contained within the framework of marriage. But organizing sexuality along these lines — in what is always called The Family, but is in fact only one kind of family form — is predicated on, indeed is virtually synonymous with, the division of labor and privilege that women are now rejecting because they are unable to survive, either materially or emotionally, within it.

The religious myths that sustain these views come from the old, patriarchal Judeo-Christian beliefs about the relative merit and place of the sexes: Woman as an extension of and servant to Man (Adam's rib); woman's sexual and sinful nature (the serpent and the tree of knowledge); woman's seduction of man and her responsibility for the expulsion from paradise (the Fall); her exclusion from supreme divinity (God is the Father and the Son, not the Mother and Daughter or even the Universal Parent); the antisexual nature of good women (Mary as opposed to Eve) and of divinity itself (Christ's chastity and the sexless pastures of heaven).

Codified in the patriarchal civilizations of Jerusalem and Rome, these ideas reflect a profound rejection and fear of women's autonomy and a consequent degradation of women's sexuality. Men's sexuality — sexuality altogether — is also feared because of the potential it has for creating feelings of solidarity in relations between equals. Most pornography for heterosexual men is loaded with sexist values. From the feminist point of view, it reinforces the heirarchy of power in masculinist society. But pornography, virtually by definition, shows sex outside of the monogamous marriage framework (indeed marriage is the only framework pornography systematically boycotts); and advocates sex for every reason but procreation. Consequently, for conservatives, pornography, like prostitution, is an agent of corruption, subverting the nuclear family and the patriarchal authority based in it by sanctioning those old devils, licentiousness and vice.

But as recent events in Canada and the U.S. have demonstrated, any alliance of feminists and conservatives against pornography is built on quicksand because nonsexist sexual material, pictorial or otherwise, is inevitably judged doubly evil within the patriarchal scheme of things. Not only does such material suggest that sex can be a vehicle for pleasure for people of all ages, colours, sexual preferences and gender combinations, but it also threatens directly or indirectly, our current sexual norm. Where heterosexual porn for men is at least a celebration of masculine dominance and feminine acquiesence, dissident sexual material undermines even this. Smut is bad enough; "feminist" and "gay smut" are intolerable.

That these ideas still have such a strong hold on so many people is telling evidence of how far we have to go ourselves before the values and institutions of patriarchal culture wither away. As long as these continue to be cultivated and manipulated, so long as they are promulgated by the male-dominated heirarchies of church power throughout the world, there is not much hope for their gradual disappearance. From Pope John's latest encyclical reaffirming patriarchal views of sex, marriage and procreation to the offerings of such TV evangelists as Jim Bakker and his wife, Tammy, sexism continues to be sanctified by religious bodies whose power and privilege are thereby augmented.

The power structures that organize religious movements have been around for a very long time, and they are deeply committed to maintaining authority over sexual matters. For it is through these that they tap into powerful, often unconscious, feelings, and through appeals to these feelings that they are able mobilize their adherents into armies on the political field. From the Islamic fundamentalism of Khomeini and his followers to the aggressive evangelism of many American fundamentalists to the enormous rallies organized around the globe for Pope John Paul, religious heirarchies are working very hard against equality for women as an integral part of their larger agenda of political influence. They have been a major force in history, and they continue to wield great influence in many national governments.

Of course the organized religions are not monolithic. Catholicism contains an extraordinary spectrum of political forces, from Latin American worker priests and reform-oriented nuns to Opus Dei, the international organization that exerts power inside the repressive structures of governments and right-wing movements. Bishop Remi de Roo of the Canadian Conference of Catholic Bishops may represent the former pole and the best of Canadian Catholic conscience on economic questions and the political morality of unemployment. The American bishops may have taken an exemplary stand on the immorality of nuclear weapons. But unfortunately neither they nor others in the church's heirarchy have spoken up against the anti-woman and reactionary policies of the Vatican and the continued sexual oppression of women and sexual minorities. In Canada, the Catholic heirarchy has supported censorship and Ontario's crusading Mary Brown, who represents a traditionalist view of gender and sexual matters that she aggressively implements. In the U.S., they actively campaigned against the Catholic Democratic vice-presidential candidate, Geraldine Ferraro, because, though personally antiabortion, she was prochoice.

Though they have neither the history nor the international scope of Catholicism, the North American-based Protestant fundamentalist churches are just as aggressively political. Their militant support of Ronald Reagan and other New Right politicians in the U.S. is well known, and homosexual panic campaigns in a number of states (remember Anita Bryant and the Dade County, Florida, initiative?) played a major role in consolidating their political strength. They are aggressively propagandistic, owning and operating several radio and television networks, as well as a rapidly expanding number of churches, schools and publishing houses. In Canada, they are becoming increasingly active in the Conservative party, which itself is adopting Reaganite politics in the name of "good relations with our neighbor to the south." In the winter of 1984, for example, a young Baptist was able to win the PC nomination in London, Ontario, away from a senior colleague of Brian Mulroney's — cabinet material, said *The Globe and Mail* — on the strength of 800 new members signed up through the local evangelical churches.

Although many people subscribe to traditionalist-patriarchal beliefs from what they feel is a deeply moral stance, until now, today's feminists have confronted the conservative and authoritarian movements almost as natural foes. This is because conservative views of family and sexual relations, by their very logic, perpetuate women's second-class status, dependent economically and psychologically on men (whether individually or, in the case of welfare mothers, widows and other poor single women, through the state). Feminism has therefore constituted the clearest expression of an opposite pole to the growth of conservatism during the late '70s and early '80s.

Nowhere has this polarization been more pronounced than on sexual issues. Feminism has insisted that women, like men, must have the ultimate decision-making power with respect to their own bodies in reproductive and erotic matters; conservatives, on the other hand, have insisted on continued masculine control through the notion of the rights of the unborn and the punitive intervention of the state. Equally contentious has been the struggle for civil and social rights for homosexuals, who have been zealously repressed and scapegoated by the Right. Feminism, in contrast, has for the most part viewed gays and lesbians as allies in the larger struggle for sexual pluralism and self-determination.

Conservatives have carried through all kinds of antifeminist censorship, particularly around birth control and women's health publications; they have firebombed abortion clinics; they have been responsible for censoring and banning much art and educational material, thereby catching in their wide and paranoid net even liberal work not in active sympathy with gay and feminist ideas. In this way they have invidiously narrowed the range of knowledge, vision and choice in society, harming us all, not just the politically active. Indeed, until the pornography issue came along, feminism and the Right had no common ground.

Conspicuous by their absence from the conservative clerical contingent are the United Church of Canada, many Anglican and Unitarian congregations, segments of Conservative Judaism and virtually all of Reform Judaism. The United Church particularly has chosen a very different path. In contrast to the Catholic and evangelical churches, for whom feminism truly is evil incarnate, threatening by definition the philosophies and the power heirarchies within them, United Church members have spent much time considering how feminist and gay issues might be relevant within their faith. Such discussions are not easy, and the heated controversies that have recently emerged over whether homosexuals may be ordained is an indication of how challenging these topics can be. (The United Church, unlike the Catholic church, has already agreed to ordain women.) Internally divided over this issue, the church's members and heirarchy are struggling through very important issues. But many of the United Church's most progressive impulses around sexuality are threatened by the procensorship stance it has taken, motivated by an analysis of pornography that is at least in part informed by the feminist critique.

Some similar developments have occurred within Anglicanism and Judaism, which also boast a few women clergy. Their sexual philosophies and political positions, like those of the United Church, have fanned out on the spectrum usually found among both small- and large-l liberal views on sex. These in turn have found their clearest political expression over the last 15 years in the contradictory approaches of the Trudeau government. Like the different positions within the churches, liberal policies have been akin to unsorted laundry that is now being divided into rather different piles.

The best of the liberal approach has been the live-and-let-live spirit behind the legal reforms of 1969. The state has no place in the bedrooms of the nation, Trudeau declared magnanimously; whatever consenting adults did was fine as long as they did it in private and it harmed no one else. In theory this stance seemed reasonably enlightened, but it was belied by a very different reality at all three governmental levels: the continued prosecution of Dr. Henry Morgentaler for performing safe, wanted abortions, while access to therapeutic abortions in hospital settings decreased; a refusal to remove abortion from the Criminal Code; a series of mass arrests at gay baths in various cities; persistent entrapment and consequent disgrace of gay men in numerous communities; continued denial of custody rights to lesbian mothers; continued persecution of prostitutes through a variety of laws — all this in addition to the kinds of censorship that have been documented in this collection.

In the face of growing political polarization over sexual matters, the liberal position, so welcome (if so tepid) in the '60s, is now collapsing as it encounters conservative opposition in today's political climate. The pornography debate has been playing an important and problematic role in this process, splitting liberalism itself into a number of factions. One wing is moving toward censorship and legal reform. Many of its adherents are feminists who have been concerned about women's issues in the past. But many of its other members — especially politicians of both sexes — have adopted this perspective due in part to two less appealing motives: their desire to cater to a constituency itself favoring these positions; and because censorship, legal reform and social control strategies reinforce the power of politicians and officials. While there may be some sincerity in this camp, there is also a lot of opportunism, which is further fanned by the prospect of support from a different group of women's grassroots radical feminists who have done pioneering work on violence against women, and want more government action against this violence.

Moving in another direction is a wing composed primarily of men who oppose censorship from a classic, prefeminist liberal position. They have belittled women's pain and anger when confronting pornographic imagery, dismissing women's concern with the messages about sex, women and men that much pornography contains. This group has painted women who have been critical of pornography as totalitarians attempting to impose a sanitized version of politically correct sexuality on everyone. They suggest that feminists are just frigid, politically backward puritans against whom they, the men, will champion the right of freedom of expression.

The problem is that most women feel that for them freedom of expression is largely an abstraction. In fact, when freedom of expression is measured in terms of the capital it takes to start a noncommercial magazine, radio or television station; in terms of the money it takes to mount campaigns that reach a fraction of the people that advertising reaches; in the time and money it takes to make successful films or to run for Parliament — women's sense of disenfranchisement is substantively correct. Those who deny this reality only alienate women further.

And indeed, faced with these kinds of insensitive arguments — transparent covers for a sexist disregard of feminist concerns — many women have been impressed by the ongoing shift of liberal feminists toward censorship and legal reform, and have begun to identify these strategies and the analysis that informs them as "the" feminist position. Almost no other view has been publicized, no other bears the stamp of approval of the National Action Committee on the Status of Women in Canada. The liberal masculine denial of women's concern about pornography has pushed many angry, worried women — and many men who share their concerns — away from considering a feminist anticensorship position and into the waiting arms of procensorship feminists and conservatives.

Our own debates about sexuality, pornography and censorship are concerned with late twentieth century developments. But it is not difficult to see how today's trends threaten to replicate the treacherous alliances that brought about the misguided use of state machinery to regulate sexual life during the nineteenth century. What now must be seen is how this trend is developing at present and what can be done to reverse it.

The Censorship Trap

I began this article by talking about the period of transition in which we are living: the transition, if the best in humans wins out, from a society in which men have power and privilege to a society in which the sexes are equal. I want to move into the conclusion by emphasizing that when the social relations of masculine dominance, male supremacy, partriarchy — any one of these labels will do — are challenged, the reverberations affect every important social institution. Masculine dominance is not something that can be neatly removed, like a decrepit porch off an otherwise strong house. It is more like the frame of a building, shaping family life, the paid workforce, political institutions, education, art and science. Women and men working for equality are in effect asking for changes throughout every level of society.

Because of the far-reaching implications of feminism, the basic principles of the women's movement — equality in social standing, opportunity and remuneration, a change in the antagonistic relations between the sexes — have come to embody the aspirations of great numbers of women and men for a better life for all. Over the last 20 years, there has been an enormous change in expectations and desires. But though ideas have changed, with the exception of a recent influx of young, middle-class women into professions, no parallel change has occurred in the material conditions of the majority of women and men. If anything, conditions for most women are deteriorating with the effects of chronic recession — due to last at least until the end of the decade — and the lives of men and children are directly affected as a result. Women's earnings continue to average less than 60 percent of men's. In the U.S., sociologist Lenore J. Weitzman estimates that upon divorce, a woman's standard of living falls, on average, 73 percent during the first year, while the standard of living for her ex-husband rises by 42 percent. The Canadian reality is likely very similar. We know that the majority of women and children in a family headed by a woman are poor, and that more than two-thirds of men default on their child support payments. Not only does women's poverty victimize women and their children; it also places pressures on responsible men to live as the main provider within the constraints of unsatisfactory relationships and gender scripts that they would prefer to leave behind.

Despite the enormous change in consciousness, material conditions have changed so little compared with some changes in law, for example, because it is harder to alter economic stratification than to change ideas. To bring about equality means reorganizing the economics of our society in both the private and state sectors. Two major shifts in wealth distribution would be minimally necessary: First, resources would need to be redirected from the private to the public sphere, for example from arms manufacture and subsidies to corporations to social programs and community organizing. But when feminists talk about this kind of shift, they do not have in mind the kind of priorities indicated by an October, 1984, CBC newscast, which announced, first, that Metropolitan Toronto will donate $30 million to the construction of a domed stadium for (men's) professional sport, and, second, that the province of Ontario will spend $400,000 on a campaign to raise public awareness of domestic violence. Second, then, the shift in wealth must take place from men as a class to women as a class and children, who have the least access to and control over the deployment of that wealth.

Clearly, these kinds of changes cannot be undertaken without major political commitment, since public planning, economic reorganization and a lot of political clout are prerequisites. It has been estimated, for example, that introducing equal pay measures in Ontario, a province with a current population of 8.7 million, would cost an additional $3 billion annually. This staggering figure illustrates how extensively the profit system is based on what is known as the superexploitation of women and explains why any serious attempt to implement equal pay will encounter massive corporate resistance — a key factor behind the defeat of the Equal Rights Amendment in the U.S. Changes in government and state life are as important as changes in economics. The two fronts are complementary, and change cannot proceed very far on either one without similar progress on the other.

Sexist pornography is a product of the economic and social conditions of our society — not vice versa. Societies that are not based on profit, industrialization and male dominance have sexual culture — but this material looks and functions nothing like pornography. It follows that these are the conditions we must change if we want sexist pornography to disappear. Like other forms of sexist culture, pornography will go away when women no longer need to sell their sexuality and when men no longer need or want to look to sexist pictures to find out about sex, to learn what they are supposed to want and be as men and to support their need to feel superior to women. Likewise, violence against women will continue to plague us until we are able to bring such changes about. As long as women cannot support themselves and their children — and all the economic, social and sexual rights that this entails — they will be abused by brutalized men who feel that it is either acceptable or safe to lash out at women.

It is precisely because feminism implies such basic and far-reaching change that the institutions of corporate capitalism and masculine privilege that are built on a foundation of women's second-class status must find ways of resisting it. It is not a question of conspiracy on the bad side, or good intentions on the positive, but of the logic of institutional imperatives. And it is within the logic of these imperatives that ways must be found to undermine the potential for change embodied in broad profeminist consciousness. Politicians who support the status quo play a pivotal part in the management of dissident political movements and interests. Because they are commited to present institutions, they must find ways to weaken the women's movement and dilute its influence in society. Depending on circumstance and inclination, they may employ a variety of means: pure diversion is preferable; containment and cooption are a good second choice; and turning feminism against itself and repressing it, while messy and often risky, will be undertaken if necessary.

Given the many changes in consciousness that the current wave of feminism has already brought about and the deep polarization between conservatism and feminism, this kind of manipulation has not been particularly easy. In British Columbia, the crushing blows dealt to the unions by the Social Credit government simultaneously swept away all the gains made by the women's movement over the last 20 years. But in the rest of Canada, such a frontal assault would bring about electoral defeat, as Brian Mulroney's need to make election promises to retain social services and work for women demonstrated. It is within this delicate political situation — a need both to defuse feminist potential and to appear profeminist — that the pornography debate has unfolded. The convergence between conservatism and important sectors of feminism has offered politicians and bureaucrats a wonderful opportunity to undermine feminism while appearing its champions. In the drama that is now unfolding, all three elements of subversion — diversion, cooption and represssion — are working together.

The successful diversion of any movement requires that its members become involved in something that softens their impact. In the case of feminism, the issue of pornography need not, by definition, be diversionary. Women's sexuality and the battle over its control are central issues for feminism. If the approach to pornography had served to highlight the causes of women's oppression through a critique of women's sexual exploitation, its galvanizing effect would have been very different. But as Ann Snitow writes in this volume, there has been, among the antipornography feminists, a series of subtle shifts in ideas about the forms and causes of women's oppression. From an appreciation of the multidimensional reality of masculine dominance, vocal feminists have been increasingly narrowing their focus to one dimension: the sexist and sexually explicit representation of women: pornography. Women's attention has been diverted from the causes to the depictions of their oppression.

Once this happens within feminism, other institutional responses occur. Public debate in our society is orchestrated primarily through the mass media — central institutions very much marked by sexist values and power structures — and these, unfortunately, systematically divert attention away from root causes and structural problems. Perhaps this explains why most feminist issues gain so little attention from the media while pornography, censorship and related issues have received lavish, if carefully manipulated, coverage. Most media have taken care to present only procensorship feminists, so that they can claim to be "socially responsible" at the same time as effectively caricaturing feminism as monolithic, puritanical and even, yes, totalitarian. This is usually done by counterposing "sensible" (male) civil libertarians or good old-fashioned pornographers (Bob Guccione of *Penthouse*, for example, or Al Goldstein of *Screw*) who extol freedom of speech and the wonders of the free market. Anticensorship feminists, on the other hand, have been systematically ignored by most media presentations.

But government itself has also aggressively participated in the debate, rapidly capitalizing on the controversy. Not only have film censors and attorneys-general cloaked their repressive activities in feminist rhetoric in recent years, but at the federal level in Canada, the creation of the Fraser committee bound the issues of pornography and prostitution to the single line of legal reform. A master stroke, this effectively preempted any viable public discussions of the conditions that create sexist pornography, prostitution and violence against women, and so trapped feminists in the dead end of legal responses to social and economic problems. In the U.S. a president's commission on pornography is likely to be created and child pornography hearings are underway. These too will manipulate feminist concerns to provide cover for an antifeminist agenda.

As a result of the interaction between feminist debate, media treatment and government response, pornography — its content and "solutions" understood in these simplistic terms — has come to be seen as *the* feminist issue. More feminist meetings, institutional seminars and political discussions, and the resultant media coverage, are devoted to pornography these days than most other feminist issues combined. And as the many facets of women's oppression get conceptually eradicated and as the government road shows and increased prosecutions capture public awareness, attention gets diverted from the fact that fewer and fewer resources are being devoted to improve the conditions of women in general, and women sex-workers — prostitutes, body-rub parlor staff, porn models and actresses — in particular; that real life for large numbers of people is getting worse, not better.

The tradeoff in state priorities and resources is very real. It takes a lot of money to mount a really good spectacle to divert public attention: millions of dollars to finance government studies and special committees and censor boards; additional millions to prosecute dissidents, artists, gays and feminists (as well as the odd pornographer); more money yet to charge and imprison prostitutes and other sex offenders. These dollars should be devoted instead to job training and work creation programs for sex-workers; to self-help groups for victims (and perpetrators) of sexual abuse, programs organized with the help of skilled feminist services; to the subsidizing of feminist media; and to the many other positive measures that are outlined in the final article in this book. Censorship and prosecutions contribute nothing positive to solving sexual problems in our society. But they do take the heat off the economic and social institutions that create the workers, producers and buyers in the sex industry. And in comparison to the measures necessary to make that industry wither away, they are, not surprisingly, very cheap indeed.

When diversion works at this level, it becomes more than simply a shift of feminist attention. It actually succeeds in coopting and containing the energies of feminism and its supporters by involving feminists in expanding and reorganizing what the social scientists call "the apparatus of social control": the police, the courts, the jails. By contrast, desperately needed social services — unemployment insurance, health care, special educational services, pre- and postnatal centres, child-care facilities, rape crisis and battered women's shelters — shrink or disappear entirely. Those few that remain become increasingly oriented to minimal, emergency service — and, unfortunately, to greater forms of regulation and control, rather than self-help and empowerment. And as a rule, the programs that utilize the courts and prisons to intervene in sexual life primarily affect poor and working-class families, who already suffer disproportionately in recessionary times. While there seems no shortage of lawyers to prosecute child abusers, there are pathetically few resources to help devastated family members cope with the abuse, and the trauma of intervention and public exposure.

There is a painful irony in the kind of reorganization now taking place in government: the support feminists give to it in theory will be used against women in practice in yet additional ways. Camouflaged by the appearance of responsiveness to feminists' demands whenever political priorities permit (they do not, for example, in British Columbia, where Milton Friedman presided from the wings over the first Bennett budget that nearly precipitated a general strike), Liberal and Conservative governments have been creating their own services for women. But the women appointed to head these services are not those who pioneered the grassroots programs to aid women. They are either nonfeminists or women who have succeeded in modulating their feminism sufficiently to reach relatively high positions. As a result, the values and methods of a sexist and class-based bureaucracy come to predominate. Worse, having created "parallel" services, governments then starve the feminist-built projects of funds, arguing redundancy and duplication, and thus further impoverishing a whole layer of feminist experts and activists. The result is substitute, divide and conquer — all with the feminist stamp of approval — when the women's movement gives government the power to organize social services from above, rather than forcing it to finance services that are directed and controlled by users and workers.

It is true that social services have been slashed in the last decade in Canada. But as in other Western countries, this has not been because there is any real reduction in state expenditure — far from it, as the current record deficits of the Canadian and American governments demonstrate. As the work of criminologists and sociologists like John McMullen and Bob Ratner of the University of British Columbia and Ian Taylor of Carleton University shows, it is the systems of social control — the police, the courts, the prisons and the military — that have benefited from the diverted funds (in addition to the private sector, which has received billions in subsidies and tax writeoffs — $24 billion federally in Canada over the last 10 to 15 years). The pornography crusades have intersected with this potentially explosive dynamic — explosive because of the anger that knowledge of such a trend would spark should it become widespread. Prior to the feminist and conservative alliance, this trend was largely and quite consciously hidden by the rhetoric of "state fiscal crisis." Now feminism has been enlisted to reinforce the trend, directly if inadvertently.

Given the prognosis for the rest of the decade — the lean, mean '80s, as many economists have dubbed it — the growth of repression will inevitably rebound against women. Not all women will feel — do feel — it equally. For the woman supervising a team of provincial youth workers or working as Crown prosecutor, life is very different than for the woman fighting the police over the right to a first contract on the picket line outside her plant; or the secretary facing government inaction on the downgrading of her job to keypunch operator; or the teacher facing ever larger classes of ever more alienated kids; or the nurse fighting a losing battle with cuts in health care — as worker and as client; or the immigrant woman facing the threat of deportation should she so much as raise a word of protest against her appalling exploitation.

It's not only the pay, the quality of working life and the social respect that are so different. It's also the relative safety of the streets they live on. It's access to information on sexuality and safe contraception; to a therapeutic abortion, if necessary; to a variety of cultural institutions that provide alternatives to the models of sexuality offered in pornography; to a discreet psychiatrist, feminist support services and economic resources if incest or battering become problems in the family; the resources to avoid the agonizing disruption by police and social workers of family and sexual life. If all women do not gain the (still insufficient) opportunities that now exist for a minority of urban professional women, nothing fundamental will change for women in general; pornography and prostitution will continue to flourish; violence against women will remain a reality — indeed worsen. And in the context of recession, all of women's limited gains will continue to be eroded. If this happens, the real advance of feminism will come to a halt.

Because sexist sexual repression, already present, will intensify if we let it. For every gain we now make — a sex abuse education program here, a community health program there — we pay in new crackdowns on prostitutes, new attacks on feminist cultural producers, further and heavier assaults on reproductive rights, lost ground in the media and arts circles, intensified entrapment of gays, and pressure for much more of this from conservative forces heavily represented in government. The legacy of the first wave of feminism suggests that it is very easy for women who are relatively privileged vis-à-vis other women, who have greater access to — and confidence in — government to lose sight of the potential treachery of a male-dominated, profit-protecting state; of the way in which such a state, even when parts of it are staffed by women, can work against the interests of the majority of women — those caught in the female ghettos; of how, in a matter of a few years, well-intentioned feminists can be involved in undercutting their less privileged sisters, and with them the power of organized feminism as a whole.

But that legacy, by giving us the power of hindsight, can also help us to find an alternative route. Having seen how women have been divided by their differences in social position and the illusion of power offered by integration into sexist institutions on those institutions' terms, we can refuse to be divided again. Having seen how alliances with non- and antifeminist forces have eroded our strength, we can avoid those alliances now. Having seen how preoccupation with laws and state control worked to displace concern with and action on the real conditions of women's lives, we can choose not to be diverted and coopted.

If we simply step over the censorship trap, if we renew our determination to fight for economic and institutional change, we can increase the power of modern women to bring about a better life for all. Instead of championing censorship, we can organize so that a multiplicity of feminist voices speaking about sex and gender are heard. Instead of seeking top-down state control, we can demand public resources for social services organized on the basis of self-determination and social empowerment. These are the principles of a living, growing, transforming feminism, one that extends and gives real meaning to democracy.

Acknowledgments

Without the work of feminist historians Judith Walkowitz (*Prostitution and Victorian Society: Women, Class and the State*, Cambridge University Press, 1980) and Carol Lee Bacchi (*Liberation Deferred: The Ideas of the English Canadian Suffragists 1877-1918*, University of Toronto Press, 1983), this article would not have been possible. I have also learned a great deal about the history of the politics of gender and sexuality from the work of Anna Davin, Barbara Ehrenreich, Deirdre English, Barbara Epstein, Michel Foucault, Linda Gordon, Atina Grossman, Rachel Harrison, Joseph Interrante, Gary Kinsman, Carol Lasser, John Mitzel, Frank Mort, Dorothy Smith, Meredith Tax and Jeffrey Weeks — lessons that have informed my general approach.

I am also profoundly indebted to all the contributors to this book. Their work and ongoing discussions about history, analysis and strategy throughout the last year have helped me to clarify my own thinking on these matters. I would like to thank in addition John McMullen, Cyndra McDowell and Renee Baert, Deirdre Gallagher and Judith Weisman.

Of course, though enriched by these writers and colleagues, I alone am responsible for the contents of this article.

References

The figure of $3 billion, which represents the discrepancy between wages actually earned and wages potentially earned under equal pay legislation, comes from *Costing Equal Value Legislation in Ontario*, prepared for the Ontario Ministry of Labour by Morley Gunderson, professor of economics and industrial relations at the University of Toronto, and released in 1984. Population figures are projected from the 1981 Canada Census.

On social versus repressive expenditure, see R.S. Ratner and John McMullen, "Social Control and the Rise of the Exceptional State in Britain, the United States and Canada," in *Crime and Social Justice*, Summer, 1983, and Ian Taylor, "Justice Expenditure, Welfare Expenditure and the Restructuring of the Canadian State," in *Crime, Capitalism and Community: Three Essays in Socialist Criminology*, Toronto, Butterworth, 1983.

Leonore J. Weitzman's study of the relative economic conditions of separated spouses was cited by Barbara Ehrenreich in *Ms.* magazine, June, 1983 (Vol. xi, no. 12).

Second Thoughts
Myrna Kostash

Once upon a time I thought I had pornography all figured out. Its meaning and signification. Its purpose. How it could be combatted. The alternatives to it. On rereading my first analyses and critiques of the phenomenon, I am struck by the self-confidence of my theoretical assertions, my conviction that I had confined this many-headed beast neatly within the frame of my feminist understanding. Specifically, I wrote confidently of the difference between erotica and pornography and of the possibility that we could produce the erotic in our subterranean feminist cells. I entered assuredly into the debate around sexuality that the antiporn campaign enjoined; that porn is about this and that aspect of hetero-sex. I spoke of the perfect victimization, the categorical objectification of women in the pornographic image, that we are imaged *out there* outside our consciousness, our subjectivity. And I called, unproblematically, for the banning of that image.

Nowadays I am not so sure. As the antipornography debate and campaign have matured, broadened, become more complex, *I* have become more confused. Now, I cannot present anything definitive or conclusive or *correct*; I can only offer my tentativeness, my doubts, my second thoughts, so as to, I hope, encourage other women to express all the contradictoriness of our collective thinking and feeling about pornography, as painful as it is to acknowledge. Of course, in doing so we make ourselves vulnerable to those with more doctrinaire views who would see us as irresolute, but that is the price we pay for intellectual and political growth. And we owe it to the women's movement to do so publicly and not yield the terrain of debate to polarized argument.

"In the best of possible worlds, how would we represent sex? With tenderness, affection, respect, with humour, playfulness. We would take delight in the sensuous detail, we would caress, we would be open, psychically, to the 'lunar,' to that part of our nervous system which is intuitional, which apprehends patterns, which is artistic. The 'erotica' which corresponds to this ideal would represent freely chosen sexual behaviour in which the partners would serve each other's (and Eros'!) pleasure equally and in which the 'I love you' is made flesh." I wrote that in 1981. You can see that I attempted a definition of the erotic in what I hope are feminist terms, but the trouble with this is that it is, of course, a utopian vision: necessarily vague, evasive, dreamy, because we are not much used to contemplating a condition of sexual happiness. What we are used to is sexual terror and guilt and disappointment. What we are used to is our silence on the subject.

When we attempt such definitions, therefore, we are talking about what is *possible*, not what is already realized. And if our sexual happiness is *not* a realized thing — socially, culturally, psychologically — in the real world, then who are we trying to fool when we say we can draw the line, *in the real world*, between the erotic and the pornographic? The erotic, in feminist terms, does not exist. The erotic will be the project of a postpatriarchal, postcapitalist culture of lovers. What does exist at this point is the difference between the more and the less pornographic: at one end, "snuff" films, at the other, *Cosmopolitan* magazine covers, and, somewhere between, crotch shots from *Penthouse*. By trying to draw lines among these phenomena — by saying that scenes of sexual torture are what we're worried about, not soft-focus "pussy," or that the explicitly sexual, not the soft-core suggestive, is problematic — we are being naive.

I know that we have attempted to draw these lines because we do not want to march under the same banner with the antismut brigades, nor do we want to seem like poor sports, and we especially don't want to be drawn into a position where to be antipornography is just a smokescreen for disgust with female sexuality. And we have focused on violence as the quintessential component of porn and have said of an image that is "just" a crotch shot, "Well, *that's* not pornographic." *That*, I suppose, is erotic?

What has in part happened here, I think, is what American feminist sociologist Kathleen Barry calls the "erosion of sensibility and sensitivity": to attack *Playboy* is now seen, even by feminists, as somehow excessive, somehow not the point. (As the pornography subcommittee of the Metropolitan Toronto Task Force on Violence against Women discovered, 89.6 percent of the pornography available in 1983 was unavailable or sold under the counter in 1970. In 13 years much of what we used to call pornography became normal.) Compared to images of torture, I suppose crotch shots *are* relatively harmless — and I have heard decent men argue that they are beautiful because "pussy is beautiful" — but somewhere along the line we have lost our original insight into the misogynist nature of *all* exploitative images of women and have diluted our critique of the objectification inherent in almost any representation of our sexuality in the culture of a male-dominated society. We have lost or forgotten what we originally knew to be true: that, for our purposes as feminists, the iconography of heterosexuality is, by definition, a representation of dominance/submission, activity/passivity, power/powerlessness. Is, by definition, pornographic. To try to separate the "pornographic" from the everyday is an exercise requiring some imagination.

Here, for instance, is a definition of pornography used by Vancouver sociologist Jillian Ridington in a discussion paper she presented to the Association of Women and the Law in 1983: "Pornography is a presentation, whether live, simulated, verbal, pictorial, filmed or videotaped, or otherwise represented, of sexual behaviour in which one or more participants are coerced, overtly or *implicity*, into participation; or are injured or abused physically or *psychologically*; or in which an *imbalance of power* is obvious, or *implied* by virtue of the immature age of any participant or by contextual aspects of the presentation, and in which such behaviour can be taken to be advocated or endorsed" [emphases added]. Now this is one of the stricter definitions I have come across, but I have to ask: By this definition, *what* in popular culture, in elite culture, in advertising, in best sellers, in movies, in all those places where heterosexual coupling is portrayed or implied, where the turn-on is psychological, where an imbalance of power is of the essence in the message, what is *not* pornographic?

I can't believe I just wrote that. Do I mean it? If, by the logic of definitions and, let's face it, by the logic of our own feelings as we make our way through the streets, our culture is profoundly and pervasively pornographic, then what does it mean to say, "We are going to examine pornography," as though we could pick it up where the erotic — whatever that is — leaves off?

It seems to me that we've laid another sort of trap for ourselves as well in this attempt to distinguish erotica and pornography: we continue to talk about all this as though it were only about sex; as though the one is to be distinguished from the other by the way it depicts sex. What we need, we say to one another, is another way of making love, other sorts of turn-ons, new routes of sensuality, and so on. Are we not at the same point of our understanding here as we were of rape just before we made the analytical breakthrough that rape is not about sick male sexuality but about *power*? We argue that pornography can somehow be cleaned up, its worst aspects deleted so as not to offend feminist sensibilities. We talk about deprogramming the male sexual imagination by offering mastur-batory fantasies from the women's movement, as though pornog-raphy were only about sexual immaturity. Even if we can create small spaces of sexual alternatives, we would still be left with the source of our malaise (of which pornography is only a symptom): social and cultural powerlessness.

We are also evading our own complicity in the reproduction of the pornographic. And this brings me to the second of my con-fusions: fantasy. Kathleen Barry has said of pornography that in its imagery woman is the "naturally masochistic sexual object" who exists only for men's sexual use and satisfaction. That it is organized entirely around erection and ejaculation. That women are simply consumed. But here's a curious thing: I have noticed that in this imagery, by and large, in spite of the ropes and chains, the leather accoutrements, the gloved fists, the boots, and so on, we do not look as if we have been beaten up. Where are the bruises, the wounds and welts of *real* violence? It may be, as Kathleen Barry suggests, that this is due to the "reality distortion" of porn, the make-believe that sadism is the other half of the duality that women complete with masochism; the make-believe that "it doesn't really hurt." Or that the pain has been transformed, in the very moment of its experience, into pleasure. And that that moment, by yet another reality distortion, is therefore something we participate in of our free will because it feels good after all. I would go further. What this paradigm also seems to say is that our consent is necessary in order for the image to have its orgasmic effect, in much the same way that a rapist requires his victim to say she "likes it" or "loves him."

What is going on here? Why must we be seen to like and want such treatment? Here are a couple of ideas. Suppose that somewhere deeply hidden is the primal male desire to make a connection with the female, to unite, to mate. You do not devour your mate; you lie down with her, and she with you. Is it possible that even in pornography, in spite of its distortion and its viciousness, in spite of the systematic organization of male desire in paradigms of power, men want to be close to women? Of course, given their social and economic superiority in the real world, men find it difficult, if not impossible, to desire this intimacy and connection without simultaneously needing to reconfirm their power in fantasies of sexual dominance. Given their fear of bewilderment at autonomous female sexuality, men likewise find it difficult to seek knowledge of their mate without first rendering her manageable through fantasies of her quiescent availability. But the possibility remains: the pornographic image contains a projection of the male need for sexual partnership.

Suppose also that the pornographic image includes our consent and our pleasure because, at the level of fantasy, we *do* consent, we *do* take our pleasure? There is evidence from consciousness-raising-group discussions, at least, that the orgasms of a lot of women are orchestrated around fantasies of submission to the penis (or penises, in the case of more elaborate fantasies). We've all been made to feel guilty about this and various feminist therapies have offered to purge us of such atavism, but the fact is that, even outside masturbatory fantasies, there is a lot of very sexual, not to say pornographic, suggestion aimed at us and that it works: we become aroused. A lingerie ad playing on the fantasy of the older woman and her boyish lover (she is cool as a cucumber in black silk; he, dishevelled, is offering her her morning coffee). The famous scene of sexual consummation between the heroine and the priest in the novel *The Thornbirds*. Richard Gere in any of his movies where he takes off his shirt. Television cable porn programs — 60 percent of whose urban viewers are women, according to one source. I'm not arguing that our arousal extenuates such calculated imagery. But I do want to suggest that it is far too simple to see pornography just as something "done" to us. We women have our own pornographic imagination and I wonder if these fantasies aren't necessary in some way. In them we can be really sexy without suffering the social consequences; we can experiment with all the different ways of "getting off"; we can *enjoy* ourselves, where in real life our guilt about our own sexuality is so easily turned into hostility to men's desire. Of course, just as with men's fantasies, the materials of such arousal are very limited and crude, but until there is a revolution in the institutions that regulate sexual relations — the family, the school, the workplace — perhaps the pornographic fantasy is one of the few ways that women and men, captives together of those institutions, victims alike of their alienating procedures, are permitted connection.

Finally I come to my confusion around censorship. There was a time I felt clear about this: pornography is dangerous to women and should be banned, like a toxic substance polluting our environment. That was my feminist position. However, I am also a writer. And as a result of debates within the Writers' Union of Canada concerning freedom of expression and the freedom to read, I found myself arguing from another position altogether. To paraphrase Albert Camus, freedom to publish and read does not necessarily assure a society of justice and peace, but without these freedoms it has no assurance at all. Since these two positions are irreconcilable (and calling pornography a "commodity" is no help at all: an image, a word, is not a can of soup), I have flipped and flopped.

While I am deeply sympathetic to the impulse to, say, burn pornography in a big bonfire downtown, trash the video shops, string up the publishers and distributors, put my boyfriend in a political reeducation camp whenever he buys *Penthouse* (and send my own fantasies there too), I can't act on it.

Some feminists argue that the issue is to, as the feminist newspaper *Broadside* has expressed it, "regain control of the State's power by redefining and refining the definition of obscenity so that it meets our standards and needs." But like other contributors to this book, I argue that the state is hardly a neutral, let alone prowoman, institution that can be captured and directed toward our projects; it is specific to the development of capitalist patriarchy; its capture and transformation require a revolution. In any case, obscenity is not the issue. The Criminal Code, in reference to obscenity, talks about the "undue exploitation of sex," as though there were some we could put up with. Is explicit sex obscene? Are suntan lotion ads okay? It seems that, in practice, it is only the police who are sure of the difference between the tolerable and intolerable. And that censor boards tend to find noncommercial explicit sex unacceptable and the commercial variety quite tolerable. And that the courts find prosecution of obscenity costly and difficult. And that, in the case of Victoria-based Red Hot Video, three tapes were found to be obscene and the shop fined $100 for each one. At the time of writing, the decision was still under appeal. That's liberal democracy for you. The authorities aren't just being coy. They really aren't sure what is hateful and what isn't, what is offensive to women and why. A perfect example of this, and for me a very persuasive argument against giving the authorities any jurisdiction in this matter, is what happened to the May, 1983, issue of *Penthouse*.

It gained attention when, because of a feature entitled "Wonders of the Eastern World" — reproductions of sexual art from India, China and Japan — it was seized by customs officers in Ontario and sent back to the U.S. The offending (obscene?) parts were the great number of erect and penetrating penises, but, when these were blacked out with big dots, the magazine was allowed to be sold in Canada. The customs officers, needless to say, did not find offensive or obscene the usual pages of "split beaver" shots. Nor were they offended — and this is the crux of the story — by a cartoon near the front of the magazine. It shows a man and woman on a bed, making love doggie-style. The man is holding a pistol to the back of the woman's head and the caption reads: "Oh, you don't have to worry about getting pregnant. I've taken all of the precautions." To me this is the ultimate pornographic fantasy: the masculine wish for our death. And yet no state authority found it obscene. So much for strategic alliances with the state. So much for hoping that in the application of censorship the state will be sensitive to the distinctions between erotica and porn, between porn and explicit sexuality, between desire and hate.

By way of conclusion let me try this out on you. I have argued that pornography is not about sex. What is it about? Given the fact that sexual repression in the family together with prostitution and pornography (which originally meant "writing about prostitutes" and what can be done to them and, these days, also to wives, daughters, lovers) are one highly interdependent system, at the heart of which is the "exchange of women"; and given the fact that this exchange of women (in which a man gives another man a woman as a gift in order to establish kinship between them) means that women are for men to dispose of and we are in no position to give ourselves away (which describes our situation in pornography as well); and given that the exchange of women is otherwise known as marriage, may I suggest that pornography is about marriage? Smash monogamy! Remember that one? Maybe we were onto something. . . .

Pornography: Image and Reality
Sara Diamond

It's not surprising that feminists have become fascinated with pornography. After all, it is the only visible, publicly accessible information about men's attitudes toward sexuality in general and women within sex in particular. For many women, the distorted images of pornography have become the symbol of men's hostility and violence against women. Women have expended tremendous effort to control the proliferation of pornography, seeking increased intervention by the police, courts and various levels of government.

Surprisingly, however, feminism and porn have something in common. Both insist that women are sexual beings. Both have made sex an experience open to public examination and, now, debate. This difficult process of extricating sex from its once private domain cannot be abandoned in the fight against pornography. Feminist support for state censorship will lead us at a dead run into a dead-end. We will find the exit blocked by highly organized conservative governments and male-dominated courts and police and the sexual freedom and control we require will be lost. Instead, we must work to repossess our sexuality, through sex education and the production of sex-positive imagery, and through changing the economic and social position of women and men — steps that will undermine the demand for sexist sexual imagery.

To explain these conclusions I plan to answer a series of questions. What is pornography? Who produces it? Who buys it and why? How does porn work as a set of images? What is the relationship of pornography to reality, fantasy and behavior for men and women? What bearing does pornography have on sex? I want to suggest that pornography is complex and multilayered, with a number of different — sometimes even contradictory — dimensions, which we oversimplify at our peril. I then want to suggest what feminists should do about pornography and what kind of alternative images we must develop.

You Can Tell a Magazine by Its Centrefold

One of the greatest dangers we face when trying to understand pornography is confusing explicit sex with sexism. It is possible to create images of sexual experience that do not perpetuate the current imbalance of power between men and women. Other cultures have produced humorous, visually pleasurable or powerful images of lovemaking, free from degradation. Sexism enters the picture in the ways that the porn industry creates images and in the assumptions that people call upon when interpreting them.

In order to free sex from its armor of sexism, I want to talk about pornography in a different way from some feminists. In the 1983 Minneapolis ordinance they were instrumental in drafting, Andrea Dworkin and Catharine MacKinnon defined porn as "the sexually explicit subordination of women, graphically depicted, whether in pictures or in words." The legislation went on to outline in detail what specifically they considered to be oppressive (see Appendix II). But this view of pornography is too simplistic, for it suggests that images of sex are the same as real sex, and that the images themselves are responsible for women's subordination.

In fact, pornography is many things: a product made to be sold by a multimillion-dollar industry; a set of coded messages about sex, and male and female roles in this culture; and a specific form of sexual and cultural activity.

Pornography is produced by business interests for sale within an increasingly competitive market. To turn a profit, management must consider factors such as payment of models, camerapeople and distributors and the cost of production equipment. These concerns influence both the quality of the product and the nature of the images that are produced. Much pornography is low budget and shoddy; little money is invested in script development. Some porn seems unrealistic, even ludicrous, unless the viewer is particularly interested in the activities shown.

Recently, increased competition in the industry has meant that porn producers have had to find new markets while keeping old customers satisfied. But while magazines such as *Playboy* may adapt to conform to changing standards of "sex appeal" or beauty, the central image in the vast majority of heterosexual pornography — that of a willing, sweet, young "girl" — remains the same. The constant nature of this ideal of womanhood provides reassurance and security for the consumers of pornography, who in buying a magazine or viewing a movie can possess in fantasy women (and their associated accoutrements) who would be unattainable in real life. In this sense, pornography is similar to advertising in that the consumer can buy the product but not the happiness or status that it promises. This unbridgeable gap between reality and fantasy encourages further purchases, whether of an advertised product or of pornography, which is a kind of advertising for — among other things — male power.

Pornography both directly exploits and indirectly exerts power over women. In the cutthroat and often coercive businesss they do not control, women are the critical raw material that is exchanged and molded. Not only do the images portray real women, but the finished product, which shows men symbolically controlling women during sex (either directly or through repeated scenarios of acquiescence and service), is then sold to men so that they can reassure themselves that they remain in positions of power socially and sexually. Heterosexual pornography expresses the industry's ideas about men's fantasies of sexual fulfillment and its own ideas of how men need to remain if they are to continue to buy pornography.

The industry's version of the man who reads pornography has a female corollary: the woman in pornography. Porn often pretends that women are malleable, obsessed with sex and willing to engage in any sexual act with any available partner. In violent pornography, men's supposed ability to control women is symbolized through degradation and destruction of the female body. Racist stereotypes are common; much pornography suggests that women of color are animallike, insatiable. The plotlines or articles that accompany pictorials imply that gender identity and sexual behavior are "natural" and biologically determined. By portraying male aggression within sex as being perfectly natural, much pornography actually validates socially learned machismo.

Most pornography assumes an all-male audience. Porn movie houses and live theatres are environments where men find their response constantly reinforced by other men. Whatever doubts men may have about the accuracy of the images and the messages are repressed, for to acknowledge uncertainties would be to threaten the bonds of masculinity confirmed in these settings. Similarly, home video and magazines, which also rely heavily on the same stereotypes and conventions of action and narrative, also express an implied male agreement about sex, women and by extension men.

In daily life a woman's stance and facial expression communicate her sense of self, how she wants to be treated and what can be done to her. In pornography, the woman is often posed facing the viewer, her expression expectant or eager; or with her back to us, face turned over the shoulder to look at the viewer, waiting or even cowering submissively. When a man is shown, he is frequently positioned so that it is easy for the male viewer to imagine himself in the male model's place. The pleasure here is not about rejoicing in mutual seeing and touching, but about the clothed and invulnerable male observer watching and controlling the naked woman in the fantasy. (Female nakedness in this culture is most often interpreted as sexual availability, for it is in this way that the female nude has been presented and interpreted since the advent of the oil painting tradition.)

The visual nature of porn images reinforces perceptions of male control over female bodies in another way as well. Because of the tendency in sexist culture to reduce women to functions rather than to cherish their individuality, feminists have rightly criticized the way pornography concentrates on fragments of the female form: a breast, foot, mouth. This allows the viewer to distance himself from the real person to whom the fragment belongs, avoiding the demands of relating to a whole, intelligent, emotional and active woman. But it is also true that photography as a medium captures living, moving people and dynamic processes, immortalizing them outside of time and change. So while people may read images of fragments as frozen or deathlike, and hence when depicting women, as containing an added measure of misogynist feeling, this need not always be the case, nor is it inherent in visual fragmentation.

The immortalization effect of fragmentation also does something else: it gives the image another level of meaning, making it symbolic of memory or sentiment, seeming to express the "essence" of the complex process represented on the film. And, sexism aside, fragments are often more erotic than the whole image because they are associated with memories or dreams of pleasure for all of us. The prevalence of breasts, vaginas, women's mouths and buttocks says as much about the power men have to fill social space with images of their dreams and desires as it does about the tendency of our sexist culture to fragment women. And given that power, it is not surprising that women's body parts have become symbols of het-erosexual pleasure for both women and men.

On a different but related level, pornography also provides men with opportunities to indulge in "scopophilia" —the voyeuristic pleasure of simply looking without acting. This kind of sexual ac-tivity allows men to remain passive. They can be sexually unassertive as the images or narrative act to arouse them, without having to deal with potentially awkward or frightening social dynamics if they take the passive — the traditionally feminine — role in a sexual encounter. There are other aspects to voyeurism. We are inundated with visual imagery in North America, and I believe that the in-creased popularity of visual pornography can in part be attributed to this phenomenon. We have become used to experiencing pleasure and gathering information from visuals, so that while the voyeurism that pornography encourages is an ideological confirmation of men's power, it is also a contemporary way of fulfilling curiosity about sex in general, and about others' sexual activities.

All these aspects of pornography are in some sense easily visible, understandable and evident. But there are other dimensions that do not immediately meet the eye and, almost paradoxically, seem to contradict pornography's more obvious aspects — at least those that claim that men are in complete control. Because I believe that in terms of *unconscious* messages, much pornography is ultimately about men's fears: of inadequacy, of being controlled by women emotionally and sexually through dependency, of losing power.

In recent years women have demanded sexual as well as social and economic equality. The fact that women can have clitoral orgasms independent of penetration has become widely known, as have many women's choices for lifestyles autonomous from men. Both these recent developments directly threaten culturally formed masculine sexual identities, and feminists have suggested that the recent boom in pornography may be part of the resultant antifeminist backlash, for it reassures men that women are still under men's thumbs. There is no doubt in my mind that these recent developments are being felt at a deep level by many men. But they are not alone the cause of men's existing fears of women, fears that are old, deeply ingrained and part of very traditional gender socialization.

Susan Lurie, writing from a neo-Freudian perspective, suggests the following process of psychological formation, one that could be described as "womb envy." According to Lurie, male babies and young boys identify with their mothers, who have nurtured them both physically and emotionally. But our society demands of young boys that they break the bond with the mother early in life. In this process, Lurie says, they learn that their penis — signifying their membership in the dominant group — is the source of their pleasure, individuality and power in the world. They are forced to choose between identifying with their fathers or with their mothers — whom they love, but who have no penis and therefore no power. Given this training, boys fear being seen as women — without a penis, castrated — and thus losing their growing power in the world.

Lurie suggests that heterosexual intercourse simultaneously promises men self-fulfillment through pleasure and conquest and threatens a loss of identity through contact with the vagina, the symbol of female sexuality. That a man experiences arousal from sexual contact with women is delightful, but also recalls his early childhood love for his mother, a love that he was forced to reject and fear. The heterosexual relationship becomes laden with conflict for men. The female sexual organs seem to represent the latent power of women, for unlike the exposed penis, women's genitals are self-contained and invulnerable. In intercourse the vagina acts upon the penis to change it, from erect, to orgasmic, to flaccid. In Lurie's view, "The vagina is like the imagination; not only does it take in and transform, it is internal." The woman's body appears to be what he has learned that only he as a man can be: active and transforming in the world. The womb, to which the vagina leads, has an even greater creative power; it can produce babies, again reminding the man of his former childhood dependency. For men, intercourse involves the contradiction of allowing an expression of individuality while threatening to destroy that sense of self by making them vulnerable.

The sexist messages within pornography offer comfort in the face of these fears. The exposure of women's sexual parts demonstrates both women's vulnerability and men's ability to control them. Violent images of sexual mutilation of women, by themselves and others, proves that women can be castrated instead of castrating. Sexist pornography provides a set of mythic ideas — feminists have said that mythic or not, they amount to lies — that serve to allay men's fear of losing power. They thus assuage deeply felt anxieties that, no doubt, are hard to live with for many men, even if the distress is unconscious. But these fears can only be deprived of their crippling effect on men if they are made explicit and analyzed, or defused through different erotic messages and surpassed (as suggestsed later) — not if they are constantly reinforced by the sexist symbolism inherent in most pornography. Other possibilities of identity and pleasure need to come alive in images and in life.

And this is not impossible. When a critical mixed setting exists — one in which men can allow themselves to identify and feel solidarity with women and resist the sexist masculine bonding encouraged by much pornography — the spell of porn can often be broken. A good illustration of this was the experience of Vancouver antipornography organizers when they showed three excerpts from Red Hot Video's particularly violent tapes in 1983. Those attending, including male reporters, were unanimously disturbed by the images. The usual porn theatre environment — the sense of an enclosed space controlled by men — was dispelled. By contrast, a woman reporter later showed one of the tapes to colleagues in the newsroom. Here she was the only woman in a group of men. They ridiculed her and belittled her discomfort, telling her that the tape wasn't "real," just fantasy. In the first case, men's potential to identify with women was accentuated and produced positive results. In the second, men's fear of breaking masculine identification got the better of them.

Image, Reality and Behavior: A Complex Interface

There is a prevalent belief in our culture that images represent reality in a literal way, when in fact they are the result of a whole series of manipulations. Camera angles (direct, from above or below); framing (close in to long shot); the composition of the picture (what comprises a scene and what in that scene is included in the final frame); the relationship of audio to visual images (think of the difference between "No, no" and "Yes, yes" in a sex scene); editing styles (fast cuts versus real time, what is included and excluded); and sequence and implied plotline all intervene between the real experience and the image. These elements work together to provide a specific message, one constructed by the maker of the image, which is then interpreted by viewers who impose the conventions they have learned to use when "reading" visual symbols.

Just as images do not present a literal view of reality, so there is no direct relationship between what an image shows and what its viewer acts out. Feminist theorists such as Kathleen Barry and Laura Lederer espouse a version of behaviorist psychology, according to which the human male runs the treadmill of sexual violence for gratification in the same way a caged rat will run for cheese. Because some pornographic images suggest that sexual violence gives men more power and because the images result in orgasms (that is, this theory goes, positive reinforcement), pornography therefore conditions men to rape and abuse real women. While some men may be aroused by images of violence against women (including in nonsexually explicit contexts), few men will act on these images. The idea that every time women get a thrill from watching women TV cops Cagney and Lacey shoot a crime suspect we want to kill, or that scenes of destruction, bombing or torture in which "our side" wins trigger our desire to hurt other human beings runs counter to most women's experience. The suggestion that consumers of pornographic material or other media products respond in zombielike, imitative fashion to all powerful images is both false and frightening.

A similar misconception about the relation between image and experience is that the pornography viewer gets everything he needs — his whole sexual experience — from the image itself. In fact, there are other important contributing factors. In addition to the preconscious fantasies or memories pornography stimulates, its taboo nature combines with and accentuates the expectation of arousal virtually on its own. (I am watching porn, therefore I'm supposed to get turned on, therefore even if it's an image of a lettuce leaf I am going to get turned on.) Again the all-male, high-pressure environment in which a lot of porn is viewed may provide enough of a context for stimulation that the storyline or images don't really matter. In fact, men's responses are influenced by a wide range of elements, from the viewing context, to the specific images seen, to the relative absence of responsibility offered by the fantasy portrayed. While the porn industry (and some feminist theorists) may argue that men's attitudes toward sex are universal, there is actually an infinite variety of individual differences interwoven with their group similarities. There are men, for example, who enjoy being made love to, abandoning the role of aggressor/initiator; while others cannot relinquish their macho control. (Many men's experience and desire exist somewhere in between these poles.) It is quite possible that two such men would have very different emotional experiences when confronted with identical images.

Another aspect of the conditioning theory is the idea that men's response to pornography follows a continuum, that viewing soft-core porn inevitably leads men to seek out hard-core, violent material. Certainly both men's and women's definitions of what is "normal" in terms of sexual behavior changes over time, shifts that are related to social and economic trends. For example, the pressure from women for more sexual autonomy that began in the late '60s can be linked to such factors as the greater number of women entering the workforce, the availability of effective birth control and a general questioning of other social norms. But the notion that porn is addictive relies on the same faulty thinking that suggests that use of marijuana leads inevitably to heroin — patently untrue, as the experience of millions of North Americans proves. And the greater general visibility and acceptability of sexual imagery reflects not only the backlash against women but also real gains by the women's and gay movements in making sexuality an area of more open and explicit discussion and depiction.

In fact, one of the attractions of pornography is that it shows illicit acts that are safer, both legally and emotionally, when kept in the realm of fantasy. For some people *not* believing the fantasy psychologically allows arousal that the guilt of believing or doing would destroy. I am not saying, as the pornography industry often does, that pornography is a healthy release for violent men, but I do think there is a wide gulf between the fantasy, no matter how grotesque, and the reality. In trying to understand this fantasy/reality relationship it's useful for us as women to recall our own fantasy life: our imagination shifts and changes based on how much power we have in our lives and our relationships, as well as on the basis of our early patterns of sexual response. We, too, often engage in fantasies that we would not like to act out in our real lives. We may fantasize about sexual activity or people we have left behind; our fantasies are sometimes even the converse of our real lives.

Admittedly violent pornography and other violent media such as television do provide models for the minority of men who do act out sexual violence against women. But pornography influences reality in much the same way as the idea that "a woman's place is in the home" does, because both reinforce existing social structures.

Our male-dominated legal system makes it easier for men to get away with violent behavior toward women; and pornography further pressures some — possibly many — women to do what is asked of them without complaint. (Check out the *Cosmo* sex advice columns too.) But these are problems with our values, our mass media and our system of justice. Censorship won't make general ideas of violence against women go away; it won't make pornography disappear, just move underground. And even if porn were to miraculously disappear, violence against women would continue as long as other oppressive structures remained in place.

This Is Who You Would Be and Could Be if You Weren't You

The female viewer seldom sees her experience reflected in pornography or mainstream films or television. Consequently women have the difficult choice of either identifying with the man's point of view as expressed through script and image, or identifying with the screen woman and her experience, again created by men. The alternatives force women to choose between sustaining false expectations of women's behavior by objectifying other women or trying to live up to standards that usually defy experience.

For women, watching porn can draw us into a complex knot of pleasure and discomfort. While we may be aroused by the sexual activities depicted, most of us cannot avoid identification with the woman in the image, even if we occasionally and sometimes simultaneously identify with the man in the fantasy. Whatever pleasure we experience is often mixed with anxiety about our own sexuality being so different from that shown and anger at being forced into a role that does not represent who we are and what we need sexually. One Vancouver antipornography organizer studying violent pornography described the importance of understanding what aspects of the images she found pleasurable and the ways that these were immediately followed by images of pain. The *structure* of the video linked pleasure and pain again and again through fast editing, yet this bore no relationship to her own concept of enjoyable sex. She described her anger at having to constantly step backwards and remember that the images were constructed by real people to create a specific effect.

Women are taught to identify our own sexuality with an ideal of femininity. Many women describe a sense of being always watched, and of performing. Our culture equates women's sexuality with sexual availability; we learn from an early age to be coy, to flirt, to move seductively to make men respond to us. We learn to feel pleasure at the other's pleasure, to project sexuality in response to men's desire. This way, we are continually told, we will be desired, loved and taken care of. When we see images of other women being sexual with men, we project our identities onto the image, feeling the power relative to men. The depiction of sex can trigger memories or fantasies that are quite separate from that shown in the picture. The problem is that when we return to the actual image, we are usually confronted with a message that destroys our power and pleasure.

For many women sexual fantasy involves not only participation in a set of actions, but certain emotional settings and coordinates. Love magazines and mass-market romances are the equivalent of women's pornography. They often contain explicit details of love-making, but always in the framework of passion, "true love" and "tenderness." Invariably the stories include details of the setting, the heroine's wardrobe, the obstacles in her immediate situation. The descriptions of the dynamics in the relationship with the man (he is her boss, married to someone else, has denied her, is pursuing her, and so on) and the feelings before, during and after intercourse are also always included. These and their placing in a larger narrative context are the things that differentiate women's from men's sexually explicit literature. But these "feelings" and descriptions are not necessarily benign or even positive frameworks for sexual experience. Indeed they are often vehicles that convey strong messages about the dangers of pre- and extramarital sex and many other types of behavior proscribed by traditional (that is, patriarchal) morality. In these, too, pleasure is often linked to issues of punishment and loss of power.

In fact, there is nowhere we as women can exist freely without being castigated for our sexuality. Part of many women's aversion to graphic sexual imagery may well stem from the literal or figurative kick in the teeth that comes with being a sexual woman. We are well-taught that to be treated properly we must keep our legs crossed at all times. Explicit sexual imagery makes us uncomfortable because it is public, and we have learned that to engage in public displays of sexuality is to be defined as a slut. Where boys learn that sex makes them powerful, we learn that it makes us powerless and bad.

Given the way that our sexuality is repressed and channelled in our childhood, it's no wonder that women often recoil from the idea of the depiction of sex. Thirty years ago, studies such as Kinsey's indicated that women responded less to visual stimuli than did men, and women's greater sexual repression (relatively speaking) has often been cited to explain what they found. In part this explanation is probably valid. But there are other factors too: visual imagery is often inaccurate in representing what gives *us* pleasure; we may feel humiliated at the display of women in sexist poses; we may think that the men who are depicted in conventions which represent men's mistaken views of what turns us on look ridiculous.

The growing availability of pornography geared toward women and men and the increasing popularity of events such as male strip shows for women audiences indicate that women's lack of enthusiasm for sexually explicit visual stimulation may be changing as women become more skilled and assertive about seeking something for themselves within the current male-dominated sex culture — a concept that is backed up by recent studies. Still many factors will have to change — childhood and adult treatment of our sexuality, the representation of women and men within our visual culture — before we can evaluate with any objectivity if there is anything to the notion that women are less interested or moved by imagery per se.

One important example of the discrepancy between women's internal erotic experience and most pornographic depictions is the area of submission. There is a wide gap between the fantasies of submission that we construct for ourselves and those that porn fabricates for us. Most women seldom imagine being hurt by men in a sexual context, but many women do fantasize about being ravished. It is not surprising that women daydream about being uncontrollably desired in a culture in which our value as human beings is based on our attractiveness, and in which we are constantly prevented from acting out our desires. If we fantasize a partner taking complete control of a sexual encounter, then we are absolved from responsibility for our abandoned behavior. In this way we can mentally break sexual taboos that still remain in place in practice. We can also use fantasy to confront and explore what we are afraid of. But no matter how passive a woman is in her fantasy, she is still in control of it, she can end or change it as she desires. This is very different from the male variations on these fantasies created by the pornography industry. Needless to say, it is an entirely different situation from real rape and abuse.

Because pornography itself has so many levels and dimensions, it is my conclusion that strategies related to pornography must develop on a series of levels as well. However, it's important to begin by noting that fundamental changes in how sexual identities and behaviors are learned will not come about through suppressing images. No matter how insidious and antiwoman much pornography may be, it is not the primary cause of the repression of women's autonomous sexuality and the continued existence of male domination. Social and economic structures that create dependency on the sex market, reproduce the powerlessness of women and perpetuate women's cultural objectification create misogynist culture, and it is against these we must take aim. Porn will exist either underground or in the mainstream, as it currently does, until the roots of sexism are uncovered and broken.

In fact, nothing short of the full feminist agenda outlined elsewhere in this book will resolve the problem of pornography. We need economic equality and to win the right to free sexual expression, and control of our bodies, so that women will no longer be forced to work in the sex industry or submit to sexual activity that they do not like. Sex education in the schools, birth control, day care, access to abortion, facilities for raped and battered women, rights for lesbians and gays, and education about sexual alternatives are necessary. But while there is no substitute for long-term political and economic change, in the short term feminists have an essential role to play in developing an open and comprehensive discussion of sexuality and creating alternatives to the imagery offered by the porn industry.

We need to really talk about sex within the women's movement and within society in general. Narrowing such an exploration to porn inevitably leads to the idea that images cause the problems with sexuality in this culture, rather than simply portraying the problems. It reinforces in men's and women's minds the age-old notion that women are victims requiring protection rather than subjective sexual beings. Sexuality is a difficult and sometimes painful subject to discuss openly; we need a minimum of moralizing and a maximum of analysis.

Porn remains about the only source of explicit information on sex for young people. I can remember hours poring over my parents blue novels or rifling secretively through *Playboy* at the corner drugstore. (And I wonder how many other feminists have emerged, critical perspectives intact, from an early flirtation with pornography.) Unless women provide alternative — and accessible — information and instruction about sexuality, porn's appeal as one of the few sources of information about sex, no matter how distorted, will remain.

This discussion can expand to include the ways that we are delighted and empowered by sexual experience. Men can challenge their response to pornography and engage male viewers in analysis and anti-porn organizing. It is important for men to understand the ways that some components of their emotional and sexual selves are denied and others warped by pornography. Porn is in many ways less a women's issue than a men's issue, for the consumer is male and the product exists to assuage men's insecurities and fears.

Any tactics that we use that would directly affect the availability of porn should be chosen for their educational value: to show that this misrepresentation of women's bodies and identities makes us angry and to pose alternate ways of approaching sexuality in this culture. Community picket lines and sit-ins aimed at porn outlets can be effective, but only if we are careful about who we ally ourselves with and channel our anger, not calling for state censorship, but for consumers and communities to take responsibility for the images that they accept.

While images do not determine reality, they are unquestionably powerful. The women's movement is currently devoting vast economic and human resources to fighting existing pornography and other media imagery. It is my feeling that we would gain more by seeking resources to allow women to flood the market with feminist productions and to have access to the mass media in positions of real power and in large numbers. Imagine the impact that a woman-controlled television station could have. Widely distributed feminist imagery would be a provocative and active contradiction to the sexist imagery of all the current mass media.

While we are organizing for such access, a broad range of productions are needed. Documentary work needs to move beyond simply showing the content of pornography to examining the ways in which the meaning of porn images are created. One of the problems with existing educational material such as *Not a Love Story* and the slide show put together by the New York-based Women against Pornography is that the format and camera positions force us to look over the shoulder of the viewer or through his eyes. If we are to look at pornography, we must recognize the way the images work so as not to feel victimized by its content or be unwitting collaborators in its voyeurism. We must also leave room in the discussion for our emotional and sexual responses to emerge.

An analysis of the relationship, historic and current, between the repression of sexuality and the appeal of pornography is needed and it could perhaps coincide with a feminist history of censorship. Cross-cultural work that examines alternative ways of representing sexuality could illustrate how our society isolates and contains sexuality in a limited and limiting framework. There is tremendous power in realizing that pornographic images are created by people and that we as women can construct imagery of equal or greater impact.

Many women would like to see their sexuality not as a separate part of their lives, but as an empowering aspect of who they are as individuals and in relation to others. We catch glimpses of this possibility when we experience our eroticism in creative work and play outside the sex act. Such feminist critics as Audre Lourde have argued that the power of pornography can be usurped by demonstrating the eroticism embedded in everyday experience and emotion; by framing sex within the context of other activities, rather than elevating it to a romanticized or lowering it to a "dirty" event; by showing women as multidimensional human beings. Work that indicates that men and women's experience of sexuality integrates intellectual, emotional and physical processes is important in challenging porn's assumption that sex is naturally an uncontrollable, cathartic and independent force.

But there must be, as well, a place for imagery that is totally concerned with sex. Our society is one in which sexuality is isolated and treated as a category onto itself. While expanding the definition of eroticism is valuable, we need to retain contact with sex in our creative work. Unless we directly address the issue of what gives us pleasure, we will again abandon that terrain to pornography. Some feminists have defined erotica as images about sexuality that show equal power relationships and exchanges between mutually loving and committed people. But who will define what constitutes "equality," "love" and "commitment"? And even if we agree on the meaning of these words, one woman's dream may be another's prison. This society has traditionally chained women's sexuality to a love/ monogamy ideal. Let's not create new constraining ideas of what women's behavior should be, ideas that would rob us of our right to explore our desires on our own terms. We need to examine our feelings of lust, our desire for power, our objectification of others, how anger can be expressed within and through sexuality, our attraction to particular aspects of others' identities and images, and more, and not demand that our or others' fantasies conform to an abstract idea of politically correct sex.

At the same time as we examine erotic content, we need to look at visual stereotypes. In part, we can break the code through which images are read by contradiction, for reversing rules can force viewers to challenge their assumptions. We could put overalls onto women in lingerie; show men's fascination with their own image; challenge the stereotype of what a sexually active woman looks like; clothe women and leave men naked; interrupt standard porn scripts (for example, women breaking in on a rape scene and freeing the victim as they did in *Born in Flames*, or the victim resisting, defeating her rapist and punishing, perhaps dismembering him.) As well, we can blur sexually explicit images, create an ambience of desire, invest men with caring, sensitivity and the desire to be made love to. Women can also exert control in the way that they compose images; through the placement of camera and those within its frame the ever present, invisible male voyeur can be banished.

Inevitably, given our individual differences and the vast, unexplored terrain of our sexuality, one woman's porn is another's erotic art. If we are honest about images and ideas that inspire our sexuality, I think we will find a combination of the old castoffs of our training in a patriarchal culture, the ignored and frustrated elements of our present sexuality and new glimpses of pleasure, freedom and power. It is from the struggle with these conflicting feelings and impulses that really thoughtful and powerful imagery can emerge. It is impossible to completely separate images from their historic contexts; even pleasant images of cabbages that unroll like labia or fields reminiscent of the folds and curves of women's bodies are rooted in a long-standing romantic ideal of feminine beauty, one created by men. We need to think through the images that we use and to understand what of our current sexuality we want to retain and develop.

In the last decade, women cultural producers have been creating all kinds of work that grapples with sexual themes. In the last three years, several feminist-organized erotic art shows have been mounted in Vancouver, Toronto and Montreal, featuring multimedia presentations. The 1981 Herotica erotic art show in Vancouver developed dynamic processes in choosing and making images for a show. Organizers first looked at porn and other "suggestive" images of women, then discussed the imagery that they found most appealing within the traditional ways of representing women and then consciously developed images that did not correspond to these categories. While the final visions were somewhat abstract and highly individual, the process of developing the show is a valuable model for work of its kind.

Entre Nous, directed by Diane Kurys, explored the deep friendship and erotic attraction that women can feel for each other, and though it studiously avoids explicit imagery, it gives us a sense of erotic tension very different from most "malestream" films. Persimmon Blackbridge is a Vancouver artist who also conveys sexual energy in unusual, moving ways. In one of her sculptures two women hold hands, their bodies molded as though they were floating down a river, alive with the current, pushed apart by the water's force but held together by their touch. The piece evokes a sense of orgasmic transcendence and individual integrity.

Feminist images often contain the impulse toward self-validation, of reassessing and enjoying our bodies. These examples also bespeak an alternative lesbian vision, and in doing so state that lesbianism exists as a positive form of sexuality. This is important in a culture in which heterosexuality is perceived and shown time and again to be "natural" and absolute. Concurrently, the development of alternate heterosexual imagery is very important for it is heterosexual women's experience that is most often distorted by porn. Women can exert control over where and to whom we show our work. We can choose whether we want to show our fantasies (whether lesbian or heterosexual) to women alone or also use them to reeducate men. Showing erotic work in a context where it is discussed and analyzed helps to break down the traditional private space reserved for porn.

A number of feminist critics of pornography have resisted the idea of creating alternative imagery. They have said that such activity would only reinforce the male viewer's response to sexual images of women, and believe that even feminist erotica would support the market framework of pornography if it were produced to be sold within a capitalist culture market.

After examining the ways that pornographic images work, it is clear that there is no simple solution to the first issue. Male viewers of feminist-created erotica may well derive pleasure from the imagery, but surely feminists' objections are not to men's sexual pleasure per se, but to its current dependency on degrading images of women. Indeed, enjoying powerful images of women may break down men's fears of women by destroying the lies that porn tells about women's passivity and desire to be dominated. There is an additional concern that some women express: Does the male viewer reinterpret even positive images of women through oppressive conventions by, for example, assuming that any naked woman is available? But there are two other factors whose importance overrides this. First, for most men skillful images that empower women are not easily assimilated into patriarchal and misogynist interpretations, so that the very notion of "availability" would dissolve if an image could signal that women were self-defining and in charge. Second, and most important, women must become less concerned about men's response to our images than with creating visual material that helps us define and fight for our own sexuality.

There is a great area of exploration that is in its infancy, despite important developments in video, film, visual and performing arts. Increased censorship and other forms of institutional control over our sexual experience are on the upswing. The organized right and the state want to silence our visions, for they understand their potential power, at the same time as they enforce their traditional vision of the family, suppress abortion, birth control, lesbian and gay sexuality and sex education. Feminists can succumb to the pressures for censorship or we can aggressively present educational and artistic images that show the world as we view it and wish to see it, as part of a fight for a prowoman and sex-positive society.

A Capital Idea: Gendering in the Mass Media

Lisa Steele

A critique of the pornographic image *is* possible. I, however, will not be offering it for one simple reason: such an activity in isolation, can lead — directly or indirectly — to this particular set of visual representations being used as *the* operative "sieve of meaning" through which *all* representations of women must pass on their way to interpretation. And given the sea of images within the mass media that profess to be authoritative sources for what it is to be a woman, it is important to remember that the images of women that exist within hard- and soft-core porn are but one part of this process of representation — a process that is more characterized by continuity between the various sectors — that is, television programming, advertising, mass-circulation porn publications and so on — than it is by discord. All these sectors, having identified an "appropriate" market (audience, viewers, readers), undertake to provide it with the right product (program, ad, packaging, whatever) in order to make profits.

When pornography is removed from the overall continuity of image production within our society, severed from its roots as a form of industrially produced material several things happen. First, and almost immediately, porn — particularly the material that combines elements of violence with sexually charged pictures — is equated with disease. It is seen as the cankerous sore, the rapidly spreading infection within the body politic, a sickness so life-threatening that only the sharp lance of state censorship will save the dying patient (society).

This state intervention is supposedly undertaken on behalf of women. But legislation that focuses its attention on the elimination of "bad" images will do little to "protect" women in the long run. Only equal representation on our own terms within all areas of society — including media imagery — will accomplish this. We shouldn't settle for state censorship, which is about as effective as applying cardiopulmonary resuscitation to a mastodon, when what is needed is a whole new system for creating and distributing cultural information within our society, a system that is able to more adequately reflect how we will live our lives, and is structured more democratically in terms of production and dissemination of imagery and information.

There are other problems with the separation of pornography from the general realm of mass media images. When the question "Is this image pornographic?" becomes primary, when it becomes the "sieve of meaning" through which all images of women are sifted, a binary system for evaluating imagery is suggested. But when answering yes to this question becomes a prerequisite for criticizing how women are portrayed within all levels of the mass media, we're in trouble.

"Pornographic imagery" and "sexist imagery" are not interchangeable terms. If they are used as such, the term "pornography" will become devalued and be transformed into a generalized and meaningless catchphrase. And what about those images that have not registered in the red on the pornometer? Are they to be automatically given the stamp of approval by feminists? I'm not suggesting that those engaged in the anti-porn movement are uncritical of representations of women present in all forms of the mass media. It's just that any systematic analysis of imagery that posits porn as the bad end of the visual spectrum is bound to run out of steam before it gets to the overwhelming banality of most television and advertising, which are by far the more prevalent influences in our media landscape.

Here, images of women that could just as easily be subjected to a vigorous critique are allowed to pass as harmless, even entertaining. What is forgotten is that commodity fetishism is a two-way street: humans cannot be made into objects without a concurrent "humanization" of objects taking place. Is a "sexy" automobile in a television commercial — or a dancing candy bar, for that matter — any less harmful visually and psychically than a fragmented female form displayed on a newsstand shelf? All are products of an economy whose system of distribution relies on display for its most obvious purpose: to encourage consumption. Porn is just a small part of capitalism's attempt to turn us all into the proverbial kid in a candy store. By the time most of us get to porn, we've already seen prime time and we're well-trained to overspend our allowance, if only in our dreams.

So what are women to do? I would agree with British feminist Rosalind Coward, who has said, "Pornography as such is the wrong object of attack. Unless we refine our ways of talking about sexist codes in general, how they operate and produce their meanings, and why they are offensive, we run the risk of constantly being misunderstood." In this vein, I would offer the following examples of material that would not be considered pornography in the usual sense of the term but which nonetheless offers oppressive images of gender and sex, either overtly or as part of an embedded message. I did not have to go out of my way to locate any of these examples; all were readily available via television, billboards and magazines. All are, in fact, a structural part of our visual environment.

In September, 1984, in Canada, Pope John Paul II is just winding up his latest visit to the New World and in true small-c, catholic form, his homilies have offered something for almost everyone. Generally recognized as the first leader of the Roman Catholic church to have taken a leaf from the evangelists' book and seriously embraced the television age, John Paul has been the central figure in a triumphant union of the sacred and the venal, which, if Canadian broadcasters are to be believed, rivals both the 1984 Olympics and Michael Jackson's Victory Tour as media spectacle.

For women, however, the pope's messages remain rooted in prehistory, in spite of their newfangled packaging. The idealized family — which exists only for a minority of the population — must remain strong; no methods of artificial birth control are permissible; women must continue to merely support male frontline workers, who are allowed to serve their God on the altar of the church. Many Catholic women were more than a little discouraged by the pope's pronouncements, including his beatification of Sister Marie-Leonie, founder of a religious order dedicated to doing housework for priests. The symbolism of this elevation of a traditionally defined Ultrawoman — a woman both "married" to God and acting as "wife" to his celibate priests — was not lost on the feminists within the church, many of whom were openly critical of this action.

But enclosed within this very hidebound dogma regarding "a

woman's place" was John Paul's nod to modernity. The pope, it seems (along with the leaders of the three major political parties in the Canadian federal election in the fall of '84, all of whom were male), is against pornography. Two very obvious questions arise from this papal opinion. First, what does the pope know about porn? And second, if he, along with so many other powerful men, is opposed to porn, why is it still so pervasive? While I can't respond to my first question I would like to suggest a possible answer to the second: Few men in positions of power and influence really care about porn at all. Porn is simply the part of women's agenda that they — politicians and others in power — can most easily buy into. They may hedge around equal pay, abortion rights, universal day care, but ask them about porn and they're ready to rewrite the laws tomorrow, so deep is their "concern." And, to be realistic, censorship is the cheapest item on the shopping list of the women's movement.

But returning to the pope, one event in his Canadian tour illuminates John Paul's avowed "opposition to pornography." For a crowd of 60,000 in Montreal he conducted a youth rally, a spectacle *The Globe and Mail* called "a magnificently choreographed morality play in which the forces of chaos, anxiety and unemployment were overcome with love and emotion." The conduit for this most holy message was a huge group of young girls, clad in white chiffon dresses, who performed synchronized movements, drifting into various symbolic shapes, including a dove the size of an outdoor playing field. The girls looked "virginal," according to the newspaper account. Not an accident, one might assume, in view of John Paul's oft-articulated definition of "womanness": to be subservient, to lack autonomy, and certainly to lack autonomous sexuality. The pope's views of women are, in effect, in agreement with many of the values present in pornography; the image of the "virginal" girls in the Montreal event only underlines this confluence.

The point here is that while many North American church women felt obliged to protest the pope's beatification of the Most Holy Housewife, they failed to register any complaints about the football-field full of vestal virgins in Montreal. Now, had the girls been more nubile *and* clad in bikinis — well, we might have had the makings of a protest over visual representation. But this is precisely the problem that arises when porn is seen as the key that will unlock the syntax of women's oppression.

A similar problem can occur when analyzing advertising, one of the primary sources of visual imagery within our culture. Ads are packed with meaning, values, representations and misrepresentations of women and women's roles. At present, however, the strongest protests by women are often directed at imagery that can most easily be labelled "pornographic." A 1982 ad for Sanyo stereos featured various pieces of equipment stretched across a young woman's reclining, bikini-clad body. The only text, other than the corporate logo, was the word "components." The ad, which appeared on billboards, on public transit vehicles and in bus shelters, was the subject of a vigorous and very thoughtful critique by individual women and women's groups in Toronto. This kind of image, they said, presented Woman as a bunch of sexualized fragments available for consumption by the, presumably, male spectator. The ad's opponents demanded that this image be removed from public circulation because of its potentially damaging effect on women, charging that it could lead to violence against women. This, of course, is the reasoning behind many of the current procensorship drives undertaken by women in the anti-porn movement. The result is a reduction of the very complex issues surrounding visual representation to "porn leads to — and thus equals — violence against women."

While those who support this position often refer to an ad such as the Sanyo one as "the tip of the iceberg," exactly what constitutes the "iceberg" isn't clear. Many people are profoundly uncomfortable with overtly sexual images; it is not difficult for them to spot the continuity between these and the Sanyo ad because the signifiers are so similar: the objectification of a woman's body, fragmentation, and so on. To them, the iceberg is the whole range of pornography (the boundaries of which they draw quite individually). But the women who organized the Sanyo protest may have been concerned about the more general environment of sexist imagery and sex-role stereotyping of women that pervades the mass media. If they were, the tactic of using this one image, in isolation, as the centrepiece for a public protest seems to me have been incomplete. Granted, this particular ad was eventually removed, after much discussion and defence by Sanyo. But, I would argue, this victory was limited. Having focused on such an extreme example and "won," the critical community was in a very real sense disarmed.

(A similar controversy erupted in Canada over the December, 1984, issue of *Penthouse* magazine, which featured — along with the standard sexist *Penthouse* fare — a series of sadistic photographs of bound women. In the current climate of feminist protest over such imagery, the publication of these photographs could be viewed as a kind of market test — one that is useful, for the publishers, in deflecting criticism from those other images that are seen to be "less bad" by comparison. Not unexpectedly, there was a massive uproar from women over these photos, which continues at the time of writing. Canadian politicians and bureaucrats, mostly men, eager to voice their "concern," became enmeshed in a comic round of hot potato, as various departments tossed the issue from customs to Parliament to the police and back again. In the meantime, two very important things were accomplished: first, sales of *Penthouse* increased — which is not to say that this should be a primary concern when individuals or groups are considering mounting a public protest, but it should be noted nonetheless; and second, the rest of *Penthouse*'s contents were seen as "less bad" compared to the overtly offensive nature of the sadistic photographs. In other words, by exceeding what was acceptable to the Canadian public and ending up with a protest that called for the removal of this particular issue of *Penthouse* from distribution in Canada, the publishers got a reprieve of sorts for the other contents of their publication. I would suggest that this was, in part, why the magazine published the photographs in the first place.)

Sexist representations of women are not a question of degree: they are deeply embedded in the entire symbolic code of our culture, both visual and linguistic. Treating *any* imagery that is generated within the mass media as an aberration is a mistake. It is all part of the same system that, in the service of profits, reduces society to "consumer groups." And marketing is every bit as conservative as the military, and only slightly less costly.

It is important to remember that as individuals and as a culture we pay dearly for the "rights" of a few to make profits from the rest of us. At times, women claim that we are "paying" more than our share, as happened in the case of the Sanyo ad protest. But particularly now, when "free enterprise" is being touted as a solution to all our economic and social ills, it's also important for feminists to view those images that are blatantly pornographic within the context of what amounts to an increasingly controlled environment of thought and action — an environment that, sadly, we're becoming accustomed to.

When I say controlled, I mean that while we are often quite prepared to label other societies as repressive — particularly in terms of the state's relationship to the individual — we are less willing to name those aspects of our own society that exert influence, even control, over us. We are not willing to admit that turning over the process of mass communication to commercial interests may not have been a very good idea. Living in the "free world," it's hard to accept that the multitude of products the mass media make available to us allow for little real "choice."

Certainly as feminists we must begin to question whether the market studies and demographic statistics used to establish "norms" adequately safeguard our right to see ourselves justly reflected within our own culture. We can't focus on pornographic images, hoping that removal of these overt symbols of an antiwoman culture will cause the others — the ones that are just sexist — to fall like the proverbial house of cards. Focusing on porn or pornlike images only delays the process of critique of the media from a feminist perspective, the only thing that will lead to a full assault on the repressive production and distribution systems that currently exist within the mass media.

The impact of advertising on contemporary life lies not only in its ability to sell a product, but also in how this exchange is encouraged. Some advertisers are as blunt as the Coca Cola campaign that blasted the world with "Coke is it," while others rely more on persuasion: the McDonald's jingle, "You, you're the one." But regardless of the product or approach, most corporate advertising draws heavily on what are considered to be "gender-appropriate" representations when it comes to making pictures of men and women — after, of course, the potential market has been thoroughly assessed. Thus advertising offers discrete and compartmentalized views of gender, depending upon the sector of society the product is being pitched to.

The Sanyo ad for stereo components was aimed primarily at men, those who were presumably accustomed to the fragmented female anatomies present in soft-core porn, and offered an equivalent visual image as a set for the company's product. Ads for dishwashing detergents, on the other hand, are aimed at the female consumer; sexuality is seldom enlisted in the service of selling these products, which involve domestic labor. Here, the image of the "ordinary woman," sans bikini, is used to conjure up the right feeling in the potential consumer. Is one of these views of Woman more false than the other? More damaging?

Filmmaker Joyce Bunuel has provided very humorous insight into this rather random assignment of "appropriate image type" in her film *Dirty Dishes*. At one point, her main character, a young housewife played by Carole Laure, auditions for a dishwashing detergent commercial. About to go loony within the isolating routines of her life, she seeks a job outside her home. The producers, however, reject her. As the camera scans Laure's beautiful features, we hear them say, "No one would ever believe she does dishes." Up until this point, of course, we have seen Laure do nothing but wash dishes, clean and care for her children and husband. The wonderful irony of this moment was lost on the male reviewers of this film, all of whom declared Bunuel's casting of Laure wrong because she was "too beautiful to be believable." It is not only ads such as Sanyo's ad, with their obvious links to porn, that fragment women and women's experience; the entire structure of the mass media institutionalizes fragmentation in the name of "target marketing."

Fashion advertising is no different. But again, critiques of this imagery should encompass the whole genre rather than focusing only those images that seem most offensive. Consider, for example, some of the Calvin Klein ads. First, there was the 1980 ad featuring a barely pubescent Brooke Shields in jeans, provocatively declaring, "You know what comes between me and my Calvins? Nothing." Outraged feminists decried this ad's overt sexualization of a young girl. Several years later, however, these same jeans turned up on a group of beautiful young women in Klein's television ads. The young women were still provocative, but now they were grotesquely inarticulate, rambling on about their likes (the color blue, a ride in a convertible in the moonlight) and dislikes (phony people, and so on). They sounded as if they were reading from a high school yearbook. They were *meant* to. These women embodied Woman as a powerless class. One of them actually said, "When I lose my mind, I can always fall back on my body," and giggled.

Feminists can hardly claim a victory because Shields or some other girl-child is no longer modelling Calvin Klein's jeans; the reincarnation is more terrifying than the original because it's more difficult to criticize. Remember, Brooke Shields was only 14 years old; her successors were in fact older, but they were required to present themselves within the immature persona of woman-as-child. Which is worse? The Shields ad was attacked because of its use of a sexualized image of a child; further, a causal relationship was drawn between images such as this one and the sexual abuse of children. The ads that followed couldn't be directly implicated by that particular charge. But all imagery must be subjected to close scrutiny and, while a critique that says "it makes women look dumb" may seem pale compared to "it looks just like kiddie porn," both must be recognized as manifestations of the need to objectify women that is present in the mass media as a whole.

But, you might be asking at this point, if objectification is the issue, surely the Calvin Klein enterprise is one company that has made some concessions to the feminist critique of sexist advertising. After all, it gave North America its first taste of the male as public sex object through the huge billboards of the young, muscular guy in his underpants (which were Calvin Klein "originals"). But is equal-space-for-exploitation-of-equal-value really equality? I don't think so, especially in view of the *almost* mirror-image quality of the billboards advertising Klein's underwear for women. The strived-for similarity between these two images is obvious; the differences are telling. The young man is quite muscular; the young woman, who is also basking in her briefs, is very thin. He is at ease, but powerful in his pose, and photographed frontally; he is erect in his posture. She seems less relaxed, photographed from the side, her reclining figure positioned diagonally in the frame; her spine arched — a pose that, despite its use as a signifier of female pleasure in porn photos, is a singularly ineffective one for achieving orgasm.

On examination, these two images are neither as androgynous as one might assume — both are wearing the same underpants, after all — nor does the combination of the two produce the exact symmetry that would seem to be suggested. Why? Because gender difference is highlighted in such a way as to visually reinforce the very traditions of male dominance. Why? Because the Calvin Klein enterprise is no more interested in promoting androgyny and sym-metry — thus equality — between the sexes than it is in nationalizing its bank accounts. The company knows as well as any of us that its sales might drop dramatically if its customers were less anxious about their own sexuality. But the company is extremely interested in the *appearance* of equality because its customers are very much the New Woman and Man. Thus, the aggressive campaign to sex-ualize the male image and also the presentation of apparently sym-metrical ads for male and female products.

Another set of ads of this kind was created for Calvin Klein's perfume and cologne. Each features a man and a woman in bed together. He is dark haired, deeply tanned and muscular; the woman is blonde and almost frail. In the ad for the men's product, the man is on top; in the other, the woman is on top — sort of. Here again, as in the previous set of representations, gender difference is predominant. Furthermore, in the ad where the man is on top, he is shown poised over the supine woman in a position that would enable him to achieve sexual satisfaction, should he so desire. In the other photo, the woman is in no such position. She lies draped decoratively over the man's back, her face resting on his shoulder; the man in this photo is face down on the bed. So in this set of pictures, not only is gender difference important, it is also a determinant in who gets what he or she wants sexually. The man dominates in both photos in that he controls the potential sexual experience, whether he's actively engaged or passively turned away. He holds the power to say yes or no, and asserts this power through the sheer presence of his obviously stronger body. So much for equality. These pictures are a sociobiologist's dream of what the world will be like after women stop being so uppity.

And there's the lexicon of Modern Man and Woman according to Calvin Klein — from Baby Brooke to the Big Baboon. Personally, I can't decide which of these images is worse; all are oppressive in relation to the women pictured; some are just more blatant than others. All emanate from a company that has made hundreds of thousands of dollars on its products, which include umpteen overpriced little suits/jackets/trousers/skirts/blouses for the "working woman," a company that helped to pioneer the concept of "investment dressing" for women entering the managerial class, encouraging them to leave behind the "look" — as well as the price tag — of the pink-collar ghetto. But no one ever said that profit making was without its contradictions.

Many who are reading this may be thinking that surely fashion advertising has been raked over the coals of feminist analysis enough; that its attempts to misrepresent the human condition are well understood; that by definition fashion imagery is false, with its obvious manipulative attempts to portray ideals of beauty and perfection; that most people in our society know this and consequently read the visual imagery as not being real. This may be so, but many also admire the craft and so-called creativity present in such modern-day icons as Calvin Klein ads; many would say that they can sort out the artistic values from the social values, and admire the former while remaining critical of the latter. I do not think this is possible. In advertising, as in most of the rest of the mass media, form follows function. The purpose of advertising is not simply to decorate our environment, although ads also do that to a much greater extent than fine art does, but primarily to sell products and services.

David Imber, a 10-year veteran of the advertising business in New York, has noted: "Research is extremely important in adveritising. Art in advertising is essentially painting by numbers. You put a skin around a mathematical number; that skin, that veneer, is the art. The mathematical formulae are demographics, qualitative and quantitative research analyses, sales records, etc."

Imber went on to say that ad agencies are conscious of the values they are putting forward; this consciousness is built into the personnel composition of these companies. Artists play an extremely unimportant role. Those who control the decisions in advertising are experts in manipulation; they often hold two degrees, usually in psychology and business administration, sometimes with some sort of specialty in group dynamics added for good measure. This is hardly a system that can be expected to serve individuals' or group's rights to see themselves accurately represented within their own society. To consider advertising, in particular, or almost any form of mass media, as a type of artistic production is to miss the point: advertising is an integral part of our social system, just as capable of transmitting values and ideas as religion or education. As Vivian Gornick says in her introduction to Erving Goffman's book *Gender Advertisements*: "Advertisements depict for us not necessarily how we actually behave as men and women but how we *think* men and women behave. This depiction serves the social purpose of convincing us that this is how men and women *are*, or want to be, or should be, not only in relation to themselves but in relation to each other. They orient men and women to the *idea* of men and women acting in concert with each other in the larger play or scene or arrangement that is our social life. That orientation accomplishes the task a society has of maintaining an essential order, an undisturbed on-goingness, regardless of the actual experience of its participants" (emphasis in original.)

We now live in a visual culture, primarily generated by mass media industries, that is blurring the distinctions between advertising and content. This compounds the problems of those of us who wish to structurally alter the entire system of mass media communications (including feminists who are critical of porn), by expanding the boundaries of what material must be considered in a feminist critique of the media.

Esquire magazine, a self-defined men's magazine that would not be classified as porn, is an interesting example to consider. What does *Esquire* have to say about women? Not much directly; but the content that includes women is revealing. When I reviewed several issues from 1983 and '84, and compared *Esquire* to porn publications, which are also magazines directed to a primarily male audience, *Esquire* looked good; if anything, women were almost absent in a visual sense. It should have been a relief, given the more common distortions of women's images within most other magazines. It wasn't. Somehow, the conspicuous absence made those images of women that were present even more important, especially those that appeared in a 12-page fashion spread entitled "The Men's Club" that ran in March, 1983. The six full-color, double-page photos feature a group of five barely postadolescent males and the short text that accompanies each photo instructs the potential buyer on what to wear in order to (presumably) enter The Club. The striking thing about this series as a whole is the way the other "characters" — particularly the three women who appear — are juxtaposed to the five young men.

In the first photo, the five guys at the water cooler are all looking down on a young woman who is crouched in front of them, at (their) crotch level getting a cup of water. She is wearing high heels and a straight skirt unbuttoned to expose most of her thigh. She looks "in a flap" as she gazes distractedly into the camera, wildly self-conscious in the presence of the men. She has good reason to be. Each holds an object — a water gun, a plant, an Aspirin bottle, a cup — that symbolizes their need for "service." Surrounded by The Club, she sees the politics of the workplace from her (structurally) inferior position: she is aware that more than her secretarial skills may be necessary in this environment; that, as well, she may have to act as wife and mother, and ultimately employ her own sexuality just in order to survive in her job. The Boys, meanwhile, are confident. Even at their young age, they know how to assert their class through their gender. And, more important, this photo says that it works.

The second woman portrays a manicurist in an old-fashioned barbershop. In this photo, something has caught the attention of half of the group; two of our young heroes stare out of the page, leaning forward expectantly, almost in a trance. The barber, an older, balding man, looks but is less involved, almost cynical. The young attractive manicurist also looks, but she giggles and covers her mouth demurely, aware of her status relative to the customers, who are in fact her employers. There are obvious class distinctions present in this photo. The reactions of the barber and manicurist are similar; as service workers, they see things differently from their upper-crust clientele. The obvious intention of this photo is to encourage this separation — along class and gender lines — among the viewers, most of whom would be upwardly mobile males.

The third woman is part of a wedding party in the last photo of the series, one that is edgy to the point of vertigo in its depiction of women's place within marriage. We have seen the lads triumphant and confident in each of the previous social settings. Here, something has come between them; and that something is not "a wife" in traditional terms, but female sexuality.

In this photo four of the men are looking straight into the camera. "The groom" has a pure white suit on, a flower in his lapel and he holds "the bride," gripping her little finger between the knuckles of his semiclenched fist. Three of the others bear the bright imprint of a recent kiss near their lips; they appear composed, almost — but not quite — smiling. The groom, however, is tense, the muscles of his prominent jaw visible. The bride is in the act of turning her attention — and her lipsticked mouth — to the remaining member of the group. Her hand is draped casually around his shoulder; her back is to the groom. Her expectant recipient leans into her offer, his face toward the camera, his eyes locked in a conspiratorial gaze with the bride. The groom, meanwhile, maintains his grip not only on the bride, but also on a bunch of white lilies (purity? death?), overwrought by this scene of loss. What exactly has been lost here? Property, plain and simple. The groom is visibly ill with the knowledge that he cannot "own" his newly taken wife.

These photos are part of the editorial content of *Esquire*, not ads. For lack of a better term, I would call them educational. The models chosen to wear both the clothes and the stories are, in fact, very young. Readers are being explicitly told to acquire certain clothes, the overt subject of this series of photos, and certain values, implicit in the mininarratives, in order to get ahead. These values are continuous with those of pornography. But, if danger is the question, they are more dangerous than even the most sadistic images within hard-core porn. Instead of conflating violence and sexuality, they conflate economics and sexuality by equating male dominance with economic and social status. And even the (former) sanctuary of marriage induces paranoia, not comfort, for the *Esquire* man. If boys are to become men — enter the men's club (read patriarchy)

— they must learn to look down on women, to put them in their place, to distrust them and, finally, to renounce the possibility of close emotional ties with them.

Of course, not all these messages were *consciously* included, nor are they necessarily consciously experienced by the men aspiring to or already members of the "Men's Club." No self-respecting magazine editor, fashion or otherwise, would ever admit, "My job is to produce copy that accentuates men's masculine bonding and undermines the possibility of their identifying with women, thus destroying men's potential for more androgynous and less dominating behavior." Yet this is precisely what this feature does, though it achieves it symbolically, at the unconscious level. The suppression of this potential for empathy between the sexes reinforces the unequal arrangement of power and privilege — the basis of the men's club — in our society.

To me, this series of photos is infinitely more depressing than any image within the genre known as porn because it depicts structural sexism, giving a "normal," conservative and rather genteel face to the preservation of gender inequality, in economic, social and sexual terms. Also, it's harder to "read" at first glance. But few would call for the banning of this series of photographs precisely because it is so "normal." The values may be offensive, but everybody's dressed, right? Nobody's getting hurt, beaten, whipped, raped. Come to think of it, there's no sex anywhere, right?

Wrong. And this is the central problem with the current anti-porn movement: without nudity, violence and other blatant representations of oppression, there's no protest. As I have tried to point out in examining the series of photos in *Esquire*, while there may be no pornography, there's plenty of implied sex and a huge helping of sexism. But sex, per se, is not the problem; sexism is. As women, we have had little opportunity to either produce or witness woman-positive representations of sexuality — certainly not in mass communication forms. Censorship strategies being suggested by the anti-porn movement are not going to work, because censorship is essentially an attempt to *reform* the mass media by removing from public view those images that are most offensive to women. "Most offensive" is the key phrase here; in order to determine which images are most offensive, one must by default declare other images to be "less offensive," and others, finally, "inoffensive." Clearly, this is a useless exercise for women today. Reform is simply not possible.

If the mass media are about representation and communication — which they are supposed to be — then a useful comparison could be with government. Imagine, for a moment, a system of government that only allowed for representation of its citizens at a federal level. Could democracy flourish in this kind of environment? The mass media are just this sort of system of representation. With their "high production values," their centralized distribution networks, they almost completely displace and overshadow all other forms of cultural production. If women feel unrepresented by porn, we have to begin to accept that neither are we very well served by the more apparently benign aspects of our cultural environment. Censorship will never truly alter or eradicate sexist imagery. It focuses on "bad" material and leaves the nexus of power within the communications/ entertainment industries unchallenged, allowing the same values to persist.

So if we are going to consider pornography, we must begin to be critical not only of material that is produced for men, but also that which is produced for women — and I'm not talking about *Playgirl* magazine. There's romance fiction, which encourges women to mainline marriage fantasies and domination on a weekly basis; *Cosmopolitan* magazine, which teaches women, step-by-step, how to become sex objects; fashion magazines such as *Vogue* or *Bazaar*, which offer in-depth instruction in the narcissistic pastime of turning oneself into a living sculpture; soap operas, which actively conflate genuine problem-solving and upward mobility into tight, consumable narrative packages, so slick you can almost taste the hair spray. The list could go on.

The anti-porn movement often says that pornography is "instructing men in sexism." Well, if you ask me, *Cosmo* "instructs" women along the same lines. And what about kids? I'm not talking about kiddie porn; I'm talking about television for children. Even if they only watch the programming specifically geared to them — no sex and no porn — they approach their adolescence with certain shared cultural perceptions. They will "know" that boys get dirty as a result of active movement, while girls get dirty as a result of "an accident"; that women are more likely to be cooking, cleaning, washing and tending to the needs of others than they are to be in the workplace; that when men do any domestic chores — with the notable exception of barbecuing in the backyard — they are all thumbs; and, most important, that everyone is capable of having fun — provided, of course, they are able to connect with the correct product. Now, these "facts" will be in conflict with the circumstances of their own experiences (their mothers may work; their fathers may cook; their sisters and all the women around them may, in fact, be athletic; they themselves may be unhappy). But this conflict is an important part of "growing up"; properly channeled, at least in terms of media culture, this conflict can be transformed into personal anxiety by the time puberty sets in.

But earlier, much earlier, children learn to trust certain sources. They "learn," for instance, that delight can be made to conform to predictable patterns when their favorite cartoon character turns up on their very own pajamas (sleeping with Snoopy, as it were). This delight can be extended almost infinitely, they find, by the acquisition of accessories (the joy of brand names, trademarks). As they grow older, their vocabulary of values begins to expand as they come to understand that, for some reason, long-distance telephone calls and life insurance are meant to bring a lump to one's throat; that tampons and "freedom" mean sort of the same thing; that frozen baked goods and canned soups contain "love." In short, they will have become consumers, fully capable of forming an emotional relationship with a specific range of products.

Todd Gitlin, in his essay "Prime Time Ideology" in *Television: The Critical View*, discusses the indirect consequences of television advertising, saying: "[Commercials] get us accustomed to thinking of ourselves and behaving as a *market* rather than a *public*, as consumers rather than as citizens. Public problems (like air pollution) are propounded as susceptible to private commodity solutions (like eyedrops)" (emphasis in original.) I'm not suggesting that North Americans actually believe that "nothin' says lovin' like something from the oven," but it definitely seems to strike a chord — the child within us all. And this is exactly what advertising is designed to do.

Assisted by staff psychologists, armed with reams of demographic surveys, advertising agencies are in an ideal position to "give the people what they want." And what do we want? Love, comfort, sexual satisfaction, to be attractive to others, to be an individual and yet to fit in, to have some kind of status within society and, above all, be happy. Advertising — and the editorial content that surrounds ads but is essentially continuous with the value system of the ads themselves — would seem to provide "what the people want" not by actually delivering any of these desires directly but by telling us what to buy in order to become the people we're told we want to be. The mass media sells men and boys, women and girls different packages, but each contains its own quotient of gender-appropriate sexism.

The problem with challenging this structural sexism is that it appears to be "natural," "the way things are," in spite of the obvious contradictions between how people actually live their lives and the media's depictions of current society. I would argue that if the images and values presented by the mass media currently are indeed "natural," then porn is equally "natural."

In fact, neither is natural; both are highly manipulated, carefully constructed kinds of discourses that are products of industrial information industries whose driving imperatives are not the communication of infomation but, to state the obvious once again, the making of profits. The lies that are told about women in the mass media reflect the sexism of the culture as it is filtered through this imperative, as well as the industrial forms of research, packaging and marketing that have grown up to serve it.

And so we finally arrive at what I have been referring to throughout this essay as the structural change that is necessary in cultural production. For women concerned with the images of women, the question becomes, How do we rescue our images from their virtual control by the mass media? How do we project our own views of ourselves into the mainstream? How do we begin to redefine "the mainstream" so that circulation of information, images, cultural work within smaller, more specific groups is given value within our society? How can we replace the homogenized stereotypes with our own individual and group portraits?

One of the most serious — and negative — consequences of the anti-pornography movement for women is that we have suspended these discussions in our own organizations and in the political and cultural arenas. We have to begin them again. Four years ago, the National Action Committee on the Status of Women, the voice of very considered, even moderate, feminism in this country, made a presentation to the Applebaum-Hébert committee then studying cultural activity throughout Canada. NAC suggested that in order to adequately address the need for women to be fully represented within the culture, a women's television network should be established. The committee members were rather flabbergasted by what they termed "a separatist demand"; their final report omitted NAC's recommendation. Today, women should revive this idea, turning it into an election issue, as well as staging demonstrations, lobbying and generally developing the demand for a change in the structure of television representation. Thus, the young women who are being trained in the broadcast field would have a choice when they want to enter the media. Just as Studio D at the National Film Board created openings for women who wanted to make films, a women's television network would, by its very presence, encourage women to begin to represent themselves and their concerns within the broadcast media.

If this plan seems long range, many other courses of action are possible today for women who want to begin to challenge the mass media. Right now, in every city and town, there are women artists and cultural producers writing or creating films, visual art, dance, videotapes, performances, magazines. Often their work remains unknown to all but their own immediate community, kept from the majority of women (indeed, audiences in general) by virtue of its noncommercial and threatening nature. Instead of organizing antipornography campaigns, we should devote our energy to becoming acquainted with this work; to learning about the feminist cultural resources in our own communities; to utilizing the talents and efforts of feminists in the activities and movements of which we are a part; to integrating feminist material into educational and community activities; to ensuring that women's books, magazines, films and videotapes are included in our libraries and schools, in our community centres, in our homes.

We've gone off in the wrong direction. Instead of using our anger and energy to simply fight "against," we really need to be fighting "for." For example, if a film is offensive, pornographic, violent — don't just call for its removal, go down to the theatre with a list of woman-positive, woman-produced films that you want to see screened. Don't stop your protest, your letter writing until this is accomplished. The same action could be undertaken in the case of an offending magazine. Demands for equal distribution space for feminist publications serve to highlight woman-produced media rather than strengthening the economic position of porn — as many current anti-porn protests do.

In terms of publishing in general, the concerns of the small Canadian publishing houses should be a feminist cause célèbre — including struggles over postal rates, tax breaks and other forms of economic and distribution regulations — given how crucial these issues are for publications whose first goal is publishing, not profits. Why can we buy *Playboy, Penthouse, Cosmopolitan, Sports Illustrated* and *Bride* magazine on every newsstand but can never get our hands on feminist or gay material except in downtown bookstores in major cities?

And then there's the question of advertising's open access to our public spaces. Consider the fact that Media Watch, a national group with headquarters in Vancouver, which was established to monitor the media vis-à-vis the representation of women, announced in 1984 the results of a two-year experiment in "voluntary controls" on the part of the advertising industry in terms of sex-role stereotyping. Media Watch reported that these voluntary controls were a failure; sex-role stereotyping of women in advertising did not decline, and in some cases actually increased. With popular support from women across the country, Media Watch is in an ideal position to lobby for airtime, billboard space, magazine space on behalf of women in order to redress our disgraceful treatment. That, I would say, is just the beginning.

Women need to take action at community, metropolitan, regional and federal levels in order to deal with these issues if we ever hope to eliminate sexist representations — including pornography — from our culture. We need to organize ourselves to make our own media; to popularize the work of women and feminist cultural producers; to establish our own production centres; to encourage young women who are just beginning to work; and to make feminism, through culture, part of the life of our communities. And we need to take political action in order to come to terms with such issues as financing, distribution, broadcast licensing, all of which require action at a federal level. In other words, we need to put all the energy that has been devoted to the anti-porn cause into this kind of organized strategy for building women's culture. Up until this point, many women have said that culture was not a "real" political issue; that we had to work on those issues that were more important: employment, equal pay, reproductive rights, violence against women. Culture would have to wait its turn. I think, as women, we can no longer afford to wait.

As a kind of epilogue, I would offer the following images as representative of the portrayal of women in Canadian mass media late in 1984.

Now, with unemployment unlikely to fall much below the current 12 to 14 percent (and with fully 25 percent of those between 18 and 25 unemployed), with women likely to continue their trend of being employed outside the home, with 40 percent of the paid labor force being women, with the impact of high technology restructuring the workforce and affecting the jobs women do, consider the following:

• The "I adore my 64" ad for Commodore 64 home computer systems that features four men intently performing various functions on their systems, including composing a song, designing computer graphics, doing calculations and an Einstein lookalike who is said to be "scheming." Nestled comfortably within this all-male cast is one lone woman who is using her Commodore 64 as a kitchen aid. Dressed in outdated kitchenwear, including a ruffled apron, she stands over her terminal, spoon poised in mid-air, reading (one assumes) her favorite recipe for chicken à la king.

• An ad for the Commodore Vic-20 with Edu-pak, a low-cost computer and software package being pitched at the high school crowd. The camera pans along a brick wall, catching a full range of male teen-types — the brain, the athlete, the punk — and each extols a different feature of the system. The girls — also types — are only there to present the software and carrying case to their respective mates.

• A commercial for Texas Instruments' home computer system featuring a father sitting in front of the computer with a small child on his lap. The child's hand touches the keyboard as the voice-over intones, "He's only three and already he's reaching out."

• The ad for the Adam computer, a low-priced package being sold as the least expensive "complete system" on the market, which features a high school-age couple in front of the computer. He is doing her homework; she is watching. He is showing her how the system works; she is in awe. He prints it out; she is grateful. He never looks at her.

• A line of computer software called Women's Ware, which features such vital programs as Recipe and Checkbook and comes packaged on a little plastic hanger — presumably to hang in the closet with the owner's other fashionable bits of women's wear. Not included in the Women's Ware packages is any program with word processing capabilities. Better seen than heard?

Women currently earn approximately 58 cents for each dollar earned by male workers. If computer literacy continues to be defined in advertising as yet another male preserve, the little girls of today will have to fight their way into what will have become a "nontraditional" job by the end of the century. If you think that porn is the central problem facing women today, I urge you to watch TV for about two days.

Acknowledgments

Many people assisted me in organizing the material for this essay, including John Greyson, Edythe Goodridge, and especially Kim Tomczak and Varda Burstyn, both of whom contributed significant amounts of time and thought to helping me sort out my thoughts around this topic.

Censorship and Law Reform: Will Changing the Laws Mean a Change for the Better?
Lynn King

Much pornography is abhorrent. No one denies that. So is chauvinism, patriarchy and misogyny. The challenge is how to rid society of these evils. Law reform in the guise of tightened censorship laws, expanded human rights codes, a redrafted Criminal Code and new civil suits has become the latest panacea for abolishing pornography. But law reform in this area is no answer. Legislation, if carefully drafted, is and will continue to be useful in many ways in improving women's rights in the realm of family law, equal pay and other areas. But when dealing with images — which ones should go and which ones can stay — no amount of tinkering with words can guarantee women a just law.

First of all, pornography is a telling symptom of a patriarchal society and censoring pornography is like using an Aspirin to cure cancer: it might ease the pain, but does not eliminate the disease, and may well have serious side effects. Second, freedom of expression is a fundamental right only tentatively secured and ought not to be dismissed lightly, especially for at best a doubtful result. In fact, censorship in all its forms has historically been used against women — remember that it was not long ago that any public advocacy of birth control was forbidden, even illegal.

As a feminist, a lawyer and someone who has worked in the area of women's concerns for many years, it is my belief that focusing our efforts on law reform in an attempt to abolish pornography is fraught with danger. In this chapter I want to illustrate the traps in present and proposed antipornography laws in the hope that women will be more cautious before adopting this tactic. It is not my intention here to examine in detail the censorship laws of every province, or the other laws, such as the Criminal Code, that control means of expression. Rather I will explore how certain laws have been and will be applied — an exercise that will serve to demonstrate the futility of the antipornography law reform measures currently being proposed.

Censorship exists in a variety of forms in Canada: customs regulations, sections of the Criminal Code, local retail bylaws. But most notorious are the provincial laws that empower censor boards to cut or ban films and videos prior to their release. Such schemes were implemented in the early 1900s, with the advent of films, and have changed little to this day. Basically, they require that any film or video, before being shown publicly, must be approved by a province's censor board. It does not matter what the content of the film is — it can be anything from a travelogue to a thriller. Nor does it matter whether it is for screening at a Famous Players theatre or a women's meeting in a church hall; if the public can attend, prior approval of the film by the censor board is necessary.

All provinces and territories except the Yukon classify films, dictating which audiences can see them; all but Manitoba and the Yukon also have the power to demand cuts or ban films outright. A fee, sometimes considerable, is almost always charged for this "service," and the process of submitting films for approval can be a lengthy and bureaucratic one. These factors alone effectively censor the activities of those who lack funds, time or the knack of dealing with bureaucracies.

In recent years, the Ontario Board of Censors has become the most influential — and infamous — of the provincial bodies. It has been challenged more often in the courts than any other board in the country and has been the subject of the greatest amount of scrutiny and criticism from both filmmakers and the public. And its power does not stop at the Ontario border. Because many films are first released in Toronto, and hence vetted by the Ontario board, distributors often incorporate cuts demanded by the board in prints destined for distribution in other provinces. Consequently, Ontario is an interesting laboratory for testing the efficacy of law reforms aimed at eliminating pornography.

In 1984, Dr. Robert Elgie, the minister for consumer and corporate relations, under whose jurisdiction the censor board falls, stated: "The government [of Ontario] has always been concerned about violence, degrading and often violent pornography." Yet when one looks at what guidelines the Ontario Board of Censors uses and what works it actually cuts and bans, the discrepancy between the high-sounding words of elected officials and the day-to-day practice of bureaucrats is obvious — and it is the day-to-day practice that counts. The board identifies as its areas of concern "indignity to the human body; explicit scenes of defecation, urination or vomiturition; blasphemous or sacrilegious presentations." The guidelines that the board has established for itself also identify the types of scenes it believes should be eliminated from films: "Explicit portrayal of sexual activity; sexual exploitation of children; undue and prolonged scenes of violence, torture, bloodletting; ill-treatment of animals; undue and prolonged emphasis on genitalia." Such broad statements leave immense discretion to the board.

Obviously, those who think that the censor board is in operation primarily to curtail degrading images of women have chosen the wrong protector. The board's concern lies not with eliminating misogynist images but mainly in ensuring that explicit sexuality is avoided and traditional values upheld. Indeed, Mary Brown, the current head of the board, has said that "many films now ridicule the values most families live by, promoting promiscuity at an early age, attacking parental and school authority and demeaning religious faith." In her view, *Breaking Away* and *Coming Home* should have been banned, the former for debasing parental authority and the latter for promoting extramarital affairs. She has not yet banned these films, but there is nothing in the law to stop her. More important, though, her statement gives an indication of the values the censor board wants to protect — hardly feminist values.

It is not surprising that in 1981 the board did ban *Beau Pere*, directed by Bertrand Bleir, whose *Get Out Your Handkerchiefs* had won an Oscar for best foreign film three years before. *Beau Pere* is a gently comic and ironic film about a 14-year-old girl dealing with the death of her mother and her relationship during the crisis with her dead mother's boyfriend. The sexual scenes between the girl and man are discreet; in the board's view, however, "the sexual relationship between the girl and her stepfather is quite explicit." Worse, the board believed that "the affair is condoned as a means of helping the man through an emotional and psychological crisis — it tends to 'normalize' incestuous relationships with a minor."

Do we really want a censor board writing film reviews for us and deciding what we can and cannot see? If the question becomes whether a film condones or normalizes an action, where does censorship stop? By the same logic, *Reds* should be banned for condoning or normalizing communism and *Terms of Endearment* for condoning or normalizing extramarital sex.

The board's concern with the contravention of traditional heterosexual values makes films that treat homosexuality as an acceptable, even positive, aspect of social life particularly vulnerable. One, at least, has been banned outright: *Taxi to the Loo*, a nonviolent, nonexploitive film dealing with homosexuality and the importance of integrating sexuality with emotional involvement and personal growth. In 1984, the board initially ordered cuts in the militantly feminist and prolesbian *Born in Flames* and only retreated after a public outcry. In fact, many distributors of films about gays or with gay content will not send their films to Ontario.

The power of the board does not stop with determining what films can be viewed, in what form they appear and by whom they can be seen. It also dictates where films are shown, and these decisions, too, leave no doubt about the board's views and values. In 1981, *Rameau's Nephew*, directed by the internationally renowned artist Michael Snow, was ordered cut because it contained an explicit scene of penetration and another of urination. (Neither of these scenes was in any sense "pornographic," just graphic.) When Snow refused to make the cuts, the board gave permission for the film to be shown at the prestigious Art Gallery of Ontario in Toronto, but turned down a simultaneous request from The Funnel, a Toronto experimental film theatre. When asked to justify this discrimination, the board cited the art gallery's "tradition and stature in the community" and the Funnel's obscurity. Similar elitism has characterized the board's decisions about where the National Film Board's documentary on pornography, *Not a Love Story*, can be shown. The board has allowed it to be screened in an "environment of concern" like the posh St. Lawrence Centre in Toronto, but not at regular movie theatres frequented by ordinary, everyday people. The message seems to be that sexual representation, whether "art" or "porn," will not adversely affect upper-class or educated people but will harm everyone else. In 1981 it even threatened to withhold approval of *Trace*, a 20-second experimental film, because the board found the film's structure unacceptable: "It has no beginning or end. All it was was a lot of flashing symbols on the screen," it declared.

Given that the censor board is an appointed state body whose head moves in ruling circles, its decisions are not surprising. Both in terms of film content and state authority, it is consistent with the interests of established power. Nor is the never-ending vigilence of the board incidental or idiosyncratic. As writer John Jeffries has noted:

> The administrative apparatus erected to effect preclearance may screen a range of expression far broader than that which otherwise would be brought to official attention. The relative ease and economy of an administrative decision to suppress may make suppression more likely than it would be without a preclearance requirement. Under a system of administrative preclearance, suppression is accomplished "by a single stroke of the pen." At that point the burden falls on the would-be speaker to indicate his right. Without administrative preclearance, the government's decision to suppress may be constrained by the time and money required to demonstrate in Court an appropriate basis for such action. And the fact that those exercising the authority of preclearance operate in the relative informality of administrative action may tend to shield their decisions from effective public scrutiny. Most important, administrative preclearance requires a bureaucracy of censorship. Persons who choose to fill this role may well have psychological tendencies to overstate the need for suppression. Whether or not this is so, *there are powerful institutional pressures to justify one's job, and ultimately one's own importance by exaggerating the evils which suppression seeks to avoid. . . . The function of the censor is to censor. He has a professional interest in finding things to suppress* [emphasis added].

In other words, once the nets are cast, the fishing expedition never ends. As the Court of Appeal noted in a 1984 decision involving a challenge of the censor board: "The section [authorizing censorship] allows for the complete denial or prohibition of expression in this particular area and sets *no limits* [the court's emphasis] on the Board of Censors." In fact, at the time of writing the board was engaged in expanding its fishing grounds into previously sacrosanct territory, seeking the right to review and censor all films and videos, even those available only for private viewing, thus abolishing the (always dubious) distinction between public and private use that it previously recognized. It has also moved against Toronto art spaces and made it clear that it intends to clamp down hard on minority, dissident and feminist voices who challenge its authority. In practice it has demonstrated what John Jeffries described in theory.

Once a law or regulation is on the books, it is the personnel of the state — its bureaucrats, its judiciary — who enforce it. Feminists may think that a particular law looks good as written and may be assured repeatedly that it will be used to stamp out misogynist pornography and nothing else. But feminists do not control the censors who demand the cuts; feminists do not control the attorney-general or the police who initiate the prosecution; feminists do not control the courts that decide the fate of the accused — nor will we for a long time to come.

I doubt whether feminists would have wanted Al Razutis's *A Message from Our Sponsor*, an experimental film that was very critical of the exploitation of women in advertising, censored. Yet the censor board demanded cuts and, when Razutis refused, it became illegal to publicly show the film in Ontario. I doubt whether feminists really wanted Canadian Images, a Peterborough, Ontario, film festival that consistently programs feminist films, to be prosecuted under the Theatres Act for screening *A Message from Our Sponsor*, and yet this is precisely what happened in 1981, at great expense to the state — yes, it's your tax dollars — and the accused. And I doubt whether feminists really wanted the conviction that ultimately resulted.

The vast and complex body of the state is not neutral, but works along clearly patriarchal lines. It is therefore irrational to expect that same state to adopt feminist principles when dealing with sexual representation. The censor boards of a male-dominated state will never view films through a feminist's eye; the logic of sexism will even find positive what many feminists deplore. For example, one of the very mainstays of the present retail system is the use of women's bodies to sell everything from candies to cars, a situation feminists find offensive; the Ontario Board of Censors, however, ruled that Razutis's film critique of this system could not be shown. The board does not stand apart from the way power and privilege work in our society but is part of this system and reflects its values every day. Those values are not feminists' values.

These problems are not peculiar to the area of film censorship. Another method of state control is the Criminal Code sections dealing with "Offences Tending to Corrupt Morals," which include publishing or distributing obscene material; exhibiting a disgusting object or indecent show; presenting an immoral, indecent or obscene performance; and mailing anything that is obscene, indecent, immoral or scurrilous. (At present any work whose dominant characteristic is found to be undue exploitation of sex, or sex and crime, horror, cruelty or violence is considered obscene.) There are even more provisions, but these examples serve to show how all-encompassing the attempts to control all forms of expression, including books, paintings and movies, are.

It is obvious that these laws are not intended to prohibit degrading images of women but rather to impose and uphold the sexist values and morals of the state. It is no accident that *The Body Politic*, a Toronto gay journal, has been prosecuted repeatedly under this section of the code, nor that a Toronto gay bookstore, Glad Day Books, has been frequently harassed under the same section. Even though it is not illegal for consenting homosexuals to engage in sex, the state still harasses gays by prosecuting depictions of their sexuality and will continue to do so as long as there are anti-porn laws allowing it to.

One of the factors that enables such state action is the present concept of "community standards." When an obscenity case is heard, the court must determine whether the work on trial exceeds the accepted standards of tolerance in the "contemporary Canadian community" — that is, whether the "exploitation" is "undue." Some feminists have naively endorsed this concept, believing that through the application of this test, those materials they find unacceptable would be judged illegal. But such a system has dangerous implications, for "community," in the court's view, must encompass everyone, including those who oppose abortion, premarital sex and birth control. Even if a book or movie is for and about women, everyone, including the most chauvinistic of men, is taken into account when the community's standard of tolerance is determined. Furthermore, the Crown is not even required to call expert evidence as to what contemporary community standards are.

Ultimately it is the presiding judge who must endeavor to decide what he (almost invariably he), in the light of his experience, believes the community's standards to be. A recent example of how this concept can be applied was the 1983 case involving the interpretation of the Customs Act. Under this act, books, printed papers, drawings, paintings or representations of "an immoral or indecent character" are prohibited from entering Canada. When a Mr. Tom Luscher of British Columbia attempted to import one issue of a magazine for himself alone, he was prohibited from doing so by customs officials. Luscher appealed to the federal court and the judge found that the magazine in question was simply concerned with the sexual activity of a man and a woman from foreplay to orgasm. The judge ruled that these actions were in no way unnatural or unlawful and, indeed, that they were a common part of the lives of Canadian men and women; he also found that Luscher had no intention of circulating or selling the magazine; and only planned to use it in the privacy of his bedroom as a means of fantasy enhancement. Nonetheless, the judge found when measuring the magazine against *his* assessment of the current community standards of tolerance, that the customs officials had been correct in prohibiting the magazines as immoral or indecent.

In 1983, Ontario County Court Judge Stephen Borins pointed out the absurdity of attempting to interpret community standards when he was required to determine whether 25 videotapes were obscene (although, despite his reservations about the undertaking, he did uphold the charges for 11 of the tapes):

> This is a very difficult judgment to make in a community of 24,000,000 people who inhabit the second largest country in the world. . . . No doubt very different levels of tolerance exist in small communities such as Goose Bay in Labrador, Dawson in the Yukon, and Nobleton in Ontario, and the large metropolitan centres of Montreal, Toronto and Vancouver. As well, Canada is a pluralistic society and different parts of that society will have different points of view. Yet it remains the task of the trier of fact, who is assumed to have his finger on the "pornographic pulse" of the nation, to assess objectively whether or not the contemporary Canadian community will tolerate distribution of the motion pictures before the Court. There is some irony to this requirement. The Judge, who by the very institutional nature of his calling is required to distance himself or herself from society for the purposes of the application of the test of obscenity is expected to be a person for all seasons, familiar with and aware of the national level of tolerance. Thus the trial Judge (or jury) is required to rely upon his or her own experience and decide as best he or she can what most people in Canada would think about such material to arrive upon a measure of community tolerance of that material. Judge or jurors lacking experience in the field of pornography and the attitudes of others toward it face a substantial challenge in making the findings demanded by the law.

Some feminists support an amendment to the Criminal Code introduced by former justice minister Mark McGuigan that would substitute the word "pornography" for "obscenity." Others, including the National Action Committee on the Status of Women, have

endorsed changing "undue exploitation" to "degrading representations" or "coercive representations." However, these terms would
still have to be interpreted first by the police, then by judges, in
light of contemporary standards. It is easy to imagine the judge
finding two lesbians making love a "degrading representation," perhaps even "coercive" ("How else could it have happened?") There
is no reason to believe that tinkering with the words of this section
of the Criminal Code will alter the court's ingrained biases. Words
do not change the system; they can simply mislead us into believing
the system is responsive.

The 1984 experience of the Maximum Art Gallery in Toronto
illustrates the perils of believing otherwise. The gallery had displayed
in its front window a painting by Bill Stapleton that showed a
Mayan woman being raped by Guatemalan soldiers, the artist's
representation of an incident he had been told of while visiting a
refugee camp in southern Mexico. Stapleton said of the painting:
"It was a hard subject to do, and I considered the effect it would
have on people, but that's what is happening down there. . . . It's
just awful, and it's my responsibility as an artist to reveal what's
happening."

But shortly after the picture went on display, the gallery's curators
were told by police to remove it from the window or face obscenity charges under the Criminal Code. The police had apparently
polled several people passing the gallery about their reactions to the
painting and "every one of them said it was horrible, disgusting,
obscene. . . . You're talking about a painting of a gang rape scene."

Many feminists concerned about the consequences of such measures as tightening film censorship laws and amending the Criminal
Code have been drawn to another possibility: amending the hate
propaganda laws. These forbid "the advocating or promoting of
genocide of an identifiable group or inciting hatred against an identifiable group where such incitement is likely to lead to a breach of
the peace." At present the identifiable groups protected are those
distinguished by color, race, religion or ethnic origin; it has been
proposed that gender be included in the list. I was drawn to this
idea initially, as were a number of the other contributors to this
book. But on consideration we realized this approach was as problematic as others discussed earlier.

First, although pornography is frequently misogynist, it is unlikely
that the courts would conclude that it "advocates or promotes genocide of women." Similarly, it is unlikely that the present legal

system, even if it acknowledged that pornography incites hatred of women, would consider such incitement is likely to lead to a breach of the peace. Nor is changing the wording of the hate laws the answer. One of the differences between pornography and hate propaganda directed against the groups currently included in the law is that pornography usually involves the depiction of sex in some way. Although this may be primarily sex based on hatred, introducing the concept of sex could lead to the stifling of sexual imagery that has nothing whatsoever to do with hatred. Margaret Laurence's beautiful and at times sexually explicit novel *The Diviners* was almost removed from the Grade 13 curriculum and school libraries in some Ontario areas several years ago because some book banners believed that her "aim in life is to destroy the home and family." They might have as erroneously said that she hated women, that destroying the home and family was tantamount to hatred of women and hence the incitement of harm against women.

A system whose very structure protects and perpetuates the privilege of men as a group will not — cannot — fulfil a feminist mandate in the area of image depiction. The idea that we can develop a "feminist jurisprudence" is appealing in the abstract, but in practice it involves a fundamental contradiction in terms that is never systematically resolved in women's favor. As proof we need only examine some of our other experiences with law reform, for by looking at areas other than censorship we can clearly see the problems inherent in relying on changing laws and can better put the censorship/sexual representation debate into perspective.

The creation and enactment of Ontario's Family Law Reform Act is one such example, for it is representative of similar developments in other provinces and countries. The genesis for the change in the province's family law was the 1973 Supreme Court of Canada decision that deprived Iris Murdoch, an Alberta farm wife, of most of her interest in the family farm when her marriage dissolved. Outraged, feminists and others lobbied for more equitable laws. In retrospect, however, we settled for high-sounding principles rather than real rights. Some of the wording in the new legislation was appealing: "it is necessary to recognize the equal position of spouses as individuals within marriage and to recognize marriage as a form of partnership"; "it is necessary to provide in law for the orderly and equitable settlement of affairs of spouses upon the breakdown of the partnership."

But the legislators failed to guarantee a 50-50 split of all assets after a divorce, leaving the division largely to the interpretation and discretion of the courts. As a result, the courts basically decide on a case-by-case basis whether a woman should receive an equal share of such family assets as the house and car, and whether she is entitled to *any* portion of the husband's nonfamily assets.

One section of the act, for example, states that where one spouse has contributed "work, money or money's worth" in respect to the acquisition, management, maintenance, operation or improvement of property other than family assets, the court may compensate the spouse. Many women assumed that if a wife worked in the home, thereby enabling her husband to acquire and build up nonfamily assets, such as a business, she would be able to claim compensation under this section. The Supreme Court of Canada disabused women of this notion in 1982, when it found that a trial judge was wrong in considering the work of a wife in the home as any sort of contribution to the husband's ability to acquire nonfamily assets, although there is nothing in the legislation that suggests this dismissive interpretation of housework.

Even the section relating to spousal maintenance and support has been used against, rather than for, women. This section begins by stating "every spouse has an obligation to provide support for himself or herself" — a clause that has haunted women since its enactment. Although the unemployment rate is higher for women than for men and women's salaries on average are less than 60 percent of those of men, this section has sometimes been used by judges to force women who have been out of the workforce for years, laboring in the home to care for their husbands and children, to obtain menial, dead-end and low-paying jobs to supplement the minimal support they receive from their previous husbands.

In the end, the Family Law Reform Act that was hailed as "pro-woman" has saved men considerable money and cost women a fortune in lost expectations and uncompensated work.

Equal pay laws have created similar problems for women. Again, the lesson is instructive; again, Ontario's experience is typical. Ontario's present system provides that an employer is not allowed to pay female employees less for substantially the same kind of work performed in the same establishment and under similar conditions, the performance of which requires substantially the same skill, effort or responsibility. When this particular wording was introduced in 1974, feminists saw it as a means of ensuring that, for example, nurses and orderlies working in the same hospital would receive comparable pay. The courts, however, rejected this view, ruling that "substantially the same work" means "substantially *similar* work" — work must *look* the same — thus ensuring that the majority of women who labor in all-female job ghettos remain unprotected. This unnecessary interpretation has cost women more than can ever be regained in lost wages.

These experiences with the Family Law Reform Act and equal pay legislation offer an important lesson: we must always distinguish between laws that protect women's right to public resources, such as funding for day care or battered women's shelters, and those over which we have no control. These have been and will continue to be used to maintain women's second-class status. And while further lobbying may eventually bring about improvements in the areas of family law and equal pay, laws dealing with pornography and censorship are fundamentally different and far more dangerous, for they are totally subject to interpretation by people who are selected by an antifeminist system. Politicians may express their sympathy with feminist concerns when courting votes or giving speeches. But deeds speak louder than words. For feminists who are concerned about sexism, sexuality and sexual representation, legal reform is a trap. Let's leave it unsprung and move on to better ways.

Women and Images: Toward a Feminist Analysis of Censorship
Anna Gronau

At times it has been very difficult to reconcile my feelings about censorship as an artist and curator with my feelings on the matter as a woman and feminist. A few years ago, when I was the programmer for The Funnel, a Toronto theatre for experimental film, censorship became a repressive presence in my life. That experience forced me to confront my beliefs and the ways in which they appeared to conflict. My analysis of censorship has had to take into account both feminism and art, and I have concluded, ultimately, that my personal and political interests are no better served by censorship than are my artistic interests.

We had shown films freely for a number of years at The Funnel, unaware that Ontario's censorship laws could affect us. Our "education" began, however, in 1980, when a representative from the censor board visited our office and informed us that all films we planned to screen had to be submitted to the board for prior approval. Our naive contention was that The Funnel was comparable to an art gallery, and thus this requirement should be no more applicable to us than to a place that exhibited paintings. Despite this argument, the letter of the law prevailed.

For our small, artist-run organization, the time and money involved were practically more than we could handle. Films had to be shipped, at our expense, to and from the censors' offices, and fees had to be paid for censoring "services." Our schedule was put under tremendous strain, since visiting artists who often delivered their films in person now had to arrive much earlier, in time for the censors to preview their work. There were other, less tangible but more damaging costs: most filmmakers objected strongly to submitting to a kind of regulation that was unheard of in other parts of Canada and the world, and to the added wear and tear on their films. Others refused outright to comply. Censorship, in addition to being a bureaucratic burden, was philosophically repugnant and an embarrassment internationally.

The problem did not remain confined to The Funnel. In the course of the following year, as Lynn King's article explains, the arts community experienced an unprecedented invasion of censorship. By the end of 1981, The Funnel, the Canadian Filmmakers' Distribution Centre, Canadian Images Film Festival in Peterborough and *Fuse* magazine were all engaged in court cases arising from the censor board's new zealousness.

Armed with numerous lawyers and seemingly endless resources, the Ontario Board of Censors won its case against Canadian Images in 1984 and succeeded, meanwhile, to have the cases launched by *Fuse*, The Funnel and the Canadian Filmmakers' Distribution Centre dismissed. At the same time, The Funnel had become the object of intense scrutiny by a variety of officials. Fire and building code regulations were rigidly imposed upon us, forcing us to undertake thousands of dollars' worth of repairs and renovations. Already under financial strain as a result of the costs of complying with the censorship regulations and meeting our lawyers' bills, we wondered for a time if we would be put out of business. Fortunately, the artists' community rallied and we managed to pull through, finally paying off our debts in 1984.

It was this same group of independent producers, exhibitors and distributors that began to organize in 1981 to fight censorship when the censor board started its campaign against galleries and festivals. Alarmed by the Orwellian implications of the board's actions, we formed Film and Video against Censorship (FAVAC) and began a long process of lobbying for change.

In 1982, once the Canadian Constitution had been enacted, we saw a new opportunity to challenge the board's powers. Two other FAVAC members, Cyndra MacDowall and David Poole, and I formed the Ontario Film and Video Appreciation Society (OFA-VAS). We submitted four films to the board that had previously been prohibited from being screened in Ontario: *Amerika, Rameau's Nephew. . . , The Art of Worldly Wisdom* and *Not a Love Story*. (Not one of these films, it should be noted, has ever been charged with obscenity under the Criminal Code.) An accompanying letter stated that in light of the freedom of expression clause in the Constitution's Charter of Rights, we believed that we had unlimited freedom to screen them. Predictably, the board disagreed and OFAVAS launched its suit.

Both the Ontaio Supreme Court and the Ontario Court of Appeal upheld OFAVAS's case; undeterred, the board appealed to the Supreme Court of Canada, a case that is still pending at the time of writing. Concurrently, obviously unconcerned that two Ontario courts had ruled that the law under which it operates is unconstitutional, the board sought legislation, Bill 82, that would expand its powers to include the right to censor films and videos intended for noncommercial and private use; this bill was passed in late 1984.

In the face of dissent, the Ontario Board of Censors has recently tried to make its actions more palatable by claiming that one of its priorities is protecting women by eliminating violent pornography. This is a tactic that typifies the philosophy and practice of censors. A brochure produced by the New York Public Library for its 1984 exhibition, "Censorship: 500 Years of Conflict," points out that justification for censorship has shifted over the years, while its true purpose — social control — has remained constant:

Historically, censorship has taken many forms. Roman censors sought to determine who was morally suited for citizenship; religious censors held heresy to be an impediment to salvation; moral censors in the nineteenth century passed judgment on what was suitable for family reading and viewing; and governments have restricted the circulation of information in the interest of national security, national dignity, or the stability of particular regimes. Censorship has always been justified in the name of public good and social order and has always been opposed in the name of freedom of expression and progress.

The censor board's claims have convinced many people, among them, unfortunately, a number of feminists. But as one who has experienced being censored, I have become deeply suspicious of those arguments. Looking closely at the way censorship operates, I have found that beneficiaries of film censorship are not women, or even society as a whole. Ironically, however, producers and exhibitors of pornography do have something to gain. Making demanded cuts in films destined for public release reduces their chance of being prosecuted under the Criminal Code. If a film is not approved for public exhibition, it may well become more sought after underground.

In the case of commercial distributors and exhibitors, who may disagree with censorship in principle, compliance is nevertheless seen as a form of insurance against obscenity charges. Some may even welcome the interpretation of conservative, mainstream stand-ards that censorship provides, since their films must be acceptable to a broad segment of the population in order to turn a profit. For artists, however, the form or content of a work of art tends to be much more important than its commercial potential. In fact, artists may often consciously make a work radically divergent from the status quo — not out of a desire to be perverse, but to pose new questions and offer fresh perspectives. Given this, it is not surprising that artists seldom support censorship, for they understand that art, in order to express new ideas, may be surprising or shocking in form. At the same time, because their work is necessarily public, it is artists who are most likely to bear the brunt of censorship, to be intimidated into silence or euphemism by it, or forced into con-frontation and martyrdom. Freedom of expression, an abstraction to some, is to artists as essential as their raw materials — paint and canvas, film and cameras.

It is no less important, in my view, for women. Some of the most important work on why people invest images, particularly moving ones, with so much authority has been done by feminists, who have found that social conditioning plays an important role in this pro-cess. According to people such as Laura Mulvey and Peter Wollen in Britain or Kaja Silverman in the United States, we project our values and experiences onto the images that we view, reading mean-ing into them. The ideology of sexism, for instance, structures the very way we think and perceive. We can no longer view certain films or other images that once seemed benign without being aware of sexist characteristics; our way of perceiving has now changed to the extent that what once was "natural" (that is, in line with the predominant cultural pattern) is now imbued with different mean-ing based on new ideas. A look at different periods and societies supports this theory. Some cultures have believed in the superna-tural power of imagery; others have regarded the possession of, for example, a painting, as symbolic of its owner's power over or priv-ileged relationship to what was depicted; and when films were first introduced they were viewed by some as a frightening breach of the laws of nature. There is no reason to think that the ways in which people understand images will not continue to grow and change.

In contrast, supporters of censorship hold the dangerous belief that all images have a fixed meaning and can seduce viewers into imitative action. Those who have the most power in this society have a vested interest in our believing that this is how images affect us: a population with such an outlook is more susceptible to both advertisements and propaganda. Worse, if we feel we require protection from the image, we may abdicate the power to make and interpret images to the few who control the mass media.

Following on this reasoning, there is good cause for alarm about censorship. If pornography is seen as a contributor to misogyny, and censorship is advocated as a means of eliminating this misogyny (the view held by procensorship feminists and nonfeminists alike), a regrettable corollary is the assumption that society and individuals are incapable of change — either at a deep personal level or through conscious work and social programs. Censorship, paradoxically, enshrines the present inequality of the sexes in law: it implies that women are by nature weak and powerless creatures who require protection from men, who are in turn violent and aggressive by nature. Yet these same "aggressors" are cast in the role of protectors. As long as the law suggests that sex (both in the sense of gender and the drives of sexuality) is identical with, or the cause of, sexism the world will continue to regard being a woman as a liability.

There is another compelling argument against censorship that feminists must consider: knowledge gives us the power to progress, and without access to information, such as our history, we cannot engage in the necessary process of redefinition and reevaluation. Censorship removes the evidence and hinders the acquisition of knowledge. I believe that this hurts feminism a great deal, for being able to document our oppression has been, and continues to be, of inestimable value in battling sexism. It was only when pioneering thinkers began to systematically study the great and small documents of social history that they discovered the complicated religious, psychological and medical theories that had been employed through the centuries to prove the "inevitability" of male dominance. Until this evidence was produced, sexism, as a word or a concept, did not exist. Women who rebelled against a system that relegated them to second-class status had instead to grapple with the fact that their perceptions were considered wrong, that they were at odds with the "natural" order of things.

The recent rise of violent pornography has coincided with increased power on the part of women. Censoring this material, I believe, only abets those who seek a return to the former distribution of power, for such action will remove the public proof that violence and other wrongs against women continue to exist in society. We may, once again begin to doubt our perceptions; censorship seeks to hide the evidence of sexism, silencing those who try to confront it. Without that evidence we will have no concrete, visible proof. It is a short step from not having the means to protest to being unable to protest. There are already too many impediments to our being heard; we must not be complicit in the creation of another barrier.

Feminists studying the culture of male-dominated society have also tried to understand why and how women have been excluded from the cultural process for so long. We came to realize that we have lacked a voice; that we had been both prevented from speaking and impeded in developing a language in which to articulate our experiences. Just as a new branch of science must create names for new ideas and phenomena, so women have to build a language that will allow us to communicate. Many of our experiences have existed too long in the realm beyond words.

Our sexuality is a prime example of this voicelessness. Generations of women, unable to express their sexual desires — indeed, prohibited from doing so — have had to endure unsatisfying, if not painful, sexual relations. Even today, women are still regarded more readily as sexual objects than as sexual "subjects." As yet, there are almost no words or images to describe our sexuality as we experience it, and without a language, women will be unable to reach out to men to explain, or to one another for understanding and support. So far feminism has been quite successful in communicating many ways in which we have always been defined in relation to men, and thus restricted. But there are still a great many unanswered questions. To what extent can or should men and women be defined separately? Are there intrinsic psychic differences between us, or only socially determined ones? How can we overcome sexist limitations and come to know who we are and what we want? How can we articulate our identities and desires?

The arts are one area where those experiences that are yet unvoiced can begin to be communicated. Using the conventional vocabulary of words and images, but in an unconventional way, art may reveal the flaws and inconsistencies in the established, commonsense view, a questioning that is central to the development of women's voice. In learning to speak with that voice we must be open to experimentation, risktaking and playful investigation, just as children are when they learn to walk and talk. Censorship disrupts our ability to learn.

Take, for example, what would happen were a government to censor images of violence. The conventional, commonsense view deplores violence and would applaud such a move on any government's part. But "violence" can mean many things. In dreams, psychotherapy and art, particularly, perhaps, feminist art, it often symbolizes a problem that needs to be confronted, or a breakthrough in relation to a problem. It may indicate release from an oppressive aspect of the psyche or a self-destructive pattern. Censorship, however, based on a narrow, conventional definition of violence, is unable to differentiate between the expressions of violence necessary to developing new ways of thinking and speaking about ourselves and those without redeeming aspects. Nor can censorship laws be drafted so as to exempt women's — or anyone else's — new language, for it is still unformed. The limited, bureaucratic forces of censorship are capable of dealing only with what exists, not with what has yet to be created.

Artists of both sexes and women in general are particularly vulnerable if their search for ways of expressing new ideas includes such taboo subjects as sex and violence. Human sexuality has been formed by a society that assumes the sexes are unequal, and notions of a sexuality based on equal power remain tentative, hypothetical. If we should want to explore the deep psychological and social links between violence and sex as part of the process of gaining knowledge and understanding of them (and, by extension, about our own sexual repression and potential), our own productions may well be both disturbing and explicit. Censorship can only accentuate the taboos that already surround women's open exploration of their sexuality. There are too many other obstacles now in place to women becoming artists or writers, or even speaking out publicly, without inviting the judicial control of censorship.

I consider myself to be a feminist, and I believe that sexism is the enemy of women, but I have also come to the conclusion that censoring pornography is like killing the messenger who brings bad news. It offers a paternalistic, catchall solution to our problems and distracts our attention from the less visible but more insidious injustices we suffer by focusing on the symptom rather than the disease.

The more we can confront and understand violence and sexuality, and the machinations of power — both in the world and in ourselves — the better we will be able to take actions that are best for us. There are a great many social programs that can and should be put into place to better the lot of women so that we no longer see protection by men as our only option. As someone who works with images, I also believe that we can confound and confront sexism through our work, discrediting pornography where we need to, by creating work that reveals its hidden subtext, by juxtaposing it with images that challenge its usual meanings, or by satirizing it. (Sara Diamond examines these strategies at greater length in her article in this volume.) We can also use our art to discover new ways of expressing our sexualities and identities. And we can continue to name the real forces that oppress women and speak loudly against them. But in an atmosphere of censorship, our voices may well be silenced.

Thrills, Chills and the "Lesbian Threat" or, The Media, the State and Women's Sexuality

Mariana Valverde and Lorna Weir

When feminists discuss pornography, one often hears that lesbians have nothing to lose if porn is banned or censored. Lesbians, after all, are living embodiments of women's struggle for sexual autonomy, and thus have special reasons to object to heterosexual porn. But even if this is true, we think that lesbians have a lot to lose if censorship of pornography is instituted (see pages 79 and 91). This article explains why we have come to this conclusion, and why the problems of porn and lesbian oppression affect all women.

Throughout most of this century, lesbians have existed in a limbo somewhere between invisibility and persecution. Male children call each other "faggot" constantly, but one seldom hears the word "dyke" in playgrounds. Lesbian culture has not gained the attention of the police nearly as much as gay male culture. It is difficult to say if this is because we haven't been as active as the gay movement or because, as French feminist Luce Irigaray has pointed out, the language and culture of women's desire has been suppressed since the time of the Greeks. A well-known example of this was Queen Victoria's famous refusal to sign a law against lesbianism because, she said, women just didn't do that sort of thing.

To explain sexuality historically, we need to understand that, contrary to popular belief, sexual relations are not static, but change a great deal through history and across cultures. To understand modern-day lesbianism, we need to know how both homo- and heterosexuality have become what they are.

Furthermore, both forms of sexual preference need explanation, not just homosexuality. They constitute a complementary whole, and mutually shape each other. In fact, both homosexuality and heterosexuality underwent tremendous changes around the turn of the century.

In the 1880s and 1890s, a series of sexual practices began to be studied and classified. The theories of German psychologist Richard von Krafft-Ebing and other experts in medicine, criminology and allied disciplines reconceptualized sexuality in terms of a heterosexual norm with attendant specific deviations. Then various governmental bodies and the newly emerging mass media popularized these new ideas, with the result that educators and parents began to worry about the sexual identity of their children. For the first time in history, people began to interpret their sexual acts and desires in terms of two mutually exclusive sexual identities. Opposite-gender relations were intensified as a heterosexual identity was created against which other desires appeared as perverse. This is what is known as *heterosexism*.

An example of how this was used was the moral fervor with which authorities turned against all-female and all-male environments, such as boarding schools. Around 1900, same-sex intense friendships, which had traditionally been encouraged, began to be seen as corrupt and perverse.

We can see, then, that the invisibility of lesbianism is not an oddity of history, but rather the flip side of coin whose other, "normal" side is institutionalized, compulsory heterosexuality.

Of course, long before the 1880s sex took place both between and within the genders. But the point is that earlier opposite-gender sex did not have a distinct name for itself as a sexual identity. Earlier on, all sorts of violations of sexual propriety had been lumped together under the term "sodomy," which covered a wealth of same- and opposite-gender sexual acts. A sodomite was someone who engaged in nonreproductive sex of any kind; but after he confessed his sins, he was essentially the same as anyone else. On the other hand, the modern homosexual is perceived to have a different, abnormal personality. According to Freud, abnormalities in childhood sexual development cause (or at least tend to cause) homosexuality, and this marks one for life, regardless of whether one acts it out. Thus, the sodomite *did* certain things to set him or her off from other people, while the homosexual *is* different from other people.

Just as homosexuality today is not merely an act but an identity, so modern heterosexuality is also a whole identity. This identity is a very particular form of opposite-gender desire. It has been actively fashioned by psychology and medicine, through the police, courts and social agencies.

Associated with the growth of compulsory heterosexuality was the increased isolation of the nuclear family. Individual men and women were now expected to seek companionship and fulfilment in each other to a far greater degree than before. Whereas romantic love had been previously regarded as disruptive of social relations, and had been associated more with adultery than with marriage, the newly married couples of the 1920s began to expect "to keep the sizzle in marriage," as a *Reader's Digest* article advised them to do. Married couples were perceived to be attached not just by property considerations, by affection, by wanting to bring up children and by male lust: they were supposed to be bonded with the glue of mutual heterosexual desire.

This bond was not purely mystical. It had to be embodied in material possessions. As feminist historians have pointed out, the heterosexual couple became a vehicle for consumer capitalism during the 1920s. The respectable working-class couple no longer lived in a rented home with aunts and lodgers, but instead saved up for a single-family home. The advertisements of the 1920s show a shift away from largely asexual appeals and toward an increasingly (hetero)sexualized message in which social status and sexual normalcy reinforced each other. Since then, the advertising industry has been telling us that consumer capitalism and heterosexual fulfilment are two hearts with but a single beat.

The massive social approval bestowed on brides, thrifty housewives and model mothers is not innocent. It hinges on the victimization and suppression of single women, "masculine" women, lesbians and anyone else who does not conform. The elevated status of women with men is gained at the expense of women without men. We do not point this out in order to make anyone feel guilty; clearly many women do have a sexual passion for men, and it's not their doing that their desire is rewarded while ours is punished. But all women should understand that the heterosexist division of society into "normal," coupled womanhood and "abnormal" single or lesbian existence works to undermine our collective independence. To defend the existence of lesbianism as a viable and visible choice is to create more social space for all women.

The oppression of lesbians, then, is not just a result of old-fashioned prejudices or individual bigotry. It is intertwined with structural social and political trends affecting everyone in many areas of their lives. Some heterosexist policies, such as rules governing child custody, are aimed specifically at lesbians. But others are aimed at all women without men, for instance the measurement of the Canadian standard of living according to the income of the increasingly mythical "average family." The myth of the average family income obscures the poverty of lesbians and other single women and reinforces the notion that if we don't live with a man, then it's our own fault for being poor.

It is essential that we see heterosexism and lesbian oppression in their full scope, and not just concentrate on sexual activity. Lesbianism as a sexual preference has political and social consequences. As lesbians, our aim must be broader than the limited freedom to do as we please in the bedroom. With particular reference to the issue of porn, we have two tasks. One is the attempt to create, invent and imagine our own self-image as lesbians through lesbian song, poetry and art. The other is to participate in the joint effort by all women to destroy the edifice of heterosexism, to abolish the distinction between normal and abnormal sexuality, and bring about real sexual choices. One cannot proceed without the other.

Since the word "lesbian" was coined, we have struggled for the right to define ourselves and create our own image of who we are. This may seem trivial in comparison to such basics as job security. But male experts have not merely studied us: they have defined us as perverts and outsiders, and on the basis of these definitions we have been politically oppressed. Lesbian-negative theories convinced many lesbians that there was something wrong with their biology or that some early trauma had caused them to reject "normal" heterosexuality. Practically everyone they consulted agreed that lesbianism was a deviation from normal womanhood; only the degree of tolerance or persecution that ought to be directed at such deviants was in question.

Before the late 1960s, a homosexual subculture existed, consisting of bars, some legal reform groups, a few periodicals, books (often tragic, such as *The Well of Loneliness*) and supportive friendship networks. During the teens and '20s there were a few attempts at organizing, but the homosexual movement was crushed in the 1930s along with the women's movement. Between the 1930s and the late '60s, the homosexual subculture had for the most part an underground existence, for homosexuals of both genders were potentially subject to psychiatric and medical persecution, not to mention job loss and disgrace.

Until the 1970s, the lesbian did not exist openly in society: if she was acknowledged at all, it was most often in the sensationalistic style of '50s pulp novels. It was only with the growth of feminism and gay liberation in the '70s that lesbians developed networks that enabled us to talk about our lives. There are now a number of organizations, some books, a bit of music and a scattering of periodicals through which we are defining ourselves to one another.

However, while we spend vast amounts of energy producing a few lesbian cultural events and some slim volumes of poetry, the images of lesbianism produced in our society on a mass basis change little. Our alternative lesbian culture is politically crucial to protect us and gives us personal strength, but it is in an economically precarious position (as are most alternatives to the dominant media). As long as it remains on the margins of society, it cannot present real choices for women at large. Until the media conglomerates are attacked head on, lesbian images of lesbians will remain on the fringes — and hence our very existence will be seen as "fringe."

There is one exception to this general invisibility, and it is important because it is the same place where most men acquire their ideas of what a lesbian is: the pornographic bookstore. Indeed, it is curious that the phrase "lesbian porn" does not refer to sexual imagery produced for lesbian delight, but rather to images of alleged lesbian acts produced for heterosexual men. Men's pornography is for men; lesbian pornography is also for men.

This is a great patriarchal coup: extending the male gaze into an area of female experience that by definition is closed to men. Of course, when men look at "lesbian" porn, they do not get an accurate view of lesbian sexual activity. They only see their own fantasy of women displaying themselves for the pleasure of male voyeurs/participants. But even this imaginary and distorted access to lesbianism confirms men in their "right" to have unlimited access to any and all women, even women who are explicitly uninterested in sex with men. Lesbian porn thus undermines all women's right to say no and erodes the foundations of choice and consent.

Reduced to the level of kinkiness, lesbian sexuality is trivialized and robbed of its radical passion. Lesbians are merely a special challenge, a kind of sport or an exotic spice to revive the audience's presumed heterosexual interests.

A 10-page photo spread from the May, 1976, issue of *Penthouse* is typical. The front cover of the issue promises much: "Fulfilling Your Freakiest Fantasy: Thrills, Chills and the Lesbian Threat." Inside, a lesbian "spider" has caught a "fly" and is shown having sex with her prey; both "insects" are typically young, blonde and flawless. The text reads: "We [men] always suspected there was more to insect sexuality than preying and stinging. As revealed by the probing lens of microphotography [note the phallic reference], this bit of business looks particularly intriguing." The fly is no mere prey: "It is a defeat worth savoring, a killing passion that bridges the gap between rival species." (Even in describing lesbian sex the men who write the copy are intent on seeing feminine "rivalry" — between different species, no less.)

We purposely chose an example from *Penthouse* rather than from one of the publications catering to more specialized markets. Feminist critiques of porn have tended to concentrate attention on violent porn, neglecting analyses of soft-core, mainstream material. It is, however, the soft-core conglomerates that control the dominant representation of sexual expression. They should be understood as part of the culture industry, a major capitalist growth sector since World War II; this industry has created virtual information monopolies and elaborated new forms of cultural control. Porn is not just a form of patriarchal power; it is big business, the capitalization of sexual images. *Penthouse* magazine has a world-wide circulation of 3.2 million readers per month. The monthly budgets of all lesbian publications combined probably do not equal what it cost to finance this one photo spread.

Precisely because sexual images have become big business, we believe that those anticensorship advocates who base their position exclusively on the principle of individual freedom of expression are being naive. In theory, we may have the same rights as Bob Guccione, but we hardly have equal power. To paraphrase A.J. Liebling, freedom of the press belongs to those who own the press.

However, censoring pornography is not an appropriate strategy for feminists, particularly lesbian feminists, to pursue. Legislation of this kind will only undermine our attempts to give birth to a lesbian culture. Under stricter pornography legislation, the sexist and antilesbian feature in *Penthouse* might be prohibited — but such tougher laws could be applied equally to lesbian sexual representation, written and visual. Even the current laws have been used against lesbians.

In his 1982 judgment on the Glad Day Books gay pornography trial, Provincial Court Judge David Vanek shed an eerie judicial light on lesbian porn/erotica. Referring to a 1970 case in the Manitoba Court of Appeal in which some pornography magazines had been found to be obscene because of "lurid scenes of lesbianism," Vanek argued that although certain sexual acts (that is, homosexuality) had been decriminalized in 1969, the photographic portrayal of such acts was not necessarily legal. Why? Because photography implies the presence of a photographer, which meant that the acts were not taking place "in private," as required by the law.

This interesting double standard suggests that representations of homosexual sex will be allowed into the public realm only at the discretion of government officials. Homemade lesbian erotic films are in principle illegal, and the authorities are the ones to decide when our private acts are public enough to prosecute. The Glad Day decision — in effect prohibiting the production and distribution of lesbian and gay male images — poses a serious threat to any attempt to contest heterosexual supremacy. It places the control of sexual expression back firmly into the hands of the porn industry. It is thus a step backward for all women and for sexual minorities. (This decision was, however, subsequently appealed, and the legal wrangles continue.)

To develop a lesbian culture that would include both sexual and nonsexual representations of women who love women, we have to actively work for the creation of a public culture. Our desire has so far remained private and hidden, and in that sense we have not yet challenged the public lies of heterosexual men's porn. Ironically, however, we will have to live with those distortions even as we create our own images, for any attempt to ban manmade lesbian images would undoubtedly result in the persecution of lesbian-made images as well.

At the same time, a liberal approach that promises us moral support in case of unusual persecution is not very helpful either. Lesbians have few, if any, bookstores to be raided or defended: for us, freedom of speech is not an existing freedom to be defended but a goal to work toward. It is a project requiring a collective attack on the media conglomerates that monopolize public images and confine us to the fringe. Our strategies for displacing the ideology of the soft-core industry and creating lesbian culture cannot be achieved through the law, police and courts. We do not need a legal defence as much as a cultural offence. Lesbians and other sexual minorities are beginning to provide alternative, nonsexist and non-heterosexist representations that can help to disrupt and subvert the sexual regime that is at present produced over our heads.

At stake for lesbians, and for all women concerned about autonomy, is the creation of a society of genuine sexual pluralism. Pluralism means more than the absence of discrimination; it implies positive measures to protect diversity. Under a pluralistic regime, life for lesbians would be pleasantly humdrum. Government laws would not favor heterosexual couples or discriminate against singles; textbooks would have lesbian characters no better or worse than heterosexual characters; women's groups would no longer be lesbian-baited. Sexual pluralism would help to lessen everyone's sexual anxiety, and we could all relax about sexual issues a lot more than we do now.

Anti-porn legislation can only hinder the making of a sexually pluralistic society, through suppressing discussions by those whose views differ from those of the porn industry and government bodies. The differential impact of current obscenity legislation on sexual minorities is becoming better known; we have no reason to believe that the effects of the proposed porn legislation would be any different.

As lesbians, we want to pose alternatives to heterosexist and sexist depictions of women. And our struggle for self-determination is intimately linked to that of all women, for when an assertive woman is dismissed as "only a dyke," the independence of all women suffers. When lesbian mothers are free to be open about their lives without fear of losing custody of their children, all single mothers struggling against a hostile society will benefit. Heterosexism is like the police: it may put only a few of us in jail, but its existence affects the lives of us all. The struggle against the enforced myths of heterosexism, the fight for lesbian culture and for woman-positive sexual representations, belongs to all women.

Acknowledgements
We would like to thank Gary Kinsman for contributing information and suggestions for this article.

Retrenchment Versus Transformation: The Politics of the Antipornography Movement
Ann Snitow

This piece is drawn from a talk that was given to a number of groups between March and September 1983. Since that time, a whole new strategy for antipornography organizing has been developed in the U.S. by Andrea Dworkin and Catherine MacKinnon. Though I do not deal here with the specifics of the new laws they propose, much that I have written has critical bearing on their claim that "pornography is central in creating and maintaining the civil inequality of the sexes."

There is a storm brewing in the women's liberation movement over sexual politics. This is not to say the women's movement is by any means limited to the current debates about pornography but when a woman today goes searching for the feminism she's heard about, that has called her, she is likely to encounter the antipornography movement, with its definition of sex and sexual imagery as continuous zones of special danger to women. Of late, this has been one burning tip of feminism where energy and feeling collect.

These heated feelings recall the passions that fueled the early days of the present wave of feminism, that fueled the proabortion movement and the women's health movement — both also about that contested terrain, the female body. As a veteran of those years, I remember how empowering that anger was, how it opened the eyes and cleansed the blood. We must indeed act out of what we feel or be cut off from the deepest sources of energy and political authenticity.

Nonetheless, I want to argue here that we need to know more about these feelings, or else run the risk of creating a strategy likely to move us away from the very things we say we desire. I want to argue that, in general, today's antipornography campaigns achieve their energy by mobilizing a complex amalgam of female rage, fear and humiliation in strategic directions that are not in the long-term best interests of our movement. A politics of outrage — which can be valuable and effective – can also seriously fail women in our efforts to change the basic dynamics of the sex-gender system.

Both in Canada and the United States in 1984, feminists have moved in the forefront of new political alliances pledged to combat pornography through legal means. Canadians have emphasized municipal bylaws, licencing and reforms to the Criminal Code, while U.S. antipornography activists are trying to use civil rights legislation as the basis of civil suits. These U.S. laws — now being proposed and tested in court — would allow an individual to claim damages if a public utterance could be defined as "the sexually explicit subordination of women." What does it mean in Mulroney's Canada or Reagan's America to demand new legal means to regulate public sexual imagery? How have we come to this strategic and theoretical point in the history of feminist thinking and activism about men's and women's sexuality?

All that I think about activism centred on the symbolic terrain of the sexual has developed in the atmosphere of the remarkable new work of feminist historians and theorists such as Carl Degler, Ellen DuBois, Barbara Epstein, Kate Ellis, Linda Gordon, Mary Hartman, Carroll Smith-Rosenberg, Gayle Rubin, Carole Vance and Judy Walkowitz. They provide a frame through which I see women's present efforts to gain sexual autonomy. This work suggests that though there were exceptions, most of the North American activist women who spoke of the importance of sex in the course of the nineteenth century spoke of how hard it was for women to gain control of their bodies within marriage — to control pregnancy. In this effort, middle-class women struggled to establish themselves as moral authorities. Even some of the most radical nineteenth-century activists accepted a general moral scheme in which men were sexual predators, fallen women were victims, and married, middle-class women were sexually pure.

In other words, the vast majority of nineteenth-century feminists accepted a model of society that not only assumed that men and women live in separate spheres, do different social tasks, but also that they have essentially different sexual and moral natures. Vulnerable on many fronts, nineteenth-century women chose organizing strategies to gain protection that *confirmed* gender differences.

If one narrows one's focus to these women, to the last major wave of feminism in the nineteenth century, male and female can look like two fixed, clearly defined categories, almost like two species. But as soon as one draws back and takes a longer view, these sharply defined gender distinctions begin to blur and shift. In the West in the last 150 years or so, the idea that gender is a particularly clear or useful principle by which to organize social life has been steadily eroded. We continue to cling to gender identity, of course — who, we wonder, would we be without it? — but gender keeps changing on us. Take, for example, the mothers of the young women who initiated the present wave of the women's movement. Born into a world where women couldn't vote, either forced to work or discouraged from working, depending not on gender but on class, rushed into the factories during World War II, then out of them again when the real men came home, this generation of women experienced — within one lifetime — four or five fundamentally different versions of what a woman is and does. They had reason to whisper into their daughters' ears that a woman might need to be any number of things.

Each wave of feminism has come a bit closer to facing this frightening malleability of gender. At the start of the present women's movement, we flirted with this idea as never before. Though Anne Koedt wrote in the germinal essay, "The Myth of the Vaginal Orgasm," that female sexuality was utterly different and out of synchronization with male, other theorists, such as Shulamith Firestone (*The Dialectic of Sex*), were saying the opposite, that gender and sexuality were separable, that sex could be set free from the old gender boundaries, that birth control and the chance of economic independence outside the family were going to make a tremendous difference, were going to change what *being a woman is*. For a brief, heady moment, women as different as Koedt and Firestone joined to proclaim the right to demand a sexuality more centred on female pleasure. Though consciousness-raising groups discussed rape and spent long sessions detailing "what men do to us around sex," their predominant mood was one of internal hope: we felt we could fight our oppression effectively.

But gradually the mood of the women's movement changed and its organizing shifted in emphasis. In general, there was a move away from insisting on the power of self-definition — think of the Lavender Menace, or the early celebration of the vibrator, or the new heterosexual imperative that one should demand from men exactly what one wanted sexually — to an emphasis on how women are victimized, how all heterosexual sex is, to some degree, forced sex, how rape and assault are the central facts of women's sexual life and central metaphors for women's situation in general. How did a sector of the movement come to say that violence and rape are the fundamental causes of sexism, rather, say, than child-rearing practices or economic inequalities? Why did the many powers of men to control women in a complex and heterogeneous society such as our own get telescoped into the single power of the male fist?

My answers to these questions are speculative and the following generalizations are not meant to imply that all antipornography campaigns have the same sources, content or political goals. Nor do I want to overstate the shift in movement priorities. Nearly all the current formulations of sexual issues in this wave of feminism were already present in the intense intellectual melee of 1969 to 1972. The changes are of emphasis, of visibility, of strategy. We are faced now with the task of exploring the various strands of the ideological web we've been weaving all along, discovering and facing the contradictions that are inevitable in a movement as rich, as broadly based, as our own. There are many variables here — both inside and outside the dynamics of our own political groups.

Let me take it as emblematic and not a coincidence that in the United States pornography became a much publicized focus for feminist organizing around 1977, the same year that the U.S. Supreme Court began seriously to undermine the right to abortion it had only established in 1973. By ruling that women could not use Medicaid funds for abortions, the court returned abortion to the status of privilege for those who can afford it. This failure of movement momentum got publicity, while at the same time the Equal Rights Amendment to the U.S. Constitution, which would have rendered hundreds of discriminatory laws illegal, was beginning to run into serious political trouble. The popular backlash against the political program of feminism was in full swing, with the New Right stealing media attention and gaining clout as a powerful, growing lobby.

In spite of a mass-based women's movement, by the late '70s it was also plain that women were not making economic gains. Though token women were appearing in high places, most women without economic support from men continued to live in poverty, a situation that has steadily undermined the allure of feminist enthusiasm for female independence. Without public support for day care and other family services, the working woman had reason to see her job not as a new access to power, but as one more instance of exploitation. Feminists have mounted a campaign against the "feminization of poverty," and, here and there, the fact that working women put in a double day has been acknowledged, but no social movement has yet succeeded in significantly altering this unfairness.

In such a political climate, feminists felt disappointment and frustration: How could it be that, in spite of the vitality of our movement, change was so much slower than we had hoped? The lively antipornography campaigns of this period are one expression of a general discouragement among women, and among all progressive movements during this period of backlash. The terms the antipornography movement uses to describe women's condition betray a loss of heart about women's ability to challenge men's power directly.

In this time of backlash, some feminists seem to be reasoning that if the state is impervious to our demands, perhaps we can compel its strength to our service. Maybe, this argument goes, the masculine power structure that resisted the ideology of equality will listen more attentively to the ideology of difference. The antipornography movement posits a male sexual drive that is intrinsically violent, different in kind from a more consensual and loving female sexual nature. If equality and gender-blind institutions are unobtainable, if they are fantasies of sameness that bury women's particular sexual and psychological condition and obscure the phobic male reaction to women, then, these feminists reason, why continue demanding equality? Why not demand instead specific recognition in law and custom of women's special nature and vulnerability?

The logic of this argument is compelling, but it collapses a theoretical tension that was clear and vibrant earlier, a tension between recognizing the specific situation of women with all the strengths that proceed from it and, at the same time, attacking the female role, the female myth. In other words, female difference, the special culture of women, is a source of movement strength and authenticity while the idealization of femaleness tends to undermine the movement's power to challenge the status quo. Though some antipornography theorists pay lip service to this distinction between women and the abstraction, Woman, almost all opt for a politics that defines male and female as relatively fixed, timeless categories. For these theorists, history is nothing but a record of female frustration and sexual slavery. Things are going badly now because for women they always go badly. For these feminists, only a profound and enduring difference between the sexes seems an adequately powerful explanation of why changes we wish for are so slow in coming.

One reason, then, why the antipornography movement became a focus of feminist energy in the late '70s lies in its claim to explain the recalcitrance of the male power structure. But at the same time external events seemed to mock earlier feminist high expectations, internal movement difficulties also made this emotionally vivid, symbolic campaign attractive. We had created revolutionary institutions, battered women's shelters, rape crisis centres, and the women who worked in them began to explore the complexity of female victimization. We learned from them not only about the variety of ways in which men brutalize women but also about how women internalize this oppression, weakening our capacity to resist. The women's movement set out to name male crimes formerly invisible — rape, wife battering, sexual harassment — and at first this naming was power in itself. For example, sexual harassment at work used to be socially invisible; it was accepted as a natural event, never seen as an injustice. Now, after years of effective feminist political action, in many an administrator's drawer lies a plan for what to do with a sexual harassment charge.

But rather than seeing this as a step forward in economic and social power, however small, our movement began to be frightened by what it had brought to light. Visibility created new consciousness, but also new fear — and new forms of old sexual terrors: sexual harassment was suddenly *everywhere*; rape was an *epidemic*; pornography was a violent polemic against women. It was almost as if, by naming the sexual crimes, by ending female denial, we frightened ourselves more than anyone else.

Pornography became the symbol of female defeat: Look, they hate us, we could say, pointing to a picture. Far less colorful instances of male dominance surround us: institutionalized sexism that needs no lurid, not to mention stigmatized, representations of naked women to make itself felt. But this engrained system of masculine power has proved far harder to attack.

Antipornography theory offers relief in the form of clear moral categories: there are victims and oppressors. As in the nineteenth-century debates on sex, lust is male, outrage female. But why should such solid, high boundaries between the genders comfort modern feminists? One reason must be our own uncertainties and anxieties about the present fluidity of gender imagery and identity. Nor are these anxieties unjustified: There is no guarantee that shifting gender definitions are in themselves progressive, leading inevitably to increased flexibility and choice. Nonetheless, in the midst of disturbing change, we must recognize, too, our opportunities — and celebrate our triumphs. In spite of backlash and our own failures, the women's movement has made enduring changes in how everyone thinks about women.

Instead of recognizing that the new visibility of women's sexual victimization is a great leap forward, some feminists are drawing energy from the assertion that women's situation is fast deteriorating. They have, I believe, lost sight of the larger historical truth: the women of the nineteenth century *belonged* to their husbands or fathers. Under such conditions, wife beating and marital rape could barely be conceived of as crimes.

Our situation is profoundly different. Women are flooding into public space. Exploitation, new forms of sexual anomie, backlash, phobic resistance from men, new impediments to women's autonomy are all inevitable; but we must not misinterpret these as defeats, nor lose heart about our long-term ability to change the state, nurture our own institutions and protect ourselves without restricting ourselves.

The antipornography movement has attracted women from many sectors of women's liberation. But this unity has a high price, for it requires that we oversimplify, that we hypothesize a monolithic enemy, a timeless, universal, male sexual brutality. When we create a "them," we perform a sort of ritual of purification: There are no differences among men or women — of power, class, race. All are collapsed into a false unity, the brotherhood of the oppressors, the sisterhood of the victims.

In this sisterhood, we can seem far closer than we are likely to feel when we discuss those more basic and problematic sources of sexual mores: ethnicity, church, school and family. We are bound to disagree once we confront the sexual politics implicit in these complex social institutions, but from just this sort of useful debate will come the substance of a nonracist feminist concept of sexual freedom. Sometimes, ironically, our drive toward a premature feminist unity through female outrage has led to scapegoating inside the women's movement, as if we were already agreed about which sexual practices belong beyond the feminist pale. I find such internal attacks particularly terrifying now at a time when sexual minorities are increasingly harassed by the state. Given the sexual ignorance, fear and oppression in a sex-negative society, it is a false hope that feminist unity can rely on a premature agreement on sexual expression.

What *are* the feminist grounds of unity in a discussion of pornography, or of women's sexual freedom in general? Feminists on all sides of this debate share the desire to "take back the night"; to own our sexual selves; to express these selves in images of our own choosing. We share a feminist anger about women's sexual exploitation and a desire to leave the impress of this feeling — our recognition of profound injustices that reach to the core of identity — upon the consciousness of the world.

We also share the belief that sex is primarily a social, not biological, construction; hence social power relations have everything to do with who can do what to whom sexually. Since sex is social, we agree that its symbolic representation is important, that the imagery of sex is worth feminist analytical attention. We agree, too, that in sex, as in everything, women are sometimes right to fear: misogyny permeates our social life and men dominate women. But finally, and significantly, we disagree about the best route to liberation — or even to safety.

Present antipornography theory, rather than advancing feminist thinking about sexuality, continues sexist traditions of displacement or distortion of sexual questions. Instead of enlarging the definition of sexual pleasure to include a formerly invisible female subjectivity, antipornography thinking perpetuates an all too familiar intellectual legacy, one that defines male arousal as intrinsically theatening to female autonomy. Once again, women's experience fades into the background while men fill the foreground. Antipornography theory limits this focus further by collapsing a wide range of sexually explicit images into only one thing: violence against women.

But feminists have little to gain from this narrowing idea of what pornographic imagery contains. A definition of pornography that takes the problem of analysis seriously has to include not only violence, hatred and fear of women, but also a long list of other elements, which may help explain why we women ourselves have such a mixture of reactions to the genre. (I have heterosexual porn in mind here, but some of this description applies to other types of pornography; generally, porn is a much more varied genre than antiporn activists acknowledge.)

Pornography sometimes includes elements of play, as if the fear women feel toward men had evaporated and women were relaxed and willing at last. Such a fantasy — sexual revolution as *fait accompli* — is manipulative and insensitive in most of the guises we know, but it can also be wishful, eager and utopian.

Porn can depict thrilling (as opposed to threatening) danger. Though some of its manic quality comes from women-hating, some seems propelled by fear and joy about breaching the always uncertain boundaries of flesh and personality.

Hostility haunts the genre, but as part of a psychodrama in which men often imagine themselves women's victims. Mother is the ultimate spectre and women, too, have moments of glee when she is symbolically brought low.

Some pornography is defiant and thumbs a nose at death, at the limitations of the body and nature, indeed at anything that balks the male (perhaps potentially the female?) will.

Porn offers men a private path to arousal, an arousal that may be all too easily routed by fear or shame.

Though pornography often centres emotionally on dramas of dominance and submission, anyone who has looked at the raging dependence or the imagined omnipotence of a one-year-old has reason to doubt that patriarchy is the only source of our species' love/hate relationship to the emotions of power and powerlessness. Pornography is infantile then, but "infantile" is a word we use as a simple negative at the risk of patronizing some of our own sources of deep feeling. In many of the guises we know, such infantile feelings give rise to images of the brutal or the coldly murderous; in others, however, childishness can be more innocently regressive, potentially renewing. As Kate Ellis and others have argued, we can indulge in fantasies of childish ominipotence without having these define the entire field of our consciousness or intentions. Particular deep feelings may be neither valuable or liberating, but they demand understanding; they cannot be sanitized through mere will.

Ridden with authoritarian fantasies as it is, pornography also flouts authority, which no doubt in part explains its appeal to young boys. Certainly while porn remains one of their few sources of sexual information we should not marvel at the importance of the genre. But porn as we know it is, of course, a miserably skewed source of information. While it does offer taboo, explicit images — however distorted — of the bodies of women, the male body usually remains invisible. Since men control porn, they can continue to conceal themselves from inquisitive female eyes.

The same people who want sex education removed from schools now join feminists in the fight against porn. If this odd alliance prospers, we will hear the crash of successive doors closing in the faces of curious but isolated children. In the present political context, pieties about protecting children are passive and reactive; we are not protecting them so much as abandoning them to silence. Pornography as we know it requires a social context of ignorance and shame that present feminist campaigns against it do nothing to alter.

Finally, antipornography theory's central complaint about pornography is that it is objectifying and fragmenting. The genre makes women into things for male pleasure and takes only that part of the woman that pleases without threat. Once again, the danger of objectification and fragmentation depend on context. Not even in my most utopian dreams can I imagine a state in which one recognizes all others as fully as one recognizes oneself (if one can even claim to recognize oneself, roundly, fully, without fragmentation). The real issue is a political one. Antipornography activists are right to see oppressive male power in the gaze of men at women: Women cannot gaze back with a similar, defining authority. But, while we all want the transformed sexuality that will be ours when we are neither dependent nor afraid, the antipornography campaign introduces misleading goals into our struggle when it intimates that in a feminist world we will never objectify anyone, never take the part for the whole, never abandon ourselves to mindlessness or the intensities of feeling that link sex with childhood, death, the terrors and pleasures of the oceanic. Using people as extensions of one's own hungry will is hardly an activity restrained within the boundaries of pornography, nor is there any proof that pornography is a cause rather than a manifestation of far more pervasive imbalances of power and powerlessness.

Antipornography activists argue that pornography is everywhere, both the source of woman hatred and its ultimate expression. This is an effort to have it both ways: woman-hating is everywhere, but the source of that hatred is specific, localized in pornography, the hate literature that educates men to degrade women. The internal contradiction here is plain. If misogyny is everywhere, why target its sexual manifestation? Or if misogyny collects around the sexual, why is this so? Why assume that the cordoning off of particular sexual images is likely to lessen women's oppression? This over-emphasis placed on sex as cause is continuous with the very old idea that sex is an especially shameful, disturbing, guilt-provoking area of life. To accept rather than struggle against the idea that sex is dangerous and polluting is to fear ourselves as much as the men who rape and hurt. We need to be able to reject the sexism in porn without having to reject the realm of pornographic sexual fantasy as if that entire kingdom were without meaning or resonance for women.

Without history, without an analysis of complexity and difference, without a critical eye toward gender and its constant redefinitions, without some skepticism about how people ingest their culture, some recognition of the gap — in ideas and feelings — between the porn magazine and the man who reads it, we will only be purveying a false hope to those women whom we want to join us: that without porn, there will be far less male violence; that with less male violence that will be far less male power.

In the antipornography campaign, the thing we have most to fear is winning, for further legal control of pornography would, first, leave the oppressive structures of this society perfectly intact, even strengthened, and, second, leave us disappointed, since crimes against women are not particularly linked to pornography and indeed have many other highly visible sources.

Women will be victimized while we lack power. But even now we are not completely powerless. In fact, we are in the midst of complex power negotiations with men all the time. One of the basic themes of porn is the taming of the beast, Woman who if not bound, will grab; if not gagged, will speak. Pornography's fantasy penis is meant to tame the little bitch as it rarely can in real life.

However silenced and objectified we may be in the prevailing culture, we are not *only* silenced, not *only* objectified. Porn cannot fully define the situation in which we find ourselves. It symbolizes some, but not all, of our experiences — with men, with sexuality, with culture. In the liberation struggles of the '60s, American radicals insisted that everything is connected: what was happening in Vietnam was connected to what was happening in imperialist America. In the analysis and rhetoric of the antipornography movement, this tendency is carried to a distorting extreme. Instead of seeing connections among very different elements in our culture, some antipornography activists conflate things, see them all running together down a slippery slope. Pornography leads to rape, which leads to the rape of the land, which leads to international imperialism.

I'm not arguing that these things are not connected, only that by connecting them too quickly, too seamlessly, through the evocative power of metaphor, we fail to see the all-important differences. We must make distinctions of kind and of degree. For it is in the places where things don't fit together neatly that we can best insert our political will toward change.

If we leave this discussion in the realm of moral absolutes, of slippery slopes on the road to sin, we have chosen a rhetorical strategy that can arouse and enrage but that cannot lead us to a position beyond the old moral categories of female righteousness.

Ironically enough, the slippery slope model isolates sex from all other issues, since all other issues collapse into sex, are only sex. Once again, differences, varieties of power and powerlessness, get lost in a false unity. A frame is drawn around women's sexual exploitation and we are told this is the whole picture, the essence, the core truth. Women's sexual suffering becomes women's sexuality itself.

We do particular injury to feminist work by conflating sex with violence. This is to cede precious territory to the political opponents of feminism. It may be the female legacy of shame and fear that makes us accept this equation so quickly. Is it in our interests — not to mention in the interest of truth — to say that because husbands often rape wives, all marriage is rape? Or to say that women who reject this equation have been brainwashed by patriarchy? This is to deny women any agency at all in the long history of heterosexuality.

It is hard to imagine good organizing that can emerge from this insulting presumption. In her book *Right Wing Women*, antipornography theorist Andrea Dworkin argues that there are but two models for women's roles in society: the farm model and the prostitution model. Women are either fields to be plowed, cows to be milked; or they are meat to be bought. This is a pornographic reductionism of the role of women in history.

The antipornography world view purports to solve several problems at once: it explains movement failure; it downplays what is unnerving in our successes; it reenergizes honorably weary activists; it reestablishes unity at a time when differences among women are increasingly visible and theoretically important. But, built on weak foundations, these political gains will not endure. When maleness is defined as a timeless quality, it becomes harder rather than easier to imagine how it can ever change. The politics of rage tapers off into a politics of despair — or of complacency — and gender, which at moments has seemed very fluid and variable, suddenly seems solid and reliable again, If, as Mary Dale generalized in *Gyn/Ecology*, footbinding in China and suttee in India and child molestation in Manitoba are all identical, seamless, essentially male acts, where is the break in this absolute tradition, the dynamic moment when female will can prevail?

Since one of the faults of antipornography theory is its misplaced concreteness, I can't be correspondingly specific about how I would go about working to alter the often limited rapacious or dreary sexual culture in which women — and also men — now live. There are a lot of questions to answer: Does a disproportionate amount of misogynistic feeling cluster around sex? Why? How deep does sexual phobia go? Is sex in fact an area of experience that will need to be seen as separate, with its own inner dynamic, even perhaps its own dialectic? If we reject the strategy of repression and banning, how *do* we raise self-consciousness and political consciousness about the aspects of porn that express sexual distress, derangement, hostility? (It does seem obvious to me that banning is a step in the opposite direction, away from learning, from unmasking, and toward a suppression that ignores meaning.) What is the actual content of porn and how is porn related to the broader questions of arousal? In other words, what makes something sexy, and what part does power play in the sexualization of a person or situation? Is it a feminist belief that without gender inequality all issues of power will wither away, or do we have a model for the future that will handle inequalities differently? Are there kinds of arousal we know and experience that are entirely absent in porn? How expressive is it of our full sexual range? How representative? How conventional and subject to its own aesthetic laws?

We must work to answer these questions, but we know a lot already. We know that women must have the right to abortion, to express freely our sexual preferences; that we must have the control of the structure and the economics of health care, day care, and our work lives in general. All these levels of private and social experience determine the degree of our sexual autonomy. The New Right is sure *it* knows what women's sexuality is all about. We must reject such false certainties — in both the feminist and New Right camps — while we set about building the nonrepressive sexual culture we hope for, one in which women's sexual expressiveness — and men's too — can flourish. In her essay "Why I'm against S/M Liberation" (in *Against Sadomasochism*), Ti Grace Atkinson says, "I do not know any feminist worthy of that name who, if forced to choose between freedom and sex, would choose sex." While women are forced to make such a choice we cannot consider ourselves free.

Acknowledgements

I thank my coeditors of *Powers of Desire: The Politics of Sexuality* (Monthly Review Press), Christine Stansell and Sharon Thompson, and Carole Vance for many months of invaluable discussion. Nadine Taub helped me broaden and support my argument that disappointment is an unspoken theme of recent organizing, and Alice Echols was the first to develop the theme of false unities. Thanks, too, to e members of my study group: Julie Abraham, Hannah Alderfer, Meryl Altman, Jan Boney, Frances Doughty, Kate Ellis, Faye Ginsburg, Diane Harriford, Beth Jaker, Barbara Kerr, Mary Clare Lennon, Marybeth Nelson, Paula Webster, Ellen Willis and Carole Vance.

This piece is a talk that was delivered to a number of groups during 1983. Thanks to the following sponsoring organizations: Calgary Status of Women; the San Francisco Socialist School and Women against Violence in Pornography and the Media; the Fourteenth National Conference: Women and the Law; Lavender Left and Philadelphia Reproductive Rights Organization; New York University Colloquium on Sex and Gender.

Feminist Debates and Civil Liberties

June Callwood

First, I should get some personal pain out of the way. In the summer of 1984 a letter attacking me appeared in *The Globe and Mail*; the writer was a woman I see almost every week at a meeting of an organization called The Issue Is Choice, a small working group that raises funds for the defence of Dr. Henry Morgentaler, the Montreal physician who has defied the law in order to win women's right to abortion. Her letter was prompted by a column I had written for the *Globe* on pornography, and in it she said that if I would only inform myself of the extent of violence against women, I would realize that my views were harmful.

That letter hurt. I don't suppose this woman really believes that I don't know women are battered. It is general knowledge that more than 10 years ago I was one of two women who started Nellie's hostel for women in Toronto. Over the years, Nellie's has sheltered some 18,000 women in crisis, many of them abused. I frequently volunteer at Nellie's, usually taking the 14-hour night shift, during which it is not uncommon to share a 3 a.m. cup of coffee with a woman who can't sleep for nightmares of the rape she suffered, or worry with a woman six months' pregnant and punched in the belly that her labor has begun, or open the door to police bringing to safety a limp, dazed woman with her arm in a fresh cast.

What concerned me about my colleague's angry letter was that she felt she couldn't discuss her feelings with me personally, either because she was too furious or, more likely, certain that I would reject her arguments. We have continued to work together in the cause of abortion reform, but the ice between us is palpable.

Similarly, my longtime friend Doris Anderson, former editor of *Chatelaine* magazine, a woman I hail as one of the founders of feminism in this country, past president of the National Action Committee on the Status of Women, has entered into agreement with me that we won't talk about pornography when we meet. We've tried, and we sincerely respect one another's position, but she thinks a certain degree of censorship is essential in order to protect women, and I believe that censorship will change nothing for the better and has the potential to make matters worse.

My personal experiences around the issue of pornography and censorship mirror those of thousands of women in this country who have become estranged from feminist colleagues and even from close friends. What alarms me most is that this polarity might well cripple our efforts to work together in the future on such common — and vital — causes as day care, reproductive rights, equal pay for work of equal value and adequate pensions for women. As lawyer Mary Eberts once said, "Pornography is our Skokie." Just as the American Civil Liberties Union's controversial decision to support the rights of self-styled Nazis to demonstrate in Skokie, Illinois, in 1977, divided that organization, so the pornography debate is splitting the women's movement into separate, often hostile, camps.

What is lost in the nasty turn that many relationships have taken is that we all feel the same about pornography. None of us believes that hard-core pornography is harmless. We all see it as a gross dehumanization of women, and we all know that whenever one group in society — in this case, men — convinces itself that another group is a subspecies, it becomes permissible to inflict suffering and humiliation on the inferiors.

Unhappily, most forums where reasoned discussion of strategies and solutions might take place are soon stampeded by women, often feminists, who show films of men putting meat hooks in women's vaginas or talk about films where men put meat hooks in women's vaginas. Most of the audience erupts like a lynch mob, and those who dare to rise in the tumult to say that censorship isn't the answer are accused of insensitivity or worse.

The issue is such a powerful one that even university women's clubs and other organizations that rarely become exercised about women's issues have been heated in their advocacy of censorship. But what puzzles me most is that some of the women who support censorship hold otherwise very liberal views. Something has obviously touched them deeply to cause them to align themselves with the most reactionary and punitive elements in our society.

A possible explanation is that pornography releases our almost primeval obsession with protecting our bodies. It is this atavistic need for security that explains our distaste for impersonal sex and fondness for romantic literature, our modesty — even shame — about exposing ourselves, our sense that our bodies are sacred chalices, life carriers, exclusive. We cannot, we feel, be whole and invincible unless our bodies are safe. Pornography, like rape, views women as receptacles, and so stirs our deepest fears.

It is exactly because of this, I believe, that the schism in the women's movement caused by the pornography issue is so wide. Those who oppose censorship sometimes imagine that their opponents are simpletons who believe that the porn industry will collapse under the impact of new, tougher laws and that men, once the influence of pornography is removed, will immediately stop hurting women. In fact, most feminists in the procensorship camp know that pornography will only be driven further underground, where it will continue to flourish. Rather, they see stiffened censorship laws as symbolic of society's determination to end the abuse and humiliation of women, a legal torpedo across the bows. Supporters of this position dismiss those who strive to protect freedom of speech as naive and out-of-date, unwilling to accept that a genuine emergency exists. Most wounding is the accusation that my collegue on The Issue Is Choice made: that civil libertarians don't know, or don't care, that women are beaten and raped.

Fueling this debate is the erroneous impression that many Canadians have that we are sinking under a sea of filth. In 1983, *Globe and Mail* writer Bryan Johnson reported that Canada has virtually no pornography industry, aside from duplication and distribution of foreign videotapes. (Liss Jeffrey, writing in the November, 1984, issue of *Canadian Business* magazine estimated that 90 per cent of the print and video porn available here comes from the U.S.) The following year, after an exhaustive investigation to determine how much hard-core porn was actually available, Johnson wrote that he found almost none. Members of Project P, the antipornography squad that is a joint effort of the Ontario Provincial Police and the Metropolitan Toronto Police, informed him that there was little around, despite their diligent efforts to find it. Nor had police in North America been able to verify that a real "snuff" film, one in which a woman is actually mutilated and murdered, has ever been made.

Kiddie porn, dubbed the "heroin of the porno trade" by a Project P officer, is repellent to almost everyone, but its incidence, too, has been exaggerated. The Badgley Commission on Sexual Offences against Children and Youth, which spent four years studying the incidence of child pornography in Canada, discovered that the problem has been greatly overblown. While wary of the potential for videotapes to evade the network of law enforcement in the future, the commission reported that in 1984 kiddie porn wasn't a major problem. It noted that of the 26,357 seizures by customs of material deemed obscene that occurred between 1979 and 1981, only 1.3 percent involved children — a number that is confirmed by Project P, which estimates that less than three percent of the print and video material its officers find is kiddie porn. Such material "generally is not imported for commercial distribution in Canada," the Badgley commission reported, noting also that "there is virtually no commercial production of child pornography in Canada." Those few Canadian producers that do exist are "small, without exception, unsuccessful and relatively promptly identified by enforcement services." At present, the commission concluded, "the various enforcement agencies are effectively and efficiently controlling the problem."

The commission's members also agreed that while Canadians are divided on the question of adults' access to pornography, there is almost unanimity that children and teens should not be exposed to it. The Badgley report indicated that three out of four Canadians believe that only those over 18 should be allowed to purchase porn, and many municipalities are introducing bylaws that enforce this limitation. When the bylaws are reasonable, few Canadians would quarrel with their existence — certainly not this one.

Much of the pressure from feminists for tough new laws to deal with material involving women is based on the belief that men who view violence toward women tend to imitate such behavior. Capitalizing on this prevalent view, judges pronouncing sentence on men who have raped, battered or killed frequently treat themselves to front-page attention by denouncing pornography as a causative factor. It's something of a chicken-and-egg situation; surely it is at least as likely that violent men seek out violent pornography than that mild men are corrupted by exposure to sadism. Indeed, to date there have been no studies that have conclusively proved the monkey-see, monkey-do theory. On the other hand, several researchers, notably Thelma McCormack of York University in Toronto and Susan Gray of Fordham University in New York, have reported finding no correlation between exposure to violent pornography and increased violent behavior. (Thelma McCormack's study, "Making Sense of Research on Pornography," originally prepared for the pornography subcommittee of the Metropolitan Toronto Task Force on Violence against Women, appears in Appendix II.) Professor Jonathon Freedman, chairman of the department of psychology at the University of Toronto, supports this view. In an appendix to the brief on pornography presented to the Fraser Committee on Pornography and Prostitution by the Canadian Civil Liberties Association in 1984, he wrote, "The basic situation is that we do not have sufficient scientific evidence to draw any clear conclusions."

The same CCLA brief pointed out that even if it were true that pornography influences behavior, it does not follow that it is wise for society to deal with the problem by enacting censorship laws. "Couldn't it also be said," wrote Alan A. Borovoy, general counsel of the CCLA, "that exposure to communist material could gradually erode the taboos against totalitarianism? And don't some people say that exposure to certain feminist literature could gradually erode society's commitment to the family? . . . There is a widespread pragmatic realization that a legal prohibition could wind up nailing the wrong material."

This is the point that most concerns civil libertarians. Pornography cannot be defined to everyone's satisfaction. For instance, Mary Brown, the head of the Ontario Board of Censors, believes that anything that undermines the values of the traditional family is pornographic. As Michael Barrett, chairman of the Sex Information and Education Council of Canada, noted in his association's newsletter in 1984, some people consider all sexually explicit material is pornographic. He continued: "That over-reaction has been the legacy of our society, to lump together as obscene or pornographic all depictions of sexual activity including those that were joyous, consenting and egalitarian. We have deprived ourselves of those positive images we claim to value and would wish to endorse for our chidren. . . . Some now use the term 'pornography' to imply depictions of violence or brutality with or without 'sexual' overtones (i.e. violent pornography). Others attach the distinction 'hard-core' vs 'soft-core.' Still others use the word as an umbrella term to include all sexual images of which they disapprove."

In 1984 the Fraser committee was presented with literally hundreds of wordings for proposed amendments to the obscenity section of the Criminal Code, no two the same. The most carefully narrow came from some thoughtful feminists, among them lawyers, who sought to rephrase the law so that it would permit depictions of consenting sexuality while prohibiting the portrayal of sexual activity that involved coercion or force. Even these failed to find common ground. Each differed from the others and none was sufficiently airtight that it couldn't potentially be applied to material that its drafters sought to exclude. Even the Supreme Court of Canada can't agree on what obscenity legally means. In the more than 30 years since obscenity was last defined in the Criminal Code, there has never been a unanimous decision of the court on an obscenity case.

A 1983 case involving 25 videotapes seized by police as obscene further illustrates the difficulty of legally determining what is acceptable and what is not. At the time, Ontario County Court Judge Stephen Borins, who was required to rule on the tapes, observed that obscenity is the only offence in the Criminal Code that citizens don't know they've committed until the judge says so. ("It is not like walking into a bank with a gun and holding up a teller," he commented dryly.) Judge Borins ultimately decided that 11 of the 25 tapes were obscene, saying that they would have exceeded the community standards of Sodom and Gomorrah — yet six of these are available in Quebec, having been approved by that province's censors. More tellingly still, a year after Judge Borins's decision, the proprietor of a video outlet in a small Ontario town was charged for distributing two of the tapes that the judge had found *not* to be obscene; despite this, the dealer, unable to afford a lengthy legal case, pleaded guilty. Several months later, a Scarborough, Ontario, video retailer was also charged for distributing another of the tapes Judge Borins had passed. (At the same time the hapless dealer was charged for carrying *Andy Warhol's Frankenstein*, a movie that has been aired on pay-TV in the province and had even met the standards of Ontario's antediluvian board of censors.)

Significantly, Canadian police are not among those calling for new laws to curb pornography, saying that they're satisfied that the existing laws are adequate to curb the industry. In fact, Canada's anti-porn laws exceed only those of the resolutely sanitized nations under totalitarian rule, and there is no indication that these laws are not effective. Project P obtains convictions in 99 percent of its cases.

A change in the obscenity laws would raise many questions that feminists have not yet resolved. Women attending conferences have been known to make scenes at hotel newsstands because they object to such magazines as *Playboy* being sold, yet those publications rarely feature depictions of cruelty to women. Many of those who support suppression of porn have stated that they are all in favor of erotica, but have not attempted to explain the distinction. If the Criminal Code is to be amended, somebody certainly should decide whether *Playboy* and its ilk are a) erotic, b) pornographic, c) degrading, or d) silly. Efforts to suppress the puerile maunderings of undergraduate engineers raise similar questions. If these publications were to be classified as pornographic under new, broadened Criminal Code legislation, does it follow that everything crude, unflattering to women and not funny should become illegal?

A number of feminists who support some form of censorship attempt to make another distinction. They are not against sex, they say, but sexism. But while *Hustler* is clearly sexist, so is *Cosmopolitan*. A Miss Bikini Contest is sexist. So is patting women on the bum. To draft legislation that would prohibit *Hustler* while allowing *Cosmo*, which presumably is not the target, would be an impossible task.

And if it is the element of coercion that should distinguish what is pornographic from what is not, as a number of feminists have proposed, one of the problems that arises is that much sadomasochistic material does not involve women victims. Men are shown chaining and whipping other men; women are shown chaining and whipping men. Are those who support banning depictions of coercive sexuality opposed to all sexual coercion or only that in which women are apparently coerced?

In 1983, the Canadian Association of University Teachers tried to make an end run around these and other thorny problems raised by obscenity legislation. In all seriousness it proposed that pornography legislation exempt the work of all academics and all those with permission from a psychiatrist to have pornography in their possession. But such Alice-in-Wonderland schemes won't work, if for no other reason than that laws designed to make the subtle distinction between what is legal and what is not are not enforced by the well-intentioned people who advocate them. Power to decide what is offensive lies with policemen and -women who are trained to be literal. Civil libertarians are not being alarmist when they warn that laws meant to catch pornography that shows the mutilation of women could also be applied to war coverage on the news.

Inevitably, though, those who espouse the civil libertarian philosophy in regard to pornography have been the targets of considerable hostility. This antagonism is firmly rooted in our history, and can be traced to the mood of the country at the end of the eighteenth century, when American Tories who fled north to escape the excesses of the Sons of Liberty vowed eternal vigilance against the emergence of civil rights in their new country. Scarred as they were by their experiences with mobs shouting slogans about freedom, these neo-Canadians regarded talk about the rights of individuals to be the highest form of treason. Accordingly, they molded a nation in which the state was enthusiastically given the authority to control its citizens — creating what Northrop Frye has called Canada's "fortress mentality." When something worries Canadians, the solution they embrace is having the government move in to suppress it. It is not surprising that the most popular act in our history, according to a Gallup Poll, was the imposition of the War Measures Act in 1970. Consistent with these attitudes are the current initatives to apply a good housekeeping solution to the problem of pornography: roll up the sleeves and get out the legal lye and ammonia.

Because of this legacy, Canada has never been fertile ground for civil liberties. Associations created earlier in this century folded for lack of support. The present good health of the Canadian Civil Liberties Associaton, formed in 1965, seems to its founders, of which I am one, nothing short of a miracle. What perhaps accounts for the CCLA's current strength is a tentative change in the Canadian public, the awakening of concern over abuse of bureaucratic and police powers. The same awareness has led to the establishment of federal and provincial human rights commissions and the Charter of Rights and Freedoms enacted in 1982, although it is typically Canadian that the commissions are frail, underfunded, underfanged and curtailed by the anxious governments that spawned them and that most judges seem never to have heard of the charter.

The country's advances in civil rights are fragile. They would be undermined profoundly if state power became the tool for solving the problems of pornography. For feminists to make gains we need a country that tolerates all expression, however unpopular. Legislation designed to suppress what one group considers to be unseemly can always be interpreted to stamp out what another group does not like.

Mistrust of civil liberties reveals a lack of historical perspective.

The freedom of dissent enjoyed by today's feminists owes everything to civil liberties groups who 30 years ago fought for the right of marginal organizations and minorities to disagree with the majority. It was a civil liberties organization that sought to make covenants on the sale of land to Jews illegal. It was a civil liberties group that in 1965 fought a Toronto bylaw that would have allowed police to censor placards in demonstrations. Today, it is the Canadian Civil Liberties Association that protests such draconian welfare laws as the man-in-the-house rule and campaigns against inequities in the country's abortion laws.

No sane civil libertarian is an absolutist. When there is a compelling need to limit freedom of speech, as in the areas of libel and slander, no one argues against such legislation. The tests of limitations on free speech are that a clear and present danger exists and that the law proposed to address the danger will not cause more harm than the problem it is intended to overcome. Laws against pornography meet neither of these criteria. There is strong reason to doubt that pornography is as prevalent and horrific as the public has been led to believe, and arguments about its power to influence behavior have not been convincing. Nor is there agreement on a definition of pornography. There are shoals of hazards when a law seeks to prohibit something it can't describe.

Laws against pornography will do nothing to change the bully-victim relationship that is sustained by the poverty of women. The demand for porn laws is welcomed by politicans: for no expenditure or inconvenience whatsoever they can give women legislation that will please many of them mightily and alter nothing. But the most effective way to get across to society that women are not numb and dumb is to ensure that women's incomes equal those of men. When women have the same economic power that men do, the male-female relationship will begin to be egalitarian rather than coercive.

Feminism and civil liberties are inextricable. The goal of both is a society in which individuals are treated justly. Civil libertarians who oppose censorship are fighting on behalf of feminists, not against them.

False Promises: Feminist Antipornography Legislation in the U.S.

Lisa Duggan, Nan Hunter and
Carole S. Vance

In the United States, after two decades of increasing community tolerance for dissenting or disturbing sexual or political materials, there is now growing momentum for retrenchment. In an atmosphere of increased conservatism, evidenced by a wave of book banning and anti-gay harassment, support for new repressive legislation of various kinds — from an Oklahoma law forbidding schoolteachers from advocating homosexuality to new antipornography laws passed in Minneapolis and Indianapolis — is growing.

The antipornography laws have mixed roots of support, however. Though they are popular with the conservative constituencies that traditionally favor legal restrictions on sexual expression of all kinds, they were drafted and are endorsed by antipornography feminists who oppose traditional obscenity and censorship laws. The model law of this type, which is now being widely copied, was drawn up in the politically progressive city of Minneapolis by two radical feminists, author Andrea Dworkin and attorney Catharine MacKinnon. It was passed by the city council there, but vetoed by the mayor. A similar law was also passed in Indianapolis, but later declared unconstitutional in federal court, a ruling that the city will appeal. Other versions of the legislation are being considered in numerous cities, and Pennsylvania senator Arlen Specter has introduced legislation modeled on parts of the Dworkin-MacKinnon bill in the U.S. Congress.

Dworkin, MacKinnon and their feminist supporters believe that the new antipornography laws are not censorship laws. They also claim that the legislative effort behind them is based on feminist support. Both of these claims are dubious at best. Though the new laws are civil laws that allow individuals to sue the makers, sellers, distributors or exhibitors of pornography, and not criminal laws leading to arrest and imprisonment, their censoring impact would be substantially as severe as criminal obscenity laws. Materials could be removed from public availability by court injunction, and publishers and booksellers could be subject to potentially endless legal harassment. Passage of the laws was therefore achieved with the support of right-wing elements who expect the new laws to accomplish what censorship efforts are meant to accomplish. Ironically, many antifeminist conservatives backed these laws, while many feminists opposed them. In Indianapolis, the law was supported by extreme right-wing religious fundamentalists, including members of the Moral Majority, while there was *no* local feminist support. In other cities, traditional procensorship forces have expressed interest in the new approach to banning sexually explicit materials. Meanwhile, anticensorship feminists have become alarmed at these new developments and are seeking to galvanize feminist opposition to the new antipornography legislative strategy pioneered in Minneapolis.

One is tempted to ask in astonishment, how can this be happening? How can feminists be entrusting the patriarchal state with the task of legally distinguishing between permissible and impermissible sexual images? But in fact this new development is not as surprising as it at first seems. For the reasons explored by Ann Snitow (see page 107), pornography has come to be seen as a central cause of women's oppression by a significant number of feminists. Some even argue that pornography is the root of virtually all forms of exploitation and discrimination against women. It is a short step from such a belief to the conviction that laws against pornography can end the inequality of the sexes. But this analysis takes feminists very close — indeed far too close — to measures that will ultimately support conservative, anti-sex, procensorship forces in American society, for it is with these forces that women have forged alliances in passing such legislation.

The first feminist-inspired antipornography law was passed in Minneapolis in 1983. Local legislators had been frustrated when their zoning restrictions on porn shops were struck down in the courts. Public hearings were held to discuss a new zoning ordinance.

The Neighborhood Pornography Task Force of South and South Central Minneapolis invited Andrea Dworkin and Catharine MacKinnon, who were teaching a course on pornography at the University of Minnesota, to testify. They proposed an alternative that, they claimed, would completely eliminate, rather than merely regulate, pornography. They suggested that pornography be defined as a form of sex discrimination, and that an amendment to the city's civil rights law be passed to proscribe it. City officials hired Dworkin and MacKinnon to develop their new approach and to organize another series of public hearings.

The initial debate over the legislation in Minneapolis was intense, and opinion was divided within nearly every political grouping. In contrast, the public hearings held before the city council were tightly controlled and carefully orchestrated; speakers invited by Dworkin and MacKinnon — sexual abuse victims, counselors, educators and social scientists — testified about the harm pornography does women. (Dworkin and MacKinnon's agenda was the compilation of a legislative record that would help the law stand up to its inevitable court challenges.) The legislation passed, supported by antipornography feminists, neighborhood groups concerned about the effects of porn shops on residential areas, and conservatives opposed to the availability of sexually explicit materials for "moral" reasons.

In Indianapolis, the alignment of forces was different. For the previous two years, conservative antipornography groups had grown in strength and public visibility, but they had been frustrated in their efforts. The police department could not convert its obscenity arrests into convictions; the city's zoning law was also tied up in court challenges. Then Mayor William Hudnut III, a Republican and a Presbyterian minister, learned of the Minneapolis law. Mayor Hudnut thought Minneapolis's approach to restricting pornography might be the solution to the Indianapolis problems. Beulah Coughenour, a conservative Republican stop-ERA activist, was recruited to sponsor the legislation in the city-county council.

Coughenour engaged MacKinnon as consultant to the city — Dworkin was not hired, but then, Dworkin's passionate radical feminist rhetoric would not have gone over well in Indianapolis. MacKinnon worked with the Indianapolis city prosecutor (a well-known anti-vice zealot), the city's legal department and Coughenour on the legislation. The law received the support of neighborhood groups, the Citizens for Decency and the Coalition for a Clean Community. There were no crowds of feminist supporters — in fact, there were no feminist supporters at all. The only feminists to make public statements opposed the legislation, which was nevertheless passed in a council meeting packed with 300 religious fundamentalists. All 24 Republicans voted for its passage; all five Democrats opposed it to no avail.

A group of publishers and booksellers challenged the law in Federal District Court, where they won the first round. This legal setback for the ordinance may cause some other cities considering similar legislation to hold off until the final resolution of the appeal of the Indianapolis decision; meanwhile, however, mutated versions of the Dworkin-MacKinnon bill have begun to appear. A version of the law introduced in Suffolk County on Long Island in New York emphasized its conservative potential — pornography was said to cause "sodomy" and "disruption" of the family unit, in addition to rape, incest, exploitation and other acts "inimical to the public good." In Suffolk, the law was put forward by a conservative, anti-ERA male legislator who wishes to "restore ladies to what they used to be." The Suffolk County bill clearly illustrates the repressive, antifeminist potential of the new antipornography legislation. The appearance of a federal bill, together with the possibility of a new, Reagan-appointed commission to study new antipornography legislation, indicates how widespread the repressive effects of the ordinances may become.

Yet it is true that some of the U.S. laws have been proposed and supported by antipornography feminists. This is therefore a critical moment in the feminist debate over sexual politics. As anticensorship feminists work to develop alternatives to antipornography campaigns, we also need to examine carefully the new laws and expose their underlying assumptions. We need to know why these laws, for all their apparent feminist rhetoric, actually appeal to conservative antifeminist forces, and why feminists should be preparing to move in a different direction.

Definitions: The Central Flaw

The antipornography ordinances passed in Minneapolis and Indianapolis were framed as amendments to municipal civil rights laws. They provide for complaints to be filed against pornography in the same manner that complaints are filed against employment discrimination. If enforced, the laws would make illegal public or private availability (except in libraries) of any materials deemed pornographic.

Such material could be the object of a lawsuit on several grounds. The ordinance would penalize four kinds of behavior associated with pornography: its production, sale, exhibition or distribution ("trafficking"); coercion into pornographic performance; forcing pornography on a person; and assault or physical attack due to pornography.

Under this law, a woman "acting as a woman against the subordination of women" could file a complaint; men could also file complaints if they could "prove injury in the same way that a woman is injured." The procedural steps in the two ordinances differ, but they generally allow the complainant either to file an administrative complaint with the city's equal opportunity commission (Minneapolis or Indianapolis), or to file a lawsuit directly in court (Minneapolis). If the local commission found the law had been violated, it would file a lawsuit. By either procedure, the court — not "women" — would have the final say on whether the materials fit the definition of pornography, and would have the authority to award monetary damages and issue an injunction (or court order) preventing further distribution of the material in question.

The Minneapolis ordinance defines pornography as "the sexually explicit subordination of women, graphically depicted, whether in pictures or words." To be actionable, materials would also have to fall within one of a number of categories: nine in the Minneapolis ordinance, six in the Indianapolis version. (See Appendix II for text of the original Minneapolis ordinance, from which the excerpts of the legislation quoted in this chapter are taken.)

Although proponents claim that the Minneapolis and Indianapolis ordinances represent a new way to regulate pornography, the strategy is still laden with our culture's old, repressive approach to sexuality. The implementation of such laws hinges on the definition of pornography as interpreted by the court. The definition provided in the Minneapolis legislation is vague, leaving critical phrases such as "the sexually explicit subordination of women," "postures of sexual submission" and "whores by nature" to the interpretation of the citizen who files a complaint and to the civil court judge who hears the case. The legislation does not prohibit just the images of gross sexual violence that most supporters claim to be its target, but instead drifts toward covering an increasingly wide range of sexually explicit material.

The most problematic feature of this approach, then, is a conceptual flaw embedded in the law itself. Supporters of this type of

legislation say that the target of their efforts is misogynist, sexually explicit and violent representation, whether in pictures or words. Indeed, the feminist antipornography movement is fueled by women's anger at the most repugnant examples of pornography. But a close examination of the wording of the model legislative text, and examples of purportedly actionable material offered by proponents of the legislation in court briefs suggest that the law is actually aimed at a range of material considerably broader than what proponents claim is their target. The discrepancies between the law's explicit and implicit aims have been almost invisible to us, because these distortions are very similar to distortions about sexuality in the culture as a whole. The legislation and supporting texts deserve close reading. Hidden beneath illogical transformations, nonsequiturs, and highly permeable definitions are familiar sexual scripts drawn from mainstream, sexist culture that potentially could have very negative consequences for women.

The Venn diagram illustrates the three areas targeted by the law, and represents a scheme that classifies words or images that have any of three characteristics: violence, sexual explicitness or sexism.

Clearly, a text or an image might have only one characteristic. Material can be violent but not sexually explicit or sexist: for example, a war movie in which both men and women suffer injury or death without regard to or because of their gender. Material can be sexist but not sexually explicit and violent. A vast number of materials from mainstream media — television, popular novels, magazines, newspapers — come to mind, all of which depict either distraught housewives or the "happy sexism" of the idealized family, with mom self-sacrificing, other-directed and content. Finally, material can be sexually explicit but not violent or sexist: for example, the freely chosen sexual behavior depicted in sex education films or women's own explicit writing about sexuality.

As the diagram illustrates, areas can also intersect, reflecting a range of combinations of the three characteristics. Images can be violent and sexually explicit without being sexist — for example, a narrative about a rape in a men's prison, or a documentary about the effect of a rape on a woman. The latter example illustrates the importance of context in evaluating whether material that is sexually explicit and violent is also sexist. The intent of the maker, the context of the film and the perception of the viewer together render a depiction of a rape sympathetic, harrowing, even educational, rather than sensational, victim-blaming and laudatory.

Another possible overlap is between material that is violent and sexist but not sexually explicit. Films or books that describe violence directed against women by men in a way that clearly shows gender antagonism and inequality, and sometimes strong sexual tension, but no sexual explicitness fall into this category — for example, the popular genre of slasher films in which women are stalked, terrified and killed by men, or accounts of mass murder of women, fueled by male rage. Finally, a third point of overlap arises when material is sexually explicit and sexist without being violent — that is, when sex is consensual but still reflects themes of male superiority and female abjectness. Some sex education materials could be included in this category, as well as a great deal of regular pornography.

The remaining domain, the inner core, is one in which the material is simultaneously violent, sexually explicit and sexist — for example, an image of a naked woman being slashed by a knife-wielding rapist. The Minneapolis law, however, does not by any means confine itself to this material.

To be actionable under the law as pornography, material must be judged by the courts to be "the sexually explicit subordination of women, graphically depicted whether in pictures or in words that also includes at least one or more" of nine criteria. Of these, only four involve the intersection of violence, sexual explicitness and sexism, and then only arguably (see Appendix II). Even in these cases, many questions remain about whether images with all three characteristics do in fact cause violence against women (see Appendix I). And the task of evaluating material that is ostensibly the target of these criteria becomes complicated — indeed, hopeless — because most of the clauses that contain these criteria mix actions or qualities of violence with those that are not particularly associated with violence.

The section that comes closest to the stated purpose of the legislation is clause (iii): "women are presented as sexual objects who experience sexual pleasure in being raped." This clause is intended to cover depictions of rape that are sexually explicit and sexist; the act of rape itself signifies the violence. But other clauses are not so clearcut, because the list of characteristics often mixes signs or byproducts of violence with phenomena that are unrelated or irrelevant to judging violence. We might be willing to agree that clause (ii) — "women are presented as sexual objects who enjoy pain" — signifies the conjunction of all three characteristics, with violence the presumed cause of pain, but the presence of the words "and humiliation" at the end of the clause is problematic. Humiliation may be offensive or disagreeable, but it does not necessarily imply violence.

A similar problem occurs with clause (iv): "women are presented as sexual objects tied up or cut up or mutilated or bruised or physically hurt." All these except the first, "tied up," generally occur as a result of violence. "Tied up," if part of consensual sex, is not violent and, for some practitioners, not particularly sexist. Women who are tied up may be participants in nonviolent sex play involving bondage, a theme in both heterosexual and lesbian pornography. (See, for example, *The Joy of Sex* and *Coming to Power*.) Clause (ix) contains another mixed list, in which "injury," "torture," "bleeding," "bruised" and "hurt" are combined with words such as "degradation" and "shown as filthy and inferior," neither of which is violent. Depending on the presentation, "filthy" and "inferior" may constitute sexually explicit sexism, although not violence. "Degradation" is a sufficiently inclusive term to cover most acts of which a viewer disapproves.

Several other clauses have little to do with violence at all; they refer to material that is sexually explicit and sexist, thus falling outside the triad of characteristics at which the legislation is supposedly aimed. For example, movies in which "women are presented as dehumanized sexual objects, things, or commodities" may be infuriating and offensive to feminists, but they are not violent.

Finally, some clauses describe material that is neither violent nor necessarily sexist. Clause (v), "women . . . in postures of sexual submission or sexual servility, including by inviting penetration," and clause (viii), "women . . . being penetrated by objects or animals," are sexually explicit, but not violent and not obviously sexist unless one believes that penetration — whether heterosexual, lesbian, or autoerotic masturbation — is indicative of gender inequality and female oppression. Similarly problematic are clauses that invoke representations of "women . . . as whores by nature" and "women's body parts . . . such that women are reduced to those parts."

Texts filed in support of the Indianapolis law show how broadly it could be applied. In the amicus brief filed on behalf of Linda Marchiano ("Linda Lovelace," the female lead in *Deep Throat*) in Indianapolis, Catharine MacKinnon offered *Deep Throat* as an example of the kind of pornography covered by the law. *Deep Throat* served a complicated function in this brief, because the movie, supporters of the ordinance argue, would be actionable on two counts: coercion into pornographic performance, because Marchiano alleges that she was coerced into making the movie; and trafficking in pornography, because the content of the film falls within one of the categories in the Indianapolis ordinance's definition — that which prohibits presenting women as sexual objects "through postures or positions of servility or submission or display." Proponents of the law have counted on women's repugnance at allegations of coerced sexual acts to spill over and discredit the sexual acts themselves in this movie.

The aspects of *Deep Throat* that MacKinnon considered to be indicative of "sexual subordination" are of particular interest, since any movie that depicted similar acts could be banned under the law. MacKinnon explained in her brief that the film "subordinates women by using women . . . sexually, specifically as eager servicing receptacles for male genitalia and ejaculate. The majority of the film represents 'Linda Lovelace' in, minimally, postures of sexual submission and/or servility." In its brief, the City of Indianapolis concurred: "In the film *Deep Throat* a woman is being shown as being ever eager for oral penetration by a series of men's penises, often on her hands and knees. There are repeated scenes in which her genitalia are graphically displayed and she is shown as enjoying men ejaculating on her face."

These descriptions are very revealing, since they suggest that multiple partners, group sex and oral sex subordinate women and hence are sexist. The notion that the female character is "used" by men suggests that it is improbable that a woman would engage in fellatio of her own accord. *Deep Throat* does draw on several sexist conventions common in advertising and the entire visual culture —

the woman as object of the male gaze, and the assumption of heterosexuality, for example. But it is hardly an unending paean to male dominance, since the movie contains many contrary themes. In it, the main female character is shown as both actively seeking her own pleasure and as trying to please men; a secondary female character is shown as actually directing encounters with multiple male partners. Both briefs described a movie quite different from the one viewers see.

At its heart, this analysis implies that heterosexual sex itself is sexist; that women do not engage in it of their own volition; and that behavior pleasurable to men is repugnant to women. In some contexts, for example, the representation of fellatio and multiple partners can be sexist, but are we willing to concede that they always are? If not, then what is proposed as actionable under the Indianapolis law includes merely sexually explicit representation (the traditional target of obscenity laws), which proponents of the legislation vociferously insist they are not interested in attacking.

Some other examples offered through exhibits submitted with the City of Indianapolis brief and also introduced in the public hearing further illustrate this point. Many of the exhibits are depictions of sadomasochism. The court briefs treat SM material as depicting violence and aggression, not consensual sex, in spite of avowals to the contrary by many SM practitioners. With this legislation, then, a major question for feminists that has only begun to develop would be closed for discussion. Instead, a simplistic reduction has been advanced as the definitive feminist position. The description of the material in the briefs focused on submissive women and implied male domination, highlighting the similarity proponents would like to find between all SM narratives and male/female inequality. The actual exhibits, however, illustrated plots and power relations far more diverse than the descriptions provided by MacKinnon and the City of Indianapolis would suggest, including SM between women and female dominant/male submissive SM. For example, the Indianapolis brief stated that in the magazine *The Bitch Goddesses*, "women are shown in torture chambers with their nude body parts being tortured by their 'master' for 'even the slightest offense'. . . . The magazine shows a woman in a scenario of torture." But the brief failed to mention that the dominants in this magazine are all female, with one exception. This kind of discrepancy characterized many examples offered in the briefs.

This is not to say that such representations do not raise questions for feminists. The current lively discussion about lesbian SM clearly demonstrates that this issue is still unresolved. But in the Indianapolis briefs all SM material was assumed to be male dominant/female submissive, thereby squeezing a nonconforming reality into prepackaged, inadequate — and therefore dangerous — categories. This legislation would virtually eliminate all SM pornography by recasting it as violent, thereby attacking a sexual minority while masquerading as an attempt to end violence against women.

Analysis of clauses in the Minneapolis ordinance and several examples offered in court briefs filed in connection with the Indianapolis ordinance show that the law targets material that is sexually explicit and sexist, but ignores material that is violent and sexist, violent and sexually explicit, only violent or only sexist.

Certain troubling questions arise here, for if one claims, as some antipornography activists do, that there is a direct relationship between images and behavior, why should images of violence against women or scenarios of sexism in general not be similarly proscribed? Why is sexual explicitness singled out as the cause of women's oppression? For proponents to exempt violent and sexist images, or even sexist images, from regulation is inconsistent, especially since they are so pervasive.

Even more difficulties arise from the vagueness of certain terms crucial in interpreting the ordinances. The term "subordination" is especially important, since pornography is defined as the "sexually explicit subordination of women." The authors of this legislation intend it to modify each of the clauses, and they appear to believe that it provides a definition of sexism that each example must meet. The term is never defined in the legislation, yet the Indianapolis brief, for example, suggests that the average viewer, on the basis of "his or her common understanding of what it means for one person to subordinate another" should be able to decide what is pornographic. But what kind of sexually explicit acts place a woman in an inferior status? To some, *any* graphic sexual act violates women's dignity and therefore subordinates them. To others, consensual heterosexual lovemaking within the boundaries of procreation and marriage is acceptable, but heterosexual acts that do not have reproduction as their aim lower women's status and hence subordinate them. Still others accept a wide range of nonprocreative, perhaps even nonmarital, heterosexuality but draw the line at lesbian sex, which they view as degrading.

The term "sex object" is also problematic. The City of Indianapolis's brief maintains that "the term sexual object, often shortened to sex object, has enjoyed a wide popularity in mainstream American culture in the past fifteen years, and is used to denote the objectification of a person on the basis of their sex or sex appeal. . . . People know what it means to disregard all aspects of personhood but sex, to reduce a person to a thing used for sex." But, indeed, people do not agree on this point. The definition of "sex object" is far from clear or uniform. For example, some feminist and liberal cultural critics have used the term to mean sex that occurs without strong emotional ties and experience. More conservative critics maintain that any detachment of women's sexuality from procreation, marriage and family objectifies it, removing it from its "natural" web of associations and context. Unredeemed and unprotected by domesticity and family, women — and their sexuality — become things used by men. In both these views, women are never sexually autonomous agents who direct and enjoy their sexuality for their own purposes, but rather are victims. In the same vein, other problematic terms include "inviting penetration," "whores by nature" and "positions of display."

Through close analysis of the proposed legislation one sees how vague the boundaries of the definitions that contain the inner core of the Venn diagram really are. Their dissolution does not happen equally at all points, but only at some: the inner core begins to include sexually explicit and sexist material, and finally expands to include purely sexually explicit material. Thus "sexually explicit" becomes identified and equated with "violent" with no further definition or explanation.

It is also striking that so many feminists have failed to notice that the laws (as well as examples of actionable material) cover so much diverse work, not just that small and symbolic epicentre where many forms of opposition to women converge. It suggests that for us, as well as for others, sexuality remains a difficult area. We have no clearly developed framework in which to think about sex equivalent to the frameworks that are available for thinking about race, gender and class issues. Consequently, in sex, as in few other areas of human behavior, unexamined and unjustifiable prejudice passes itself off as considered opinion about what is desirable and normal. And finally, sex arouses considerable anxiety, stemming from both the meeting with individual difference and from the prospect — suggested by feminists themselves — that sexual behavior is constructed socially and is not simply natural.

The law takes advantage of everyone's relative ignorance and anxious ambivalence about sex, distorting and oversimplifying what confronts us in building a sexual politic. For example, antipornography feminists draw on several feminist theories about the role of violent, aggressive or sexist representations. The first is relatively straightforward: that these images trigger men into action. The second suggests that violent images act more subtly, to socialize men to act in sexist or violent ways by making this behavior seem commonplace and more acceptable, if not expected. The third assumption is that violent, sexually explicit or even sexist images are offensive to women, assaulting their sensibilities and sense of self. Although we have all used metaphor to exhort women to action or illustrate a point, antipornography proponents have frequently used these conventions of speech as if they were literal statements of fact. But these metaphors have gotten out of hand, as Julie Abraham has noted, for they fail to recognize that the assault committed by a wife beater is quite different from the visual "assault" of a sexist ad on TV. The nature of that difference is still being clarified in a complex debate within feminism that must continue; this law cuts off speculation, settling on a causal relationship between image and action that is starkly simple, if unpersuasive.

This metaphor also paves the way for reclassifying images that are merely sexist as also violent and aggressive. Thus, it is no accident that the briefs supporting the legislation first invoke violent images and rapidly move to include sexist and sexually explicit images without noting that they are different. The equation is made more easy by the constant shifts back to examples of depictions of real violence, almost to draw attention away from the sexually explicit or sexist material that in fact would be affected by the laws.

Most important, what underlies this legislation and the success of its analysis in blurring and exceeding boundaries is an appeal to a very traditional view of sex: sex is degrading to women. By this logic, any illustrations or descriptions of explicit sexual acts that involve women are in themselves affronts to women's dignity. In its brief, the City of Indianapolis was quite specific about this point: "The harms caused by pornography are by no means limited to acts of physical aggression. The mere existence of pornography in society degrades and demeans all women." Embedded in this view are several other familiar themes: that sex is degrading to women, but not to men; that men are raving beasts; that sex is dangerous for women; that sexuality is male, not female; that women are victims, not sexual actors; that men inflict "it" on women; that penetration is submission; that heterosexual sexuality, rather than the institution of heterosexuality, is sexist.

These assumptions, in part intended, in part unintended, lead us back to the traditional target of obscenity law: sexually explicit material. What initially appeared novel, then, is really the reappearance of a traditional theme. It's ironic that a feminist position on pornography incorporates most of the myths about sexuality that feminism has struggled to displace.

The Dangers of Application

The Minneapolis and Indianapolis ordinances embody a political view that holds pornography to be a central force in "creating and maintaining" the oppression of women. This view appears in summary form in the legislative findings section at the beginning of the Minneapolis bill, which describes a chain reaction of misogynistic acts generated by pornography. The legislation is based on the interweaving of several themes: that pornography constructs the meaning of sexuality for women and, as well, leads to discrete acts of violence against women; that sexuality is the primary cause of women's oppression; that explicitly sexual images, even if not violent or coerced, have the power to subordinate women; and that women's own accounts of force have been silenced because, as a universal and timeless rule, society credits pornographic constructions rather than women's experiences. Taking the silencing contention a step further, advocates of the ordinance effectively assume that women have been so conditioned by the pornographic world view that if their own experiences of the sexual acts identified in the definition are not subordinating, then they must simply be victims of false consciousness.

The heart of the ordinance is the "trafficking" section, which would allow almost anyone to seek the removal of any materials falling within the law's definition of pornography. Ordinance defenders strenuously protest that the issue is not censorship because the state, as such, is not authorized to initiate criminal prosecutions. But the prospect of having to defend a potentially infinite number of privately filed complaints creates at least as much of a chilling effect against pornographic or sexual speech as does a criminal law. And as long as representatives of the state — in this case, judges — have ultimate say over the interpretation, the distinction between this ordinance and "real" censorship will not hold.

In addition, three major problems should dissuade feminists from supporting this kind of law: first, the sexual images in question do not cause more harm than other aspects of misogynist culture; second, sexually explicit speech, even in male-dominated society, serves positive social functions for women; and third, the passage and enforcement of antipornography laws such as those supported in Minneapolis and Indianapolis are more likely to impede, rather than advance, feminist goals.

Ordinance proponents contend that pornography does cause violence because it conditions male sexual response to images of violence and thus provokes violence against women. The strongest research they offer is based on psychology experiments that employ films depicting a rape scene, toward the end of which the woman is shown to be enjoying the attack. The ordinances, by contrast, cover a much broader range of materials than this one specific heterosexual rape scenario. Further, the studies ordinance supporters cite do not support the theory that pornography causes violence against women (see Appendix I).

In addition, the argument that pornography itself plays a major role in the general oppression of women contradicts the evidence of history. It need hardly be said that pornography did not lead to the burning of witches or the English common law treatment of women as chattel property. If anything functioned then as the prime communication medium for woman-hating, it was probably religion. Nor can pornography be blamed for the enactment of laws from at least the eighteenth century that allowed a husband to rape or beat his wife with impunity. In any period, the causes of women's oppression have been many and complex, drawing on the fundamental social and economic structures of society. Ordinance proponents offer little evidence to explain how the mass production of pornography — a relatively recent phenomenon — could have become so potent a causative agent so quickly.

The silencing of women is another example of the harm attributed to pornography. Yet if this argument were correct, one would expect that as the social visibility of pornography has increased, the tendency to credit women's accounts of rape would have decreased. In fact, although the treatment of women complainants in rape cases is far from perfect, the last 15 years of work by the women's movement has resulted in marked improvements. In many places, the corroboration requirement has now been abolished; cross-examination of victims as to past sexual experiences has been prohibited;

and a number of police forces have developed specially trained units and procedures to improve the handling of sexual assault cases. The presence of rape fantasies in pornography may in part reflect a backlash against these women's movement advances, but to argue that most people routinely disbelieve women who file charges of rape belittles the real improvements made in social consciousness and law.

The third type of harm suggested by the ordinance backers is a kind of libel: the maliciously false characterization of women as a group of sexual masochists. Like libel, the City of Indianapolis brief argues pornography is "a lie [which] once loosed" cannot be effectively rebutted by debate and further speech.

To claim that all pornography as defined by the ordinance is a lie is a false analogy. If truth is a defence to charges of libel, then surely depictions of consensual sex cannot be thought of as equivalent to a falsehood. For example, some women (and men) do enjoy being tied up or displaying themselves. The declaration by fiat that even sadomasochism is a "lie" about sexuality reflects an arrogance and moralism that feminists should combat, not engage in. When mutually desired sexual experiences are depicted, pornography is not "libelous."

Not only does pornography not cause the kind and degree of harm that can justify the restraint of speech, but its existence serves some social functions, which benefit women. Pornographic speech has many, often anomalous, characteristics. One is certainly that it magnifies the misogyny present in the culture and exaggerates the fantasy of male power. Another, however, is that the existence of pornography has served to flout conventional sexual mores, to ridicule sexual hypocrisy and to underscore the importance of sexual needs. Pornography carries many messages other than woman-hating: it advocates sexual adventure, sex outside of marriage, sex for no reason other than pleasure, casual sex, anonymous sex, group sex, voyeuristic sex, illegal sex, public sex. Some of these ideas appeal to women reading or seeing pornography, who may interpret some images as legitimating their own sense of sexual urgency or desire to be sexually aggressive. Women's experience of pornography is not as universally victimizing as the ordinance would have it.

The new antipornography laws, as restrictions on sexual speech, in many ways echo and expand upon the traditional legal analysis of sexually explicit speech under the rubric of obscenity. The U.S. Supreme Court has consistently ruled that sexual speech defined as "obscenity" does not belong in the system of public discourse, and is therefore an exception to the First Amendment and hence not entitled to protection under the free speech guarantee. (The definition of obscenity has shifted over the years and remains imprecise.) In 1957 the Supreme Court ruled that obscenity could be suppressed regardless of whether it presented an imminent threat of illegal activity. In the opinion of the Supreme Court, graphic sexual images do not communicate "real" ideas. These, it would seem, are only found in the traditionally defined public arena. Sexual themes can qualify as ideas if they use sexuality for argument's sake, but not if they speak in the words and images of "private" life — that is, if they graphically depict sex itself. At least theoretically, and insofar as the law functions as a pronouncement of moral judgment, sex is consigned to remain unexpressed and in the private realm.

The fallacies in this distinction are obvious. Under the U.S. Constitution, for example, it is acceptable to write "I am a sadomasochist" or even "Everyone should experiment with sadomasochism in order to increase sexual pleasure." But to write a graphic fantasy about sadomasochism that arouses and excites readers is not protected unless a court finds it to have serious literary, artistic or political value, despite the expressive nature of the content. Indeed, the fantasy depiction may communicate identity in a more compelling way that the "I am" statement. For sexual minorities, sexual acts can be self-identifying and affirming statements in a hostile world. Images of those acts should be protected for that reason, for they do have political content. Just as the personal can be political, so can the specifically and graphically sexual.

Supporters of the antipornography ordinances both endorse the concept that pornographic speech contains no ideas or expressive interest, and at the same time attribute to pornography the capacity to trigger violent acts by the power of its misogyny. The city's brief in defence of the Indianapolis ordinance expanded this point by arguing that all sexually explicit speech is entitled to less constitutional protection than other speech. The antipornography groups have cleverly capitalized on this approach — a product of a totally nonfeminist legal system — and are now attempting, through the mechanism of the ordinances, to legitimate a new crusade for protectionism and sexual conservatism.

The consequences of enforcing such a law, however, are much more likely to obstruct than advance feminist political goals. On the level of ideas, further narrowing of the public realm of sexual speech coincides all too well with the privatization of sexual, reproductive and family issues sought by the far right — an agenda described very well, for example, by Rosalind Petchesky in "The Rise of the New Right," in *Abortion and Woman's Choice*. Practically speaking, the ordinances could result in attempts to eliminate the images associated with homosexuality. Doubtless there are heterosexual women who believe that lesbianism is a "degrading" form of "subordination." Since the ordinances allow for suits against materials in which men appear "in place of women," far-right anti-pornography crusaders could use these laws to suppress gay male pornography. Imagine a Jerry Falwell-style conservative filing a complaint against a gay bookstore for selling sexually explicit materials showing men with other men in "degrading" or "submissive" or "objectified" postures — all in the name of protecting women.

And most ironically, while the ordinances would do nothing to improve the material conditions of most women's lives, their high visibility might well divert energy from the drive to enact other, less popular laws that would genuinely empower women — comparable worth legislation, for example, or affirmative action requirements or fairer property and support principles in divorce laws.

Other provisions of the ordinances concern coercive behavior: phsical assault which is imitative of pornographic images, coercion into pornographic performance and forcing pornography on others. On close examination, however, even most of these provisions are problematic.

Existing law already penalizes physical assault, including when it is associated with pornography. Defenders of the laws often cite the example of models who have been raped or otherwise harmed while in the process of making pornographic images. But victims of this type of attack can already sue or prosecute those responsible. (Linda Marchiano, the actress who appeared in the film *Deep Throat*, has not recovered damages for the physical assaults she describes in her book *Ordeal* because the events happened several years before she decided to try to file a suit. A lawsuit was thus precluded by the statute of limitations.) Indeed, the ordinances do not cover assault or other harm incurred while producing pornography, presumably because other laws already achieve that end.

The ordinances do penalize coercing, intimidating or fraudulently inducing anyone into performing for pornography. Although existing U.S. law already provides remedies for fraud or contracts of duress, this section of the ordinance seeks to facilitate recovery of damages by, for example, pornography models who might otherwise encounter substantial prejudice against their claims. Supporters of this section have suggested that it is comparable to the Supreme Court's ban on child pornography. The analogy has been stretched to the point where the City of Indianapolis brief argued that women, like children, need "special protection." "Children are incapable of consenting to engage in pornographic conduct, even absent physical coercion and therefore require special protection," the brief stated. "By the same token, the physical and psychological well-being of women ought to be afforded comparable protection, for the coercive environment in which most pornographic models work vitiates any notion that they consent or 'choose' to perform in pornography."

The reality of women's lives is far more complicated. Women do not become pornography models because society is egalitarian and they exercise a "free choice," but nor do they "choose" this work because they have lost all power for deliberate, volitional behavior. Modeling or acting for pornography, like prostitution, can be a means of survival for those with limited options. For some women, at some points in their lives, it is a rational economic decision. Not every woman regrets having made it, although no woman should have to settle for it. The fight should be to expand the options and to insure job safety for women who do become porn models. By contrast, the impact of the ordinance as a whole would be either to eliminate jobs or drive the pornography industry further underground.

One of the vaguest provisions in the ordinance prohibits "forcing" pornography on a person. "Forcing" is not defined in the law, and one is left to speculate whether it means forced to respond to pornography, forced to read it or forced to glance at it before turning away. Also unclear is whether the perpetrator must in fact have some superior power over the person being forced — that is, is there a meaningful threat that makes the concept of force real.

Again, widely varying situations are muddled and a consideration of context is absent. "Forcing" pornography on a person "in any public space" is treated identically to using it as a method of sexual harassment in the workplace. The scope of "forcing" could include walking past a newsstand or browsing in a bookstore that had pornography on display. The force involved in such a situation seems mild when compared, for example, to the incessant sexist advertising on television.

The concept behind the "forcing" provision is appropriate, however, in the case of workplace harassment. A worker should not have to endure, especially on pain of losing her job, harassment based on sex, race, religion, nationality or any other factor. But this general policy was established by the U.S. courts as part of the guarantees of Title VII of the 1964 Civil Rights Act. Pornography used as a means of harassing women workers is already legally actionable, just as harassment by racial slurs is actionable. Any literature endorsing the oppression of women — whether pornography or the Bible — could be employed as an harassment device to impede a woman's access to a job, or to education, public accommodations or other social benefits. It is the usage of pornography in this situation, not the image itself, that is discriminatory. Appropriately, this section of the ordinances provides that only perpetrators of the forcing, not makers and distributors of the images, could be held liable.

Forcing of pornography on a person is also specifically forbidden "in the home." In her testimony before the Indianapolis City Council, Catharine MacKinnon referred to the problem of pornography being "forced on wives in preparation for later sexual scenes." Since only the person who forces the pornography on another can be sued, this provision becomes a kind of protection against domestic harassment. It would allow wives to sue husbands for court orders or damages for some usages of pornography. Although a fascinating attempt to subvert male power in the domestic realm, it nonetheless has problems. "Forcing" is not an easy concept to define in this context. It is hard to know what degree of intrusion would amount to forcing images onto a person who shares the same private space.

More important, the focus on pornography seems a displacement of the more fundamental issues involved in the conflicts that occur between husbands and wives or lovers over sex. Some men may invoke images that reflect their greater power to pressure women into performing the supposedly traditional role of acceding to male desires. Pornography may facilitate or enhance this dynamic of male dominance, but it is hardly the causative agent. Nor would removing the pornography do much to solve the problem. If the man invokes instead his friends' stories about sexual encounters or his experiences with other women, is the resulting interaction with his wife substantially different? Focusing on the pornography rather than on the relationship and its social context may serve only to channel heterosexual women's recognition of their own intimate oppression toward a movement hailed by the far right as being antiperversion rather than toward a feminist analysis of sexual politics.

The last of the sections that deals with actual coercive conduct is one that attempts to deal with the assault, physical injury or attack of any person in a way that is directly caused by specific pornography. The ordinances would allow a lawsuit against the makers and distributors of pornographic materials that were imitated by an attacker — the only provision of the ordinance that requires proof of causation. Presenting such proof would be extremely difficult. If the viewer's wilful decision to imitate the image were found to be an intervening, superceding cause of the harm, the plaintiff would not win.

The policy issues here are no different from those concerning violent media images that are nonsexual: Is showing an image sufficient to cause an act of violence? Even if an image could be found to cause a viewer's behavior, was that behavior reasonably foreseeable? So far, those who have produced violent films have not been found blameworthy when third persons acted out the violence depicted. If this were to change, it would mean, for example, that the producer of the TV movie *The Burning Bed*, which told the true story of a battered wife who set fire to her sleeping husband, could be sued if a woman who saw the film killed her husband in a similar way. The result, of course, would be the end of films depicting real violence in the lives of women.

The ordinances' supporters offer no justification for singling out sexual assault from other kinds of violence. Certainly the experience of sexual assault is not always worse than that of being shot or stabbed or suffering other kinds of nonsexual assault. Nor is sexual assault the only form of violence that is fueled by sexism. If there were evidence that sexual images are more likely to be imitated, there might be some justification for treating them differently. But there is no support for this contention.

These laws, which would increase the state's regulation of sexual images, present many dangers for women. Although the ordinances draw much of their feminist support from women's anger at the market for images of sexual violence, they are aimed not at violence, but at sexual explicitness. Far-right elements recognize the possibility of using the full potential of the ordinances to enforce their sexually conservative world view, and have supported them for that reason. Feminists should therefore look carefully at the text of these "model" laws in order to understand why many believe them to be a useful tool in *anti*feminist moral crusades.

The proposed ordinances are also dangerous because they seek to embody in law an analysis of the role of sexuality and sexual images in the oppression of women with which even all feminists do not agree. Underlying virtually every section of the proposed laws there is an assumption that sexuality is a realm of unremitting, unequaled victimization for women. Pornography appears as the monster that made this so. The ordinances' authors seek to impose their analysis by putting state power behind it. But this analysis is not the only feminist perspective on sexuality. Feminist theorists have also argued that the sexual terrain, however power-laden, is actively contested. Women are agents, and not merely victims, who make decisions and act on them, and who desire, seek out and enjoy sexuality.

Acknowledgements

For stimulating discussion and political comradeship, thanks to FACT (Feminist Anti-Censorship Task Force), New York, and to members of the Scholar and the Feminist IX study group (Julie Abraham, Hannah Alderfer, Meryl Altman, Jan Boney, Frances Doughty, Kate Ellis, Faye Ginsburg, Diane Harriford, Beth Jaker, Barbara Kerr, Mary Clare Lennon, Marybeth Nelson, Ann Snitow, Paula Webster and Ellen Willis). Special thanks to Rayna Rapp and Janice Irvine for comments and criticisms, to Lawrence Krasnoff for graphics and to Ann Snitow for aid above and beyond the call of duty. We are grateful to Varda Burstyn for her helpful suggestions and patience. We remain responsible for the opinions expressed here.

Beyond Despair: Positive Strategies
Varda Burstyn

For large numbers of North Americans today, life verges on the schizoid. Abundance coexists with deep poverty. Millions of people are active in a vast, grassroots peace movement while literally trillions of dollars are spent on conventional and nuclear weapons. Technology is touted as a means of freeing workers from drudgery but brings instead downgraded jobs, unemployment and more alienation. Ideas about women's liberation and sexual equality struggle for — and within — our hearts and minds, battling notions about sexuality, reproduction and sex roles that date from Victorian times. These social splits haunt us: We live with polarization in society, and confusion, uncertainty and fear uneasily coexist with our pleasures, hopes and satisfactions.

Most disturbing is the way violence seems to permeate our culture. If we are women, however, there is an extra measure of fear, even of panic. For interwoven into women's experience of social violence is a fear unique to women: that generic form of terror, "violence against women." Because aggression against women often takes a sexual form, and because of the stigma attached to women whose sexuality is expressed outside the conventions of marriage, deep anxiety about danger colors all women's hopes for sexual pleasure.

This kind of violence is rooted in the virgin/whore, good woman/bad woman dichotomy of patriarchal cultures, where control of women's sexuality is a core mechanism in their overall subordination. It is not new nor peculiar to our times. Still, antipornography feminists claim that we are seeing a qualitative escalation, virtually an epidemic, of violence and sexual hatred. We simply do not have statistics to allow us to compare what is taking place today with what existed 15, let alone 30 or 60 years ago. When we survey the social landscape, we must be sure to register the fundamental gains women have made. But though we cannot be sure of the rates of violence against women, it is possible that some types are increasing.

First, there is a general escalation in social violence as the current economic recession continues to create anger and despair — a spiral that in turn results in increasing violence on the part of police. If young people seem surly, cynical or sinister, they are telling us they feel brutalized by a society that has no jobs and no place for them. The effects of adult unemployment put all family members under often unbearable strain, isolating parents from community and friends and depriving men and women of dignity and hope for their children — two qualities that are preconditions for an optimistic outlook on the future. While those with jobs do not suffer the same kind of devastation as the unemployed, they are subject to pressures to perform, to compete, to stay ahead of the other guy, to remain silent about injustice, to put up with awful working conditions, to put down fellow workers — these, too, lead to the weakest family members — women and children — becoming scapegoats for tension, anger and despair.

The crisis in gender relations through which we are living also colors the way people experience the strains and tensions of recessionary times. We have been experiencing an especially intense period of change during the last 15 years, change that has found its way into most households through negotiations between men and women about work and leisure, money and power, social and domestic work, warmth and sexual intimacy. These involve personal change, and because we absorb ideas about gender along with our basic sense of identity, the process has been difficult and often frightening.

Traditionally, patriarchal ideas of identity for men have revolved around notions of being the provider on the one hand and being served by women — for whom they are supposed to provide — on the other. But that identity has been falling apart, with nothing solid yet ready to replace it. As social historian Barbara Ehrenreich has noted, since the '50s there has been a general tendency among men to move away from a lifetime commitment to one woman and her children. In addition, as the real value of the average wage has dropped and today's economic pressures intensify, men simply cannot provide in the ways they were raised to believe they should.

Women are even more beleaguered. Generally poorer than men and basically responsible for children, they are no longer able to count on men's continuous financial support, and whether paired or single, must do double duty at home and on the job. Understandably many are angry and unwilling to serve men in traditional ways. They, too, suffer pain, disorientation and loneliness; they, too, feel a crisis of identity. To say that "masculinity" and "femininity" are in a state of flux does not describe a process of polite discussion and accommodation, but one of real upheaval, accompanied by a lot of pain for everyone and, for a significant minority, real violence as well.

However — and here I think we must all pause for the mental equivalent of a deep breath — the pain and fear I have described, troubling and real though they may be, are just *one part* of the picture. It is also true that the last 20 years have molded a large number of men who are supportive of feminism, both individually and institutionally, because of their love for women and because of a sense of their own enlightened self-interest. Young women today have role models and ideas about life opportunities that simply did not exist two decades ago, and this profoundly changes possibilities for men as well. The principle of equal pay is slowly being established in law, if not yet in practice. We are taking action on matters we did not even have words for a decade ago: sexual harassment, sexual preference. Society is beginning to come to accept homosexuality as a positive choice. Women have much greater access to contraception, and slowly — and always with setbacks — we are making progress toward reproductive rights. A whole body of scholarship and literature now exists on women's sexuality, making it possible for more and more women to understand their potential. The very fact that we can now speak of the issues of abortion and contraception, lesbianism and erotic pleasure (though we may only really address them adequately outside the mass media) is a major triumph for women, and thus for society as a whole. For all the pain and trouble of the intervening years, what feminist who lived through the '50s would want now to return to them?

We have precariously but tenaciously established women's studies programs in high schools, community colleges and universities and we are slowly tackling the great socialization machines: the text-books and curricula in the school system. Even unemployment for men has had, in some families, positive effects in this generation: some men at least have come to know and care for their children, to understand the kind of work women do at home, to support women more as women have traditionally supported them. And though we are confronted with violence, women as a group have begun to reclaim the strength and vitality of our bodies, through fitness and self-defence, as part of reclaiming and establishing our individual and social strength. As Ann Snitow has argued in this volume, we are in a qualitatively better position than women who have mobilized before.

It is a matter of grave concern, however, that these positive, sometimes almost miraculous, achievements get the shortest pos-sible shrift in our mass media. Why are we constantly bombarded with images of violence against women and between men? Why are all the changes that we record with such a sense of gratitude and accomplishment — men cooking, taking care of children, nurturing us as well as receiving our sustenance — trivialized and undermined by commercials for breakfast cereal, disposable diapers and frozen food? Why is our reclaimed strength negated by the sexual objec-tification inherent in TV "exercise" programs and *Cosmo* fitness spreads? Why do we never see our struggles on television — no picket lines, no women's group meetings, no community, school and church activities? The news lingers over and glorifies accidents, rapes, murders and the mayhem of war — rarely looking behind the carnage to the social, economic and human factors behind them, never discussing systematic discrimination. The mass commercial media remain bastions of exploitative sexism; we have not succeeded in reforming them. And they do us damage by editing out of the transcript of reality all the aspects of our lives that make us feel there is hope and a real possibility for ongoing change.

As women struggle to maintain a sense of continuity, worth and security amidst violence and media messages of violence, we find ourselves almost overwhelmed by the fear that we could be the next victims of the rapist-killer in the night, the brutal, jealous batterer at home. When I feel that kind of panic I want to bar my door, shut myself in, never go out on the streets. I also want to lock up everyone and everything that contributes to that violence — ban the images, imprison the perpetrators and throw away the key. I want never to trust a man and, simultaneously, to never live without one, never to have the beast in my house — and never to be without the safety of his presence. I want to stop challenging sexist rules for fear of the vicious retaliation. Susan Cole has a powerful metaphor for these feelings: she likens women's condition to that of an imprisoned population, their labor grossly exploited, liable to violence and rape at any time.

But while this metaphor is motivated by a feminist desire to describe and change sexism, it has a similar effect to that of existing media images: By showing us only the *worst* part of the picture, it anchors our response to social and sexual problems in our fear, frustration and rage. Fear, however, is paralyzing and isolating. It makes difficult problems seem overwhelming. Acting out of frustration can backfire too, if we reach for the quick solution and short-circuit important social processes. Rage, legitimate and necessary as an elementary response of rejection, is dangerous when it comes to social policy. It creates a demand for revenge and punishment and gets in the way of the kind of person-to-person, group-to-group confrontation and negotiation that alone can bring about real social healing — the precondition of real change.

But if we are to construct loving, responsible relations between people of all ages and sexes, we must ground our legal and social actions in the best of what people are living today, not the worst. For though the sexual morality of the previous period is breaking down, along with the patriarchal family, and though there are casualties from this disintegration, it is also true that seeds of a new, responsible, life-positive morality are growing, and it is these we must nurture and cultivate. The sexism inherent in so much pornography requires not the repressive response of censorship. Rather, we must make our own explorations of sexuality known throughout society. The exploitive values so obvious in pornography should not be obscured by censorship, but *challenged* by noncommercial, pluralistic and life-affirming work that reflects the variety of sexual lifeways that exist in our society, and that will, given half a chance, create new kinds of family-friendship groups.

Resolving the issues of sexuality is absolutely crucial to the continued existence and the extension of the gains we have begun to make. Feminists are correct when they insist that sexuality is central in gender politics. But a censorious focus on pornography does not adequately address sexuality. This is why this volume, though entitled *Women Against Censorship*, argues that in addition to rejecting censorship as such, we must also avoid strategies that emphasize legal reform and social control, for these give the state instead of communities of people the power to determine what can be expressed. It puts primary emphasis on the legal system and the punitive, criminal arms of the system at that, and little or no emphasis on changing the real conditions of women's and men's lives. It encourages, even if inadvertently, top-down models of state intervention into sexual life instead of fostering the more creative, organic changes that are slowly emerging — changes based on a commitment to gender equality and freedom of sexual orientation.

The final portion of this chapter is dedicated to constructive alternatives to both censorship and pornography, to giving concrete content to a strategy based in responsible pluralism in sexual life. This approach recognizes the variety of sexual arrangements that now exist in our urban, multicultural society and seeks to use this pluralism as a way of teaching mutual respect, emotional and procreative responsibility, and solidarity between the sexes in place of bitter antagonism.

Our approach has to reflect the morality we want to build, which we struggle for in our daily lives and we try to convey to our children, because it embodies our vision of the future. In order to make that future real, we need strategies that will get at all the *causes* of violence and of sexism, strategies that bring about structural and institutional change, that improve the lot of the majority of men in this society as well as that of the majority of women, that validate the notion of public sexual expression as an important part of our reshaping of gender and sexual relations in the direction of equality and freedom. The initial insights of the feminist critique of pornography were important. They contributed to our understanding of masculinist institutions by showing how sexist values were being reinforced even under the supposedly liberating guise of the "sexual revolution." But the censorship/social control strategy that has come out of the antipornography movement is now diverting the attention of feminism and society away from structural and institutional change.

The following proposals for positive action are predicated on the need to change social and institutional reality, including the pornography industry and sexist mass media. A number of these are critical short-term measures to deal with pornography, sexist media and violence against women; others represent more general, long-term goals. But pornography is both a product and an expression of many social conditions and contemporary institutions. There can be no improvement in pictures of sex if the realities of sex do not change for the better.

1. The Legal Front

All prior censorship of all media must be stopped. No exceptions to this fundamental democratic right can be tolerated, for if we censor the voices of our opponents and enemies, they will surely find ways to censor us.

All sections dealing with "obscenity" in the Criminal Code should be dropped; no sections substituting legislation on "pornography" should be added. To be judged, all sexual material must be interpreted; all interpretation is subjective; all interpretation must pass through a judicial system geared to the stabilization of the social order — currently organized along lines of economic hierarchy and masculine power and privilege.

All powers at present conferred upon customs and postal officials to decide what may or may not enter the country should be rescinded.

All laws that enshrine a double standard that treats homosexual material or practice as more harmful than heterosexual material or practice must be removed from the books.

Human rights legislation should not be used to prosecute sexual material. No matter how offensive and grotesque some material is, the problem is not the sex per se, but the violence and hatred depicted in it. In Canada, both human rights legislation and provisions in the Criminal Code prohibit inciting harm on the basis of race and religion. Each province has a human rights body, and infractions of human rights legislation can be redressed through the mediation of such groups and/or through the judgment of human rights tribunals.

A number of groups have proposed that hate literature laws, currently included in the Criminal Code, be placed under human rights legislation, which now covers sexual harassment. They have suggested that this legislation then be expanded to include incitement of hatred and violence against women, lesbians and gays. Some provinces (Manitoba and Saskatchewan at the time of writing) have already included "sex" in their human rights code in sections prohibiting all material "discriminating" and "exposing or tending to expose a person to hatred" (in the Manitoba code, additional categories are "race, nationality, religion, colour, marital status, physical or mental handicap, age, source of income, family status, ethnic or national origin." Conspicuous by its absence is "sexual orientation"). Of all the approaches to regulating offensive material, this is the most positive, but it still presents several problems.

First, the legislation is based on "generic" categories: the terms "gays and lesbians" would be unacceptable because of their specificity; "sexual orientation" (or "sexual preference") would be the only acceptable term. The problem here is that heterosexuals do not face the same kinds of institutionalized prejudice and discrimination as homosexuals. If representatives of the dominant group decided to go after dissidents — gay journalists, for example — they could find examples of the journalists' work that might be construed as inciting hate of heterosexuals. This problem is even more likely to crop up with the substitution of the term "gender" or "sex" for "women." If this sounds farfetched, recall that in December, 1984, Joe Borowski, a former Manitoba cabinet minister and well-funded anti-abortion crusader, announced his intention to seek charges against *Herizons*, a Winnipeg-based feminist magazine, for a cartoon showing a construction site exploding, supposedly as a result of women's revenge against the workers. He has stated that this cartoon represents "violence against men." When there is a fundamental clash in values and goals, even ideas about hate are not free from misinterpretation and manipulation.

In addition, as Lynn King has pointed out, we must be aware that laws, even when enacted under feminist pressure, are never enforced in a social vacuum: whether they are used for or against feminism depends much more on how strong the women's movement is than on the original initiative behind the laws.

There are, of course, appropriate cases for legal action. We must utilize and seek improvements in laws governing sexual harassment, assault, working conditions and wages. For example, women should lobby for the expansion of sexual harassment legislation to cover the display of offensive pornographic materials in their workplaces. This legislation should be used as a model to deal with all forms of unwanted pornographic display in public institutions: in medical schools, where pornographic shots are included in anatomy slides; in high schools, where the metric system is taught to physics students by discussing a woman's measurements. In several provinces, sexual harassment legislation requires that discussions take place between the two parties concerned before further action is taken. This is very important, for it encourages the kind of confrontation and negotiation (with public power on the woman's side) that create cultural change instead of relying on the external, punitive and expensive intervention of the criminal courts. (In fact, this kind of approach could serve as a good model for a number of nonsexual offenses now covered in the Criminal Code.)

This legislation should be examined and used creatively as a model for dealing on a case-by-case basis with community gathering places (for example, bars or community centres) as well. If women find that places they frequent beginning to show pornography — as has happened in some small towns in Canada — and if discussion with the proprietors fails to achieve its removal, women and supportive men may decide to approach human rights commissions or local authorities to ask that this practice be ended, on the basis that it acts as a form of sexist harassment. Sexual harassment legislation and new laws built on that model could be used to mediate *specific* conflicts in women's favor; they should not be used to prohibit the general availability of material, pornographic or otherwise, dealing with sex.

The problem with bylaws that regulate the availability of pornographic material — through licensing or other means — is that they can all too easily be applied to nonsexist sexual material, literary, educational, gay and lesbian. In the U.S. such laws have been used to control the availability of birth control, self-help, feminist, gay and lesbian information. If pornography is indeed perceived as more offensive than other kinds of materials, the answer may lie in negotiation with proprietors. In November, 1984, the Boots drugstore chain announced that it had received many letters and requests to not carry pornography, and since it considered itself a "family store," it would no longer stock "adult magazines." Other merchants have opted for less obvious display of pornographic material. This approach may take longer and require more effort, but it avoids the dangers of state determination and control, and encourages neighborhood accountability.

If women find themselves coerced into sexual activity for pornographic production, they should lay assault and rape charges against those responsible. If they are paid less than promised for their work, they can sue for breach of contract. If their pictures are published without their consent, they can sue for harassment, slander, libel and damages, or new legislation can be devised to deal specifically with this problem. Similarly, if women are coerced by their husbands or lovers into sexual acts inspired by pornography, they should lay assault and rape charges. But to suggest, as Andrea Dworkin and Catharine MacKinnon do in the U.S., and Susan Cole does in Canada, that the makers of the pornography in question be sued because the pornography itself is responsible for the assault is dangerous. In addition to all the problems outlined by Lisa Duggan, Nan Hunter and Carole Vance earlier, such an approach sets a precedent that could result in descriptions and depictions of acts — of birth control, of abortion, of extra- or premarital sex, of lesbian sex, for example — being used to penalize those who have expressed their opinions and/or desires.

If children are coerced into sexual performance, assault and abuse legislation already exists in Canada and the U.S. to deal with the problem. Several other proposals related to children follow, but the general point is that we do not need new legislation that targets "obscenity" or "pornography" to deal with problems of harassment, assault, coercion, rape and economic exploitation. Such laws only make it easier for antisexist material to be suppressed.

2. Protest and Direct Action

When opportunities for good educational work arise, people should protest grossly sexist spectacles or events, whether they are explicitly sexual or not, in the great feminist tradition of the old Miss America actions. Protests of this nature — picket lines, letters to the editor, newspaper articles or collective open letters analyzing and denouncing such events — all are an important part of the free exchange of ideas. But such protests should not call on the state to prohibit such spectacles.

3. Alternatives to Pornography

The existence of a specific genre of sexual material known as pornography is predicated on a number of important, though rarely acknowledged, aspects of our social treatment of sexuality. Isolated and, among many groups, virtually a taboo subject, it crops up again in its own genre of material, which, not surprisingly, reflects its repression and isolation from social life.

Second, our society divides "education" from "entertainment." To educational material we entrust the task of analysis, but we make the material so dull that those it is supposed to inform resist its messages. Because its role is to divert, entertainment is imbued with beauty, excitement and sensuality. But these precious qualities become distorted and degraded when they are leeched of their emotive, poetic and social content. So sex education induces boredom mixed with embarrassment; while most pornography creates a heady mixture of excitement, sexism and idiocy.

Third, sexual material has become distorted by the imperatives of profit: pornography is big business and it cultivates consumer habits that maintain industry growth. Sex education, too, is a thriving enterprise, with its own experts who jealously guard their territory. But in the case of sex education, its stated purpose and relative freedom from profit considerations make it possible for it to be transformed into a genuinely valuable instrument of social policy. On the other hand, the profit base on which the pornography industry is built and porn's reliance on the taboo nature of sex virtually preclude turning this industry to positive purposes.

We must target sexist and heterosexist values in pornography and in sex education. But this is not enough to change the way sexuality is represented in society, because the identification of sexism can't be achieved in the abstract. We must work to effect change in the very forms of culture that organize and transmit information about sexuality. We have to reclaim our right to a sexual culture, shaped by us, for us. There are many ways to accelerate the process.

(a) Community activity

At present "sex education" is included in the curricula of most primary and secondary schools; is part of, in a more extended and sophisticated way, certain courses at the university level; and in some urban centres is offered by groups such as Planned Parenthood. The curricula are shaped, in the main, by sexologists and social workers, who represent a skilled but still narrow and specialized approach to sexual questions. Opponents of sex education have argued that though we have more programs for the discussion of sex, we have not seen a reduction of such "sexual problems" as teenage pregnancy and sexually transmitted disease. Supporters of sex education are concerned about these, but their concern extends to other issues as well. Notably, many feminists are worried that due to the hypersexualization of our culture, girls are losing the de facto right to approach sexual experience on the basis of their own needs and personal timing. If 20 years ago it was difficult for a girl to say yes, today it is harder for her to say no.

In terms of sex education for children and youth in the school system, there are a number of big problems. Children often feel uncomfortable discussing sexuality with teachers, who are also authority figures and whom students fear, rightly or wrongly, may use information against them. They often do not feel comfortable talking about sex in the arbitrary grouping of a class, preferring the safety of a chosen peer group. The official programs deal not with the real-life experience of kids, but with a predetermined and not always relevant set of facts and opinions. Finally, confining sex education to schools mistakenly assumes that the only people who need to discuss and learn about sex and sexuality are students. As a beginning, the following changes in sex education would constitute worthwhile and necessary improvements:

Sex education should become much more integrated into the programs offered by community colleges, university extension facilities, libraries, local Ys, and other service organizations. Further, it must respond to the needs and concerns of people of all ages, ethnic backgrounds, sexual orientations, religious views and communities by incorporating material developed by all these groups. The pluralistic approach reinforces the idea that there are many different, satisfying and moral ways to live sexual life and encourages all people to look to their needs and desires to guide them in their own choices.

Sex education along these lines need not — should not — be confined to analytical, critical and purely informational material. Rather, it should include expressive and creative work that acknowledges confusion and pain and validates eroticism and pleasure. Thus people working with sexual themes in the arts should participate in this process, so that views of sexuality that break the pornographic conventions are integrated into mainstream life, not, as at present, confined to its fringes. This would be one of the best ways to break down the harmful barriers between "education" and "entertainment."

Educational programs dealing with the sexual abuse of children have been developed by teams of people, including feminists, throughout North America. The best ones concentrate on teaching children the difference between "good" and "bad" touching by encouraging them to decide for themselves what is right on the basis of how they feel. Linked with this focusing of a child's attention on her or his own feelings — a radical step in itself — is the notion that children have the right and the responsibility to say no to adults, and to speak up and reach out to others for help when they are threatened.

We need more of these programs, and they must be tied to educating adults on the issues involved in child abuse. At present the vast majority of abuse takes place between adult men and young girls within the context of the family. There is evidence that, through education, some men can realize how harmful their actions are and choose to change their behavior. We need, in addition, similar educational programs on rape and wife battering. But — and this will be taken up again later — these campaigns must be accompanied by great increases in the services and personnel that offer help to victims, perpetrators and other family members. Otherwise such campaigns only spark crisis, then leave people in trouble, unable to find the resources to help them deal with the consequences of raised consciousness and social intervention.

(b) Arts and the media

Cultural production is at present divided between "mass media" on the one hand — the television programs, magazines, newspapers and films that reach millions — and, on the other, "the arts," which reach a small minority of the population. Almost without exception the kind of cultural work that explores sexual themes using values and conventions that differ from pornography is confined to the world of the arts, although this does not mean that the arts are free of sexism and sexual objectification. The mass media have a virtual monopoly on large-scale communication, and they reinforce sexist values and pornographic conventions. We have to find ways to counteract this power and influence. Lisa Steele's article in this book provides a program for change on this front. I will simply add a few points here.

We must find the means and ways to substitute a true plurality of images and meanings for the false "average" or stereotyped meanings created by the mass media.

As it now stands, most commercial material is produced with corporate financing, whether through direct sponsorship (television, many films) or indirect sponsorship (some films, magazines). If noncommercial work is to succeed, it must be able to reach as broad an audience as the commercial media and be of comparable quality. To attain this goal requires a number of things.

Through government action we must put some limits on commercial access to and monopoly over the public arena. As it now stands, women, sexual, racial and ethnic minorities, lacking funds and networks of power, are disenfranchised. Ways must be found to untangle the imperatives of profit from the politics of information without substituting state control for that of commerce, thus giving voice to the true plurality of our society. As a starting measure, taxes on the commercial media — which have, it is generally acknowledged, a licence to print money — should be used to help finance noncommercial undertakings.

At present, there is very little material that is produced for television by organizations such as Planned Parenthood, and feminist, gay, even forward-looking church groups, because they do not, as a rule, have the necessary economic resources, although the talent is not lacking. Furthermore, in the case of feminist and gay work especially, were such material to be produced much of it would be censored under present laws, which, as feminist Susan Cole has observed, make it possible to depict a woman sucking a gun but outlaw images of fellatio.

Therefore government arts bodies at all levels — municipal, provincial, federal — should be involved in financing material by cultural producers who speak for those without the resources to create work on a mass scale. In the area of sexuality, this means subsidizing feminist and gay cultural workers and their projects in particular.

With respect to magazines, at present *Playboy* and *Cosmopolitan* are available on virtually every newsstand in North America, but it is impossible to obtain copies of, say, *Fuse* or *Broadside* or *The Body Politic* (have you even heard of these alternative arts, feminist and gay publications?) except in a few bookstores in major urban centres. Government action must be undertaken to enable noncommercial publications to be distributed on a much wider basis. In Italy, laws make it mandatory for booksellers and magazine distributors to carry publications expressing every viewpoint and concern. Such laws were determined to be the only effective way to break commercial monopolies and ensure democratic expression. Variations on this principle exist in law in other European countries; we should adapt measures like these to our own situation.

Regarding films, again there are a number of important tasks. More feature films must be made and distributed by noncommercially oriented filmmakers — people with the ability to reach a broad audience and a point of view not filtered through the censorship of corporate sponsorship. This means that the criteria for government subsidies and distribution plans be adjusted accordingly. Monopoly control of cinemas makes it almost impossible to distribute noncommercial films that are not geared to generate multimillion-dollar profits. We need to build a network of nonprofit film centres so that independent work can be shown.

But while we must fight for governments to develop an enlightened cultural policy, we must not wait for them to act or rely on their funding or intervention. We must become actively involved in making and promoting the use of progressive work on sexuality within our own communities and social and political movements.

All cultural organizations and enterprises need to be brought under mandatory affirmative action legislation. If women are able to make work that expresses their concerns as women without fear of reprisals and other negative consequences, particularly if they do not have to account to corporate sponsors, they will produce material that will illuminate sexuality for all. The National Action Committee on the Status of Women has recommended that women have a television station of their own. This is precisely what we need.

4. The Sex Industry

Today the market for various forms of sex and sexual products is very large, and so is the industry that in large part cultivated and created it. Its clearly defined sectors include many different forms of prostitution, pornographic production and sexual spectacle. (It is worth remembering that the boundaries of these sectors are ill-defined. Models and actors who make highly sexual advertisements or sex and violence films and television programs — how should we classify these people and their work? And what about sex education films and books?) There are a number of women who willingly work as photographers, directors, producers and madames in these sectors — an increasing number, if reports from certain parts of the industry are true. There are call girls whose conditions of work are good, relatively speaking: they have few clients, only see those they like, make a lot of money, live in relative safety and comfort, enjoy their work. Many think of themselves as companions or sex therapists.

But for the most part, women's working conditions in the sex industry are far from good, and in many cases, quite dreadful. And indeed, although it is impossible to say with accuracy what proportion of adult sex-workers perform under conditions of real coercion and brutality, for a significant number of women their "choice" of sex work is a choice only in the most literal of senses. They "choose" to work under terrible conditions, without control over environment, clientele or the nature of the spectacle, because they have no other option but to starve. Others turn to sex work because they see this course as less damaging to their health and well-being than factory work, cleaning or waitressing, which are often unsafe and frequently involve constant sexual harassment.

A feminist-oriented approach to the sex industry must ensure that women are no longer victimized by police and social policies; that greater criminalization of neighborhoods and risk to women as workers is discouraged; that the audience for sexist pornography and the market for alienated sex is reduced. This kind of approach means that we must address the needs of sex-workers both by improving the quality of their present working lives and by seeking to create real alternatives to alienating sex work. On both planes, repressive measures are harmful and counterproductive. Censorship only worsens the position of sex-workers vis-à-vis those who control the industry — pornography producers, sex emporium entrepreneurs, and pimps, corporate or individual — by criminalizing sex work and its products and putting the women who work in this field at greater risk in relation to police and the courts.

There is a debate as to whether we should legalize prostitution and regulate pornographic production and other sex work. The answers are complex. On the one hand, legalization would mean that sex-workers would be registered with the state, and therefore theoretically their working conditions, wages and other rights would be monitored. On the other hand, certain kinds of sex work — especially classically defined prostitution — would thereby be institutionalized in ways that tend to give government and corporate entities more control over the women workers in the industry, rather than increasing their autonomy in relation to clients and employers. Instead, along with the Canadian National Action Committee and the U.S. National Organization for Women, we must demand the decriminalization of prostitution. The present laws (in Canada, laws against soliciting and the keeping of a "bawdy house"; in the U.S. against prostitution per se) put prostitutes at constant risk, and create an entire group of women who are socially ostracized and saddled with criminal records, which make finding alternative employment extremely difficult. We must demand the annulment of criminal records for sex work, and find ways to deal with prostitution on a local level without victimizing women. While this is not a simple matter, if communities work in conjunction with prostitutes, and if prostitutes are allowed to operate independently and without harassment, a solution can be found. In the case of sex emporiums, strip joints and similar spots, laws regulating working conditions, minimum wages and unionization should apply, since only such regulation can prevent the worst sort of exploitation.

In terms of the longer-term fate of prostitution, again the issues are complex. Many feminists, though they argue against the victim-ization of prostitutes, nevertheless believe that sex work is more problematic than other kinds of work. In part, this evaluation stems from a sense that there is something especially alienating in intimate physical contact with strangers, particularly under conditions of poverty and stigmatization. Many sex-workers report such feelings about their work, saying that over time it affects how they feel about themselves and about men. If we believe that sexual encoun-ters are best in conditions of free affectional choice — a position that I hold both emotionally and intellectually — then we must work toward the creation of meaningful alternatives to alienated sex work. This means that in keeping with a more general com-mitment to full and meaningful employment (see below), we must demand educational and economic support for women who want to leave this work so that they can live dignified lives without economic hardship while preparing for new ways of earning a living.

But we have to also confront ideas about prostitution that are more products of patriarchal prejudice than sisterly concern, and understand how these affect our own attitudes. We often think of prostitutes as themselves degraded or as degrading women (see Appendix II) — but this comes from the "good woman/bad woman" notion of sexuality that penalizes women either way. We think of prostitution as peculiarly harmful physically and hence psycholog-ically, but as psychologist Paula Caplan has pointed out, we glorify athletes who take beatings on a regular basis; indeed, we glorify soldiers and other official dispensers of force and even death; we turn a blind eye to the way that many professionals often sell their services to business projects whose aims fall short of ethical integrity — the examples could go on. The point is that we judge women's selling of sexual service through the peculiarly harsh lens of sexist attitudes, which blind us simultaneously to forms of "fee-for-serv-ice" that, socially and individually speaking, are even more dam-aging. We must undercut women's poverty and the association of sex with commerce rather than attack sex-workers as such. It may seem paradoxical, but in order for exploitative sex work to wither away, sex-workers themselves have to be protected and integrated into the women's movement and their needs and rights defended.

5. Economic Independence for Women and Youth

University-educated women still only earn the same as men with high school education, and women with less than post-secondary education are at the bottom of the wage scale. If women did not need to sell sex, most would not, since many women sex-workers dislike their work and would prefer to earn their living doing more rewarding, less alienating things.

As far as domestic violence is concerned, for the most part women stay with men who batter because they have no alternative source of economic support for their children. The psychology of dependence and victimization is often at work here: battered girls often become battered wives; and all women must overcome the socialization that says they should "obey" men. Nevertheless, if women were economically independent, they could leave battering men. The economics of dependence underlie the psychology of sexism.

Women are often assaulted on the streets because their neighborhoods are unsafe, or because they cannot afford cars or cabs. Women actors take jobs in productions full of gratuitous violence because they cannot afford to turn them down.

Many mothers are silent when they become aware of an incestuous partner, defeated by their dim prospects on a depressed and discriminatory labor market. Young girls who are victims of sexual abuse run away and turn to prostitution because, in addition to other problems discussed below, they have no source of income. Young boys with homosexual inclinations are driven from homes and communities where their sexual preference is rejected and turn to hustling to support themselves in urban centres. While cultural messages are extremely important in shaping the way women, girls and boys perceive their choices, the economic foundations of sexual exploitation are fundamental, and no amount of wishing will make this harsh and difficult reality disappear.

Therefore, the most important action that must be undertaken to stop the sexual exploitation of women and young people is the fight for economic independence for women and youth. Far from being an evasion of the question, "What can we do about sexist and violent pornography, prostitution and other kinds of alienated sex work?", economic independence is the primary issue. It requires effort on several levels:

(a) Equal pay for work of equal value (or comparable worth, in American usage). Women are concentrated in low-paying job ghettos in which work requiring similar skill, responsibility, experience, and exposure to danger is less well paid than comparable men's work because the wage structure of our workforce rests on women as a superexploited pool of labor. Women must receive equal remuneration to men, so that "women's work" is valued as highly as men's in terms that count.

(b) Affirmative action to bring women into nontraditional jobs, professions and positions throughout society. This is mandatory to the achievement of equal opportunity; it is also crucial as a social statement of the fundamental social equality of the genders.

(c) Full employment: Not only are women suffering from unemployment and underemployment, but as long as men interpret women's need to work for wages as competition for scarce jobs, they will continue to justify their hostility and aggression toward women who are seeking economic and social equality. Structural unemployment creates a layer of people who live in a permanent state of desperation. This kind of despair — in addition to the attendant material hardships and social stigmatization — breeds violence and abuse of all kinds.

(d) Quality social services for all: Unless good child care, health care and care for the aged exist, unless welfare, workers' compensation and unemployment benefits meet the minimum standards of life with dignity and opportunity, women will never be able to participate in shaping culture and politics as men's equals. And the children of sole-support mothers — a significant and ever-growing proportion of children — will pay additional penalties. Social services — especially if they are organized communally on the basis of user and worker collaboration, rather than bureaucratically and impersonally — are not substitutes for individual care, but complements to it. Most women simply cannot handle the responsibilities of child rearing, caring for the sick and aged, household work and labor outside the home in addition to the private preparation and public activity that is necessary for them to function on a par with men. Until women are viewed as equals, not subordinates, misogyny will continue to haunt our culture.

(f) With respect to violence against women, we need, immediately, an adequately funded network of shelters and programs for battered women and their children. After *The Burning Bed*, a television special on wife-battering, aired in October, 1984, the media, stressing the negative impact of the broadcast, reported that one viewer had set his wife on fire. What they did not indicate was that shelters were flooded with women (and their children), who simply left their homes in droves; nor did they report that women's shelters are in such dire financial straits that many had to turn dozens of women away.

(g) Similarly, with respect to child abuse, social workers have found that educational and media programs bring floods of new clients into all kinds of community services. Unfortunately, most such services are already overburdened and underfinanced. Often, new requests for help are channeled toward the apparatuses of state that seem to have limitless resources: the police and the courts. Families suffer terribly when they become involved in these systems, which should be measures of last resort, at best; not the means of primary intervention.

(h) Education and jobs for youth: In Canada youth unemployment stands at 25 percent. Not only does this situation force many girls and boys into prostitution, but it also breeds extreme alienation from society, and, in its wake, violence, sexual and otherwise. It throws youth back into the family just when they should be moving beyond it, creating hardship and tension even in the most loving of situations. Young people must have decent education and meaningful jobs. These will make it possible to build solid friendships and love relationships — the fundamental bases of society. Young people also need economic stipends to enable them to leave abusive parents, from a young age if necessary. At present many children and teenagers are forced to endure such abuse or turn in desperation to painful or dangerous ways of supporting themselves.

6. Reproductive and Erotic Rights for Women and Sexual Minorities

Sexual mores and norms are not naturally predetermined but socially created. They take the raw material of sex — two sexes, a drive to find pleasure from the body and a desire to procreate — and organize it into socially ordered practices. In our society, the dominant sexual norms — those reflected in law, education, church life and the mass media — reflect men's systematic dominance in social and political life. Although there are great differences among the major cultural institutions and their views of sex (differences, for example between the old-fashioned patriarchalism of orthodox Catholicism and the slick new "masculinism" of *Penthouse*), they all reinforce men's power over women and sexual arrangements compatible with that power. From a feminist point of view, then, sexual morality must be a political issue as well. The kinds of norms we want to develop must reflect our goals of equality and self-determination.

For women, the sine qua non of sexual rights has been embodied in the slogan "Control of our bodies, control of our lives." Part of the antifeminist backlash we have been experiencing is a reaction against women's move to take control of their own bodies and lives. The key planks in a program of reproductive and erotic rights are:

(a) Safe, reliable contraception, universally available to women of all ages; increased awareness of contraception in community programs; and improved methods developed through subsidized research and government manufacture, if necessary. For example, the technology now exists to produce a condom that would be so sensitive that neither partner would feel deprived of the sensation of contact. Condom and drug companies are refusing to manufacture this condom because it would undercut existing contraceptive devices and destroy the almost criminally lucrative oral contraceptive market. The pill has many dangerous side effects, and is increasingly implicated in diseases of the endocrine and immune systems. The new "supercondom" would be completely safe and have no side effects.

(b) A woman's right to choose abortion, and to have that choice supported by safe, easily accessible medical services. Women must be able to have the procedure done in their communities and, when necessary, by staff who speak their native language. Professional, supportive counselling both before and after, should women need help to get through this often painful and distressing operation is also critical, as is the right to have the procedure covered by medical insurance.

(c) The right to choose or to refuse sterilization: All over North America, as well as in the Third World, women of racial and national minorities find themselves sterilized without their consent after childbirth or abortion. This must stop. At the same time, many white, middle-class women who want sterilization are refused because their doctors believe that they should reproduce or go on reproducing.

(d) An end to compulsory heterosexuality: We know that sex between people of the same gender is the choice of a significant minority of the population. We also know from the study of other cultures that same-sex practices have often been a central part of mainstream sexuality. From these facts we can deduce that our own sexuality is very much shaped by the taboos placed on same-sex practice, taboos that work in the context of masculinism to reinforce gender hierarchy. If these taboos were lifted, sexual encounters would likely occur between people of the same sex much more often than they do now.

The present prohibitions on homosexual practice give rise to deep prejudices, which in turn lead to fear and mistrust. People with homosexual preferences are seen as "perverted" and "deviant," hence dangerous and contaminating, while those with heterosexual preferences are considered "normal" and "healthy." These prejudices set ordinary people against one another, and divert attention from the crimes of institutionalized, compulsory heterosexuality: incest, molestation and rape, and a generalized, though rarely acknowledged, atmosphere of coercion that subtly forces women to serve men sexually and to subordinate their own needs to men. So pervasive are these values that, like the air we breathe, for the most part we do not even notice them. But they are a major part of what keeps our sexual lives in line with gender hierarchy.

Because homosexual practice — as part of or as the exclusive component of an individual's sex life — is so stigmatized, we need to take some affirmative action on this front. Sex education programs must include gay-positive content to break down the stigmatization of same-sex choices, and the way homosexual people are isolated from mainstream life. Similar measures are necessary in other spheres. Given the deep biases against homosexuality, and the way that they tend to color media productions on gays and lesbians, this material needs to be developed under the leadership of gay and lesbian people, who can speak for themselves.

7. Sexual Rights for Children and Youth

Humans do not emerge fully formed — sexually or otherwise — at the age of 16 or 18 or 21 or whatever the law determines to be the legal age of sexual consent. We learn what we are, what we should be and what we can have throughout infancy, childhood and puberty. It is during these years that we learn whether we are worthy of love and respect, or neglect and contempt; whether our bodies are a source of pleasure and strength, or shame and weakness; whether we may refer to our inner needs to decide how we will use our bodies, or to the dictates of parents, men, or even the internalized voices of rejecting peers.

As Thelma McCormack's report to the Metropolitan Toronto Task Force on Violence against Women demonstrates, there is no clear evidence that pornography leads to violence against women. But there is a relationship between brutalization, neglect and rejection in childhood and the brutalization of others. There is also a link between the more generalized and acceptable forms of male socialization, and a high level of anger toward and contempt for women, and a correlation between female socialization and a greater propensity for self-effacing, masochistic behavior.

When we learn about what we may or may not do with our bodies during our formative years — lessons always filtered through the screen of gender — we are learning about social as well as personal issues. In cultures where children are prohibited from sex play, they also learn that they must postpone or renounce pleasure in general, that they may seek pleasure only with certain kinds of people under certain kinds of circumstances. Thus children learn about social boundaries, power and privilege as much as they learn about their bodies. If children pick up strong messages from their culture about the exploitation of sexuality and its connection with sexist gender roles, as adults they will either live out those messages, or, if those messages conflict with others they have received from family, peers and teachers, spend energy and time sorting out the contradictions in their own feelings and expectations. Nevertheless, children are not equally impressionable at all times, and not all sources for ideas about sex — parents, siblings and friends, cultural material — are equally powerful. We know now that the very earliest of a child's years are all-important in developing a youngster's core sense of integrity, worth and concomitant ability to respect the worth of others. We also know that children whose parents are generally positive about sexuality are more capable of discerning and rejecting the negative messages about sex and gender that are encoded in cultural material, more capable of accepting their own sexuality and that of others.

We are also coming to realize that children who feel comfortable with their own bodies and who believe they have rights of their own are *safer* children — able to reject unwanted advances, able to say no, able to speak out for themselves. The idea of "good" and "bad" touching on which pioneering education on sexual abuse is now being based depends on children's capacity to *consciously* think about touching in the first place — about the kind of touching they like and the kind they do not want. This approach is based on the reality that being able to say no also means allowing touching that feels safe, respecting, affectionate, fun. It means encouraging children to explore and enjoy their own bodies and to feel safe in play with their peers; it means acknowledging children's physicality and sexuality.

It also means teaching adults that children are sensual and sexual in their own right; helping them to recognize their own feelings toward children; and educating them about the importance of respecting children's need for physical comfort from adults and for exploration and play with peers on the one hand, and their right to bodily integrity on the other. But bodily integrity does not simply refer to sexual contact. All forms of corporal punishment violate that integrity; they also teach children that it is acceptable for those with might to impose their wills on those without it, a lesson that will serve children ill if they face unwanted advances from those bigger than they.

In recent years, a number of youth workers and lawyers in Canada, the U.S. and Europe have been proposing the idea of a children's bill of rights. The approach is correct: children are humans, not chattels, and their rights must be acknowledged and protected. But if such a plan is carried out, it must encompass children's right to be sexual without reprisal or punishment on the one hand, and their right to say no to unwanted contact on the other.

It is within this framework that we must look at some of the thorny issues raised in the current debate about pornography and censorship: age of consent laws, sexual abuse and so-called kiddie porn.

In Canada and the U.S., major public controversies over the issue of sexual abuse of children are occurring. In Canada, the Badgley commission tabled its findings on the topic in late 1984; in the U.S., congressional hearings on child pornography are being conducted at the time of writing. It is clearly beyond the scope of this article to deal in depth with many of the issues involved. But certain themes are important because they intersect with the debate on pornography and censorship and are affected by it.

Age of consent laws were enacted toward the end of the nineteenth century, ostensibly to protect children from sexual molestation. Unfortunately, these laws have been ineffectual at this level. As we know, child prostitution, sexual abuse, rape and more subtle forms of coercion have never been curbed by these laws; instead, the laws have served as a means of sexual repression of gay boys and men (in Canada, the age of consent for heterosexual sex is 16, while for homosexuals it is 21); of working-class girls for the "crimes" of sexual precociousness or promiscuity; of many men, including very young men, for what used to be known as "statutory rape"; and of adolescent girls, who fear the consequences of sexual activity should they be discovered. We have a series of laws on assault, coercion and rape that more than adequately cover cases of forced sex with children and youths. Sentencing and penalties can be adjusted accordingly. But because age of consent laws hurt so many people — particularly young people — and protect no one, it is time to abolish them and opt for a different way of protecting young people from being coerced into sexual activity.

Another major issue is "kiddie porn" and its relationship to sexual abuse of children. In Canada, the Badgley commission found that less than two percent of pornography could be classified as kiddie porn, and that this material is not a major factor in the bulk of child abuse cases. The causes of sexual abuse of children are more complex and much more rooted in people's life conditions than in exposure to pictures or stories. Men who were abused as children or participated in abuse of siblings will often become abusers; men under stress because of unemployment, demotion or other problems and who are already alienated, isolated and unable to communicate may become abusers. Women represent less than two percent of sexual abusers; they, too, are isolated, alienated and troubled people.

As far as access to sexual material is concerned, we need to reexamine some of our previously held ideas. If we want young people to have positive sexual experiences based on self- and mutual respect, at a pace that reflects their own needs and not oppressive pressures to conform in whatever direction, we have to allow them to understand not simply the biology but also the sociology of sex. Any sex educator will tell you that most children seek out and find — from peers if not from parents and schools — whatever information they can about sex. Often, given how little they do get from these sources, they find it in newsstand pornography. Making sexually explicit material inaccessible only increases its attraction and heightens its authority. It is better to acknowledge the existence of pornography, if only to provide a critique of its values and alternative sources of information, than it is to keep it officially proscribed.

Because sexual abuse can be so devastating to the children involved, it is important that adult society distinguish between it and other types of physical contact between adults, children and youth. If we fail to make these distinctions, we may greatly exacerbate — sometimes even create — trauma through inappropriate punitive intervention caused by misunderstanding or overreaction. In legal terms we must devise ways to deal with adult-child relations on a case-by-case basis, and to devise solutions — ranging from counselling to incarceration, where necessary — on that same basis, rather than react by imposing uniform sentences for "standardized" offenses.

This is particularly important when we are dealing with relations between adolescents and adults. Present age of consent laws are predicated on the assumption that adolescents are not sexual beings entitled to sexual experience with others. In fact, physiologically and emotionally, adolescence is a time of intense sexual feeling, and many adolescents take determined action to bring about encounters with partners who are considerably older than themselves. In terms of social policy governing education, state intervention and punishment, notions such as statutory rape or variations on that theme are more dangerous than useful.

For example, most of us react differently to the idea of an encounter or relationship between a 13-year-old girl and, say, her 35-year-old teacher; or an encounter or relationship between a mature 15-year-old boy and a woman of 20, even 30; or a homosexual experience between an 18-year-old "boy" or "girl" and a 22-year-old "man" or "woman." All three of these examples are illegal, yet the differences in our intuitive reactions are meaningful for they indicate important and real differences in degrees of social power and capacity for individual consent. These hypothetical examples illustrate the problems with standardized laws, and real cases can be even more complex. Laws that punish "youth/adult" sex indiscriminately should be rescinded and young people should be educated not only to understand that they are entitled to be free of assault and coercion (including legal rights) but also that — and this is especially important for girls — they need not succumb to unwanted advances nor initiate sexual encounters only out of a desire to be approved and acknowledged. It will be a mammoth task to convey this message effectively because our mass visual culture — especially through advertising — has so thoroughly sexualized women and girls while simultaneously obscuring the value of women's other qualities.

We must also determine how we can make it possible for real abusers to change so that they actually stop hurting children. The present system of imprisonment does not rehabilitate, it makes inmates worse. We need to look at forms of treatment that stress self-help within a therapeutic environment — isolated from society if necessary — so that when offenders are reintroduced to society, as they almost inevitably are, they will not once again harm children, women or youth. At present it costs approximately $57,000 per year to maintain a prisoner in the Canadian federal system. We need to discover ways to use those funds to solve rather than reinforce the problem.

Whenever we think about solutions to violence against children — whether sexual or not — we must remember that the vast majority of it takes place not between children and strangers or institutional workers, but within the family. *Ending abuse depends upon changing the way family life is lived in our society*: changing the conditions of adults' lives, educating them about their duties and responsibilities as parents and relatives; and empowering children and youth — emotionally and economically — to say no to, and, if necessary leave, those who abuse them.

The proposals in this chapter are not easy or cheap to implement. The only way they can come about is through resources being directed toward the establishment of educational and social services organized along community user/worker lines, and based on models of self-help, not toward censorship, legal battles, police forces and expanded prisons. "Community," in our complex society, must apply to both geographic and cultural organization. We must work toward economic security for all, because it is an absolutely necessary condition to moving beyond despair and brutality. We have to find ways — cultural, economic and political — of putting human needs, including those for a safe environment, above those of profit and privilege. There can be no equality for women, no security for children, without these changes — changes that imply real improvement in men's lives as well. To win equality we must defend and qualitatively extend the processes of transformation that are already underway, but currently threatened, in our society.

It is easy enough to lose sight of these processes. This book is being compiled at a historical moment when, out of fear and confusion, many people are shifting to the right. We hear about the need for belt-tightening, for cutbacks, for "trimming the waste" in social services, for the "necessity" of unemployment, for spending trillions on weapons and war — all in the name of prosperity and peace. Not surprisingly, the political arena echoes with cries of horror at violence, rape and child abuse. Conservative forces demand censorship, harsher laws, tougher police forces, longer prison sentences. How will feminism respond to the challenges of the period?

It is a matter of fact that every rise in unemployment causes more violence; every cutback in special education breeds greater ignorance; every slashing of social programs creates further despair; every attack on public broadcasting gives the commercial media greater power and a bigger monopoly; every increase in the military budget takes money away from services for battered women and children and condones brutality as the acceptable way for the strong to deal with the weak.

Feminists who oppose censorship — a strategy that takes little time or reflection to expound — do not have another slogan, another quick solution, another panacea to offer in its place. We do have a comprehensive list of tasks we must carry out to bring sexism and violence to an end. Working on any one of these is more helpful — immediately, not in the distant future — than supporting censorship of any kind today, for these tasks get at the structural basis of sexism and violence, and thus ensure that we will have a future.

Whenever major change takes place in society, whenever people who are underprivileged challenge the structures of inequality that have kept them down, political polarization takes place. Women are challenging sexism, and the system of masculine dominance is responding in powerful ways. Its responses are interwoven with the defences of a crisis-ridden economic system based on so great a need for profits that it jeopardizes the health, well-being and even basic existence of millions of people — indeed, of the planet as we know it. Many people are afraid and confused; it is easy to lose hope, easy to fall into the politics of fear and despair; tempting to grasp at straws if, in the current troubled seas, they seem the lines that may pull us to safety. But this illusion is dangerous; it disorients us and drains the strength we need for the tasks ahead.

There is no effective — no *realistic* — substitute for basic change, no alternative to social transformation. In times of crisis, such as our own, social movements need to firmly and publicly state their overall solutions to the problems in society. Now more than ever it is madness to abandon the program for human dignity that feminism has embodied since its second wave began in the '60s. Now more than ever the women's movement must hold to the vision of a good life for all, translate it into solid, practical policy and fight to implement that policy at all levels of society. Now more than ever we must insist that public funds that finance police, jails, the armed forces and weapons manufacture be redirected to cooperation and life, not domination and death.

Women — and men who support feminism — are too important a political force to be ignored if we fight together for this vision. Remaining steadfast now will yield positive results when, inevitably, it becomes clear that the right-wing program was able to solve nothing, that the Mulroney and Reagan governments have only worsened the lot of most people. If at that point we are ready; if we have done the groundwork, fought in our communities, confronted, educated, negotiated; if we have not abandoned the arts and the media to sexists and exploiters; if we have worked hard to build profeminist political parties willing to bring about social change, then we will be in a position to offer alternative social leadership to the antiwoman, antihuman politics of the patriarchal right and the masculinist multinationals whose need for profits stands in direct contradiction to our needs for security, self-determination and community.

We will not then have to spend precious time and resources disentangling ourselves from the snares in which we have become caught. We will not have been gagged or silenced or frightened into retreat. We will not have to start over, rebuilding our forces, reeducating ourselves and our supporters. If we remain steadfast now, when that moment comes we will be able to build the power that will take us from incremental to giant steps along the road to freedom for women and sexual joy for all.

Acknowledgements

I am grateful to all the contributors to this book for many illuminating discussions on numerous aspects of the issues addressed in this article. Special thanks to Lynn King, Lisa Steele, Gary Kinsman, Gad Horowitz and Patsy Aldana, whose patient feedback was invaluable. In addition I learned much in discussions with Joel Kovel, Judith Golden and Bonnie Bean in 1983; and with Karlene Faith and Judith Walkowitz in 1984.

Of course, I alone am responsible for the contents of this article.

Appendix I
Making Sense of Research on Pornography

Editor's Note

Women have much to lose if the current opportunities for social discussion and exploration of sexual issues are lost. Who controls erotic experiences and reproductive rights is not a trivial or academic issue for women, but a matter of central concern. In this context, it is necessary to say a few words about the contested connection between pornography and sexual violence — the issue that is constantly raised as the justification for censorship. We would never suggest that sexually explicit, sexist images do not harm when we so strongly insist that sexist imagery of all kinds is a powerful force in our culture as a whole (see both pages 40 and 58). But it is another thing to state that pornography *is the cause* of violence against women. In the opinion of many informed feminists and the majority of social scientists, the case for that proposition has not been made.

In order to convey as much of the information on the research as possible in a short space and to provide a considered feminist assessment of that research by a senior sociologist that differs from that of, say, American antipornography feminist Andrea Dworkin or Canadian freelance researcher Jillian Ridington, we have included the text of a report "Making Sense of the Research on Pornography," commissioned from Professor Thelma McCormack of Toronto's York University by a subcommittee of the Metropolitan Toronto Task Force on Violence against Women in 1983. It is an important document for many Canadian feminists, as Dr. Susan Gray's article "Exposure to Pornography and Aggression Towards Women: The Case of the Angry Male" has been for American feminists, and many of the articles in this volume reflect agreement with most of its major conclusions.

It is included for another reason as well. It is tangible proof of the dangers we are facing now. Though much of the evidence is still to be assessed and the debate among women themselves only just beginning on many sexual questions, politicians, under pressure from vocal feminists and others, are moving to formulate social policy quickly and opportunistically, and dissenting opinions from feminists themselves are being ignored and even suppressed. The Toronto task force Subcommittee not only disregarded the McCormack report, it actually commissioned another from David Scott, a nonfeminist, antipornography activist.

This in itself is part of what we fear will happen on a wider scale if we decide to deal with perceived problems in sexually explicit material through censorship. Dissenting views will inevitably suffer, and thus we will deprive ourselves of the social forces that act as catalysts for change. In this way a strategy motivated — at least among feminists — by a desire for positive change becomes self-defeating as it undercuts the democratic conditions that make change possible.

Author's Introduction

This monograph was originally prepared in 1983 for the Metropolitan Toronto Task Force on Violence against Women. The author was a member of the subgroup examining advertising and pornography. While there are several ways of looking at pornography — as a moral problem, as a social problem or as a political problem — this monograph deals only with the second approach. Specifically, it was designed to examine whether evidence indicates there is any causal connection, direct or indirect, between exposure to pornography and acts of sexual aggression.

Five areas of research were reviewed: studies of sex offenders, studies of people who use pornography regularly, studies of media influence, experimental studies of aggression, and recent experimental studies of pornography and aggression combined.

Normally, the first two — studies of sex offenders and studies of people who use pornography — would be sufficient to settle the question, especially if the findings were consistent with other studies of media effects. If the findings were positive, then experimental studies might help us to isolate the factors which accounted for the behavior.

But the findings with respect to sexual offenders and pornography users were negative. They do not show any pattern to support the view that pornography is the theory, rape is the practice. However, the "user" studies are somewhat out of date, and studies of sex offenders deal mainly with convicted persons who may represent an atypical population. A few experimental studies show positive results. These are discussed and questions raised about the interpretations of the findings. Recently, the focus of studies has shifted to attitudes rather than behavior.

In any case, everyone agrees that experimental data cannot be the basis for social policy. These studies add to our knowledge about human behavior, but they are designed in a very special way and for particular theoretical purposes. In short, we could not establish any reliable statistical association between pornography and acts of sexual violence.

In an extraordinary step, the subgroup chose to disregard the report. Students, journalists, librarians and other members of the public who have tried to procure copies of it from the task force receive evasive answers about its existence. This strategy is not exactly censorship. It is, rather, that fine Orwellian tactic of making something nonexistent.

Making Sense of Research on Pornography

Research on the effects of pornography is difficult to understand; in part, because the people who comment on it may have different philosophical, scientific or political orientations; in part, because they may be discussing different aspects of the same problems.

Not all scholars are interested in the effects of pornography. There are a number of historical studies[1] as well as discussions of the aesthetics of pornography.[2] And even in the various studies that are concerned with the effects of pornography, the term "effects" is not always used precisely or consistently. For example, it has been used to refer to:

information (sexual)
fantasy (sexual)
attitudes (long term or short term)
    toward same sex
    toward opposite sex
    toward self
behavior (antisocial)
    violence
    masturbation
    rape
    incest
    child molesting
    adultery
behavioral modifications
    reinforcement (more of the same)
    change (therapeutic; overcoming sexual dysfunctions)
mood-enhancement
affective states
    embarrassment
    guilt
    aversion
    pleasure
sexual stimulation
    arousal (tumescence)
    general excitement

With few exceptions the studies have not been integrated, with the result that we do not have a cumulative and coherent body of knowledge.

In the following comments, I want to try to clarify some of the confusion and to indicate what we can and cannot deduce from existing evidence. No attempt will be made here to discuss psychological theories about why people are motivated or attracted to seek pornographic media, nor will there be any discussion of the issue of censorship. However, I will indicate, wherever appropriate, a feminist critique of the way the research has been conceptualized, its methodology and the interpretation of its results.

I

Generally speaking, there are five areas of systematic research that have a bearing on pornography and its effects.

1. Studies of *aggression*. These are usually experimental and carried out by psychologists.
2. Studies of *pornography*. Some are experimental and carried out by psychologists; others have been field surveys concerning pornography, censorship and sexual practices. In addition, there have been studies of pornography consumers and studies of antipornography social movements. Much of this work has been done by sociologists.
3. Studies of *sexual offenders*. These may be large-scale statistical studies of persons convicted of sexual offences; or small-scale clinical studies. The former are usually done by criminologists; the latter by psychiatrists.
4. Studies of *aggression and pornography* combined. Usually experimental and conducted by psychologists.
5. Studies of *media influence*. May be survey or experimental. Carried out by sociologists, political scientists and communication scholars.

In addition to the systematic studies there are analyses of pornography and interpretations of it by people in the humanities. D.H. Lawrence, Simone de Beauvoir, George Steiner, Walter Berns, Sir Herbert Read are among those who have written on pornography and/or censorship.[3]

I want to begin by examining the aggression studies because they have influenced so much of the current discussion of pornography, and because feminists have increasingly defined such sexual offences as rape as acts of aggression rather than acts of sexual gratification.

II

Aggression studies have a long tradition in psychology, but no one thought to relate them to media violence until, more by chance than design, Leonard Berkowitz used scenes from prizefight films in his research. Since then his work has been cited in discussions of *media violence* although it is generally recognized that not all violence is motivated by aggression.

The aggression (or media violence) studies can be grouped on the basis of their methodologies and theories: 1) stimulus and response; 2) social learning; 3) cultivation hypothesis; and the 4) desensitization hypothesis.

1. *Stimulus and Response*. These studies, carried out by Berkowitz and his students (1962; 1963; 1964; 1965; 1966; 1967) were experimental studies. Matched groups (usually male college students) were compared before and after exposure to some kind of stimuli, usually scenes from a well-known prizefight film, *Champion*. The experimental group had been provoked in some way prior to the experience of seeing the ring scene from the film.

The Berkowitz S-R studies are important for two reasons. First, the results are clear cut. After exposure to the stimulus, the experimental group was more predisposed to acts of violence toward others (not toward themselves) than the control groups. Second, the studies are the model for recent studies which combine violence and erotic imagery. Thus some of the criticisms which apply to the aggression studies apply, *mutatis mutandis*, to the violence and pornography studies.

First, the violence is taken out of context. *Champion*, for example, is not a particularly violent film. One scene is, but what an audience would be normally viewing is the entire film (McCormack, 1982). Moreover, the violence of a western and the violence of a boxing film may have very different dramatic meaning (McCormack, 1980).

Second, the S-R model leaves out all inhibiting variables that normally enter into human behavior. Other studies have demonstrated that despite the media examples and despite easy or unobserved opportunity, subjects resisted and did not engage in antisocial behavior (Milgram and Shotland, 1973). We are, in fact, continually surrounded by antisocial stimuli and opportunities to which we either do not respond or, if we do, it is in socially acceptable and responsible ways. Part of our socialization is learning to recognize these situations and learning how to avoid temptation or how to deal with it.

Third, the postexperimental physiological effects may be of short duration.

Fourth, prizefight films may be evoking a latent homosexual response in male subjects, which is then handled aggressively by them (McCormack, 1978). Thus the responses may be to something else, not the violence as such on the screen. Tannenbaum (1970), for example, has suggested that various contextual variables, e.g., dim lights, watching alone or watching with others, etc., can significantly alter response.

There are still other criticisms, but these are the major ones. However, a special word needs to be said here about the *catharsis hypothesis*.

Many persons regard the findings of the Berkowitz S-R studies as constituting a definitive refutation of the catharsis hypothesis. Briefly, the catharsis hypothesis (derived from psychoanalytic theory) predicts that anger or tension produced by frustration would be reduced through vicarious experience.

There are differences of opinion about how this reduction occurs — whether we "get it out of our system" by identifying with the symbolic aggressor (e.g., John Wayne) or whether the experience triggers our own inhibitory mechanisms or whether we discover through this imaginative exercise alternate nonviolent strategies for dealing with whatever is producing the hostility.

Despite all of these different theories about how it works, the outcome would be the same: less anger, less predisposition to hit. The findings are as predicted (Feshbach, 1955, 1961, 1969; Singer, 1968; Bramel et al., 1968; Feshbach and Singer, 1977). Many of these studies have been criticized for their definition of catharsis, and according to Scheff and Scheele (1980) a stronger case for catharsis could have been demonstrated. Be that as it may, most of the original studies on the catharsis hypothesis were field studies, not lab studies, and for many scholars this gives them a credibility that lab studies do not have.

Nevertheless, there has been a dissatisfaction with the catharsis hypothesis. This may reflect the suspicion in academic circles and among positivist psychologists of anything psychoanalytic. (Freud did not use the term "catharsis," but his theories of jokes, dreams, etc., have suggested something like the Aristotelian concept.) But it probably also reflects a political impatience with the notion that what might be legitimate aggression is either displaced or defused through catharsis. Instead of getting angrier and more militant about the world's injustices, we become more passive. The catharsis hypothesis offers no support for collective efforts to resolve problems; it also offers no support for those who want to intervene to change the person.

Meanwhile, we all wind down with detective stories or we take our tired, angry, depressed, information-overloaded selves off to watch violent TV fantasies or horror movies for the pleasures and the escapist gratification they offer. When it is over, we feel better: less angry, less depressed, less fatigued — at least, temporarily. But it is also true that when people are required to carry out some difficult or unpleasant task, they may use the media to get themselves psyched-up to do it. In short, whether we appeal to scientific data or common sense, the problem remains unresolved: both reactions can and do occur.

2. *Social Learning.* Some of the dissatisfaction with the behavioralism of Berkowitz and the psychoanalytic approach are reflected in the social learning or modeling studies conducted by Bandura and his associates (1963a; 1963b; 1969; 1973). Like Berkowitz, Bandura is primarily interested in aggression and only secondarily in TV or other communication media. It is Freud's theory of aggression that he objects to rather than the concept of catharsis. In any case, Bandura departs from the Berkowitz paradigm in two ways.

First, he assumes that aggression is not an instinct or a drive to be controlled, but is, rather, *learned* behavior. And second, it really does not matter whether tension is raised or lowered by exposure to media violence. What does matter is that subjects — especially young ones — imitate what they see on the TV screen, and this learning, according to Bandura, can be so powerful that any countervailing role models either on the screen or in the child's immediate social environment — family, peers — are relatively unimportant. Finally, because children observe aggression so often on television, the patterns of response learned early in life remain with them. They are carried over into adult lives and become, like phobias, operative involuntarily when certain cues are present.

The criticisms of this perspective are extensive and based on different theories of child development as well as on media studies. Since our concern here is with adults and with pornography, we have simply noted them in passing.[4] However, although the pornography question concerns adults primarily, it is in childhood that sex roles are learned; sex stereotypes in the media may reinforce these roles. And it is through the filter of sex roles that children and adults learn by means of the media and other sources the specific norms of sexual performance and sexual attitudes expected. In the Bandura studies and, as we shall indicate later, in most of the research, there are no "controls" for sex roles.

Second, it is from Bandura's social learning theories that the behavioral modification approach has been developed in which pornography may be used therapeutically to help persons overcome problems of sexual dysfunction. Feminists may object to the use of misogynist materials as therapeutic agents, however valid the ends. They may also be inclined to suggest that in a patriarchal society certain forms of sexual dysfunction, such as frigidity in women, may be more political than pathological.

Finally, there is a serious question of whether people, young or old, really do imitate what they see on television; and, if they do, why they imitate some forms of behavior and not others. In effect, there is no place here for selectivity that could reflect, among other things, social values.

3. *The Cultivation Hypothesis*. George Gerbner and his coworkers at the Annenberg School of Communication have been analyzing trends in TV violence and the effects of the media violence on how adult viewers construct social reality (1976a; 1976b). Gerbner argues that the problem is not explicit depictions of violence but what the violence represents in terms of social relationships; that is, in terms of power or dominance and submission. This is analogous to saying that it is not the sex or violence in hard-core pornography that is salient to the viewer, but the sadomasochistic relationship. It would, then, be of no consequence whether the instrument of violence were a fist or a gun, a whip or a knife since the social message is the same.

He hypothesized that the long-term effect of heavy exposure to TV crime shows, for example, is not aggression or social learning but anxiety about one's own helplessness. We begin to believe that the TV world is the real one and grow more fearful about our own personal safety on city streets. Eventually we become more supportive of extreme law-and-order measures, which in reality may be both undesirable and unnecessary.

Gerbner's thesis is particularly relevant to women because, according to his indicators, women are proportionately more often the victims of violence than men. Constant exposure, or "cultivation," to this kind of television can, Gerbner asserts, lead to a state of mind in which women retreat further from the outside world.

Gerbner's statistics on the differences between light and heavy viewers have been questioned, and the theory itself has also been criticized. Very simply, why would people who are made anxious by what they see on TV become or continue to be heavy viewers? Either there is some positive or happy outcome of these shows that is not being measured, or, possibly, apprehensive people seek out the programs that, despite the apprehension created, do provide some kind of relief (Zillmann, 1980). More broadly put, television is an entertainment medium, and the people who watch it regularly expect that there will be shock, thrills, suspense, fear but ultimately a resolution that gives reassurance and pleasure.

As for viewing rape as an aggressive act, the figures do not indicate that heavy viewers would observe more incidents of rape than light viewers. Greenberg et al. (1980) who monitored prime-time TV found that rape was infrequent. The most common form of dubious sexual morality was sexual intercourse between unmarried persons, and even this transgression was more often referred to than observed directly. Thus, heavy viewers might be made anxious by crime shows, and women, in particular, may become unnecessarily worried about being mugged or taken hostage, but not about rape.

4. *Desensitization*. Eysenk and his associates have looked upon most research on violence or pornography as specious (1978). He makes a case for his own experimental methodology and his theory based on conditioning. Without going into either his methodology or his theory, he maintains that the effect of watching a great deal of TV violence is a lowering of anxiety, a process of unlearning and the gradual extinction of any sort of strong, spontaneous reaction; in other words, desensitization.

Desensitization is difficult, if not impossible, to prove. Eysenk spends a great deal of energy discrediting other people's evidence to the contrary. He interprets, for example, the statistics on the decline of sex offences in countries where pornography has been made freely available as proof of his theory: the populations in these countries have become so desensitized that they no longer bother to report rape.

Although there are great differences crossculturally in what people regard as sexual cruelty, it is difficult to believe that the women in Denmark or Sweden would become so blasé about rape. There is some experimental evidence that when people are heavily exposed to any form of erotica, coercive or noncoercive, they are less judgmental: they do not feel as strongly about the need for censorship as subjects who had less exposure, and they are less inclined to impose severe jail sentences on rapists (Zillmann and Bryant, 1982). But is this desensitization or is it a better understanding of the phenomenon?

Apart from Eysenk's idiosyncratic view of rape, there are some larger questions about the nature of desensitization. Is it a slippery slope or can it be reversed? Is it always undesirable? It seems fairly obvious that we do become desensitized to some degree. As we listen to the news every night about violence in Northern Ireland or in the Middle East, the first surprise and anger begin to wear off. But cooling off can be desirable for a calmer and more analytic understanding of these complex events. Desensitization, then, is not necessarily maladaptive, and, it may be, to some degree, essential if we are to engage in rational discourse and arrive at wise social policies. Desensitization is not the same as moral callousness or cognitive indifference. As for the slippery slope, there are enough precedents in history to indicate that old injustices never die.

To summarize, then, the aggression studies touch on many of the issues being raised in contemporary discussions of pornography. Indeed, there is a tendency in some quarters to disregard the pornography research entirely and to generalize from the aggression studies. But what the aggression studies show is that there can be both an increase and decrease of a tendency toward aggression as a direct result of exposure to aggressive stimuli. Second, there are a variety of hypotheses about the effects of aggression stimuli on behavior and attitudes; we are not, as is sometimes said in semipopular discussions of the pornography issue, restricted to a choice between imitation or catharsis. Elsewhere I have indicated the possibilities of using "reference groups" theory (McCormack, 1978), but there are others as well.

III

Until recently, the U.S. *Commission on Obscenity and Pornography* (1970) was the major source of systematic data on pornography. The commission carried out a comprehensive examination that included experimental studies, surveys of attitudes, an examination of the economics of pornography, etc. Only those parts of the report that are relevant for our purposes here will be reviewed.

1. *S-R Experimental Studies.* These are similar in design to the earlier studies cited here on aggression, and the findings are also consistent: exposure to erotic stimuli leads to a short-term sexual arousal.

The immediate effect of the sexual arousal in the postexperimental period was an increase in sexual activity, but in a manner consistent with the subject's usual practice. Despite repeated exposure to slides showing highly aberrant sexual activity, the subjects continued to perform as they had in the past; there were no innovations, no radical experiments.

These findings are consistent with our knowledge and theories of socialization. Sex practices, like other social practices, become habitual, routinized and, however boring, conventional. Like other social habits, we do not alter or break this one without some major incentive or without some serious disruption of our lives.

Third, the studies also confirm the importance of sex-role attitudes as a mediating variable. "Macho" men — those who scored high on masculinity scales — were more aroused by the stimuli than the more androgynous or homosexual men.

The data show, too, that erotic stimuli may lead to antisocial fantasy such as gang rape but not to any corresponding behavior. However, it must be borne in mind that the subjects were university students who may well be persons who fantasize (daydream) as an end in itself more than other people. A later study looked more closely at whether or not the subject regarded the stimuli as pornographic (Fisher and Bryne, 1978). This turned out to be a better predictor — those who rated the film as pornographic increased their sexual activity in the following week more than those who thought it was not pornographic. Subjects who judged it to be pornographic had more conservative sex socialization.

Questions have been raised about the objective measurements of sexual arousal (Amoroso and Brown, 1973). The apparatus used to measure tumescence may itself stimulate response. Self-reports of sexual arousal may also be unreliable and incorrectly measured. If, for example, subjects regard the stimuli in the experiments as repugnant, they may deny any sense of sexual excitement and, indeed, their responses may be delayed (Brown et al., 1976). I call attention to these problems because they apply to the current studies done on pornography and aggression that follow basically the same methodology.

2. *Surveys of Social Attitudes.* There have been many surveys done on attitudes toward pornography, on sexual practices and on censorship. Perhaps the most important finding for our purposes is that more than half of the persons questioned in 1970 believed that pornography was harmful but not to themselves or to people like themselves.Those who were most critical of pornography and most in favor of censorship (including censorship of libraries) were persons with a generally conservative social ideology and a strong religious background. A more recent survey among Canadians indicated there was a similar correlation between religiosity (church attendance) and favoring censorship (Bibby, 1981). But apart from this group, there is the more general phenomenon of a disproportionate concern about pornography in the absence of any strong evidence of behavioral consequences (Bell, 1976).

3. *Studies of Pornography Users.* Studies of how and when people encounter pornography and become consumers of it indicate that most people discover pornography during childhood and in their own homes or through primary groups. Schoolyards, camps, the bedrooms of older siblings — these are the places that young children see the magazines, pictures and other print media. But although the prepubescent boys or girls are aware of pornography, they are not generally interested in it except as something teenagers like and collect in a clandestine way.

For obvious reasons, adolescents are more consciously interested in pornography, more motivated to acquire and share it with their friends. Depending on their sex education, they may find it more or less instructive, although their conversations with each other or the accounts given to them by others of personal experiences may function as a better source of "how-to" information and serve to demystify sexual intercourse. The evidence indicates that the most common sexual result of exposure to pornography for teenage boys is masturbation. Only later do they replace the "centrefold" female with a real one and masturbation with sexual intercourse. The point here is that there is a developmental process in the uses of pornography that is related to stages of sexual maturation.

One of the unexpected findings of the commission was that the regular adult consumers of pornography, people who regularly purchase erotic magazines, see erotic films, etc., represent a cross section of the population. The data refute the stereotypes of users as teenage boys, "dirty old men," lonely salesmen or overly repressed men. Professional people, persons active in their communities, happily married couples and highly educated persons are as represented as all other social categories. Pornography has become a part of the lifestyle of middlebrow, middle-class people who a generation earlier would either have been more secretive about it or felt more guilty about their interest.

It is this new reality of users that lies behind the discussions about "community standards" as a test of what constitutes pornography. Given the changes in our sex mores (most notably with respect to premarital sex) and changes in our attitudes toward greater tolerance of sexual diversity, there is very little that happens between consenting adults that is not within the bounds of community standards. And if the community in question is a major urban centre with its enormous social and cultural variety, community standards cover a wide spectrum of sexual practices. It follows that it will also cover a wide spectrum of sexually oriented media. Even in a small rural community there is only moderate consensus in judgments (yes-no) of a series of pictures (Brown et al., 1978).

Nothing is going to change the range of lifestyles and sexual practices that flourish in the typical urban environment. Yet there is a criticism to be made of the concept of "community standards." It is a market, or *laissez faire*, understanding of symbolic sexuality. This offends moralists who would prefer a less relative, less market-oriented and more absolute definition of sexual norms. From a feminist perspective it disguises the inequalities of power between men and women, and serves as a cover for real sexual oppression. According to this view, all men, even those who are well adjusted, have hostile feelings toward women that can be activated by pornography. Under those conditions, women can never be wholly consenting. Moreover, to the extent that men generally establish the standards of what is acceptable, "community standards" can be regarded as a sexist criterion.

4. *Antipornography Social Movements*. There is considerable literature in the social sciences on moral reform movements, which indicates that efforts to control morality are part of a broader conservative political ideology, and this, in turn, is often combined with high scores on measures of an authoritarian personality. Leaders of these movements have been described as "moral entrepreneurs" (Becker, 1963).

"Decency crusades" have been studied with this general framework (Zurcher and Kirkpatrick, 1976; Wood and Hughes, n.d.). Feminists who are antipornography differentiate themselves from the more conservative element, which is opposed to any form of social change, including the sexual division of labor, but at the level of rhetoric they often sound alike, invoking apocalyptic imagery of impending moral decay.

To summarize, the studies of pornography suggest that the use of pornography has become widespread and that it stimulates sexual activity and sexual fantasy but does not alter established sexual practices. In spite of the more permissive social environments of today, people are still ambivalent about pornography: they believe it is harmful to others, not themselves. Most of the research on pornography was carried out before the feminist movement developed its critique of pornography, so it is not surprising that feminists who are critical of pornography are often confused with members of the older tradition of decency crusades.

IV

In general, those who study sexual offenders have not given any serious attention to pornography either as a direct or indirect causal factor. Journalists frequently do, but criminologists and others who have studied sex offences are more likely to emphasize early childhood experiences, weak social integration, cultural variables and other motivational and structural factors.

The pornography issue centres largely on rape. Theories about rape range from individual pathology, or "deviance," to structural analyses that regard rape as a system of social control, a form of coercion that, like slavery, may be related to the modes of production. Feminists have been critical of both extremes: the pathology approach and the materialist Marxist one. Instead the emphasis is on rape as a criminal offence, but one that is nevertheless supported and encouraged by a variety of myths about the victims. Thus, almost any man, regardless of his personal history, is a potential participant in coercive sexuality, and, unless the coercion is of an extraordinary nature, he can count on a certain amount of public indifference and tolerance from the law enforcement system and the judiciary. As one writer put it, the association between sex and violence is so frequent in our cultural imagery that we can be described as a "rape culture because the image of heterosexual intercourse is based on a rape model of sexuality" (Herman, 1979, p. 43). The means of the coercion may be anything from the use of actual force to threats to use force to other kinds of intimidation. Rape, then, has been redefined as an act of aggression intended to give the victim pain rather than pleasure in order to demonstrate and realize control.

Regardless of the theory about rape, very little attention has been given to pornography. Goldstein and Kant (1973), however, did analyze all of the data available about the possible influence of pornography on sexual deviance. In addition, they carried out a study that looked at four matched groups: persons convicted of sexual offences; persons known to be heavy users of pornography; persons who were either homosexuals and lesbians and also included transsexuals seeking sex-change operations; and a control group.

The major finding was that sex offenders did not use pornography significantly more than the control group, but they used it differently: less in adolescence and more in adult years. But the most distinguishing characteristic of the sex offender's use of pornography was that it activated sex-guilt. In short, the sex offender is a person who has problems with his sexual development, which leads to an atypical use of pornography.

Since rape is a notoriously underreported offence, there is a question about whether a population of convicted sex offenders provides the best data. These men may themselves be atypical — the ones who are unlucky or inept or self-destructive enough to be reported, charged and convicted. But is there a better method? Cross-cultural or comparative studies are unsatisfactory, but in different ways (McConahay and McConahay, 1977).

As things stand at present there is no systematic evidence to link either directly or indirectly the use of pornography (soft core or hard core) with rape. There are many anecdotal accounts and a great deal of speculation; to many people it seems like such a plausible connection — "pornography is the theory, rape is the practice" — that it is difficult to accept.

One reason is that pornography is a major source of myths about women's sexuality, including the pleasure-pain relationship. Pornography is not the only or the most prestigious source of these myths, but it is a source that is cheap, easily accessible to the less educated and far more entertaining than textbooks in psychiatry and psychology, which it popularizes.

For women the distortion and misrepresentation of their sexuality is part of a larger devaluation phenomenon, which results in wage discrepancies, job discrimination, legal disadvantages, medical malpractice and other indices of being a "second sex." But although the myths about women and their sexuality are widespread, they are not necessarily held by men who either impulsively or systematically commit rape, nor are they necessarily the key to rape. Rape myths may enter into the male chauvinist syndrome, but to the degree that the rapist is a person whose objective is to justify himself by forceful sexual abuse of women, to the degree that rape is an act of hatred, these men do not need the myth that women desire to be raped.

V

In the original aggression studies, the stimuli were usually films or slides of men fighting men. Images of male against male are far more common in our popular culture than images of women fighting women or women and men fighting each other. More recently, however, psychologists have been looking at the symbolic presentations of sadistic sexual behavior as a stimulus to aggression. Again, these are experimental studies and many of the criticisms of this methodology discussed earlier apply. There is no reason, for example, to suppose that behavior in a university psychology lab carries over to real life, or that the subjects (usually students in introductory psychology courses either at the University of Manitoba or the University of Wisconsin) are not wise to the game. Again, there are no controls for sex roles or for sex attitudes. Finally, the samples used are small and the studies are seldom replicated.

Despite these and other methodological drawbacks, the research raises important and new questions: Does exposure to sadomasochistic pornography lead to sexual arousal? To hostile fantasies? To aggression against women? And does the sexual script itself influence the response?

These are all empirical questions and are not based on any particular theory. The closest there is to any theory is a version of behavioral modification. Malamuth and his associates (1980) cite as being analogous to their own research studies that alter the behavior of homosexual men by exposing them to heterosexual depictions of sexual behavior, which presumably lead to positive heterosexual fantasy and eventually heterosexual behavior. But in general these studies tend to be untheoretical and to account for statistical relationships one by one.

The major finding of the studies is that men are not turned on, not sexually aroused (based on measures of tumescence and their own word) by sadomasochistic depictions. The "sex revolution" notwithstanding, there are inhibitions that prevent the enjoyment of sexual cruelty even when it is so obviously make-believe.

Inhibitions, however, are part of our sex-role learning; they are not immutable, and there is always the possibility that in a sexually permissive society an individual may perceive these inhibitions as isolating him or her from the others. Thus, the next question is whether, and under what circumstances, these inhibitions could be weakened. And, indeed, much of the research could be characterized as the study of how to lower levels of inhibition.

In order to convey some notion of how these studies are conducted and how inferences are being made, I want to discuss in some detail two of them.

The first is an experiment by Donnerstein and Berkowitz that is a further extension of the latter's earlier aggression studies (1981). But instead of using *Champion*, they used a series of specially prepared five-minute films. Subjects were divided into two groups. One group was provoked by a female "confederate"; the other by a male "confederate." After exposure to the films, the subjects were given an opportunity to retaliate by inflicting shocks on the confederate.

The findings indicated that male subjects inflicted more shocks on the female confederates than on the male one. And this differential has been taken to mean that there is a willingness, innate or socially learned, to hurt women over and above what could be said to be a legitimate response to a provocation.

But does it? What these studies show is that chivalry dies easily when self-esteem is challenged. Moreover, does it prove that men are hostile to women or that they are reluctant to inflict high levels of shocks on another male who might escalate the action by retaliating in some unexpected way? Still another explanation of the differential is that the responses have more to do with men's feelings of solidarity with each other than it does with their hostility toward women.

It is also worth noting that these studies cast serious doubt on the original Bandura hypothesis, in which we would predict that after 20 or so years of watching TV where men are continually engaged in fights with other men, the male subjects would be more willing to hurt another man than they were to hurt a woman.

The second part of the experiment involved 80 undergraduate male subjects who were divided into four groups of 20 each. Each group saw a film. Two groups saw a film which depicted gang rape, but in one of them the victim, after an initial protest, came to enjoy the sexual aggression which is euphemistically called a "positive outcome." The other group of 20 saw a film in which the victim was in some pain and not enjoying the rape: a "negative outcome." In this part of the experiment the confederates were only women. And the findings showed that subjects were more aggressive (more shocks administered) in response to the script in which the rape victim was enjoying the experience.

According to the authors, their data support the view that normally men are inhibited from carrying out acts of rape, but if they can be persuaded that women enjoy it, their inhibitions dissolve and, in addition, they feel no responsibility for their obviously antisocial behavior since they can attribute their behavior to their victims. (This has come to be known as the "misattribution problem" or, as sociologists are more likely to say, "blaming the victim.")

But if rape is, as feminists have been contending, an act of aggression intended to inflict pain, not pleasure, then the findings of this research do not support their interpretation. What the findings suggest is that normal men are not so easily disinhibited, and that men inclined to rape are different. These studies establish again the deviant character of a rapist, but whereas in the earlier research the men were understood to have problems of sex-guilt, the new approach emphasizes the absence of inhibitions — too little rather than too much sex-guilt. Either way, they are different from the larger populations of men who may feel strong hostility toward women yet not carry it out. Public opinion may be changing concerning the rape myths (the feminist movement can take credit for this), but there is no evidence that the rapist ever had or needed these myths.

The second study by Malamuth and his associates (1980) looks at erotic arousal rather than aggression, and examines the responses of women to sadomasochistic stimuli as well as those of men. But, like Donnerstein and Berkowitz, Malamuth et al. are interested in learning about the conditions under which we drop our defenses, stimuli that could weaken the normal inhibitory responses.

Instead of a five-minute film, they used a one-page story about a sexual encounter, which was described differently. In one version, it is clearly rape; in another it was "mutually consenting" ("no reference was made to any force or resistance and the woman's reactions were described as being *excited, feeling sensuousness, hungrily pulling him towards her, a sigh of pleasure* and *a frenzy of bliss.*" Italics in the original.)

Within the rape version, they introduced three endings: one in which the victim has an orgasm, another where she is clearly in pain, and a third where there was both orgasm and pain.

They too found that men are turned off by depictions of rape, that sexual arousal measured either by self-reports or an apparatus attached to the penis is decreased by these depictions. Prurience seems to have its limits. However, in the small number of cases where there was evidence of sexual arousal, it was greatest in response to the story that combined pain and orgasm. For female subjects it was greatest for orgasm alone.

Again, it indicates that there are a small percentage of men who believe the testimony of some psychiatrists that pain and pleasure go together (Stoller, 1979). In any case, this study has been questioned on a number of grounds, including ethical considerations (Sherif, 1980). As Sherif points out, the findings are so low that it is incorrect to say that the study demonstrates anything except the initial finding of aversion to depictions of rape in any form. She also challenges their interpretation of the differences between male and female responses. Not surprisingly, the female responses are low. Malamuth et al. account for this by saying that the women in the study identify with the victim. In that case, Sherif suggests, the men identify with the rapist. But that is not the interpretation given; Malamuth et al. prefer almost anything else, she observes, but they settle on "false attribution" to account for the male response.

In a joint article reviewing the research, Donnerstein and Malamuth acknowledge that they are unsure themselves about how to interpret their positive (predicted) findings (1982). They speculate that in order to predict responses to pornography, they would need a complex model which at the present time they do not have.[5] Susan Gray (1982), who reviewed the studies, came to the conclusion that when all the studies were taken together they tell us about male anger rather than about pornography. They may also tell us something about male sexuality. For example, in a recent study the investigators set up an experiment in which they were looking at the responses to the quantity of pornography, comparing massive exposures to moderate and no exposures (Zillman and Bryant, 1980). And they found that subjects who received massive exposures were more hostile to women (attitudes, not behavior — no shocks) than those who received moderate or none. But what is interesting about this study was that they did not use pornography. They showed their subjects films of noncoercive sexual acts.

If, as this study indicates, noncoercive sexual depictions can induce hostile attitudes toward women, the problem then is the state of mind: how men interpret their own sexual arousal and what it means to them. And do they project their own feelings onto women? In any case, the degree to which we accept the findings of these and other studies depends on theories of rape, theories of sexuality, theories of the ease or difficulty in altering people's attitudes and behavior by manipulating normal inhibitions.

Meanwhile, we have studies of sadomasochistic fantasy (McCormack, 1980) that suggest that bondage fantasies are not uncommon, and that many persons, male and female, find fantasies of this sort enhance sexual experience (Hariton, 1973). Freud regarded sadomasochistic fantasy as pathological, but contemporary psychiatrists (Stoller, 1979) and sexologists (Francoeur, 1977) are less critical. On the contrary, Friday (1973) regards the willingness of women to engage freely in bondage and other fantasies without guilt as a measure of liberation.

Putting aside what constitutes liberation and pseudoliberation, what Friday and others are saying is that there has been a major change in our attitudes toward sexuality, and that, unlike our predecessors, we expect sexual activity to be pleasurable — if not for the other party, at least for ourselves — unspoiled by feelings of guilt. In this context, pornography and sexual fantasies, including bondage themes, enhance the mood. One wonders, however, whether some part of that mood enhancement is not related to the taboo status of pornography and lingering guilt about sexual activity. In any case, pornography in this paradigm is neither cause nor effect; it is part of a sexual environment and it contributes to what Maslow calls "peak experience."

To summarize, the recent studies of pornography and aggression have shed little light on the effects of pornography, but have sensitized us to the deeper problems men have about aggression. They alter our perception of the type of person who would commit rape, from a male whose sexual development has been disturbed leading to strong sense of self-hatred and sex-guilt, to a male who lacks the inhibitions that might deter him.

VI

Media research has, for the past 40 years, been concerned with how much influence the media have on opinion, attitudes, and behavior (Katz, 1980). Much of this research is related to political phenomena: how did the media influence public opinion, political attitudes, voting and other forms of political participation. Consistently, the findings were contrary to the popular view of the media exerting a powerful influence, the image of "brainwashing" (Katz, 1980). About all that could be claimed was that the media helped to set a public agenda, and even that was open to question.

Media research established a model of communication that was interactive rather than one way from the media to the receiver. Audiences of all ages were not passive in this process, they were not sponges soaking up media messages; on the contrary, they were active: selective in their choices and selective in their interpretations of programs, books, newspapers and other media (Blumler and Katz, 1974). Thus, the real message of the medium was a joint outcome between sender and receivers, and, in order to understand this process, attention had to be given to the public, the newspaper readers, TV audiences, library users, magazine subscribers and others.

Attention, then, was directed to the people who were consumers of the media: what sense did they make of what they were listening to, reading or seeing? And what was the process by means of which groups would arrive at a consensual agreement? The studies documented very clearly that the major influence the media have is to reinforce existing opinions, established attitudes and behavior of individuals who are exposed. Only under the most exceptional circumstances do the media ever convert a person from one point of view to another. Thus, it is naive to expect that pornography could do more than generate interest in sexual activity and arouse some of the ambivalence a person may have about sexual activity. How people engage in sexual activity depends on a great many factors in the prior socialization process and in the social groups with whom individuals feel they belong, their "reference group."

In recent years this interactional approach has been challenged by Marxists who regard it as too benign. The media, they argue, are part of a culture hegemony that legitimates American imperialism in the Third World and capitalism in the rest of the world. Applying this reasoning here, the argument would be that pornography that may be acceptable in terms of community standards is, nevertheless, harmful to the weaker parties in a scenario of sexual conflict. Women and children become the victims in a symbolic environment that does not advocate their exploitation in any open way but, indirectly, legitimates it.

This type of argument has been used by those who oppose sex education in the schools. Even if the materials used do not advocate teenagers having sexual relations, they claim, the fact that sex is discussed at all is enough to give young people the message that it is within the range of allowable behavior.

Liberal thinking on this has always stressed the educational value and the demystification process. But since it is not possible to test either of these hypotheses, there is no evidence that the issue can be resolved through empirical research.

More amenable to testing are some of the hypotheses proposed by the late Marshall McLuhan, who urged that we look at the medium rather than the content. But this implies that pornography is not in the content but in the style, and that the pornographic experience is a conjunction of the structure of the text and the cognitive predispositions of the individual. The latter is, of course, much influenced by age and mental development.

To summarize, studies of media influence look at both the content and the audiences in a paradigm that emphasizes communication as an interactional process. Attention is given to the characteristics of audiences: age, socioeconomic status, measures of social integration and other variables that might predispose individuals or groups to experience the pornography differently. Thus, whether pornography was seen as amusing or disgusting, harmless or a danger to the moral fabric of society, a fantasy or a manual of instruction, could not be predicted on the basis of content analysis.

Second, media influence, even when it is consistent with our values, tends to be weak. It would be good to persuade people to get cancer checkups, for example; and messages of this sort would not meet with too much resistance in terms of our values of good health. Yet, even here, intensive campaigns rarely succeed in doing anything more than persuading people who were already on the way to the clinic that they were doing the right thing.

VII

Cultural analyses of pornography are diametrically opposite from the behavioral studies just discussed. For one thing, cultural studies are concerned with meaning rather than psychological or social effects. For another, cultural discussions are concerned with values: how values are dialectically embedded in pornography and how values shape our responses to phenomena. Third, cultural studies assume that pornography, like any other text, has multiple meanings, and that the literal text that the psychological experiments regard as the only text may be the least significant. Finally, cultural studies regard pornography as a reflection of the culture, a mirror through which we can reconstruct the inner life of our own culture and of older ones — a symptom rather than a cause.

There is no consensus about what pornography means as a distinctive genre (the profane), how it differs from graffiti and other forms of the profane. Nor is there any agreement about what it means philosophically or socially. Kaplan (1965) compared pornography to the black mass; Susan Sontag (1969) compared it to science fiction; McCormack to a Herman Kahn scenario; Marcus (1966) to a computer program. Simone de Beauvoir, in her essay on de Sade, saw in his work the sensual converted into the authentic (1962). (Sartre saw the same thing in the writings of Genet.) Both writers, Sartre and de Beauvoir, were making their own oblique comments on the intolerance of Gaullist France.

Other writers have addressed the political implications of pornography more directly. George Steiner (1967), for example, has suggested that pornography obliterates the line between private and public, and in doing so, creates a condition of total surveillance. By eliminating all forms of privacy, he argues, we eliminate the very experiences that give us our capacity to resist political manipulation.

Walter Berns (1971) similarly examines the relationship between pornography and politics. Pornography, he claims, turns us all into voyeurs. But to be a voyeur is to deny all shame, and shame, he postulates, is the foundation of humanness. Without this humanness there can be no civilized public life. Thus, censorship of pornography, he claims, is not in conflict with democracy; it is an essential precondition of it.

Clor (1969) is more liberal than either Steiner or Berns. Yet he, too, sees a conflict between pornography and democracy. Democracy, he says, requires a rational, analytic citizen. The challenge to it, he suggests, is not shame but sensuality. Sensuality, he suggests, may be the key to a great artistic tradition, but not to political rationality.

There are still other cultural discussions, but those noted here convey some sense of how they differ from the behavioralist studies.

VIII

What can we conclude about pornography and its social effects?

I have tried to indicate that there are a number of hidden scenarios that might not be apparent to anyone trying to make sense of this research. One is the controversy about psychoanalytic concepts versus behavioralism among psychologists, many of whom accept neither. Among sociologists, there is the ongoing debate on the nature of social deviance, which is reflected in discussions about the rapist. Because of these hidden scenarios we very seldom have studies of pornography as such; instead, we have experiments that use pornography as a stimulus. The cultural theorists have come closer to studying pornography as a phenomenon, but as I indicated, scholars in the humanities are not especially interested in the social or psychological effects of pornography.

In addition, I have tried to suggest that much of the research itself can be described as having a sexist bias. The failure to understand the importance of sex roles in the socialization process, the tendency to define male-initiated sexual activity as "mutually consenting" contributes to some of the reservations about the various empirical studies.

Bearing this in mind, we can summarize the research around certain issues:

1. *Pornography and Rape.* Pornography is a major source of rape and other sexual myths. Although these same myths are found in more respectable literature, they are found most easily and by large numbers of people in pornography. The feminist movement has been a major source in challenging the myths about rape and female sexuality in general, but there is no reason to suppose that the rapist or potential rapist shares these myths. Studies of sex offenders provide no basis for establishing a connection between pornography and rape.

2. *Pornography and Sexual Fantasy.* Explicit depictions of sexual activity, coercive or not, can induce states of sex arousal and sexual fantasies in both men and women. The fantasy may act as a substitute for an overt sexual act; it may act as an enhancement of sexual activity; it may lead to sexual activity. All of these responses have been documented. Sexual fantasy, then, is a poor predictor of behavior, though the content of sexual fantasy may serve as a good diagnostic.

There is no systematic evidence that people copy what they see or read about in pornography. On the contrary, there is strong evidence that sex patterns, once established, are as difficult to change as any other social habits, and, in addition, there are strong inhibiting factors that intervene to keep our responses within the cultural norms. These norms are changing, and the changes may be very threatening to people who, for various reasons, would like them to remain as they were. There is a tendency to attribute changes in sexual mores to pornography, but it is more likely that as our sexual mores changed the use of pornography as mood enhancement became more widely acceptable as well. Similarly, the desensitization phenomenon, if it exists, may also reflect the reality of social change rather than social indifference.

3. *Pornography, Children and Sex Socialization*. Sexual behavior is learned behavior and develops over time, corresponding roughly to stages of sexual development from infancy to old age. The process of learning includes not only a knowledge of what parts of the body can produce erotic pleasure, but sex identity and sex roles as well.

Media images, particularly with respect to sex roles, may enter into the child's socialization and reinforce the parental models. But, Bandura notwithstanding, television and other media are unable to give what real parents can: reward, approval, acceptance and reassurance about basic security. However, the real role models that children observe in their homes and on the streets may be aggressive and predisposed to violence.

Although young children have access to pornography, it means less to them than it does to their older siblings. Whether pornography does any harm to the adolescent boy or girl depends on: a) prior sex education; b) sex roles; and c) the availability of alternative imagery of sexual performance. The absence of alternative imagery probably deprives women more than men of a knowledge of their own sexuality.

Parents differ with respect to whether they wish to protect young children from erotic materials on the grounds of their immaturity or whether they see their responsibility as one of teaching children to live in a very diverse urban environment that includes pornography among other offences to our values and taste.

4. *Pornography and General Social Effects*. Although it is not possible to demonstrate a causal relationship between pornography and any specific outcome, such as rape, it is possible to say that a cultural milieu in which women are always perceived as sex objects contributes to the devaluation of women. Goals such as greater participation in public life, equal pay for work of equal value, day care, etc., are that much more difficult to achieve without the strong positive images that establish credibility. Pornography demeans men as well as women, but men have so many more positive images that they are not disadvantaged by it.

In reviewing the literature I have not tried to discuss some of the other questions about pornography — whether more is available today and whether what is available is super hard core; how other societies handle sexual obscenity; and, above all, what our responses should be to it in a free society. It is hoped, however, that research will have a bearing on policy questions.

Notes

1. Among the historical studies are D.F. Foxon, *Libertine Literature in England 1660-1745*. New York: University Books. Montgomery Hyde, *A History of Pornography*. London: Heinemann; Roger Thompson, *Unfit for Modest Ears*. London: Macmillan, 1979.

2. See Abraham Kaplan, "Obscenity as an Esthetic Category," *Law and Contemporary Problems* 20, no. 4: 544-559. Steven Marcus, *The Other Victorians*. New

York: Basic, 1966. Susan Sontag, "The Pornographic Imagination," in *Styles of Radical Will* New York: Farrar, Straus & Giroux, 35-73.

3. D.H. Lawrence, *Pornography and So On*. London: Faber & Faber, 1936. Simone de Beauvoir, *The Marquis de Sade*. London: Calder, 1962. Sir Herbert Read, "Does Pornography Matter?" in C.H. Rolph, ed., *Does Pornography Matter?* London: Routledge & Kegan Paul. George Steiner, "Night Words" in *Language and Silence*. New York: Atheneum, 1967. Walter Berns, "Pornography vs. Democracy — A Case for Censorship," *The Public Interest* 22: 3-24.

4. Alarming statistics are often given of how many hours children watch television and how many incidents of violent crime they see in an average week. Appeals are made to our common sense, which suggests that children will be strongly influenced by this viewing experience. But children themselves may not always rate programs by their violence. In a study conducted by the BBC, families were invited to the studio and after dinner they were shown a particularly violent film. After viewing the film, they were encouraged to talk about it. Contrary to expectation, they seldom mentioned the violence (Shaw et al., 1972). One criticism of the social learning studies is that the investigators interpret program content through their own eyes and not those of children (Himmelweit, 1958). Bruno Bettelheim in his study of children's fairy tales (1976) argues that children need the fantasies of violence as part of their emotional growth. One might consider that the bondage fantasies of pornography begin in classical fairy tales and touch on a child's own bondage experience as a child who can be punished and learn to love the punisher. In addition, the Bandura studies have been criticized for assuming that the subject, child or adult, is a blank. On the contrary, it is almost axiomatic to say that the attitudinal effects that any program has on persons is largely dependent on the social and psychological predispositions brought to an interactional communicative act. Many persons have made this point, but the most recent is Dorr (1980). Black children, for example, do not respond the same as white ones (Greenberg, 1972), nor do boys and girls react the same way (Cantor and Orwant, 1980). Furthermore, context may influence what children chose to see or not to see (McCormack, 1962). But perhaps the most important criticism of these studies comes from contemporary developmental theory, which examines the growth of thinking, information processing and conceptual development. As children develop, their critical skills are more developed and they are more aware of the difference between fantasy and reality, between themselves and what the TV people are trying to do to them. Thus the long-term process is not reinforcement of childhood experience with television images. Rather it is toward greater detachment (Noble, 1970; Kelley and Gradner, 1981).

5. The mindlessness of this research is illustrated by the following. It is customary after these experimental studies that use so much deception to "debrief" the subjects, to tell them, as in this case, that it is just not true that women enjoy being raped.

"The findings of these studies consistently show that the overall impact of research participation (including the debriefings) is to *reduce* subjects' acceptance of rape myths. While the data indicate that the information contained within the debriefings may be sufficient for some attitude change, the combination of exposure to violent pornography that portrays rape myths appears to be most effective in reducing rape myth acceptance. However, as an after-thought they do not recommend it. Knowledge that a debriefing may result in the total research experience having a beneficial impact is likely to en-courage future work in this area. These data, however, should not be taken as a carte blanche to justify any pornography exposure-debriefing proce-dures." (Donnerstein and Malamuth, 1982, p. 129)

References

Amoroso, Donald M., and Brown, Marvin
1973 "Problems in Studying the Effects of Erotic Material." *Journal of Sex Research* 9, no. 3: 187-195.
Bandura, Albert
1969 *Principles of Behavior Modification.* New York: Holt, Rinehart and Winston.
1973 *Aggression: A Social Learning Analysis.* Englewood Cliffs, New Jersey: Prentice-Hall.
Bandura, Albert; Ross, Dorthea; and Ross, Sheila A.
1963a "Imitation of Film-Mediated Aggression Model." *Journal of Abnormal and Social Psychology* 66, no. 1: 3-11.
1963b "Vicarious Reinforcement and Imitative Learning." *Journal of Abnormal and Social Psychology* 67, no. 6: 601-607.
Beauvoir, Simone de
1962 *The Marquis de Sade.* London: Calder.
Becker, Howard S.
1963 *Outsiders.* Glencoe, Illinois: Free Press.
Bell, R.
1976 *Social Deviance.* Homewood, Illinois: Dorsey.
Berkowitz, Leonard
1962 *Aggression.* New York: McGraw-Hill.
1964 "The Effects of Observing Violence." *Scientific American* 21, no. 2: 35-41.
1965 "The Concept of Aggressive Drive: Some Additional Considerations." In Leonard Berkowitz, ed., *Advances in Experimental Psychology,* vol. 2, New York: Academic: 301-329.
Berns, Walter
1971 "Pornography vs. Democracy — a Case for Censorship." *The Public Interest* 22: 3-24.
Bettelheim, Bruno
1976 *The Uses of Enchantment.* New York: Alfred A. Knopf.
Bibby, Reginald W.
1981 "Crime and Punishment: A National Reading." *Social Indicators Research* 9: 1-13.

Blumler, Jay G., and Katz, Elihu, eds.
1974 *The Uses of Mass Communication*. Beverly Hills: Sage.
Bramel, Dana; Taub, Barry; and Blum, Barbara
1968 "An Observer's Reaction to the Suffering of His Enemy." *Journal of Personality and Social Psychology* 8, no. 4: 384-392.
Brown, Marvin; Amoroso, Donald M.; and Ware, Edward E.
1976 "Behavioral Effects of Viewing Pornography." *Journal of Social Psychology* 98, 235-245.
Brown, Coke; Anderson, Joan; Burggraf, Linda; and Thompson, Neal
1978 "Community Standards, Conservativism and Judgments of Pornography." *Journal of Sex Research* 14 (2), 81-95.
Cantor, Muriel, and Orwant, Jack
1980 "Differential Effects of Television Violence on Girls and Boys." In Thelma McCormack, ed., *Studies in Communication*. Greenwich, Conn.: JAI Press, 63-83.
Clor, Harry M.
1969 *Obscenity and Public Morality*. Chicago: University of Chicago Press.
Donnerstein, Edward, and Berkowitz, Leonard
1981 "Victim Reactions in Aggressive Erotic Films as a Factor in Violence against Women." *Journal of Personality and Social Psychology* 41, no. 4: 710-724.
Dorr, Aimeé
1980 "When I Was a Child I Thought as a Child." In Stephen B. Withey and Ronald P. Abeles, eds., *Television and Social Behavior: Beyond Violence and Children*. Hillsdale, New Jersey: Lawrence Erlbaum Associates, 191-230.
Eysenck, H.J., and Nias, D.K.B.
1978 *Sex, Violence and the Media*. New York: St. Martin's Press.
Feshbach, Seymour
1955 "The Drive-Reducing Function of Fantasy Behavior." *Journal of Abnormal and Social Psychology* 50: 3-11.
1961 "The Stimulating Versus Cathartic Effect of Vicarious Aggressive Activity." *Journal of Abnormal and Social Psychology* 63: 381-385.
1969 "The Catharsis Effect: Research and Another Review." *Commission on the Causes and Prevention of Violence*, vol. 9: 461-472. Washington, D.C.: U.S. Government Printing Office.
Feshbach, Seymour, and Singer, Robert D.
1971 *Television and Aggression*. San Francisco: Jossey-Bass.
Fisher, William A., and Bryne, Don
1978 "Individual Differences in Affective, Evaluative and Behavioral Responses to an Erotic Film." *Journal of Applied Social Psychology* 8 (4): 355-363.
Foxon, D.F.
1965 *Libertine Literature in England, 1660-1745*. New York: University Books.
Francoeur, Robert
1977 "Sex Films." *Society* 4: 33-37.
Friday, Nancy
1973 *My Secret Garden*. New York: Trident.

Gerbner, George, and Gross, Larry
   1976   "The Scary World of TV's Heavy Viewer." *Psychology Today*, April, 41-45.
   1976   "Living with Television: The Violence Profile." *Journal of Communication* 26 (2): 172-199.
Goldstein, Michael, and Kant, Harold Sanford
   1973   *Pornography and Sexual Deviance*. Berkeley: University of California.
Gray, Susan H.
   1982   "Exposure to Pornography and Aggression toward Women: The Case of the Angry Male." *Social Problems* 29, no. 4: 387-398.
Greenberg, Bradley S.
   1972   "Children's Reactions to TV Blacks." *Journalism Quarterly*, Spring, 5-14.
Greenberg, Bradley S.; Graef, David; Fernandez-Collado, Carlos; Karzenny, Felip; and Atkin, Charles C.
   1980   "Sexual Intimacy on Commercial Television During Prime-Time." In Bradley S. Greenberg, *Life on Television*. Norwood, New Jersey: Ablex, 129-136.
Hariton, Barbara E.
   1973   "The Sexual Fantasies of Women." *Psychology Today* 6, no. 10: 39-44.
Herman, Dianne
   1979   "The Rape Culture." In Jo Freeman, ed., *Women: A Feminist Perspective*. Mayfield: 41-63.
Himmelweit, Hilde; Oppenheim, A.N.; and Vince, Pamela
   1958   *Television and the Child*. London: Oxford.
Hyde, Montgomery
   1964   *A History of Pornography*. London: Heinemann.
Johnson, Pamela Hansford
   1967   *On Iniquity*. New York: Macmillan.
Kaplan, Abraham
   1965   "Obscenity as an Esthetic Category." *Law and Contemporary Problems* 20, no. 4: 544-559.
Katz, Elihu
   1980   "On Conceptualizing Media Effects." In Thelma McCormack, ed., *Studies in Communication*, 1, 119-141. Greenwich, Conn.: JAI.
Kelly, H., and Gardner, H., eds.
   1981   *New Directions for Child Development*, no. 13. San Francisco, CA: Jossey-Bass.
Lawrence, D.H.
   1936   *Pornography and So On*. London: Faber & Faber.
Liebert, Robert; Neale, N.J.M.; and Davidson, E.S.
   1973   *The Early Window: Effects of Television and Children and Youth*. Elmsford, N.Y.: Pergamon.
Malamuth, Neil; Heim, Maggie; and Feshback, Seymour
   1980   "Sexual Responsiveness of College Students to Rape Depictions: Inhibitory and Disinhibitory Effects." *Journal of Personality and Social Psychology* 38, no. 3: 399-408.

Malamuth, Neil M., and Donnerstein, Ed
1982 "The Effects of Aggressive-Pornographic Mass Media Stimuli." In *Advances in Experimental Psychology* 15, Academic Press: 103-134.
Marcus, Steven
1966 *The Other Victorians.* New York: Basic.
McConahay, Shirley A., and McConahay, John B.
1977 "Sexual Permissiveness, Sex-Role Rigidity and Violence Across Cultures." *Journal of Social Issues* 33, no. 2: 135-143.
McCormack, Thelma
1962 "The Context Hypothesis and TV Learning." *Studies in Public Communication*, no. 4: 111-125.
1972 "Censorship and 'Community Standards.'" In B. Singer, ed., *Communications in Canadian Society*, Toronto: Copp Clark, 242-263. Reissued and original article revised. Addison-Wesley (1983): 209-225.
1978 "Machismo in Media Research: A Critical Review of Research on Violence and Pornography." *Social Problems* 25, no. 5: 544-555.
1979 "Television and the Changing Cultures of Childhood." In K. Ishwaran, ed., *Childhood and Adolescence in Canada.* Toronto: McGraw-Hill Ryerson, 302-321.
1980 "Feminism, Censorship and Sadomasochistic Pornography." In Thelma McCormack, ed., *Studies in Communication* 1. Greenwich, Conn.: JAI, 37-61.
1980 "Passionate Protests: Feminists and Censorship." *Canadian Forum*, LIX, no. 697, March.
1982 "Hollywood's Prizefight Films: Violence or 'Jock' Appeal?" Paper given to North American Society for the Sociology of Sport.
Milgram, Stanley, and Shotland, R. Lance
1973 *Television and Antisocial Behavior. Field Experiments.* New York: Academic Press.
Noble, Grant
1970 "Concepts of Order and Balance in Children's TV Programs." *Journalism Quarterly* 47: 101-108.
Read, Herbert Sir
1961 "Does Pornography Matter?" In C.H. Rolph, ed., *Does Pornography Matter?* London: Routledge & Keagan Paul.
Scheff, Thomas J., and Scheele, Stephen C.
1980 "Humor and Catharsis: The Effect of Comedy on Audiences." In Percy H. Tannenbaum, ed., *The Entertainment Functions of Television.* Hillsdale, New Jersey: Lawrence Erlbaum Associates.
Shaw, Irene S., and Newell, David S.
1972 *Violence on Television.* London: British Broadcasting Corporation.
Sherif, Carolyn Wood
1980 "Comment on Ethical Issues in Malamuth, Heim and Feshbach's 'Sexual Responsiveness of College Students to Rape Depictions: Inhibitory and Disinhibitory Effects.'" *Journal of Personality and Social Psychology* 38, no. 3: 409-412.

Singer, David
1968 "Aggression Arousal, Hostile Humor, Catharsis." *Journal of Personality and Social Psychology*. Monograph Supplement, vol. 8, no. 1, part 2: 1-14.

Sontag, Susan
1969 "The Pornographic Imagination." In *Styles of Radical Will*. New York: Farrar, Straus & Giroux, 35-73.

Steiner, George
1967 "Night Words." In *Language and Silence*. New York: Atheneum.

Stoller, Robert J.M.D.
1979 *Sexual Excitement*. New York: Pantheon.

Tannenbaum, Percy H.
1970 "Emotional Arousal as a Mediator of Erotic Communication Effects." *Technical Report of the Commission on Obscenity and Pornography*, vol. 8. Washington, D.C.: U.S. Government Printing Office.

Thompson, Roger
1979 *Unfit for Modest Ears: A Study of Pornographic, Obscene and Bawdy Works Written or Published in England in the Second Half of the Seventeenth Century*. London: Macmillan.

U.S. Commission on Obscenity and Pornography.

White, Howard D.
1981 "Library Censorship and the Permissive Minority." *Library Quarterly* 51 (2): 192-207.

Wood, Michael, and Hughes, Michael
n.d. "The Moral Basis of Moral Reform: Status Discontent vs. Culture Socialization Explanations of Generalized Beliefs about Pornography." Unpublished.

Zillman, Dolf
1980 "Anatomy of Suspense." In Percy H. Tannenbaum, ed., *The Entertainment Functions of Television*. Hillsdale, New Jersey: Lawrence Erlbaum Associates, 133-163.

Zillmann, Dolf, and Bryant, Jennings
1982 "Pornography, Sexual Callousness, and the Trivialization of Rape," *Journal of Communication* (32) no. 4: 10-21.

Zurcher, Louis A. Jr., and Kirkpatrick, George
1976 *Citizens for Decency*. Austin: University of Texas.

Appendix II
Excerpts from the Minneapolis Ordinance

The key provisions of the original Minneapolis ordinance are reprinted below:

(1) *Special Findings on Pornography*: The council finds that pornography is central in creating and maintaining the civil inequality of the sexes. Pornography is a systematic practice of exploitation and subordination based on sex which differentially harms women. The bigotry and contempt it promotes, with the acts of aggression it fosters, harm women's opportunities for equality of rights in employment, education, property rights, public accommodations and public services; create public harassment and private denigration; promote injury and degradation such as rape, battery and prostitution and inhibit just enforcement of laws against these acts; contribute significantly to restricting women from full exercise of citizenship and participation in public life, including in neighborhoods; damage relations between the sexes; and undermine women's equal exercise of rights to speech and action guaranteed to all citizens under the constitutions and laws of the United States and the State of Minnesota.

(gg) *Pornography*. Pornography is a form of discrimination on the basis of sex.
(1) Pornography is the sexually explicit subordination of women, graphically depicted, whether in pictures or in words, that also includes one or more of the following:

> (i) women are presented as dehumanized sexual objects, things or commodities; or
>
> (ii) women are presented as sexual objects who enjoy pain or humiliation; or
>
> (iii) women are presented as sexual objects who experience sexual pleasure in being raped; or
>
> (iv) women are presented as sexual objects tied up or cut up or mutilated or bruised or physically hurt; or
>
> (v) women are presented in postures of sexual submission; [or sexual servility, including by inviting penetration;]* or
>
> (vi) women's body parts — including but not limited to vaginas, breasts, and buttocks — are exhibited, such that women are reduced to those parts; or
>
> (vii) women are presented as whores by nature; or
>
> (viii) women are presented being penetrated by objects or animals; or
>
> (ix) women are presented in scenarios of degradation, injury, abasement, torture, shown as filthy or inferior, bleeding, bruised, or hurt in a context that makes these conditions sexual.

---

* The bracketed phrase appears in an early version of the Minneapolis ordinance but may have been removed before the bill was formally introduced in the city council. It has reappeared, however, in subsequent defences of the ordinance by its supporters. See J. Miller, "Civil Rights, Not Censorship," *Village Voice*, Nov. 6, 1984, p. 6.

(2) The use of men, children, or transsexuals in the place of women . . . is pornography for purposes of . . . this statute.

(1) *Discrimination by trafficking in pornography.*

The production, sale, exhibition, or distribution of pornography is discrimination against women by means of trafficking in pornography:

> (1) City, state, and federally funded public libraries or private and public university and college libraries in which pornography is available for study, including on open shelves shall not be construed to be trafficking in pornography but special display presentations of pornography in said places is sex discrimination.
>
> (2) The formation of private clubs or associations for purposes of trafficking in pornography is illegal and shall be considered a conspiracy to violate the civil rights of women.
>
> (3) Any woman has a cause of action hereunder as a woman acting against the subordination of women. Any man or transsexual who alleges injury by pornography in the way women are injured by it shall also have a cause of action.

(m) *Coercion into pornographic performances.* Any person, including transsexual, who is coerced, intimidated, or fraudulently induced (hereafter, "coerced") into performing for pornography shall have a cause of action against the maker(s), seller(s), exhibitor(s) or distributor(s) of said pornography for damages and for the elimination of the products of the performance(s) from the public view.

(1) *Limitation of action.* This claim shall not expire before five years have elapsed from the date of the coerced performance(s) or from the last appearance or sale of any product of the performance(s); whichever date is later;

(2) Proof of one or more of the following facts or conditions shall not, without more, negate a finding of coercion:

(aa) that the person is a woman; or

(bb) that the person is or has been a prostitute; or

(cc) that the person has attained the age of majority; or

(dd) that the person is connected by blood or marriage to anyone involved in or related to the making of the pornography; or

(ee) that the person has previously had, or been thought to have had, sexual relations with anyone including anyone involved in or related to the making of the pornography; or

(ff) that the person has previously posed for sexually explicit pictures for or with anyone, including anyone involved in or related to the making of the pornography at issue; or

(gg) that anyone else, including a spouse or other relative, has given permission on the person's behalf; or

(hh) that the person actually consented to a use of the performance that is changed into pornography; or

(ii) that the person knew that the purpose of the acts or events in question was to make pornography; or

(jj) that the person showed no resistance or appeared to cooperate actively in the photographic sessions or in the sexual events that produced the pornography; or (kk) that the person signed a contract, or made statements affirming a willingness to cooperate; or

(ll) that no physical force, threats, or weapons were used in the making of the pornography; or

(mm) that the person was paid or otherwise compensated.

(n) *Forcing pornography on a person*. Any woman, man, child, or transsexual who has pornography forced on them in any place of employment, in education, in a home, or in any public place has a cause of action against the perpetrator and/or institution.

(o) *Assault or physical attack due to pornography*. Any woman, man, child, or transsexual who is assaulted, physically attacked or injured in a way that is directly caused by specific pornography has a claim for damages against the perpetrator, the maker(s), distributor(s), seller(s), and/or exhibitor(s), and for an injunction against the specific pornography's further exhibition, distribution, or sale. No damages shall be assessed (A) against maker(s) for pornography made, (B) against distributor(s) for pornography distributed, (C) against seller(s) for pornography sold, or (D) against exhibitors for pornography exhibited prior to the effective date of this act.

(p) *Defenses*. Where the materials which are the subject matter of a cause of action under subsections (1), (m), (n), or (o) of this section are pornography, it shall not be a defense that the defendant did not know or intend that the materials are pornography or sex discrimination.

Contributors

Varda Burstyn is a writer on political and cultural issues, a teacher of film studies, a fledgling video producer and a radio broadcaster who contributes regularly to CBC's *Ideas*, which produced her four-part documentary series *Public Sex* in 1983. She has been involved in the women's movement since 1967.

June Callwood is a Toronto-based writer and journalist with *The Globe and Mail*. A feminist and founding member of Jesse's (a shelter for teenaged girls), she is the author of numerous books, including, most recently, *Emma*.

Sara Diamond is a Vancouver video artist, critic, teacher and writer of labor history. She is currently producing videotapes and a book on the history of women in the British Columbian labor movement.

Lisa Duggan is a lesbian-feminist writer and historian working on a dissertation on the history of American sexology.

Anna Gronau is a Toronto-based filmmaker currently working at Art Metropole. A longtime lobbyist and public educator, she is a founder and member of the Ontario Film and Video Appreciation Society, which is challenging the Ontario Board of Censors in the Supreme Court of Canada.

Nan Hunter is a feminist lawyer and activist in New York City. She works with the Reproductive Freedom Project of the American Civil Liberties Union.

Lynn King is a feminist lawyer based in Toronto who has acted in court for a number of arts organizations in successfully challenging the Ontario Board of Censors. As well, she has been active in family law reform, crisis centres for women and other women's lobbying groups.

Myrna Kostash is an Edmonton journalist and writer whose work covers feminism, regionalism, ethnicity, Canadian literature and radical politics. Her most recent book is *A Long Way from Home: The Story of the Sixties Generation in Canada*.

Thelma McCormack is currently professor of sociology at York University and president-elect of the Canadian Sociology and Anthropology Association. Her previous work has been on feminist theory and studies of the mass media of communication. She is at present working on a feminist approach to civil liberties.

Ann Snitow, a U.S. writer and university teacher of English and Women's Studies, co-edited *Powers of Desire: The Politics of Sexuality* with Christine Stansell and Sharon Thompson.

Lisa Steele is a video artist and teacher who has been producing videotapes since 1972. She was a founder and is a continuing contributor to *Fuse*, a cultural news magazine based in Toronto, and is a longtime collective member of the staff at Interval House, a shelter for battered women and children.

Mariana Valverde teaches women's studies at the University of Toronto. She is currently working on a book, *Sex and Power*, which will be published by Women's Press in 1985.

Carole S. Vance is an anthropologist at Columbia University in New York. She writes about sex, gender, politics and the body. She is the editor of *Pleasure and Danger: Exploring Female Sexuality* (Routledge and Kegan Paul, 1984), the volume of conference papers from the Scholar and the Feminist IX conference, which she coordinated at Barnard College in 1982.

Lorna Weir works with the Canadian Women's Movement Archives. She is preparing a book on population politics in early modern Britain.

The Desperate People

Farley Mowat

The Desperate People

with woodcuts by Rosemary Kilbourn
and a 16-page section of photographs

This is Volume II of
Death of a People–The Ihalmiut

McClelland and Stewart Limited

First published 1959 by Little, Brown and Company in
association with The Atlantic Monthly Press, Boston; published
simultaneously in Canada by Little, Brown & Company
(Canada) Limited

Paperback edition: 0-7710-6592-2

The Canadian Publishers
McClelland and Stewart Limited
25 Hollinger Road, Toronto

The author is grateful to *Maclean's* for permission to include
material by him previously published in that magazine under
the title "The Two Ordeals of Kikik."

Photo credits:
All photographs in the picture section following page 144 are
by Farley Mowat with the exception of those identified as
I, X and XII, which are by Richard Harrington.

Printed and bound in Canada by
T. H. Best Printing Company Limited

Books by Farley Mowat

People of the Deer (1952, revised edition 1975)
The Regiment (1955, new edition 1973)
Lost in the Barrens (1956)
The Dog Who Wouldn't Be (1957)
Grey Seas Under (1959)
The Desperate People (1959, revised edition 1975)
Owls in the Family (1961)
The Serpent's Coil (1961)
The Black Joke (1962)
Never Cry Wolf (1963, new edition 1973)
Westviking (1965)
The Curse of the Viking Grave (1966)
Canada North (1967, revised paperback edition 1976)
This Rock Within the Sea (with John de Visser)(1968, reissued 1976)
The Boat Who Wouldn't Float (1969, illustrated edition 1974)
Sibir (1970, new edition 1973)
A Whale for the Killing (1972)
Wake of the Great Sealers (with David Blackwood) (1973)
The Snow Walker (1975)

Edited by Farley Mowat
Coppermine Journey (1958)
THE TOP OF THE WORLD TRILOGY
Ordeal by Ice (1960, revised edition 1973)
The Polar Passion (1967, revised edition 1973)
Tundra (1973)

For the People of the Deer —
in the belief that we will make amends

Contents

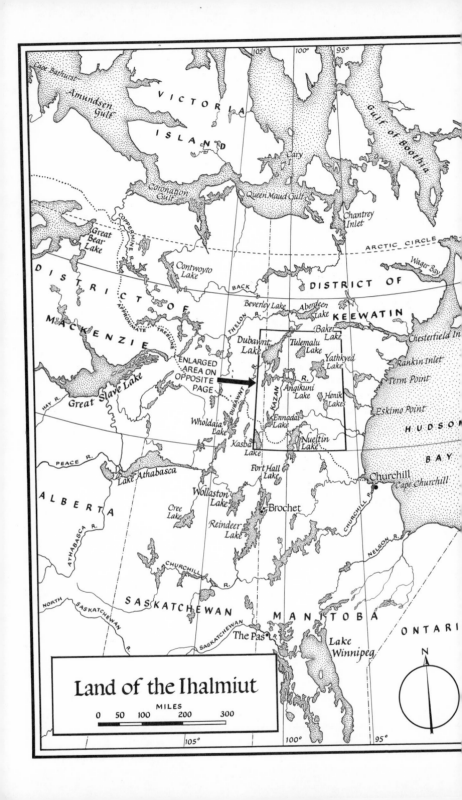

Land of the Ihalmiut

MILES
0   50 100   200   300

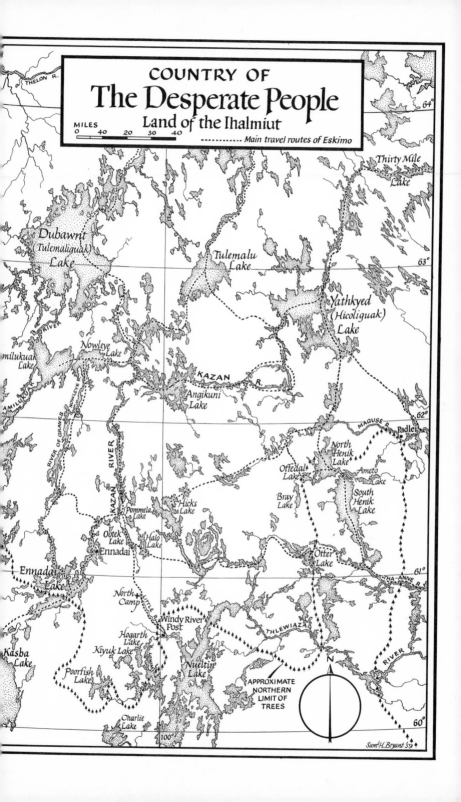

COUNTRY OF
The Desperate People
Land of the Ihalmiut

MILES
0   40   20   30   40

---------- *Main travel routes of Eskimo*

THELON R.

64°

Thirty Mile Lake

Dubawnt
(Tulemaliguak)
Lake

Tulemalu Lake

63°

Yathkyed
(Hicoliguak)
Lake

Nowleye Lake

milukuak Lake

RIVER

AMILUKU

NOWLEYE RIVER

KAZAN   R.

Angikuni
Lake

62°

MAGUSE R.

Padlei

RIVER OF GRAVES

KAZAN   RIVER

Pommela
Lake

Hicks
Lake

North
Henik
Lake

Offedal
Lake

Ameto
Lake

Ootek
Lake

Halo
Lake

Bray
Lake

South
Henik
Lake

Ennadai

Ennadai
Lake

61°

Otter
Lake

THA-ANNE R.

North
Camp

LITTLE R.

Windy River
Post

THLEWIAZA

N

RIVER

Kasba
Lake

Hogarth
Lake

Kiyuk Lake

Nueltin
Lake

APPROXIMATE
NORTHERN
LIMIT OF
TREES

Poorfish
Lake

Charlie
Lake

100°

60°

Sam H. Bryant '59

Foreword

This is the second of two books of mine about the inland Eskimos of Keewatin District in the Northwest Territories. The first, *People of the Deer,* which was published in 1952, concluded with these words:

"In the days of Inoti, the son, the strength of a great people might be made to live once more. In time it would be *our* strength, and the people would be *our* people.

"And then the dark stain which is the color of blood might at last be wiped from the record of the *kablunait* [the white men] in the place of the River of Men."

The present book is a chronicle of how, during the seven years after 1952, that stain did not disappear, but spread beyond the River of Men until it came to encompass the greatest portion of the inland plains we call the Barrengrounds — and to leave them empty of mankind.

It is a chronicle of the virtual extinction of a native people in this, the *present,* hour of Canadian history. It is also, so I believe, an irrefutable argument for the full and immediate emancipation of the surviving Canadian Eskimos from the intellectual, spiritual, economic and social domination which we have imposed upon them.

Most of the people of whom I write are gone, and cannot be recalled. It is for us to say whether the surviving Eskimos of the Canadian north will follow them or whether, as has happened in Greenland and in Siberia, they will become a revived and vigorous element in the variegated complex which is mankind.

There are now belated signs of a lightening on the somber horizon of the Canadian arctic; but this may be no more than the illusion of a false sunrise in a polar winter, unless we resolutely set ourselves to expunge a damning reflection upon our own pretensions to humanity, and unless we commit ourselves unequivocally to make amends.

The preparation of this book has been made easier for me by the degree of help which I received — sometimes from unexpected sources.

To the Hudson's Bay Company for assistance, including arctic transportation and access to certain of its records, I return my gratitude. My thanks are also due to the Royal Canadian Corps of Signals; the Territorial Court of the Northwest Territories; a number of scientists and scientific organizations; and to a great many individuals of experience in the arctic who provided me with invaluable material, including personal journals and diaries. In some cases the transmission of this material involved a considerable degree of potential risk — a fact which I am not free to dwell upon but which I feel bound to acknowledge publicly.

Finally I wish to acknowledge my debt to the several members of the Department of Northern Affairs of the federal government who gave me the most unstinted co-operation even when it was clear that the results would not redound to the credit of the Department.

All the major events in this book, and most of the minor ones, have been documented from official sources. Other sources which were used included published works, signed statements and private correspondence, together with many hours of tape-recorded conversations with survivors of the Ihalmiut, other Eskimos, and white men who were involved in the recorded events. To obviate the possibility of error, all Eskimo conversations were independently translated by at least two Eskimo linguists.

At the time *People of the Deer* was written it was impossible to obtain documentary corroboration of much of the material. Consequently I was obliged to use pseudonyms for some of the Eskimos and many of the whites as well as to deliberately misidentify some individuals. I was also obliged to refrain from identification of certain events in terms of time and place. In the present book these problems no longer exist and all names given are the correct ones, while all the events are presented in their actual spatial and temporal contexts. Where apparent discrepancies occur between this book and my earlier one, the version given here is the factually correct one.

In the Appendix I have given a detailed list of all the Ihalmiut who were alive in 1946 or who were born thereafter, together with their relationships, ages, and brief notes as to their eventual fates.

F. M.
Palgrave, Ontario
May, 1959

Foreword to the New Edition

In the original Foreword I wrote: "There are now belated signs of a lightening on the somber horizon of the Canadian arctic; but this may be no more than the illusion of a false sunrise in a polar winter . . ."

It is now fifteen years since those words were written and the sunrise has proved to be an illusion in all truth. The physical disruptions which our society inflicted on the Eskimos during the first half of this century have been ameliorated to the extent that few Eskimos now die of physical neglect. Since about 1960 we have made considerable efforts to ensure that they will survive in the flesh; but at the same time we have pursued a policy which is very efficiently destroying them psychically. We have made a ruthless and concerted effort to dispossess them from their own age-old way of life and thought and to force them into the mold of our modern technological society. Assimilation has been our goal . . . and it has failed disastrously. In 1974 almost all Canadian Eskimos have been broken away from the support of their land (which is theirs no longer) and live clustered in modern slums — many of them hardly better than ghettos — in not many more than a score of artificial settlements along the rim of the Canadian north. Here they exist for the most part on welfare payments of one kind or another — no longer taking sustenance from the land and the sea. Effectively they live in unguarded concentration camps, provided with the basic requirements for mere physical survival, but deprived of the freedom to shape and control their own lives. We have salved our national conscience by ensuring that they do not die anymore of outright starvation, but we have resolutely denied them the right to live according to their own inherent needs — the right to *function* as viable human beings according to their own desires and capabilities.

Genocide can be practiced in a wide variety of ways.

The Desperate People, of whom I wrote in 1959, are desperate still. But *now* they include *all* the native peoples of Canada — Indian, Eskimo and mixed bloods. They are making what may be their last convulsive effort to achieve survival apart from, and despite, a society which will accept them only if they transform themselves into second-class simulacrums of Western man. They are fighting what may well be their ultimate battle to exist in the world according to their own concept of what their lives should be. They are making what is probably their final effort to achieve the freedom to be themselves.

We have long prided ourselves on being a democratic nation, dedicated to the altar of freedom. Freedom for whom? If it is only freedom for ourselves to do as we please at the expense of others, then our pious stance is even more abhorrent than that of any overt tyrant — for ours is based upon a vile hypocrisy.

To have freedom one must give freedom. Let us put our vaunted belief in freedom to the test. Let us give back the freedom that we have taken from the native peoples of this land. If we cannot do this, then not only are they doomed, but we will have doomed ourselves as well.

Because the time is short, and the time is now, and that time will not come again, I am re-issuing this book in the hope that it may help us to understand and to acknowledge the crimes against humanity we have perpetrated here, *in our country*, under the aegis of a free democracy . . . crimes which we are perpetrating still in a more subtle guise.

F. M.
Port Hope, Ontario
March, 1974

1 *People of the Deer*

ACROSS the northern reaches of this continent there lies a mighty wedge of treeless plain, scarred by the primordial ice, inundated beneath a myriad of lakes, cross-checked by innumerable rivers, and riven by the rock bones of an elder earth. They are cold bones into which an eternal frost strikes downward five hundred feet beneath the thin skin of tundra bog and lichens which alone feel warmth under the long summer suns; and for eight months of the year this skin itself is wrinkled by the frosts and becomes a part of the cold stone below.

It is a naked land, bearing the deep excoriations which are the legacy of a glacial incubus of ice a mile in thickness which once exerted its colossal pressures on the yielding rock. Implacable and irresistible the ice flowed outward, crushing mountains, filling lakes with the mountains' broken bones, and lacerating the tilted planes of the land's face with great gouges, some of which are fifty miles in length. The scars made by the ice are open still; the wounds have never healed.

It is a land uncircumscribed, for it has no limits that the eye can find. It seems to reach beyond the finite boundaries of this earth. Brooding, immutable, given over to its own essential mood of desolation, it showed so bleak a face to the first white men who came upon its verges that they named it, in awe and fear, the Barrengrounds.

Yet of all the things that it may be, it is not barren.

During the brief arctic summer it is a place where curlews circle in a white sky above the calling waterfowl on icily transparent lakes. It is a place where gaudy ground squirrels whistle from the sandy casts of vanished glacial rivers; where the dun-colored summer foxes den, and lemmings dawdle fatly in the thin sedges of the bogs. It is a place where minute flowers blaze in microcosmic revelry, and where the thrumming of insect wings assails the greater beasts, and sets them fleeing to the bald ridge tops in search of a wind to drive the unseen enemy away. It is a place where the black muskoxen still stand foursquare to the cautious feints of the white wolves, and where the shambling giant of the land, the massive Barrens grizzly, moves solitary and untouchable. And, not long since, it was a place where the caribou in their unnumbered hordes could inundate the land in one hot flow of life that rose below one far horizon, and reached unbroken past the opposite one.

In all its harsh hostility it is not barren; nor has it been since the first crawling lichens spread like a multicolored stain over the scoured rocks. And through the cold millennia since the lichens came, life in ten thousand forms has prospered on the plains where the caribou became a living pulse, fleshed by the other beasts, and waiting for the day when man would come bringing sentience into a new world.

And man came early.

Three or four thousand years ago, caribou were already dying with stone points embedded in their flesh. Along the ancient gravel beaches that now cling crazily to hillsides three hundred feet above the shrunken levels of the present lakes, the quartz flakes lie profusely and the broken points made by clumsy or unlucky workmen keep them company. They are as fresh now as when men's hands gave them their present form, for no leaves have fallen in that treeless land to bury them in detritus, and the long winter winds have covered them with no more permanence than that of snow.

For all their freshness, the flaked stones have not yet been made to speak, and almost nothing is known with certainty of those first comers, nor of the manner of their passing. There is only conjecture to suggest that the first men upon the plains may have been the ancestors of the dispersed family of Athapascan Indians whose descendants include the Chipewyans of the thin forests on the Barrens' southern boundaries. There is no way of telling if these first men still held the plains when out of Asia there came a wave of new and different men.

The early history of these newcomers is not recorded either — not even upon the land which they made theirs. Skin tents, bone implements and the greater part of the tools and weapons which they possessed could not resist the years when they lay naked on the wind-swept rocks. Yet something of their early tale still lingers in the memories of surviving men whose memories are contiguous with the memory of their race. And the story says that in the opaque time which has no name, a people came out of Asia, driven from the inland plains of Siberia by encroaching hordes who were well skilled in war. The plains dwellers themselves knew almost nothing of warrior skills. They were reindeer hunters, peaceful people, and they could not fight back. So they moved west and entered a new continent along a narrow defile of tundra plain that lies between the Brooks Range of Alaska and the arctic sea.

The unfamiliar sea was close upon their left flank, and they were afraid of it, so that as they came eastward and the boundary of the tundra plains receded into the southeast, they also swung southward away from the seacoast. For a time, so the old memories insist, they lingered near two mighty inland lakes which may be those that we now call Great Slave and Great Bear Lakes. But the plains drew them on, and to the east the plains grew ever broader, and so they continued to the east. Eventually, at least as early as ten centuries ago, they reached the land which was to be their home.

They came to the heart of the Barrengrounds, which encompasses the great plateau about Dubawnt, Yathkyed and Angikuni Lakes, in the present district of Keewatin; and here they stayed. They were men belonging to the race we now call Eskimos, but who have always called themselves *Innuit*, which is to say, The People.

They were The People in truth, for if the greatest Eskimo ethnologist, Knud Rasmussen, is to be believed, it was from this reservoir of inland-dwelling Innuit that many of the coastal and sea-culture Eskimos subsequently originated. Rasmussen called the inland dwellers the proto-Eskimos, and there is little reason to doubt that he was right, for the surviving Eskimos of the great plains have no memory of life by the sea, and no knowledge of such a way of life, or of its manifest tabus and mysteries; yet they have a long memory for the past — perhaps a longer memory than that possessed by any other group of Eskimos.

People who remain in one place for a great stretch of time often have such memories; but those who drift and move before the years have shorter ones. Pommela, who was a shaman and a wise man, could, as late as 1948, recall eleven generations of his people who had lived beside the lake called Angikuni, and when he had recited to me the names of the men of each of these generations in direct descent down to himself, he concluded with the remark that the earliest of these had been no newcomer to the land.

In any event it is certainly established that when the first Europeans came to Hudson Bay in the beginning of the seventeenth century, the people who had come out of Asia millennia before had long been settled in the heartland of the Barrens. When the first whites arrived, the whole of the inland plains westward from Hudson Bay to the headwaters of the Back River and to the Great Bend in the Thelon River, and north from near timberline to the fringes of the arctic coast, were in the hands of a great multitude of inland Eskimos who depended for their whole livelihood upon the caribou, and who were in truth the People of the Deer.

They were a singularly fortunate people. Through the next two centuries, while the white men changed and mutilated the faces of the nations of coast Eskimos, and of the Indians, the People of the Deer remained remote, their presence unsuspected behind the grim ramparts of the Barrengrounds which presented such a frightening aspect to the Europeans that it was not until late in the eighteenth century that any white man dared to venture into them.

Yet, indirectly, the coming of the white men wrought a catastrophic change in the lives of the inland Eskimos.

Through countless centuries the inland people had been bounded on their southern flank by the Athapascan Indians, of whom the most important were the Idthen Eldeli — the Eaters of the Deer — who formed a major segment of the Chipewyan group. Yet, though there had always been a bitter enmity between the Eskimos and the Chipewyans, there had not been much bloodshed, for neither group knew much of war. By tacit agreement they left a broad band of unoccupied country between them, and though there were isolated massacres when a band of one race was able to surprise a smaller group of the enemy, for the most part there was a state of armed but impotent hostility.

In the middle of the seventeenth century this state of things began to change. Far to the south of the Idthen Eldeli lands, which may then have stretched as far as Churchill River, the Indians of the open prairies began to acquire firearms. With these magnificent new weapons, the Plains Crees began to strike northward against the Woodland Crees who, in their turn, edged northward into Chipewyan country. The Chipewyans had always been inferior fighters, so they gave way before the pressure; and their retreat was hastened when the Woodland Crees began to obtain guns from the outposts of the Hudson's

Bay Company. The Idthen Eldeli were rapidly driven north to the edge of the forests until they were impinging on the southern fringes of the Eskimo lands. Here they halted for a time; but before long they too began to barter for guns, mainly at Fort Prince of Wales, the present site of Churchill. Before the middle of the eighteenth century the Idthen Eldeli, made warlike by the new weapons in their hands, had begun to strike far out into the Barrens.

The inland Eskimos could not resist the invasion, and so they in their turn drew back toward the north, abandoning the land which had been theirs for many centuries.

As yet they had had no contact with the whites, and very little even with the coast Eskimos with whom the Hudson's Bay Company was now trading at Eskimo Point and Marble Island. Since they could obtain no guns, the only defense open to them was to continue to withdraw until sheer distance eased the pressure, and they were at last able to draw breath and pitch their camps in the twin valleys of the Thelon and Back Rivers.

During the years between 1770 and 1772, when Samuel Hearne became the first (and last) white man ever to traverse the Barrengrounds on foot, he found the heartland to be in the possession of the Idthen Eldeli bands. Hearne walked north to within a hundred miles of the lower Thelon River and saw no Eskimos, yet though the Eskimos were gone, the Indians held only a precarious tenure on the land, for they could not live upon it in the winter and were forced to withdraw south of timberline each autumn. Nor was even this partial possession destined to endure for long. During the final decade of the eighteenth century, smallpox came burning up from the south of the continent and it swept north in as destructive an epidemic as any known to human history. Entire Indian tribes were decimated until the dead must have numbered in the tens of thousands. The plague came at last to the Idthen Eldeli, by way of the traders at Great Slave Lake, and when it had burned its way through their scattered camps they had melted, in the space of a single winter, from several thousand people to a few hundred who clustered in fear and desperation close to the trading posts at Churchill and Great Slave. It was to take them generations to rebuild a fraction of their former strength and, before they could recoup their losses, they were again on the decline as the lesser ravagers, tuberculosis, influenza, and diphtheria, followed quick upon each other's heels. By 1800 the great plains which had been so briefly theirs were lost to them forever. For a time, small and timid parties were sometimes driven by starvation to follow the migrating deer northward into the tundra during the summer months, but even these desperate sallies eventually ceased, for the land was no longer empty.

The Innuit had returned to claim their own.

The People had been spared the plague, for they had no contact with white men. Thus, when the Indians failed to reappear in the summers immediately after the smallpox scourge, the Eskimos began to edge southward. They came cautiously up the Dubawnt River to the great inland sea which they called Tulemaliguak. They were a numerous people, and they were anxious to regain their old lands, for they had been able to obtain too little meat in the narrow confines of the Thelon and Back River valleys, and they knew, as had the Indians, that the best hunting grounds lay in the Dubawnt-Yathkyed-Angikuni country.

Before the end of the first decade of the nineteenth century the repossession was complete, and the inland people again held the whole of the central plains. To the north the Hanningaiormiut lived along the shores of Back River. South of them, on the Thelon Lakes, were the Akilingmiut. Southward again were the Tulemaliguamiut, and east of them were the Kingnetuamiut, so named after the high hill which guards the entrance to Angikuni Lake. From Angikuni the People had spread up and down the Kazan River, northward past Yathkyed as far as Thirty Mile Lake where their expansion was contained by the Harvaktormiut who held the mouth of the river. Those who lived near Yathkyed called themselves Padliermiut, and some of them spread even farther to the east, coming eventually to the lakes which we call North and South Henik, and thence down the coastal rivers to the shores of Hudson Bay.

Southward from Angikuni, along the Kazan (which they called the River of Men), the People came to Kekertarahatok, which we now call Ennadai Lake, but they did not halt until they reached the northern edge of the forests. These, the most southerly of all the People, became the Kekertarahatormiut.

The inland Eskimos were a great people in those days, numbering perhaps two thousand in their many camps; and though each group of camps had its own local identity, they were all united under a common name, Ihalmiut. It is a name with a proud ring, for it means The Other People, in the sense of those who are set apart from, and who are superior to, all others. And the Ihalmiut were indeed set apart, for it was not until the year 1867 that the first of the strangers who had already usurped a continent came into their land.

It was in 1867 that Father Gasté, an Oblate priest, set out from his mission at Reindeer Lake to proselytize the pagan inland Eskimos to the north, of whom he had heard from his own Idthen Eldeli Indians. Gasté underwent terrible hardships but, if report speaks truth, he eventually met the Kekertarahatormiut somewhere northwest of Nueltin Lake. He remained with them for most of that summer, and he may even have penetrated as far north as Angikuni Lake where the Kingnetuamiut camps were massed in such propinquity that the shores of the eastern bay were like a city of skin tents. Gasté was repulsed in his efforts to convert the Innuit, and in the autumn he fled south, barely regaining his mission post alive. It took him years to recover from the spiritual and physical ordeals he had suffered, and he never again ventured north into the tundra plains. Nevertheless, and as a direct result of his visit, a trade link was established for the first time between the inland dwellers and the whites. From 1868 onwards a small and courageous handful of the best hunters and bravest men amongst the Kekertarahatormiut each year dared the long journey south, penetrating two hundred miles into the forests, and into the lands of their old enemies the Chipewyans, in order to trade with the priest, and with the Hudson's Bay Company post at Reindeer Lake. Those were hard journeys and sometimes there was bloodshed between Indians and Eskimos. Nevertheless, having once discovered guns, steel hatchets, knives and metal cooking pots, the Ihalmiut desired more and more of these rare things.

So it happened that individuals amongst them began to engage in a series of quite fantastic trading journeys. From Angikuni and Yathkyed the Padliermiut began to drive their sleds southeastward as far as Churchill, taking a full winter season to complete the round trip; and the following winter these trading Eskimos turned north carrying trade goods clear to the arctic coast at Chantrey Inlet. The Ennadai and upper Kazan Eskimo travelers journeyed to Brochet at Reindeer Lake each winter, and in the summer they went north by kayak or with pack dogs to Beverly Lake where they and the Akilingmiut traded with the dreaded Kidliermiut — the men who kill all strangers — who came to meet them at Beverly Lake from the south shores of Coronation Gulf and from as far to the northeast as the mouth of the Coppermine River.

Yet despite these contacts with the whites, the land of the Ihalmiut still remained inviolate, and the Peoples' lives were little changed. Not more than a handful of the men were engaged in the trading journeys, and the vast bulk of the People had no contact with the world beyond the Barrens. They wished it so. They went into the strangers' lands and procured those things for which they had need; but the strangers did not come into *their* lands and force new appetites and new ideas on them.

But just before the turn of the century a stranger did come amongst them. He was J. B. Tyrrell, a geologist and government explorer, who in 1893 and 1894 made two masterful journeys through the Barrens from timberline north as far as the Thelon, thus becoming the first white man ever really to penetrate the interior plains since the time of Hearne. In 1893 Tyrrell explored the Dubawnt River system from its headwaters to

Baker Lake, and so home along the shores of Hudson Bay to Churchill. Not content with this spectacular journey he paralleled it the next year by traveling from the headwaters of the Kazan to a point north of Yathkyed, and then swinging east to reach the Bay at the mouth of the Ferguson River.

Between Ennadai and Yathkyed he found the country heavily populated and, being a scientist and a methodical man, he mapped and located the camps he passed and tabulated the number of people whom he saw. In his official report to the government, Tyrrell estimated that he *encountered* between five and six hundred Eskimos along his route of 1894; but when I talked to him in 1949 he told me that he had actually seen only a portion of the people, and that he believed they may have numbered well above a thousand on the Kazan alone.

His estimate is confirmed by the observations of the Oblate priest, Father Turquetil. Like Gasté, Turquetil was stationed at Reindeer Lake, and he too burned to establish a mission amongst the inland Eskimos. From 1901 to 1906 he made five attempts to reach the inland people, and in 1906, with the assistance of a group of Eskimo traders from Ennadai, he at last succeeded in reaching that lake. He stayed for seven months in the land of the Kekertarahatormiut, and on his eventual return south he estimated the Eskimo population of Ennadai, the upper Kazan, and Angikuni Lake as totaling 858 souls — and this estimate *did not include* the Padliermiut of Yathkyed. Including the people north of Dubawnt Lake (which would presumably embrace the Thelon and Garry Lake Eskimos) Turquetil's estimate of the total numbers of the Ihalmiut was close to two thousand.

In those days immediately after the turn of the century the Ihalmiut must have been the most numerous cohesive group of Eskimos extant. They must also have been amongst the most secure, and the most vital. Unlike the majority of the coastal and sea-culture Eskimos, they were not nomads, for they had no need to pursue different kinds of game at different seasons. They were a settled people of long-established residence in their camps along the rivers and beside the lakes. The caribou, on which their entire way of life was based, came to them twice, and often four times a year, in mighty herds that stretched as far as a man's eye could encompass. They were a people of great strength and certainty, and this they clearly demonstrated by the manner in which they rejected the attempts of Father Turquetil to Christianize them. The old men of the Ihalmiut still recount how the Black-robed One set himself against the *angeokoks* — the shamans and the wise men — whose magic defeated him so severely that he believed his life was in jeopardy, and fled the inland plains. It must indeed have been a salutary experience, for no other missionary again attempted to penetrate the heartland of the People until almost half a century had passed.

The People proved their certainty and pride by their steadfast refusal to follow the coastal Eskimos into virtual servitude to trading post and mission. They chose to remain remote, untouchable, and their own masters, and only a selected few continued to trade with the whites on the borders of the land. Kakumee, Ooliebuk, Igluguarduak, Pommela and no more than a dozen others did the trading for more than a thousand people, who refused to pursue the white fox, and their own future, into decay and ultimate extinction.

They were a people with a niche in time, for, unlike the coast Eskimos, they had a genuine sense of their own antiquity. Their legends spoke clearly of their primacy amongst the nations of the Innuit.

They were a rich people, as richness is measured in their world, for they seldom knew hunger; they had an abundance of the warmest clothing a man could want — caribou skins; their dogs were numerous and strong; the children in the tents were also numerous, and there was little or no need to face the horror of putting babies that could not be fed under the snow to die. They had no effective enemies amongst men. The deer were incredibly numerous, and the muskoxen were still abundant. The Ihalmiut had no need to suffer through bitter winter days upon the ice floes seeking seals; nor on the frozen lakes jigging stubbornly for the fish which are, at best, a starvation diet in the north. Instead of being a time of hardship and of dread, the Ihalmiut winter was a time for feasting, for visiting, for songs and stories. Almost alone amongst the Eskimo peoples the Ihalmiut possessed the rarest of all riches — time. They had time to remember what was past and to speculate upon what was still to come. They had time to dream, and time to work with words and thoughts — while their cousins on the hard seacoasts had little time for anything save the eternal struggle to survive.

Such was the hidden world of the Ihalmiut as the second decade of the present century began. Such were the people who had as much of contentment as they could desire. Such were the People of the Deer.

2 Of Many Graves

IT was in the year 1912 that the defenses which the land had built about its people were suddenly and ruthlessly pierced by an enemy which could not be denied. The assailant was brought into the land hidden within a man of the people, the shaman Pommela, who was returning from a trading trip to Reindeer Lake. When it reached the heart of the plains, it burst out of him and ran an untrammeled course along the river routes. It leapt from camp to camp with an appalling swiftness and, as it passed, the camps stood desolate and still. It had no name, this unseen nemesis, for it was a stranger. Perhaps it was influenza, but whatever we might call it, it became known to the Ihalmiut as the Great Pain.

Those who survived its passage remembered its effects with dreadful clarity. Pommela remembered it, and he spoke of how men, women and children, driven mad by the flaming fever within their bodies, flung off their clothes and plunged themselves into the last spring snowdrifts — and did not rise again. Of the countless families whom Pommela knew, half vanished within the space of a spring and summer, and those families which remained were shattered so that here a father might have survived alone of all his children and his wives, and here a young child might have survived its parents, its brothers and its sisters.

Word of the disaster was slow to reach the outer world, but some years later Father Turquetil, at his new mission post on the coast at Chesterfield, heard that between five and six hundred of the inland people had perished in that one stroke of death. No one will ever know with any certainty how many died, for no one kept count. The greatest dying probably took place at Angikuni Lake, for this was the center of the Ihalmiut country and it was here that the people were most heavily concentrated. The evidence of the plague remains there still, for the shores of the western bay are so thickly strewn with hurriedly built graves that in places it is difficult to walk between them.

When the disease had run its course, the scattered survivors of the people of the plains slowly drew together again to form new camps of widows, orphans, and widowers. The Angikuni area itself was almost abandoned, and most of the surviving Kingnetuamiut withdrew north and south along the Kazan. Thus a major break appeared in what had been a continuous population stretching from Ennadai northward to Thirty Mile Lake. The heartland came to be almost empty of the People, who were now concentrated largely in the vicinity of Yathkyed, and about Ennadai Lake, and who were therefore perilously near the north and south frontiers of their own land, and thus more easily accessible to new invasions of another kind.

These were not long in coming. Now, from the north, the east and the south, the traders began to move in upon the Ihalmiut.

In 1913 a trading post had been established at Baker Lake and the next year an outpost from it was pushed up the Kazan to a point on the edge of the Padliermiut country. For the first time the Padliermiut were in direct contact with the whites, and within a few years they became slaves to new appetites, for trinkets, flour, cloth, and much other sorcery that could wean a hunter away from his allegiance to the deer and turn him into a trapper of white foxes. They paid an early price. According to Rasmussen, about a hundred of them died in 1919 of starvation and disease.

The more southerly Padliermiut were invaded from the eastern flank. In the early 1920's traders pushed in from Eskimo Point to Yathkyed itself, with the intention of establishing a permanent outpost there. When it proved impossible to maintain such a post, due to the difficulties of supply along the wild rivers running eastward to the sea, the post (called Padlei) was built instead near the headwaters of the Maguse River, and from here it exerted its steady pull, drawing to it many of the Padliermiut and the last remnants of the Kingnetuamiut. These came to take up residence in a new country which was not generous of meat, and they, too, rapidly became slaves of the demand for foxes.

The invasion of the Kekertarahatormiut from the south moved at a slower pace, for the distances were greater there, and the defenses of the land were stronger. Nevertheless, outposts from Reindeer Lake were established at Fort Hall Lake by 1914 and then, as competing traders entered the country, the outposts began to leapfrog each other north until by 1924 they had reached the edge of the true Barrens west of Nueltin Lake, and were in direct contact with the outlying camps of the inland Eskimos of Ennadai and the upper Kazan.

The effects of the new invasion were manifold.

In the first place the People, still disorganized by the blow which had crippled them in 1912, no longer were secure, no longer felt the certainty they had once known, and they could not so easily resist the temptations which the traders offered. The old framework of their life, already cracked, began to crumble and they began to build a new structure, a slipshod, jerry-built affair whose foundation rested uneasily upon a wildly fluctuating factor — the value and abundance of the white fox. They began to spend much of their time in the hunt for foxes.

The locations of good trapping areas and proximity to the nearest trading posts came more and more to determine the places where they chose to live. They obtained rifles and almost limitless supplies of ammunition in exchange for foxes, and for a time this mighty increase in their ability to kill the deer — even at poor hunting places — compensated for their abandonment of the old camp sites at the main deer crossings, and of their old ways which had been determined by the ways of the deer. But the very efficacy of the rifle was also its most evil attribute. To a people who had known no other restrictions on their hunting than those imposed by the nature of their crude weapons, the thought that it might be possible to kill *too many* deer did not occur. Nor did any of the white strangers to the land attempt to introduce this idea into the People's minds. In truth, the white men themselves were the most pitiless butchers of the deer the land had ever seen, and by their example they greatly encouraged the People to the excessive slaughter which the rifle now made possible.

The herds of deer, mighty as they were, were delicately balanced between the toll taken by their natural enemies and their ability to reproduce. As the toll suddenly grew heavier, there was no corresponding increase in the annual fawn crop. Slowly death gained the upper hand. What had been a river of life flowing through the Barrens began to shrink; the tributaries began to dry up altogether. Where once there had been a myriad roads belonging to the deer, now there were fewer with each passing year. And in 1926 the consequence of the slaughter fell full upon the People.

Harried and decimated, the deer changed their ancestral routes in the autumn of 1926, and during the winter which followed nemesis came again to the Ihalmiut camps. That winter there was starvation on a massive scale throughout the inland plains. At Ennadai one trader heard of fifty deaths, while from the vicinity of Hicoliguak a report of the deaths of more than two hundred people filtered through to Baker Lake.

The Ihalmiut were not only wasting in the flesh; they were

also stricken in the spirit. The nature of the epidemic of the earlier decade had been completely inexplicable, and less terrible for that, since it did not strike at the familiar certainties upon which men depended. But this new catastrophe struck at the very roots of the Ihalmiut existence since, for the first time in memory, the sustainer, the foundation of life itself — *tuktu*, the deer — had failed the People.

This disaster resulted in the virtual obliteration of the Padliermiut as a people of the deer. Wracked by the terrible uncertainty which resulted from the failure of the herds, the majority of the survivors sought for a new certainty in an increasing reliance on the fox. They abandoned Yathkyed and the Kazan from Angikuni north to Thirty Mile Lake, and fled to Padlei.

There they became completely dependent on the fur trade, and although they still hunted deer, ate deermeat when they could get it, and dressed partly in deerskins, they were no longer *of* the deer. The old ways were no longer valid and, when missionaries came inland from Eskimo Point a short time later, the final dissolution was assured. The Padliermiut became mere fragments of a people whose identity and strength were gone.

But not all of the Padliermiut fled to Padlei.

There were some whose faith was strong enough so that even the inconceivable failure of the deer in the autumn of 1926 could not destroy it. Of these, about fifteen families remained in the ancestral lands, and there most of them perished before 1932 as starvation came again and again into their camps. Some, the strongest and most obdurate of all, traveled up the Kazan through the deserted land, seeking their kinsmen at Ennadai. Amongst them was the towering figure of Igluguarduak who brought his four surviving children into the camps of the Kekertarahatormiut, together with some score of relatives and followers. They were not the only strangers at Ennadai, for others of the broken people had preceded them, and still others followed. Some came from Padlei itself, and these were men who could not bear the servitude to the trap and to the Black-robes.

Some came out of the lonely country to the northeast, between Tulemaliguak and Angikuni. A few even came from the Thelon country where the Akilingmiut had also become a people of the trap — the steel trap for the fox, which had become a greater trap for the people. Throughout the lands of the Ihalmiut those who could not, and would not, discard the old for the new, drifted toward Ennadai, so that before 1930 it had become the last stronghold of the People in the southern half of the Keewatin plains. There was one other stronghold, a small one, far to the north in the vicinity of Garry Lake, but it was now cut off from intercourse with the rest of the inland people, and was to remain so until its ultimate collapse and disappearance.

The remnants of the Ihalmiut who were now concentrated near Ennadai could not have numbered more than three or four hundred. Yet, though their numbers had been so greatly reduced, they were still able to feel themselves a people, and there was strength in them. Here, through the decade ahead, they were to remain and wage their struggle for survival.

In the last years of the 1920's they consisted of four groups. One of these, under the leadership of a man called Ilupalee, occupied the pocket of tundra which thrusts south into the forests just west of Nueltin Lake, and their camps stood beside the shores of Kiyuk, Poorfish and Hogarth Lakes. A second group lived along the Nowleye River, while a third occupied the Kazan itself for a distance of some forty miles north of Ennadai. But the largest and most important group of all were those who called themselves the People of the Little Hills, and who held the northeastern shores of Ennadai and the land about the lakes which are now called Hicks, Stern, Calhoun and McCourt.

This latter band consisted of more than a hundred people, and the two greatest men amongst them were the brothers Kakut and Pommela, whose uncle was Kakumee, the most famous of all the inland Eskimos. These people occupied the central keep, while the three smaller bands held the outer bastions of the shrunken lands of the Ihalmiut.

In the early years of the 1920's there had been probing attacks upon this fortress by the traders from the south, but by 1927 a new and far more formidable invasion had begun. Out of the forests swarmed a strange breed of white men who were to become known as the Barrenland trappers. They were the last wave of the savage flood of anarchy which, a century earlier, had flowed westward to overwhelm an entire continent and to debauch the native peoples in its path. The Barrens trappers were the backwash of that flood, diverted into the bleak lands of the north, and doomed to break and disappear upon the edges of the last frontier. They were men who had cast off the ways of their fellows, or who had been cast off. Restless, unfulfilled, driven either by some consuming hunger within themselves or else by the antipathies of the herd behind them, they came thrusting north seeking to live by the white fox.

For a decade and more the land about Nueltin, Ennadai, and south of Dubawnt Lake was theirs. Most of these men had no law, nor knew of any. The majority hunted foxes not with traps, but with strychnine. They slaughtered the deer with an annihilating savagery in order to leave hundreds of carcasses strewn along the perimeters of their vast hunting areas as bait for foxes. The land was theirs, and they took what they wanted from it, and did what they wanted with it. And the People of the land had no recourse against them. Only twice in twenty years was any shadow of authority seen near the inland country and on these two occasions police patrols approached the verges of the land and then withdrew in haste, having accomplished nothing. In 1932 a Royal Canadian Mounted Police constable stationed at Eskimo Point heard rumors of what was happening in the interior, and reported to his superiors — but no action was taken. There was no law in the interior plains where the last of the Ihalmiut fought their losing battle.

There were some amongst the Ihalmiut who attempted to defend themselves. When one of the trappers entered Igluguarduak's camp and, at gun point, stole a team of dogs, a sled and a woman, he did so in the firm belief that the "Huskies" would not resist. And they did not resist. But some hours later Igluguarduak hitched up his own team of dogs, and in the dark of a winter's evening he caught up to the white man. Igluguarduak returned to his camp with the woman and the stolen team — and when the spring came and the ice melted, the body of the white man floated on the surface of the bright waters.

Yet the Ihalmiut were not fighting men. Even Igluguarduak did not have the courage to remain in that place after the deed was done. Before the spring came he had vanished, accompanied only by his wife and one child. He returned to his old lands north of Hicoliguak where he remained, almost alone, eschewing any contact with the whites at Baker Lake, until he died in 1948 — the last survivor of the Padliermiut to live in the ancestral land.

By 1930 the southern bastion of the Ennadai fortress had been reduced to dust, for Ilupalee's band was scattered and the traders had reached north as far as Ennadai itself. The Barrens trappers roamed at will over the entire area, and with their poison baits they took most of the fur that was available, so that those of the Ihalmiut who had learned to live by the trap could not live. To make matters worse, the Idthen Eldeli had again begun to push northward, drawn by the trading posts, and assured of safety by the presence of the whites.

The slaughter of the caribou became a bloodletting on an almost unprecedented scale, not only on the open plains, but also in the thin forests where the majority of the deer herds wintered. Here, too, the trappers, both white and Indian, needed immense numbers of deer to provide bait and dog feed so that they could operate their long trap lines. Where once the deer had died so that men might be fed and clothed, now these were the least of the reasons for their slaughter.

Starvation became an annual occurrence in the Ihalmiut camps. In 1929 the whole of the Nowleye River band perished of famine, and that river received a new name, becoming the River of Graves. One more bastion was gone. By 1932 the surviving Ihalmiut numbered no more than two hundred people and, in order to survive at all, these had also become slaves to the fox. They were not yet totally enslaved, for they still hunted the deer and, when they were lucky, they were still able to make good hunts. But what had been a certainty to them once had now become entirely a matter of luck, and each year saw their luck grow worse. Only a very few of the best and most determined hunters now dared depend upon the deer. For the rest, their dependence on the fox, and on the food the fox could buy, became greater with each year that passed. It was a poor support at best, for the white trappers took most of the fur, and the traders gave very little in exchange for what fur the Eskimos could catch.

Then, in 1932, the value of white fox pelts, which had declined steeply over the previous two years, suddenly and catastrophically collapsed. Within a year more than three-quarters of the white trappers and traders in the southern Keewatin plains had withdrawn from the land, never to return.

The Ihalmiut were once again in possession of their own country — but the nature of that country had altered drastically. The great and assured herds of deer had vanished, and the people who had once been the People of the Deer could no longer predicate their lives upon the caribou. Thus they were forced to turn more and more to the white fox, even as the value of the fox declined.

Never before in the history of the Barrens had the lives of man and fox been interrelated. Man had depended on the deer, and the fox had depended on the lemming. But the lemming — that mouselike creature of the high arctic — is a cyclic animal. Through four or five years its numbers mount until, usually in the fifth year, there are too many lemmings for the land to support. Then nature takes a hand and disease goes raging through the myriad runways. In the next year there are so few lemmings that many of the predators who depend on their flesh must starve. The white owls flee to the distant south. The foxes grow thin, and disease comes to them also, and in the following year a man may trap all winter and take no more than a dozen white fox pelts.

In the late 1920's when a fox pelt was worth as much as fifty dollars, the low point in the cycle of abundance could be borne by those who depended on the fox, but in 1933, when a prime white fox pelt was often worth less than three dollars, a man who depended on the fox in the years of its scarcity would starve.

It was because of this that the Ihalmiut lands were emptied so abruptly of the white interlopers — but the Ihalmiut could not flee. This was their home, their only and their final home.

So they remained, but they were no longer the People of the Deer. Now they were the People of the Lemming.

And there were fewer of them with each new year. By 1940 when the last official trader, an outpost manager for the Hudson's Bay Company, withdrew from the land, there were 138 Ihalmiut left. After 1940 their sole hope for a futurity lay in an immigrant German, an ex-manager of the company post, who had chosen to remain on in the land. He was the last of the many whites who had come to the Ihalmiut country, had taken what they could get, and who had departed when there was no more to take. He remained not because of any sense of obligation to the People but because he was married to a Cree wife, and had five children who would have found little to their taste in the color-conscious settlements far to the south. Although he continued to hold a trader's licence, he actually did very little trading. The tremendous difficulties of freighting supplies by canoe along the three-hundred-mile waterway from Reindeer Lake ensured that he could make no significant contribution to the growing needs of the Ihalmiut for white men's goods. Though he was a trader in name, he supported his family largely through the efforts of his elder children as trappers on their own account. The furs they caught were the mainstay of the family's precarious existence on the border of the Ihalmiut country.

In effect, therefore, the Ihalmiut were almost totally abandoned, and they could neither return to the old ways nor find a sufficient source of sustenance in the new ways that the whites had taught them.

In the fall of 1942 the people who lived near the head of Ennadai Lake missed the caribou entirely. No one knows which route the shrunken herds followed during that autumn's migration, but they did not come to the old crossing places. And that winter forty-four people, a third of the total surviving population, died of hunger. The trapper-trader at the mouth of Windy River on Nueltin Lake could not help them, for his family also failed to kill sufficient deer to last the winter through, and he had nothing to spare for the Ihalmiut.

By 1946 the land had become a land of graves. In all the many places where the tents of men had stood, from Ennadai to Hicoliguak and even farther north, from Angikuni west to the great sweep of Tulemaliguak, the tents had vanished. Only the circles formed by the anchor stones marked where they had stood, and only the mounded rocks upon the ridges marked where their owners lay.

The Ihalmiut of South Keewatin, who had been a great and numerous people less than forty years earlier, had vanished — save for one tiny pocket of humanity which still gave a semblance of life to a land almost dead. These were the three score People of the Little Hills who still clung stubbornly to the cluster of small lakes northeast of Ennadai, and to a way of life which had become a way of death.

3 *A Spring to Remember*

Along the borders of the Barrens, where the trees grow thin and stunted, stood a score of rough log shanties, many of them no more than hovels, which had been the transient homes of the now vanished white men. In the summer of 1946 all of these were empty; even the squat cabin which crouched below a protecting northern ridge near the mouth of Windy River on Nueltin Lake, and which was the home of the German trapper-trader, held no life. In the spring, when the ice passed from the lakes, the trader and his family had taken their canoe and had made their way southward.

The last white man had gone, but the Ihalmiut had no knowledge of his departure and so it was that in the early summer days two men whose names were Hekwaw and Ohoto set out from their camps near Ennadai to find the white man. They had urgent need of him — they and all the people; for in the hot days of July death had come in a new guise to the camps. Men, women and children lay moaning on the worn deerskin robes. Their throats were choked with swollen membranes and with mucus, and they fought desperately for breath — and none could help them fight. Pommela, the chief shaman of the band, who had many spirits at his command, could do nothing to ward off the new evil which had entered into so many of the People. Ootek, a young man, but a shaman too, had sung his magic songs and had sought out the spirits in a score of trances, but he had failed as well. The two men differed only in the fact that Pommela, recognizing the impotence of his magic, finally took his family and moved away from the tents of the stricken people so that he and his own might not be endangered — while Ootek remained and exhausted himself in the useless struggle until he too fell sick, as did his only child. One shaman had fled, and the other lay stricken in his tent, when Ohoto and Hekwaw took counsel and decided that they must seek the white man's aid.

They walked the sixty miles from their camps to Windy River in two days — and when they came to the cabin where their hopes dwelt, they found the door barred against an emptiness within. So they returned again to their own place, and they came back in time to help heap rocks over the bodies of eighteen people.

Three times during the summer men came out of the north seeking help at the cabin, and found none. But on the fourth visit, in mid-August, the door of the cabin stood unbarred at last.

The trader himself had not returned, nor was he ever to return again, but he had sent his three sons back to the land and to the river beside whose shores their Indian mother had been buried. There was Charles, who had just turned nineteen, and his brothers Fred and Mike, who were, respectively, sixteen and seven years of age. The three had come back to earn their living as trappers. They had not come unwillingly, for this was the only land that they had ever known, and they had suffered intolerable rebuffs amongst the whites during their brief excursion south, because their skin was dark and their blood mixed.

Their canoe, a nineteen-foot freighter, could carry less than a thousand pounds of ammunition, food, clothing and other essential supplies, in addition to the drums of gasoline and its human cargo. This was not enough to see the three boys through the eight months of winter which lay ahead, and it was clear to Charles that he would either have to journey south by dog team and obtain further supplies once the snows had come, or else he and his brothers would have to abandon their trap lines and retreat out of the land long before the winter ended. It is not to be wondered at that there was little space in the canoe for goods to give more than token meaning to the trader's licence which Charles carried folded between the pages of his diary.

Windy River Cabin was thus occupied when, on August 16, Pommela and three other men of the Ihalmiut came to it — but there was little enough for them at the end of their journey.

They told Charles and Fred of the events of the summer, and the two youths listened silently. There was no display of emotion on the part of the tellers, nor of the listeners, for they were equally helpless to change what was past. Charles heard that eighteen people had died of the disease, and though he knew most of them, he could do no more than echo Pommela's fatalistic conclusion to the grim tale, *ayoranamut* — it could not be helped.

Moreover, it was not on behalf of the dead that Pommela and the others had come south. The disease was gone, and the dead were dead. Now the summer was coming to its end, and in a few weeks the deer would begin to mass for the trek to the forest country. The people needed rifle ammunition in order to ensure a good hunt during those critical weeks so that the living would remain alive until spring. It was on account of the living that Pommela and the others had come for the fourth time to the cabin of the traders. There was no ammunition in the camps, nor had there been since late in the preceding winter. Throughout the summer, fear of the diphtheria epidemic had been second only to the fear that, if the traders had indeed left the land for good, there would be no more shells for the ancient rifles, and therefore no deer stored in the meat caches against the winter months.

When Pommela and his companions breasted the ridge by Windy River they carried with them a great apprehension; but the sight of smoke rising from the tin-can chimney, and of the canoe drawn up upon the shore, had seemed to mean release from fear. They had been smiling as they hurried down the slope toward the shack.

Charles knew these people, and he knew what was in their hearts. It was not easy for him, yet he had no choice but to explain that he had very little ammunition — not enough in fact for his own needs.

In the end he gave Pommela and the other men more shells than he could safely spare — but he knew that it was not enough. The Ihalmiut hunters also knew that it was not enough; yet there was nothing to be done. They took what they had been given and turned north, and Charles stood on the ridge above the cabin and watched them diminish into the illimitable distances of the great plains; and the youth was troubled for them.

He had no time to dwell upon it. He was young, and the responsibility he bore was overwhelming. Three people's lives were in his hands, and there was much to do. The deer were coming, and he and Fred must meet them, not only at the cabin, but along as much as possible of their joint trap line which extended northwest a distance of more than two hundred miles to the south shores of Nowleye Lake. Deer carcasses were the essential bait for foxes, and meat caches were the equally necessary fuel depots for the dogs which must drag the heavy winter sleds into the faceless land from which all but a few isolated deer would vanish when the snows had come.

In late August the caribou which were scattered over that measureless expanse of plain had already begun to coalesce and to drain life from the intervening spaces. As the month ended, the growing herds began to drift toward the south, drawing to themselves other small herds in the abortive migration of late summer which reaches to the edge of timber, but no farther.

There, milling in indecision on the borders of the Barrens, the herds await a signal known only to themselves which sends them surging north again, driven by the frantic madness of the rut.

As the deer drifted south in this August of 1946, the people who awaited them beside the Little Hills took toll of them, for it is at this season that the hides are best for winter clothing. The toll was small, for the herds also were small, dispersed, and therefore wary. And the hunters had few shells.

In early September the herds suddenly heard the call, and swung northward, and they were followed by Charles and Fred, who hunted while they traveled. Some of the animals which they shot were left to lie where they had fallen, to serve eventually as bait for foxes, though in the meantime they became prey for the many scavengers — the ravens, gulls, foxes and wolves. Other carcasses were cached beneath rock piles, to be used later on for dog feed. It was too early to put down meat for human use, for the weather was not yet set upon the cold of winter.

Fifty miles north of Windy, Fred turned back, while Charles continued at the heels of the herds until he came to the broad Kazan. Here he found the remnants of the People camped near to crossing places where, in the years gone by, men in kayaks armed with spears had caught the deer between the steep banks of the river, and had killed until there was no more need of killing. In those days the carcasses of the deer had been innumerable, but in this September of another time there were but few dead deer rocked down along the shore. The herds were now too small and too dispersed to give the kayak hunters what they needed, and so most of the hunters had gone out into the plains with rifles, to kill by ones and twos, where once they had killed in tens and twenties at the river crossings.

When Charles came to the camps he found that many of the men were already out of ammunition. He did not investigate the reason for this very closely, but he suspected the truth — that Pommela, into whose hands he had given most of the ammunition intended for all of the Ihalmiut, had retained the bulk of it himself.

Charles did not linger at the camps, for he did not wish to see that which he could not have avoided seeing had he remained — the stone meat caches on the high ridges standing as empty as rifled graves. He was ill at ease in that place of women and children, for he could not escape the knowledge that the children who played by the river edge, and the women who brewed tea for him in the tents, were facing a black future in the months ahead. It made things no easier that no one reproached him for having ammunition which he kept for his own use. He did not like his role, and so he took his dogs, which Pommela and Ohoto had kept for him during the summer, and quickly left the camps.

The first snows had already fallen but there was not yet enough for sled travel, so Charles walked on the frozen plains with the dogs strung out ahead and behind him, half-delirious with their freedom, and driven wild by the heavy scent of caribou which lingered on the long white plains. For the rut was over and the deer too had begun their exodus, so that now the herds were in full flight toward the distant shelter of the forests. Though their paths still seemed innumerable, Charles could remember the time when those faint paths had each been a mighty highway beaten to the rocks beneath. He could remember, as a child, watching the herds come swelling past Windy Cabin in an unbroken river that flowed for days and nights and in his own brief time he had watched that flow shrink and contract until now the remnants of the flood could pass Windy in a single day.

These thoughts were with him when he reached his home. He knew that the best efforts of himself and Fred had not resulted in the slaughter of sufficient deer for their own needs. He guessed, with accuracy, how things would be in the distant camps where the People lived.

When the snows came, and the herds vanished from the plains, most of the People abandoned the camps by the Kazan and retreated to a circlet of little lakes to the eastward where, in times past, occasional small groups of wintering deer had sometimes lingered. Only two families, those of Hekwaw and Katelo, remained beside the river where, in days gone by, they had always known an abundance of deermeat. They remained, partly because of an ephemeral hope that the dead days might again vouchsafe some semblance of their former generosity, and partly because Hekwaw and Katelo, being past the prime of life, could no longer undertake the lean and savage winter hunting expeditions on the wind-swept plains. There were other reasons too. Hekwaw had, in his time, been a great hunter and a famous man, and not the least of his fame was based upon his generosity. Through the long decades he had often taken into his tent unwanted women and orphaned children who might otherwise have perished. In the autumn of 1946 there were many such who had turned to Hekwaw in their extremity. In his skin tent, therefore, there was himself, his two elderly wives, and his two grown sons, together with the widows of two men who had died of disease that summer, and five children who had lost both parents. One of these was an adopted daughter of Pommela's who, in this time of extremity, he had cast off as being only a useless mouth to feed. Thus, even had he wished to follow the rest of the People to the Little Lakes, Hekwaw could not easily have done so.

Hekwaw was sometimes affectionately called *Akla* — the bear — in recognition of his vast bulk, his shambling gait and his broad and placid face. Until the mid-1930's he had resolutely refused to yield his old allegiance to the deer in exchange for the new allegiance to the fox. For years after most of his contemporaries had died, or had moved closer to the trading posts, Hekwaw and his family remained on the Kazan not far south of Angikuni, in the place where he was born. In those days he was like the gray rocks of the Barrens and neither starvation nor disease could break him. Yet it was a lonely life he and his family led, and the Eskimos are a gregarious people. One spring Hekwaw finally succumbed to the nagging of his younger wife and reluctantly joined the remainder of the People near the Little Lakes.

Then his rocklike strength, and his great skill as hunter and provider, proved of no further avail against the fates. From this time onward he shared the torment of the People fully and in his own flesh, for he saw six of his children perish in the country of the Little Lakes, and at the age of fifty he had become an old man.

The tents of the ten families who had moved east from the Kazan were established in two different camps, for though the Ihalmiut were now so few in numbers, they were nevertheless divided against each other. The smallest of the camps was under the hegemony of Pommela and was established by a little lake which bore his name. It consisted of his own two tents and the single tents which housed the families of his followers Alekahaw and Onekwaw.

The members of the other group, who looked to Owliktuk for leadership, had pitched their tents by Halo Lake, five miles from those of the old shaman. The families here were those of Owliktuk, Halo, Yaha, Miki, Elaitutna, Ohoto and Ootek.

Since the days of his youth Pommela had always been full of unpredictable actions and of dangerous passions. He was the antithesis of a true Innuit, for he lived almost entirely for himself, and within himself, and he had early discarded his adherence to the ancient and primary law which binds all Eskimos together in a co-operative way of life. He had been one of those who traded to Brochet and even to Churchill in the early years of the century, and the unique position he had gained as an intermediary between the Ihalmiut and the whites had early given him a taste for personal power. The taste had developed to a consuming hunger as the years advanced, and he had fed it freely. Though he despised all white men, he was astute enough to realize that the source of their power lay in material possessions, and so he had set himself to become something which no Eskimo could ever have envisaged in the past — a wealthy man.

He had succeeded. Now he had two tents, and one of these was filled with an incredible miscellany of useless things purchased over the years from the traders, or taken by stealth or force from his own people. He had not even hesitated at robbing the graves of his dead friends in order to possess himself of their belongings. His second tent was filled with such things as ancient gramophones, rusted and useless rifles, a cast-iron stove for which there was no fuel in this treeless land, and three brass-bound trunks filled with an array of junk of indescribable origin and nature. This rusting wealth was not only of no practical value — it was an actual encumbrance, for it made moving camp a considerable problem. Yet these possessions were more than symbols, for Pommela believed they were an actual source of power, and in the tortuous recesses of his mind, the pursuit of power had come to be the motivation of his life. He was possessed of a ruthless and unquenchable vigor which still showed clearly through the darkly wrinkled face of a man of sixty years. He was feared and hated by all the People, even by the two sycophants, Onekwaw and Alekahaw, who chose to live under his protection.

Pommela had also been cursed with the most terrible physical affliction that an Eskimo man can know, for he was sterile. The fact of his sterility was something that he had never admitted, and during his adult life he had taken seven wives, and had slept with countless other women, in his terrible desire to prove his manhood. As he grew older he had treated the women who failed him with a callousness that had often been their death. In 1946 he was still possessed of two wives, but though there were four children in his tent, none of these were his, for they were the children of his wives by other men, now dead. These children were a symbol of his failure, and he hated them for that.

Pommela was one of the two *angeokoks* — shamans — in the band. Amongst the Eskimos an *angeokok* is both priest and doctor, and, like priests and doctors amongst all races of mankind, some of the *angeokoks* are devoted to the welfare of their people, while others are devoted only to their own welfare. Long ago Pommela had turned the special power of an *angeokok* to his own ends. He controlled many spirits, possessed of a great potential for evil, so that it was a foolhardy man who would openly dare the old man's wrath.

Yet, if none could openly resist the will of Pommela, there

were those who could do so covertly, and chief of these was Owliktuk.

A darkly saturnine man of middle years, Owliktuk's brown eyes and facial cast betrayed the white blood of some vanished trapper. Within himself he had a strength to equal Pommela's, and as great a certainty. He was by far the most effective hunter and the most thoughtful man amongst the people, and he was devoted to the old ways of his mother's race. He had the gift of unobtrusive leadership, and those who chose of their own will to follow him had been spared the worst of the troubles which had afflicted the People through the past two decades. He was a lusty man whose wife had borne and raised five children. But Owliktuk was not an *angeokok,* and herein lay his weakness, for he could not openly contend against Pommela, who possessed so many allies in the world of spirits. Owliktuk could only dis-associate himself and his followers as much as possible from the old man who was so hated and so deeply feared.

There was, however, an *angeokok* amongst Owliktuk's group. This was Ootek, a young man, and a dreamer of dreams. Ootek was a true priest, for he revered the forces that are not of our world, and he was humble before them. All his talents and his energies were pressed into the search for understanding of the omnipotent forces which control human destiny. He was a seeker after truth. And he was no match for Pommela.

When Charles drove his dog team north in mid-November to prepare his trap line he paid a visit to Pommela's camp. The old shaman greeted him with an unction that lasted only until he discovered that Charles could not, or would not, give him a sack of flour. Though he invited the youth into his main tent, he did so with a brusqueness which was nicely calculated to sus-tain the faint unease Charles always felt in the old man's presence. Charles did not like Pommela, nor did he trust him, yet he had never quite dared to cross him. And Pommela, who knew much of men, was aware that the young trapper harbored the seeds of fear within himself.

Ikok, Pommela's younger wife, served the two men boiled

deer tongues on a wooden platter and, while they ate, and drank the broth in which the tongues had been cooked, Pommela dominated the conversation. He told Charles that, due to the lack of ammunition, the people had killed less than half the deer which were required to sustain them until spring. He spoke of hunger that had already come to the camps and, with a bland disregard for visual evidence, he went so far as to claim that even he and his family were on the verge of starvation. "Give me more shells," he demanded. "I will share them with the other hunters, and then we will all have meat."

It was a demand that expressed his open contempt for the younger man since Pommela knew that Charles would not credit his own protestations of hunger, and he was also fully aware that Charles suspected him of having kept for his own use most of the ammunition which he had obtained at Windy Cabin.

Charles showed no resentment. His belief in his superiority over this sparse-bearded native was not proof against Pommela's powerful presence, and he was afraid to make an open enemy of the old man. He resolved to avoid all the Eskimos as much as possible, particularly Pommela, in the months which stretched ahead. He had done what he could for them, and he could do no more.

Rousing his dogs, the young trapper drove hurriedly away into the northwest. He spent that night in his outpost cabin on the banks of the Kazan and in the morning drove on across the frozen muskegs to the River of Graves. Turning north on its slick and almost snow-free surface, he slipped and slithered along behind his dogs as they struggled for a foothold on the patches of glare ice. Two days later he reached Nowleye Lake and, after a brief night's rest, turned south again, locating and unearthing his caches of traps, and making his "sets" along the route.

Charles had expected to find some wintering deer, for although the main herds abandon the land when the snows come, there are usually a few who lag behind. In this hope he was completely disappointed, for he saw neither deer nor tracks of deer. The fact that he was thus unable to replenish the rapidly dwindling supplies of meat he had brought with him on his sled was cause enough for apprehension. But when he reached the cabin at Kazan he found new reasons for disquietude. Two of the caribou carcasses which he had cached there in the fall were missing, and it was clear from the tracks in the snow that they had been taken by Eskimos. The implications of this theft were obvious to Charles. He knew that none of the Ihalmiut, with the exception of Pommela, would ever rob a cache unless driven to it by absolute necessity. The theft of these two deer, therefore, suggested that the situation in the Innuit camps must already be very serious; yet Charles did not deviate from his route to seek confirmation. He drove on south as fast as his dogs could go until he reached the sanctuary of Windy Cabin.

A growing foreboding as to what he might encounter in the north kept him at Windy Cabin until the end of December. A dozen times he told himself that he must visit his trap line on the Nowleye River, and a dozen times he found a reason for delay. By the end of December he could no longer postpone the trip and so he reluctantly loaded his sled with dog feed for ten days, said good-by to Mike and Fred, and turned into the threatening distances of the north. He made the journey at breakneck speed, driving his dogs unmercifully. Deliberately he avoided the Eskimo camps on the Little Lakes, nor did he linger at the Kazan cabin. The weather was kind to him and there were no storms, so that by January 2 he had reached his farthest north at Nowleye Lake and was ready to turn about. Once more he had failed to find any sign of winter deer, and their continued absence gave rise to an oppressive sense of impending disaster which acted as a goad and sent him south at the best pace his tired dogs could muster. The days were short, and the nights long and very dark. It was a time for the uncouth spirits of the rocks to walk abroad, and Charles's European blood was not wholly proof against their threats.

So it was with a relief bordering on the irrational that he came again to the Kazan cabin and recognized Fred's dogs tied up outside the tiny shack. His relief was short-lived. Fred was indeed there (for this place was the northern terminus of the younger boy's trap line) but he was not alone. With him were Halo and Ootek who had walked the twenty-five miles from Owliktuk's camp, impelled by the faint hope that they might encounter Charles or Fred and obtain assistance from them.

They told their story simply, and it was a bleak account. The meat supplies with which they had begun the winter had proven hopelessly inadequate, for Pommela had refused them any of the ammunition he had obtained from Charles and they had only possessed a beggarly handful of shells which Owliktuk had managed to save over from the preceding spring. Though they had hunted hard at the river during the autumn crossings, using kayaks and spears, the herds had been few and evasive, and the water kill had provided only enough meat for a month or two at most.

With the advent of the first snows, and the departure of the herds, the land had been completely emptied of the deer. Though the best hunters had roamed the plains for days armed with crude bows which they had hurriedly built after the ancestral patterns, they had not found a single winter deer upon which to try their dubious skill with these ancient weapons. Then, in late November, even these desperate journeys had been brutally curtailed. In this of all years the fatal dog disease which comes from the foxes and the wolves (and which is probably a form of distemper) had struck their teams. The dogs, already much weakened by starvation, had so little resistance left that within two weeks only four out of nearly fifty still survived. Nor had these four long outlived their fellows, for there had been no more food to spare for them, and before the end of the month they too were dead.

The people of Owliktuk's camp were already displaying overt signs of famine. Halo and Ootek showed the onset of starvation in the tautness of the skin across the bones of their faces and in the unnatural brilliance of their eyes. They showed it too in the way they ate the meat which Fred had given them, cramming themselves with frozen slivers of deer flesh until their bellies were distended.

By the time Charles arrived at the Kazan cabin, the immediate hunger of the two men had been assuaged, but their fears for the future had been increased. They had hoped against hope that Charles might have received more supplies from the south — perhaps by airplane, as had happened once or twice in the days when the Hudson's Bay Company still operated Windy Post. These hopes dissolved when Fred told them that, far from having supplies to trade, the boys were almost out of food and would soon have to travel south for more if they were to survive.

It was a mirthless irony that this winter found the white foxes at the peak of their cycle and abundance. They had come drifting out of the north that autumn in their hundreds, like small ghosts, and their neat tracks were everywhere. Charles and Fred had already taken more than fifty pelts apiece despite the desultory manner of their trapping. But the Ihalmiut who over the years had been turned into hunters of the fox, and taught to live by the fox, had been unable to take more than a score of pelts amongst them. They had no dogs to enable them to visit distant trap lines. They had no meat for bait, nor enough even to give them strength to maintain short trap lines which could be visited on foot. And now they knew that any foxes which they might manage to procure would be worthless anyway, for there was no way that the pelts could be metamorphosed into food.

To Charles and Fred the news of the outbreak of distemper amongst the Eskimo dogs was of such frightening import that it preoccupied their thoughts to the point where the plight of the Eskimos themselves was virtually forgotten. They knew that if the disease took many of their own dogs they would not only have to abandon their trap lines, but they might be isolated at Windy Cabin without supplies, and unable to make a dash south to the trading posts at Brochet or Duck Lake in order to replenish them. They felt sorry for Halo and Ootek and the rest, but their own plight engrossed their whole attention.

The two Eskimos left the cabin that same day. They took with them a few pounds of frozen meat — but they also took the knowledge that no assistance could be hoped for from the post at Windy River.

Charles and Fred set off for Windy before dawn the following morning. They were consumed by anxiety about their dogs, and even more determined to give the Eskimos as wide a berth as possible; but they reckoned without Pommela.

The old shaman, driving the remnants of a team, intercepted the youths as they halted to brew tea at midday. He came up to the little fire as if it had been his own, and truculently announced that all the members of his band were coming south to Windy in a few days' time, and that he expected them to be supplied with food. Charles's residual fear of the shaman was heightened by Pommela's bold demeanor, and he was unable to make any effective protest.

However, Pommela did not make good his threat at once, and during the next week Charles and Fred took stock of their position. It was by no means good. They had only enough "store food" on hand to last, with careful rationing, until the end of January. Their supply of deermeat had been reduced to about forty carcasses, widely dispersed in several caches between Windy and the Kazan, and there was only enough frozen fish on hand to feed the dogs for one long trip. If the Eskimos did not come to Windy Cabin, Charles thought that he and his brothers might be able to hold out until sometime in February; but on January 18, the Eskimos began arriving. The first to come were Onekwaw and Alekahaw and their families — eight hungry people with three starving dogs. Two days later Pommela arrived with one wife and two of his adopted children. Pommela immediately demanded meat for his dogs and for his family, and without waiting for permission he went to a cache behind the cabin and helped himself. Onekwaw and Alekahaw were not slow to follow his example, and Charles made no attempt to stop them.

On the 27th, Pommela announced that he was returning north to get the rest of his family, and Charles decided to accompany him in order to bring back some meat he had cached at North Camp, which was some forty miles from Windy. When the two men reached North Camp, Charles found that the cache had been completely emptied. It was indicative of Pommela's sense of his own power that he frankly admitted to having been the thief.

Charles's anger was intense, yet he mastered it. The knowledge that Pommela had allowed him to make this trip, knowing full well he would find an empty cache at the end of it, was bitter; but neither bitterness nor rage could free him from the trepidation which the old man inspired in him. Without a word Charles turned his team and headed south.

Immediately upon his arrival at the home cabin he warned Fred that their position had now become dangerous, for they could no longer count on salvaging any of their caches on the land. It was decided therefore that Fred and Mike should take one team and head south at once in a bid to reach Duck Lake trading post and there obtain fresh supplies. Fred took with him the last of the fish that had been set aside for dog feed, and departed on that same day, traveling light and fast.

By the end of January all of Pommela's people were clustered close about Windy Cabin. They very soon consumed the remaining deermeat which Charles had held in reserve, and they were still starving — all of them, that is, except Pommela and his favorite wife who remained well fed and energetic even while Pommela's adopted children grew steadily weaker and more subdued.

Charles soon began to find the atmosphere intolerable. He was aware that Pommela probably possessed more food than he did himself, and he grew increasingly uneasy as the old man's assumption of dominance became more and more blatant. Moreover, while he could shut his mind to some extent to the agonies of famine if the evidence was not before his eyes, he could not now avoid seeing that the children and many of the adults at Windy Cabin were approaching the ultimate stages of starvation.

Five days of this was as much as he could stand. On the sixth day Charles hitched up his team and, though he was very short of dog feed, he too headed down the ice of Nueltin Lake, intending to intercept Fred at the south end, on his return from Duck

Lake Post. Charles had made up his mind that, if he could get enough supplies from Fred, he would carry on to Brochet where he could divest himself of some of the unwanted but steadily increasing feeling of responsibility toward the hungry Eskimos, by reporting their plight to someone in authority.

The two boys met near Johnstons Island in south Nueltin on February 3. Fred had a full load of flour, lard, tea and sugar, but he had been able to obtain only a little ammunition, and no dog feed. Reluctantly Charles had to abandon his plan for proceeding south. This decision was made somewhat easier for him when Fred related how he had persuaded the manager of the isolated Duck Lake Post to send out a message on his primitive wireless set, giving at least an indication of the scope and nature of the tragedy which threatened the inland Eskimos.

This message, which appears to have been the first ever to be dispatched to the outside world on behalf of the Ihalmiut, suffered an unknown fate. Almost certainly it reached the federal government department which was responsible for Eskimo affairs. Most probably it then sank into dusty obscurity in some weighty file and was forgotten. In any event, it elicited no response.

The food Fred had brought from Duck Lake was sufficient to hold the hounds of hunger at bay for a week or two, but it was quite insufficient to be of help to the remaining Ihalmiut who were still in their camps to the north of Windy. The condition of these people was now something which Charles could no longer keep out of his conscious mind. A day after he and his brothers returned to the cabin, one of Hekwaw's sons, Belikari, also arrived there, from the Kazan. Belikari was in frightful condition, barely able to walk, and clad in rags of skins. It was some time before he recovered sufficiently to tell his harrowing story. His father's tent, crowded with women and unwanted children, had seen no food for weeks, except scraps of skin clothing, and bones dug from under the snows. No winter deer had come to the Kazan, and attempts to fish through the river ice had yielded almost no results. Death for all the inhabitants of the place was no more than an arm's length away.

This account, coupled with what Charles could see with his own eyes of the apathetic lethargy of starving children at the cabin door, finally resolved the conflict in his mind. He knew he could no longer stand apart. Now he must take sides, and though he must have deeply resented his involvement in something which was, after all, none of his affair, and which would mean that he would have to abandon his own attempts to gain a livelihood from this hard land, he nevertheless consciously now chose the harder course. In doing so he became the first outlander in all time to concern himself with the plight of the inland Eskimos.

On February 8, Charles hitched up his team (from which distemper had already stolen his two best dogs) and, taking with him thirty pounds of rolled oats as food for himself and his remaining dogs, he set out on the three-hundred-mile route south to Brochet.

That was an epic journey. He accomplished it in eleven days, but during the last three days there was not a scrap of food for man or dogs. Both he and his team were so utterly exhausted before they reached the Hudson's Bay post at the north end of Reindeer Lake that they had to be helped up the slope from the lake ice to the settlement. And the hazards of that long trek had been greatly intensified by the fact that at the few isolated camps of the Idthen Eldeli which lay upon the route death stood waiting to receive the traveler. An epidemic of influenza was raging through the thin forests between Nueltin and Reindeer with such ferocity that, before spring came, it was to take the lives of 76 Indians from a total Chipewyan population of 265. Charles encountered the disease at an Idthen Eldeli camp near Kasmere Lake. He had hoped to obtain food at this place, but when no one came out to welcome him he entered the squalid cabin and beheld the naked corpses of three people who had flung off their clothing during the paroxysms of fever, and whose contorted bodies gave a terrible warning to the chance visitor.

Charles remained at Brochet, which was itself in the grip of the epidemic, only long enough to rest and feed his dogs for the return trip. He reported to the Hudson's Bay post manager on conditions amongst the Ihalmiut, and his account was relayed by radio to the Indian Affairs Department doctor at The Pas.

On February 24 he started north again. The snows lay deep and soft in the forests, and no other travelers were moving, so that there were no packed trails to follow. Charles's team could draw the long Eskimo sled only with great difficulty. They could haul no more than five hundred pounds of freight, of which a hundred pounds was frozen fish for dog feed. Even though this was a comparatively light load, Charles was still forced to cache half of it at the south end of Nueltin Lake, and when he arrived back at Windy Cabin on March 7, exhausted and with exhausted dogs, he had with him only sufficient food to last the three boys for a few more weeks.

But fortune, which had forsaken the Ihalmiut, had been kinder to the three outlanders. On March 5, Fred, hunting far afield, had encountered a herd of twenty deer at the edge of timberline and had succeeded in killing eight of them. Together he and Charles hauled the carcasses back to Windy Cabin.

Meanwhile some of the People who had come to the cabin seeking help had given up all hope of it and had gone plodding north again. Alekahaw and his family were amongst these desperate ones, but they were lucky, for they stumbled upon the frozen remains of a deer that had probably died of gunshot wounds the preceding autumn. Alekahaw, with his wife and daughter, camped by the carcass until nothing remained of it but tufts of hair and fragments of cracked bones.

Belikari had traveled with them, but he did not stay to share their good luck. He walked on into the white and hungry land toward the distant tent of his father by the banks of the Kazan, where the people who awaited his coming sustained themselves on hope alone.

At Windy Cabin the eight deer vanished with such incredible rapidity that by March 14 Charles concluded that he and his brothers would have to abandon the post and flee southward while they still could. They had already begun their preparations for the trip when they became aware of a strange sound pulsing in the hard gray sky. They ran out of the cabin in time to see the stubby silhouette of a Norseman ski-plane slip over the Ghost Hills to the south and level off for an approach to the ice of Windy Bay.

The remaining Eskimos had also heard the sound and they had come crawling from their tents to stare incredulously at this salvation coming to them from the skies. Onekwaw's wide and foolish face was contorted in an expression of almost insane relief, while his young wife swayed beside him shrieking with hysterical laughter.

She did not laugh for long.

There was no laughter at that place when the plane came to a halt and Charles, wrenching open the door, discovered that it contained no food of any kind.

The chartered Norseman belonging to Lamb Airways of The Pas, with the Indian Affairs doctor as a passenger, had carried food when it set out from The Pas — in fact it had been laden with 1300 pounds of food. At Brochet it had stopped to pick up Charles's father as a guide, but then, for some inexplicable reason, it had flown to the *south* end of Nueltin Lake, where it had landed, and the supplies had been unloaded on the ice, before the flight to Windy was completed.

There was no time for Charles to obtain an explanation. The Norseman remained only long enough for Tom Lamb, the pilot, to call out that he would return the following day bringing a second load of relief rations direct to Windy, before the plane swung into the wind and in a few more minutes had vanished over the southern hills.

The plane did not return the next day, nor the next. On the morning of the sixth day of waiting Charles hitched up his remaining dogs — four had now died of the disease — and he had already started for south Nueltin when he heard the roar of the plane approaching.

He hurried back and was in time to help unload the relief supplies. These totaled eight hundred pounds, one hundred pounds of which consisted of dried white beans that were of as little use to the starving people of the plains as lead pellets might have been. In a land where half a day's hard searching may sometimes yield only enough willow twigs to melt sufficient snow to make a pint of water, these beans were worthless. They were still lying, untouched, in Windy Cabin a full year later.

This "mercy flight" — it was later publicized as such — represented the total assistance which the authorities considered was required to meet the needs of the Ihalmiut. The doctor departed, having visited none of the camps and having seen no Eskimos at all except the watching figures of Pommela's and Onekwaw's families on the distant shore of Windy Bay.

It was a gesture which presumably served a purpose as far as Ottawa was concerned, but it had no meaning for the people of the land. It had no effect upon Owliktuk's camp, for instance, where thirty people clung upon the brink of dissolution. As early as the first week in February all the food in this camp had been exhausted and the people had been forced to scrabble beneath the hard-packed snow for refuse discarded in the fall. Huddled in their deerskin tents, which had been banked with blocks of snow, these people endured the searing cold of winter with empty stomachs, and with only remnants of fur clothing upon their bodies. They had no fires, for no one had the strength to spare for the arduous search for willow twigs beneath the drifts. They lived on scraps of skin, on frozen carrion, and some of them even searched out and ate human excrement; for there are no niceties of taste when death lies hard and cold within the belly.

Near the end of March, and at about the time that the authorities concluded their rescue mission, the situation in Owliktuk's camp reached a climax. Owliktuk was aware that if his people remained where they were for even a few more days, they would be incapable of ever moving again. They had held on at the old camp site in the desperate hope that some winter deer would come within their reach, but Owliktuk now recognized that this was a forlorn hope. He knew it would be fatal to remain, but that it might be just as fatal to risk moving camp, for there was no real prospect of finding food anywhere in all the land. Halo's and Ootek's meeting with Charles and Fred at the Kazan cabin had made it clear that nothing could be gained by attempting to reach Windy Cabin. Yet it seemed to Owliktuk that there might still be one remote chance for their survival. Ninety miles to the eastward, at Otter Lake, a tiny outpost of a Churchill trading firm had operated spasmodically for some years past. There — if the people could reach the post — they might conceivably obtain some food. It was a slim possibility, made slimmer by the fact that a march of ninety miles, in subzero temperatures and on almost empty bellies, must tax the strength and endurance of the emaciated scarecrows who were Owliktuk's people beyond all limits.

Nevertheless Owliktuk saw it as the only hope, and when he had explained his intentions to the heads of the other families, they agreed to follow him.

That incredible march began about the 1st of April. The people took three sleds which carried the younger children who could not walk for any distance. The men hauled the sleds, and the women walked behind, some of them carrying babies in their parkas. The only food they had with which to begin that journey consisted of the flesh of three dogs which had died of distemper, and which Owliktuk had kept concealed against a last emergency. The only hope they had of obtaining food along the way lay in a rusty .22 rifle — a "spit gun," as the people call such a weapon — fit only for killing such small game as ptarmigan and arctic hares, and in seven boxes of .22 ammunition belonging to Miki. Their clothes were scanty and of poor quality for, due to the shortage of ammunition, they had not been able to obtain enough prime deer hides during the late summer to provide adequate winter clothing. They were as ill equipped in almost every physical aspect as they could possibly have been for such a journey. But they were well equipped in another sense. They were enduring, and they were indomitable.

They had much to endure. For five days they walked to the eastward and found nothing for their bellies. They were by then so weak that the women and the older people could no longer walk more than two to three miles in a day. At this juncture Yaha, plodding ahead of the straggling line, came upon the remains of a caribou that had been killed and eaten by wolves. There was not much left but bones, gristle and offal, but the find represented salvation for the band. They camped here for two days, and when they moved on there were not even any bone fragments left for the lesser scavengers.

On the tenth day Ootek saw and killed a single arctic hare with the .22 rifle — a morsel of flesh amongst so many. But that hare, and the remains of the deer, comprised the total sustenance the people were able to extract from the frozen land during the entire trek.

It sufficed — almost. Near the end of the second week two of the little band reached the end of all their journeying. One of these was Epeetna, an old woman who was the wife of Elaitutna, and her journey had been long indeed, for it had spanned more than sixty years. The other was a baby less than a year old, who died at the dried-up breasts of its mother Nanuk, who was Ohoto's wife.

That any of the people could have survived that ordeal seems unbelievable, yet in the middle of April, when they were less than two days distant from the goal, all of them still clung tenaciously to life except for Epeetna, and Nanuk's child. They had come so far, but they could go no farther as a band. And so they camped — crowding together under some fragments of deer hides which served as tents — while three of the men, Owliktuk, Ootek and Ohoto, went on alone.

These three reached the tiny shanty which was the trader's home and they tried to make known their urgent need to him. But the trader either did not understand them (for they had no furs to trade) or he had no food to spare. He did accept some boxes of .22 ammunition in exchange for a small bag of flour, but that was all the help the people were destined to receive from him.

During the next few days all those who could walk or crawl to the post did so, and they tried in every way they knew to make their plight apparent to the trader. It did no good. Eventually they returned to the travel camp to await the inevitable end of their travail.

They waited almost until the end of April — but there were some who could not wait.

There was Elaitutna, Ohoto's father.

There was Nanuk's three-year-old son Aljut.

There was Uktilohik, the year-old son of Owliktuk and Nutaralik.

None of these could wait any longer, and so they died. The rest of the people must surely have followed in a little while, but in the last days of the month a single caribou, the forerunner of the northward migrating herds, appeared in the very middle of the silent camp where men lay dying. It was Ootek who found the strength to fire a shot from the despised .22 rifle — and it was he who killed the deer.

They ate that deer, even to its bones, and then they left their dead buried under the snow and turned westward on the terrible road they had followed from their home camps. It took them eighteen days to return, but they could not travel very fast, and they were often forced to spend a day or so in camp while the men hunted ptarmigan whose spring flocks were again coming back into the land. It was late in May before they reached the Little Lakes, and here they met Hekwaw. That good old man had at last obtained some ammunition from Charles, and had made a kill of the north-bound deer, so that he was able to feed the wanderers. For them that winter of torment was at an end.

Hekwaw had saved Owliktuk's band, but he could not bring his own dead back to life. In the long days before the deer belatedly returned to the plains, death had lived in Hekwaw's camp, and was only driven out at last when Charles took up the task that the authorities had laid down.

On March 21, the day after the plane had come a second time to Windy Cabin, Charles started north. His few surviving dogs were emaciated and they could only haul two hundred pounds of flour and lard, together with some oatmeal for dog feed. Even with this light load they moved very slowly and it was not until March 24 that Charles reached the first camp, that of Alekahaw. He found the family on the verge of death. He gave them food and hurried on toward the Kazan camp where he knew Katelo and Hekwaw had their tents. He did not stop at dusk, but urged his dogs forward into the darkness until they collapsed and could go no farther.

Early the next morning he reached his destination to find that death had long preceded him.

Death had indeed come early, and had stayed late amongst the two families who had waited here for help that never came. And the ones who had been unable to wait were these.

There was Oquinuk, who was Katelo's wife.

There was Homoguluk, a ten-year-old orphan.

There was Itkuk, the widow of Angleyalak.

There was Eepuk, who was one of Hekwaw's wives.

There was Pama, a fifteen-year-old daughter of the dead Angleyalak.

Of those who still lived, only Hekwaw, Belikari, Katelo, and Katelo's son Iktoluka could stand upon their feet.

Charles camped with them for two days; scoured the country about with his team to find fuel for them; fed them and watched over them. On the third day he led them south to the Kazan cabin where they joined Alekahaw's family who had already come there on Charles's instructions.

Charles himself hurried south again, for he was aware that the food he had brought would not last for many days. Reaching Windy he instructed Fred to carry a second load of food north while he himself drove to the south end of Nueltin to freight back some of the supplies which the Norseman had left there upon the ice.

From April 5 to May 31, Charles and Fred traveled more than twelve hundred miles behind their worn-out dogs, freighting supplies northward to the people in the starvation camps. They had no time to rest, no time to look at their own trap lines which had been abandoned since January. By the end of May both boys were drawn so fine that their high cheekbones seemed about to burst from the young dark skin. And it was in this condition that I found these two who had the will to do what no other human beings would do, to succor a people who had been savaged by adversity and doomed by our neglect.

4 *The Drums of Hope*

THE deer came late to the inland plains in the spring of 1947.
During the final days of May the main herds swelled out of
the forests and streamed past Windy Post, directly driven by a
nameless urgency. The does came first, their swollen bellies
swaying as they breasted the softening drifts and climbed the
ridges where the last dwarfed trees clung in mute defiance of
the endless winds which strove to put them down.

Barely pausing to snatch a few mouthfuls of lichens from the
high crests where the snows had already vanished under the
harsh impact of the spring sun, the does streamed northward
seeking the fawning grounds before their time was on them.
Before the end of the month they were passing through the
country of the Ihalmiut and, for the first time in many months,
children smiled and men went out to hunt knowing that they
would not come back empty-handed.

So the turn of May brought the familiar visitation of the deer back to the land, but it also brought another, and a stranger, visitation. On the afternoon of June 3, a twin-engined Anson aircraft of wartime vintage came rumbling out of the east and landed roughly on the ice of Windy Bay.

When I climbed down from the plane and looked about me I thought that I had never seen such utter desolation. Under a gray and scudding sky the dark snows, the black lines of treeless hills, and the crouching back of an all-but buried and apparently deserted cabin sounded no note of welcome. There was a real temptation to clamber back into the old Anson and leave this place to its own abysmal loneliness; but I had worked too hard to get here, and I had made my decision and could not go back upon it.

The manner and the causes of my coming to Windy River have been described in detail in my previous book *People of the Deer*. It will suffice now to say that I was in flight from five years of war memories and that I was in search of a people whom I had no reason either to despise or fear, and of whose existence I was not even certain. A chain of accidents led to Windy River becoming my objective in that whole vast realm of the interior Barrens; and the consummate skill of a man now dead — the pilot of the Anson — enabled me to overleap the barriers of the land.

During the first few days of my stay in the musty, frigid cabin, I was sure that I had made a blunder and that I would come no nearer to finding the people whom I sought. But after a week of gloom during which I cursed myself for my impetuous and almost completely uninformed venture into a land which seemed so desolate and hostile, the mood was shattered by the arrival of Charles. He came out of the north, driving a shrunken team, and returning from his fifth and final trip freighting supplies to the camps of the Ihalmiut.

The shock of discovering a stranger in his cabin was so great that it nearly robbed him of speech for a matter of several hours. That did not matter since, in my delight at finding him, I was loquacious enough for two. Slowly the barriers dissolved, and within a few weeks we had become friends. It was a friendship which was to grow with the passing months during which we traveled together on foot and by canoe for almost two thousand miles. And it was through Charles that I found the people I had sought — the People of the Little Hills.

In the latter part of June we visited their camps, having half-paddled and half-carried our canoe up the roaring freshet named Little River; over the height of land, and down the small stream which the Ihalmiut called Tingmeaku — Goose Creek.

When we came amongst them, the People still bore clear evidence of their sufferings of the winter in every lineament of their faces — yet they were full of laughter and of an intense vivacity which perhaps belongs only to those who have escaped from what has seemed like certain death. They received a stranger from a race they had little cause to love, without restraint, and there was no limit to their hospitality.

During the journey north I had come to some appreciation of the gigantic proportions of that land, and I had felt a growing sense of unease at the absence of human life. Nor was this sensation much alleviated at the Ihalmiut camps, for there were only forty-nine of the People left, and this minute congregation seemed frighteningly insignificant in that limitless expanse of empty plain.

In June of 1947 the Ihalmiut were camped beside the shores of three little lakes which were first mapped — from the air — and named by us in 1954. They are now officially known as Calhoun, Stern and McCourt Lakes, but in 1947 they were still known to the people of the plains by the names of Ootek, Halo and Pommela. These names have been obliterated now, for it is in our nature to obliterate even such ephemeral traces of those we have destroyed.

By the lake which bore his name lived Ootek, the young shaman, with his wife Howmik, and their daughter Kalak, who had been born just after the return from the starvation trek to Otter Lake. Kalak was born deaf and dumb, out of the sufferings of her mother, but the child was nonetheless dear to Ootek, for she was the only child surviving out of the four children to whom Howmik had given birth in the years of their marriage.

In a tent set cheek by jowl with Ootek's lived Halo and his wife Kikik. They had two surviving children out of the three which had been born to them, and this was a tribute to Halo's competence, for, next to Owliktuk, he was the best provider amongst the people, and the most indomitable man. He was a far better hunter than Ootek, yet these two were inseparable, for what the one lacked the other had. Ootek's abilities were of the mind and spirit and these were the perfect complement to Halo's competence with the hard realities of existence in the plains. They were so close, these two, that they were almost one.

The rest of Owliktuk's group — to which Ootek and Halo belonged — had pitched their conical skin tents a mile away by Halo Lake. The largest and the best-made tent of all belonged to Owliktuk, his wife Nutaralik and their four surviving children. Such was the determination and effectiveness of this man that he had lost only one child — Uktilohik — during the hungry years. Calm, reserved, yet incisive in a time of trouble, he had become the acknowledged leader of six families of the People, not by any overt domination, but solely by the power of his example. Yet leadership gave Owliktuk no pleasure, as it did Pommela. It had come to him unasked, and he bore it in the knowledge that no single man, nor yet a combination of all the men of the Ihalmiut, could forestall an inevitable end. Owliktuk had no illusions — he remembered the past, and he could understand the pattern it had made, so that he knew what the future must be. It was his tragedy that though he strove endlessly, he could find no sure avenue of escape. His dark reflections were not natural to the mind of an Eskimo, and it may be that they were a gift he had from the unknown white man who had fathered him. Yet, if he foresaw a hopeless future, Owliktuk never thought of bowing to it. He defended himself stubbornly and with such skill that it was inevitable that he should become the strong core of the decimated People.

Amongst those who looked to him for leadership were Yaha —
an amiable and gentle fellow, but a good hunter for all of that —
and Miki, who was a taciturn and withdrawn man given to
moments of bleak fatalism. Miki's father had also been a white
man, and he had abandoned Miki and his mother one bitter winter leaving the mother to die of starvation in her efforts to keep
the boy alive. Miki survived only because he was accidentally discovered in the spring by Owliktuk's father, in the tiny cabin
where he had lived for weeks with the dead and decaying body
of his mother.

There was one other who belonged in part at least to Owliktuk's group, and he was perhaps the most tragic figure amongst
the people. This was Ohoto. A squat and burly man, he was remarkable for his quick perceptiveness, his sharp intelligence —
and his consuming sense of frustration. Years earlier, when he
was still a boy, he had visited Reindeer Lake in company with
his father, and out of that visit a steadily burgeoning desire to
become one with the white men had been born within him. Like
Owliktuk, Ohoto understood that his people, and their way of
life, were doomed; but unlike the older man, Ohoto had never
accepted the hopelessness of his position. He believed, with a
blind and pitiful faith, that it would be possible to evade his
fate if he could only transform himself into a white man; and
through the long years he had labored toward this impossible
objective. He no longer really belonged in the land of his fathers,
yet he was unable to escape from it. He aped the white men and
their ways in every possible manner. Several times he had accompanied Charles to Brochet, where he had even embraced Christianity at the hands of a missionary priest. For a while he had
striven to obey the injunctions of the Church, but when he discovered that these would lead him not to equality and acceptance by the whites, but only to another kind of servitude, he
angrily discarded them; and the words *Jesoosi Kristoosi* became
a curse upon his lips.

In the summer of 1946 his wife Kekwaw, whom he had loved
deeply, died of diphtheria. Ohoto took another wife, an aging
widow called Nanuk, but she could give him no peace, and his

restless, caged and rebel spirit continued to drive him so that he moved like a snow-ghost about the land, sometimes camping near Pommela, sometimes near Owliktuk, but more often by himself — except on those rare occasions when there was a white man within reach, and then Ohoto attached himself to the stranger like a veritable leech.

Only in Pommela's camp did I encounter any indication of hostility towards my own race. The old shaman had come through the winter with still greater certainty in his own powers, and with an increased contempt for the rest of the Ihalmiut who had submitted to his tyranny. Here, in his own land, he had no doubts as to my inferiority, and he made no secret of it — though later, when it became apparent that I could be of use to him, he changed his attitude.

His camp consisted of his own two tents and those of Katelo, Onekwaw and Alekahaw. Onekwaw was a wild-visaged, half-fey fellow whose shy smile and unbridled laughter could not hide the vast uncertainty which haunted him. He was childless (though his wife Tabluk had a daughter by another marriage) and he was Pommela's sycophant and totally under his control.

Not so Alekahaw, son of the great shaman Igluguarduak. He was a sly and clever opportunist and though he adhered to Pommela's group, this was solely because he found it advantageous to do so.

Katelo, who was Pommela's younger brother, lived in company with his twelve-year-old son; and there was no longer any woman in their tent to cook and sew for them and to give comfort when they returned from the hunt. Katelo was a broken and lonely man who had all but lost the will to live. In his lifetime he had watched three wives and seven children die of hunger and disease and now he was old and very weary, and he no longer cared.

These, with Hekwaw's family, which lived apart from the two opposing camps, were the survivors of the People of the Deer when I first knew them.

At the time of that visit I had the most superficial knowledge of their history, even of their immediate past. It was not until nearly two months later, when Charles's taciturnity had melted and he had talked many a long night down, that I began to understand something of the nature of their experience. By then I had begun to be aware of the fearful want of humanity which we had displayed toward these people, and that awareness was brought into sharp focus by an event which took place in mid-August.

While the message that Charles had radioed to The Pas from Brochet had accomplished little for the Ihalmiut in an immediate sense, it had resulted in the first official recognition of the existence of the inland people by the government. Governments are notoriously ponderous and slow to act, but once having admitted that the Ihalmiut did exist the authorities were inevitably bound to display some show of interest in, and concern for, these long-lost people.

Consequently in mid-August of 1947 Tom Lamb's plane was chartered by an Indian Affairs representative. This plane made three flights to Windy Cabin. On the first flight it carried a doctor and a full load of aviation gasoline for the use of the pilot in future operations on the Barrens. The party went no farther than Windy Cabin, saw no Eskimos, and returned south. On the second flight the aircraft also carried the doctor's wife. The three visitors enjoyed a pleasant two-day visit at Windy River, caught some fish, and then flew south once more. They had still seen no Eskimos.

On the third and final trip they did much better. With Charles along, they flew to the Little Lakes and landed on Pommela Lake. The party remained with Pommela overnight, and the old man, recognizing their potential value to him, dispensed the full and fabled hospitality for which the Eskimos are commonly renowned. The doctor examined three out of the eleven Ihalmiut families and discovered that some of the children had head lice. The following day, after trading with the people for souvenirs and after removing sundry weapons and tools from the grave of Kakut, the mission to the Ihalmiut flew south and passed out of the land.

The three flights had cost the government about $3000 but, apart from the discovery of the head lice, had accomplished nothing. The mere fact that the flights were made was presumably considered to be an adequate safeguard against any further repetition of the years of our neglect. The report submitted by the inspecting official stated that the Ihalmiut were in good condition and that there was no need to be particularly concerned either about their future or their past.

This was not an opinion which I could share, and on my return to southern Canada that autumn I wrote a detailed account of what I had seen and heard, and mailed it to the Department of Mines and Resources which, at that time, was the federal agency nominally responsible for Eskimo affairs.

The following spring (by a series of rather remarkable coincidences which have no place in this book) I found myself heading back to the inland plains as an employee of that same government department. Together with a trained biologist, who was also an old friend of mine, I had been hired to assist in conducting a study of the caribou, for, though no one in authority showed the least alarm about the future of the Eskimos, there was a very real alarm about the future of the northern deer.

I spent a few days in Ottawa before flying north, and during this time I was able to talk about conditions amongst the Eskimos with several missionaries, Royal Canadian Mounted Policemen and government officials. These men represented the three groups which (with the addition of the traders) had ruled the arctic for half a century or more, and who had absolutely controlled the destiny of all Canadian Eskimos. The representatives of these groups assured me that the Innuit were a happy and contented people who wanted for nothing, and who were being well looked after. When I demurred, with the suggestion that this was too general a statement, I was instructed by the then Deputy Commissioner of the Northwest Territories — who was my superior — that I was not to interfere in, nor to concern myself with, Eskimo affairs. On that note I left Ottawa, by no means unwillingly, and journeyed north.

At Churchill I unexpectedly encountered Charles, and what

he had to tell me roused my deepest apprehensions for the People. The autumnal migration of the deer in 1947 had been so scanty that, even with ample ammunition, Charles and Fred had been unable to kill enough meat for their own requirements. Nevertheless they attempted to operate their trap lines, only to find that the disease which had harried the dogs the previous winter had now almost eliminated the white foxes. They hung on as long as they could but not even the arrival of a charter flight sent in to them during December from Churchill with additional supplies could enable them to remain in the land. By March starvation had again become a reality, and the boys fled from the country by dog team — and did not return.

When he reached Churchill, Charles reported to the R.C.M.P. detachment that there was starvation amongst the Ihalmiut; but nothing was done about this report except to forward it to Ottawa. Ottawa, in turn, authorized a shipment of emergency supplies to be sent to the Ihalmiut when, and if, a plane happened to be bound that way.

These supplies, crated without labels, were still waiting at Churchill when I arrived there in mid-May, so I arranged to have them loaded aboard the aircraft which was to take us to Windy Cabin.

Before leaving the Barrens, Charles had told the People, and in good faith, that help would probably reach them by air within a week or ten days of his departure.

Consequently the Ihalmiut left their famine camps at the Little Lakes and made the long journey to Windy River. The place was deserted when they arrived but they settled down in the filthy outhouses to await the promised help. They waited through most of March, and all of April; and for sustenance they had the carcasses of the few wolves and foxes which Charles and Fred had been able to trap. They waited. . . .

One morning in the first week of May, Hekwaw's son Belikari struggled down from the top of the ridge behind the cabin crying out an electrifying phrase:

"The deer have come!"

Within the hour a band of does began to cross the ice almost directly in front of the cabin. They were met by a ragged fusillade. A few minutes later there was fresh blood upon the lips of the starving ones, and the famine was at an end.

When they had recovered sufficient strength the People left that place of broken hopes and walked towards their homes — but they were not yet secure. They had expended their last few rounds of ammunition upon the herd of does, and now no one, not even Pommela, had any ammunition left.

By the time they reached the Little Lakes they were surrounded by deer, but they had no means even of obtaining sufficient meat to last from day to day, let alone to put by against the summer months when the deer would be absent from their country. What was even more serious, they could not obtain the necessary skins to cover their kayaks so that they would be able to make an autumn kill at the water crossings.

There was no immediate danger of outright starvation, for they knew they could survive by snaring ground squirrels, by spearing suckers in the little streams, and by killing ptarmigan and small birds with slings. They could have stayed alive, if barely, while the summer lasted — but it was to the winter ahead that their thoughts turned.

Owliktuk and Pommela reacted to the crisis in their own ways. Pommela took two of his adopted children to serve instead of pack dogs, and set out on foot for the Hudson's Bay outpost at Padlei, some two hundred miles away by the route which he would have to follow. With him he took eleven fox skins, some of which had been caught by Onekwaw and by Katelo, and some of which he had taken, by threats, from members of Owliktuk's band. These were all the fox pelts which the Ihalmiut still possessed — the only wealth they had. Pommela — who was, before all other things, a realist — was convinced that neither Charles nor a relief plane would ever appear at Windy Cabin.

Owliktuk was not so realistic. To him a promise remained a promise, and he believed that help would come. One day he took his carrying bag, empty save for a single fish, and set out for the south. He reached Windy Cabin on May 20, found it deserted still, and set himself to wait. He waited three days. On the third day he gave up hope and started on the long walk home; but he had not gone a mile when his heart leapt up within him, for he heard the unmistakable roar of the *konitaiu* — the white man's wings.

His faith seemed justified. He turned and came back toward the cabin at a trot, slowing to a walk only for dignity's sake as he topped the final ridge.

I shall not soon forget his face, nor the emotions with which he greeted us. Owliktuk was a proud man and a self-sufficient one, yet in this moment of greeting both pride and self-sufficiency were momentarily forgotten in the relief which overwhelmed him. He shook us warmly by the hand, then hurried across the ice toward the cabin carrying a load of our supplies. Before we reached the snow-buried entrance he had already vanished up the river to collect firewood so that we might have a mug of tea.

By the time the brew was ready his emotions were again under control and he sat with us, in quiet dignity, and drank his tea; nor did he indicate in any way how serious the situation had become, and how badly worried he had been about the future. He mentioned nothing of his needs, and asked for nothing. After an hour or so he politely emptied the dregs from the tea-kettle into the dirty snow outside, and told us that he must return immediately to his camp. We saw him off, and we had no suspicion of how bad things were with him and with the rest of the Ihalmiut.

Months later it occurred to me to ask Owliktuk why he had been so reticent in a time of such great need; and his reply was:

"If you had wished to give me anything you would have done so. I could not ask for anything because I had no furs to trade. The five foxes that I caught in the winter I had left in the cabin in exchange for a file and some tea which I had taken, so I could not ask you for shells. I thought that when you were ready to give out debt [an advance on the next year's fur catch] you would do so; and I was no longer worried, for you said you would stay many weeks and I thought you had come as traders. I knew that when it was time you would give us debt so that we could kill many deer."

After Owliktuk had departed, my companion and I began to sort out the mountain of freight we had brought with us. Eventually I came to the boxes which were marked "Eskimo Relief Supplies" and I opened them. They contained six sheet-metal stoves, a bundle of fox traps, a dozen large axes and twenty galvanized-iron pails.

At first we thought that this was all some ridiculous mistake, and we chuckled at the mental image of the Ihalmiut men, each shouldering a great ax, and sallying forth to cut down trees for stove wood — in a land where no trees grew. But when we had consulted the accompanying correspondence, we discovered that there had been no mistake. The stoves, pails, axes and traps had indeed been intended to relieve the Ihalmiut's desperate situation. We laughed no more.

On June 4, all of the Ihalmiut men, except Pommela who was still en route from Padlei, arrived at the cabin. Ohoto, who had no inhibitions and no dignity to protect, told us the full story of the events of the preceding months, and the rest of the men confirmed the grim details. My companion and I had already begun to realize something of what had occurred from the evidence uncovered by the melting snows about our camp, and now it required only a close look at the emaciated faces of these people to know they spoke the truth.

Yet the activities of the visitors gave no indication of what they had suffered in the flesh and in the mind. Ohoto, quite unable to control his exuberance, capered about playing the clown, turning cart wheels and engaging in mock battles with the other men until even Owliktuk could not forbear smiling at his antics. That night we had a marathon tea party, and no one went to bed until the dawn had broken. There was more laughter, and more good-natured nonsense as we smoked and drank, than I have seen elsewhere in the world. It would have been easy to believe that these were indeed the "happy and contented people who want for nothing" of whom the missionaries and the police had spoken to me in Ottawa with such conviction.

Although we had been specifically instructed not to concern ourselves with Eskimo affairs, and had been told that this was a matter solely within the jurisdiction of the R.C.M.P., we nevertheless felt that the immediate crisis amongst the inland people was so serious that we should ignore our instructions. We had a small portable radio transmitter, and so we dispatched a message to Ottawa asking for emergency supplies of ammunition and food to be flown in at once. This message was acknowledged but it brought no action.

On June 4, there were still some deer in the country — the tardy stragglers bringing up the rear of the main herds which had already passed to the north of the Little Lakes. The Ihalmiut men had guns, and we had a fair quantity of .30.30 ammunition but, except in three cases, these did not match. Apart from Ohoto, Pommela and Owliktuk, who owned .30.30 carbines, the rest of the men were armed with ancient relics of .44.40 caliber. None of these weapons were fit for service, for they had been used so long and so hard that the barrels were worn smooth and the mechanisms functioned only spasmodically. It had been ten years since any Ihalmio, except Pommela, had been able to buy a new rifle from the traders.

We gave Ohoto and Owliktuk ten boxes of ammunition each and they undertook to hunt for all the People, though both they and we were aware that they could hardly hope to kill more than enough deer to meet the immediate need. Apart from the increasing scarcity of caribou as the herds mover farther north there was the fact that the best of marksmen, armed with these almost useless guns, would have been lucky to have made one kill for every ten shots he fired.

By the middle of June the last stragglers of the herds had passed out of the Ihalmiut lands, and Owliktuk visited us again. This time he threw off all restraint and admitted that hunger was coming perilously close to starvation. My companion and I distributed some of our own supplies to the Ihalmiut and then radioed Ottawa a second time. The message was hardly worded in the correct bureaucratic manner, for it contained a thinly veiled intimation to the effect that our third message — if one was needed — would go direct to the public press.

A reply finally arrived at the end of June. It authorized us to write off the supplies we had already given to the Eskimos against the Family Allowance payments to which the people had been entitled for the last several years but which they had never received. We were further instructed that we should register the Ihalmiut in preparation for a patrol by the R.C.M.P. which was to take place "in the near future." Finally we were instructed not to visit the Ihalmiut camps nor to become any more deeply involved in the situation.

But as to that, we had no choice. On July 2, Ohoto and Ootek arrived from the north to report that things were becoming increasingly serious since many of the women would soon be unable to feed the infants at their breasts, due to their own starvation. There were then twenty-two children in the camps, and upon these depended the whole hopes of the Ihalmiut for survival. These children had already experienced a protracted period of starvation, during the early spring, and they were in no condition to undergo another one. There was no deermeat left at any of the camps, and no prospects of obtaining any more until early August. No fish were running in the streams, where they might have been speared; and without kayaks or canoes it was impossible to set nets in open waters.

So we took the remainder of our supplies, set aside sufficient food to last the two of us for three weeks, and distributed the rest. It was very little we could give — less than six pounds to each of the Ihalmiut. And we were now helpless to do more, for our radio had ceased to function and we, like the Ihalmiut themselves, could only wait and hope.

When, on July 20, we heard the distant murmur of an aircraft engine, our excitement and relief must have very nearly equaled that of Ohoto, Ootek and Yaha who were at the cabin that day.

We were convinced that the plane would be carrying a cargo of ammunition and essential food for the people, and perhaps a government representative as well; but we were wrong.

The Norseman which landed on the river below the cabin had indeed been dispatched by the Department of Mines and Resources — but by the Wildlife Section which employed us, and for the sole purpose of air-lifting us north to Angikuni Lake to continue the caribou study there. It carried supplies for us, *but nothing for the Eskimos*. Nor was there, amongst our official mail, any information concerning the government's intention on behalf of the Ihalmiut.

With some reluctance we boarded the plane and made the flight north; but when the Norseman left for Churchill it carried with it detailed reports of the current situation, and an urgent plea for immediate action. My companion and I believed that this would bring results, for we were still remarkably naive.

When we were flown back to Windy Cabin on August 14, we found, to our amazement, that nothing had yet been done. Nor was there any indication that anything ever would be done. My companion and I discussed the matter and concluded that I should return to Churchill with the plane and take direct action as a private individual.

In Churchill I accidentally encountered the official who, in his single person, was responsible for the welfare of the entire Eskimo population in the Canadian Eastern and Central Arctic. Although he was a busy man, he took time to listen to my account of conditions in the interior, and he promised that something would indeed be done. But I was no longer quite as naive as I had been, and so I visited the Canadian Army establishment at Churchill. Here, through the good offices of Lieutenant Colonel D. C. Cameron, I was able to obtain a dozen .303 army rifles in good condition, together with a thousand rounds of ammunition. Having listened to my story with deep sympathy, Lieutenant Colonel Cameron also suggested that I accept a supply of battledress trousers and jackets, for by this time the skin clothing which the Ihalmiut had been unable to replace was so far gone as to leave many of them almost naked.

On August 20, the long deferred patrol by the R.C.M.P. finally took place. A constable arrived by air; but he brought with
him not one pound of supplies of any sort for the Eskimos. Near
the completion of his visit this constable expressed it as his opinion that the Ihalmiut were simply shiftless, that they had not in
fact suffered any losses from starvation during the preceding two
years, and that, all in all, there was really nothing much to be
disturbed about. He also made it clear that Eskimos were no business of ours, and that any supplies which they might need would
be sent in, in due course, by the proper authorities, of which he
was the official representative.

These supplies arrived on September 5. They included a drum
of powdered milk, which turned out to be rancid and which
made all those who attempted to use it very ill. The balance of
the cargo consisted of some flour and lard, and two large bales of
discarded service underclothing which had originally been destined for a cloth reclamation factory, but which had been diverted to the R.C.M.P. for distribution to the Eskimos.

The milk was destroyed. We examined the bales of underwear
with some caution, for their state of cleanliness left much to be
desired; and eventually we made a pile of legless, armless, torn
and worn undergarments, in one of the outhouses. We did not
offer these directly to the Eskimos, for we would have been
ashamed to do so; but we left them to help themselves if they felt
so inclined. We should have burned those rags, but our courage
did not extend quite so far.

Nevertheless, we *were* able to issue every man with a new .303
rifle to replace the rusted antiques which had long outlived their
period of usefulness, and with sufficient ammunition to ensure a
good hunt in the fall.

They made a remarkable and strangely comic spectacle as they
left us for the north, clad in the incongruous army battledress,
and with service rifles in their hands. But they looked very different when October came.

On their first visit after the snow began to fall they came to
see us, wearing fine new suits of skin clothing. They came with
pride and assurance — and with full bellies. As he sat fingering

his new rifle, Ohoto told me proudly that he had already cached more than fifty fat deer against the winter, and that the other men had done as well, or better.

During my remaining time that season amongst the People I saw them, for the first time, as they must have been in the distant days when their camps stretched from Ennadai to beyond Yathkyed Lake; when the land was theirs, and when they were fulfilled within a land which gave them all things that a man might need.

With a resiliency which is not given to many peoples, they seemed to have recovered some of the substance of those ancient times. Hardly a day passed but a party of them came visiting to Windy Cabin, and these visits were without an ulterior motive. They were purely social events — though almost every group that arrived bore presents of one sort or another. One man might bring a bundle of caribou tongues, while another might bring two or three pairs of finely made deerskin boots. Ohoto, ebullient and irrepressible, undertook a mock courtship of my wife (who had joined us in late August), and on one memorable occasion he sneaked into the cabin during my absence to present her with an immense bouquet of marrowbones. When I selfishly refused to admit him to full cousinship, with all that this implies in Eskimo society, he brought the whole camp to a pitch of near-hysteria with a comic song which he sang to the accompaniment of a skin-drum, and which lampooned at great length the niggardly nature of the small white man called Skibby.

On another occasion Ohoto, Yaha, Miki, Owliktuk, Halo and Hekwaw came down to see us in a body, accompanied by half a dozen children. They arrived just at dusk, and after presenting us with a haunch of meat from a fat buck, they squatted on the floor of the cabin while we brewed tea for them in two-gallon pails. My wife had baked bread that day, and she distributed this with a lavish hand while she stuffed the children with cookies.

We two white men sat on the floor with our guests. As the cabin filled with pipe smoke, the tea-pails were emptied, refilled and emptied yet again until the night was well advanced and we had talked of all the important things — the numbers of the deer, their state of fatness, the hunt each man had made. Finally Yaha got to his feet with much assumed diffidence and took down the big hoop-drum which the people kept at the cabin for such occasions as this. For almost an hour he entertained us with a shambling dance while he sang long, lugubrious songs that told in detail of his shortcomings as a hunter and even as a lover. We joined in the shouted chorus of *ai-yai-ya-ya* until the old cabin trembled.

After Yaha had collapsed in wet exhaustion, his place was taken by the youngest Innuit present — little Itkilik who was then six years of age, but who had nevertheless composed a song of his own which he danced and sang with deathly seriousness — for on this occasion he was *Inuk,* he was a man, and it behooved him to act like one. His performance was greeted with such enthusiasm that he was quite overcome by the applause, and had to retreat behind the stove until he could recover his composure.

We all danced, on that memorable night. We all sang and told stories until the food was eaten and the tea-pails bubbled with a throttled sound, for they were so full of tea leaves that there was hardly any room for water. When we became too exhausted to take the floor again, old Hekwaw got out a circlet of string and for an hour he wove flashing images in space; string figures of such complexity that the movements hypnotized the watchers into the conviction that we were living, in the flesh, the stories of old hunts, and olden times, which Hekwaw wove into the movements of the string.

The late dawn was breaking through the little windows in the shack when our guests, with obvious reluctance, at last began to straggle off to the tent which we had pitched as a sort of guest house for them upon the nearby ridge. It had been a night to remember, for we had all lived, during those brief hours, in a time that had vanished, and that could not return again except in such half-magic interludes as this had been.

It was a time for laughter and for gaiety, for all across the gravel ridges near the Little Lakes were mounds of gray rock under each of which lay the gutted carcass of a deer, already frozen. And each of these little rock piles was a fortress set against the winter months which lay ahead — a fortress against the sly approach of death.

It was indeed a good time to be amongst the People of the Deer; a good time to know them . . . and it was a good time to take our leave of them.

My wife and I said our good-bys one clear October day when the ice had already begun to form on Windy Bay, and the tundra ponds and lakelets were frozen over. Halo and Ootek came down to the shore to watch us paddle through the shell ice to the aircraft that waited impatiently with its motor roaring. They did not say good-by, for they have no word for farewell.

"So you are going now," Ootek called across the water. "But you will come back, Skibby — and there will be much to talk about when you come back."

I waved, and shouted that I would come back when the deer came; for I did not know that ten years must elapse before I would see the tents of the Ihalmiut; and I had no way of knowing that I would never see Halo and Ootek again.

5 *Two Visitations*

THE early winter of 1948–1949 augured well for the People of the Little Hills. My companion of the summer remained at Windy Cabin until mid-December and he was well supplied, so that when an Eskimo needed a little ammunition, or some tea or tobacco, he could obtain it. There was nothing else the People needed, for there was meat and to spare in the camps by the Little Lakes.

There was meat in the camps, and therefore there was strength as well. Though the long winds mounted their ceaseless assaults through the shortening days and the lengthening nights, they could not reach through fur and flesh into people's bones as they had been wont to do in the years just past; for well-fed men could strive against the wind. They built high snow walls about the tents, and inside the shelters there was the comfort that comes only with full bellies, and which is proof even against the bitter arctic frost.

When the pale and shrunken sun rose in the mornings the women climbed out from under the thick robes on the sleeping ledge and lit the little fires of willow twigs in the cooking porch, while the older children, or perhaps the husbands, pulled on their double parkas and hurried down to the nearby lake armed with ice-chisels with which to open the water holes and fill the pails for morning tea. The day's first meal was meat, as were all the meals which followed, but with every meal there was hot tea. Only rarely could the women spare enough fuel to cook the meat, and for the most part it was eaten raw and frozen. Often it was accompanied by soft splinters of the rich white back fat taken from the autumn bucks, and sometimes there was a marrowbone to crack for the sweet frozen jelly which it contained. As long as there was enough fuel to brew a pint of tea, the frozen food represented no hardship — indeed to crunch the crystalline stuff between the teeth and to feel it melt against the tongue is a tactile pleasure far more satisfying than to mouth the flaccid foods which we are used to in the south.

The deer had been good to their People in the autumn, and they continued to be good to them as December passed. Several times a small herd of hardy bucks which had remained on the plains instead of seeking the shelter of the forests came within range of the hunters' new rifles. Then there was fresh meat to eat and, on rare occasions, soup of boiled meat, marrow and blood.

Hunger was banished from the camps that season. When the meat supplies stored in the cooking porch ran low, a man had only to take his light sled and his dogs (if he still had any) and travel across the faceless land to his nearest cache. The tracks of the great white wolves would be numerous around the little pile of rocks upthrust from the enveloping snows; and sometimes too there would be the prints of *kakwik,* the wolverine, who is the greatest robber of the plains. Then the hunter would anxiously pry away the heavy stones and cut down through the hard snow which had drifted between the interstices of the cache. Sometimes he would find that *kakwik* had forestalled him and there was little left but well-cracked bones and fragments of hair and skin; but that was a rare occurrence. Usually his cache would be as he had left it, and he would load the frozen quarters of deer-meat on his sled and start contentedly for home as the early winter darkness settled somberly across the land.

The People did little traveling that winter. Though three or four bitches had survived the dog disease and had given birth to litters of pups during the summer of 1947, there were still very few working dogs. But there was no need for extended traveling. There was ample meat close to the camps, and there were so few foxes in the land that there was no point in attempting to run trap lines. Even had the foxes been abundant, their pelts would have been almost useless anyway, for Charles had not returned to Windy Cabin, and there was no trader nearer than Padlei, two hundred miles away by the usual sled route.

Charles and his brothers had stayed on at Churchill with their father, for the old German seems to have concluded that there was more profit in putting his sons to work at the Army camp than in sending them back into the Barrens when the foxes were at the low point of their cycle. Nevertheless Charles did return briefly to the inland plains in January, as an employee of the Canadian Army, which was then involved in a remarkable venture that was to have a momentous effect upon the future of the Ihalmiut.

During the war the Royal Canadian Corps of Signals had been entrusted with the establishment of a string of radio and meteorological stations throughout the arctic. By 1947 stations had been built along the mainland coasts and on many of the arctic islands, but there remained the great expanse of the interior where the difficulties of transportation had made construction of such stations a seeming impossibility. The barriers which the inland Barrens posed were indeed so formidable that it was not until 1949 that our technical abilities could devise a method of surmounting them. In January of that year an audacious plan to establish a station at the north end of Ennadai Lake was put in motion.

Until this time Ennadai, and indeed the whole of the inland

plains, had only been accessible (and barely accessible at that) to canoes, dog teams, and float- or ski-equipped airplanes. None of these would have sufficed to move the tons of supplies needed to establish a radio station, to carry in the huge power plant, and to stock the place. Nothing with less cargo-carrying capacity than a ship, or a train, could have done the job. Yet for many years a kind of train that did not run on railroad tracks *had* been operating inside the northern forest regions, opening up new mines in otherwise inaccessible locations, and freighting supplies into areas which could not normally be reached except by air. These were the so-called "cat-trains" consisting of giant tractors towing strings of sleds, and it was to them that the Army turned.

This was no simple innovation. No cat-train had ever operated on the open Barrens where the land becomes a gigantic frozen sea in wintertime, without landmarks; with no routes that can be followed by the eye; where gigantic combers of black rock or steep-sided eskers bar every path. No cat-train had ever attempted to operate in the abysmal winter temperatures of the Barrens where the unchecked wind can rage for days at velocities of eighty and ninety miles an hour and make the ground drift so impenetrable that all life becomes as blind as the lemmings in their dark and hidden tunnels.

Nevertheless the Army decided to send cat-trains overland to Ennadai in midwinter, across a snow desert, unmapped and largely unexplored, for a distance of three hundred airline miles, or more than four hundred as the tractors would have to pick their ways. There were no guides to be had, for no white man knew the intervening country between Churchill and Ennadai — but Charles was at least familiar with the immediate vicinity of that distant lake and he was therefore hired to accompany the expedition.

Early in January four huge caterpillar tractors, each towing a string of heavily laden freight sleds and a heated caboose for the crew to live in, ground their way out from Churchill. They crawled up the shores of Hudson Bay for almost a hundred miles and then they turned away from the known country into the white west.

For weeks they crawled tediously into the interior, charting their courses and plotting their positions by the use of sextants, like ships at sea. They were a lumbering argosy, sailing into an unknown world which had never seen their like before.

The people of that world had no warning of this new invasion until one day near the end of January when Yaha decided to make a journey south to the now abandoned cabin at Windy River, in the faint hope that Charles might have returned to it and brought some tobacco — for Yaha was an addict, and his usually amiable temper had begun to sour a little under tobacco deprivation.

Yaha never reached the post. One morning as he topped a long ridge near the head waters of Little River, his quick eye caught a distant movement on the eastern horizon. He stared long and hard, for at first he thought it must be a herd of winter deer but, as he watched, his anticipation began to turn to rising consternation. The objects that crawled so slowly toward him were certainly not *tuktu*. They were something absolutely foreign to his experience and to his understanding. Then he remembered the old tales told in the camps of his father, of giant beasts which had once haunted the lands far to the northwest. That memory, and the sight of these mammoth entities crawling ponderously and implacably toward him, effectively nullified Yaha's longing for tobacco.

Yaha was afoot, and he wished fervently that he had many dogs to speed his departure from that place. At that it took him only half a day to retrace the full day's march to Owliktuk's camp. He was exhausted and somewhat wild-eyed when he burst into Owliktuk's shelter to report what he had seen.

Yaha was an imaginative man, and his story lost nothing in the telling. It was not long before all the people in the camp had squeezed into Owliktuk's place to hear the tale, and there were several otherwise calm and sensible men who became busily engaged in checking their rifles and counting their remaining ammunition, while the children stared at one another in half-delighted anticipation of the horrors which Yaha described so vividly.

The excitement and the apprehension which gripped the people could not be contained. Even the internecine tension which split the Ihalmiut camps was forgotten. Miki was sent posthaste to Pommela's camp for, though Pommela might be hated and feared, he remained a powerful shaman, and this seemed to be an emergency within his special province.

Pommela had not the vaguest idea as to what Yaha had really seen, but he immediately recognized an opportunity to make capital of the mystery and so he prepared to hold a spirit séance. All of the men (with one exception) and most of the women in both camps converged on Pommela's big shelter where they sat in an uneasy silence while the old man prepared to throw himself into a trance. His ritual was impressive, for he had had considerable practice, and it was not long before his shambling gyrations and his wildly inarticulate shouts began to have their effect on the watching people. Tension, and a gnawing foreboding, gripped the watchers as the old man collapsed on the dirty snow floor, went rigid, and began to foam visibly at the mouth as the spirits he had called upon began to enter into his body.

But Pommela's audience was not complete. Ohoto, the would-be white man and perennial skeptic, had listened carefully to Yaha's highly colored account and he had concluded that the visitation was somehow connected with the whites. He even had some inkling of *what* it might be, for long ago at Brochet he had seen small tractors hauling supplies along the ice road of frozen lakes and rivers which stretched southward to The Pas.

Thus, while the rest of the People were succumbing to Pommela's spell, Ohoto quietly borrowed Owliktuk's three dogs, hitched them to a small sled, and slipped off to the south.

He arrived back in darkness, and went straight to Pommela's camp where the séance was still in full swing. The shaman had been seized by three spirits in succession and all had prophesied a great evil entering the land. When Ohoto pushed back the deerskin flap and stomped in amongst the tense and frightened audience, he interrupted Pommela's impassioned interpretation of the spirit voices, but Ohoto could not have cared less. He was bursting with his news, and he gave no thought to the fact that he was about to earn Pommela's undying enmity.

Grinning from ear to ear, and as brash as a street urchin, he announced that the "things" were by no means supernatural, but that they were new and mighty machines of the white men hauling sleds which appeared to be laden with an enormous amount of trade goods. The séance broke up as fear gave way to a gathering anticipation and excitement at the prospects for the future. The traders had come back! There would be no more shortages of ammunition or of tea and tobacco. It was indeed exhilarating news.

The cat-trains made three trips to Ennadai that winter, and the mountains of material which they brought were unloaded on the shore at the north end of Ennadai, covered with tarpaulins, and left unguarded, against the return of summer and the arrival of the construction crews by air. When the trains were returning eastward after the completion of the second trip, they dropped Charles off at Windy Cabin with his dogs and his supplies, for he had not yet been entirely able to rid himself of the desire for his old way of life, and he intended to make one more attempt at living in the land. It was a brief attempt. After only a few weeks he found that he could no longer bear the lonely wilderness and he hitched up his dogs and left the Barrens, this time forever. His passing marked the final end of that chaotic and tragic period when the white traders and trappers had dominated the country of the People. Now the land was to come under the domination of a new kind of white man, motivated by inscrutable purposes which the Ihalmiut would never comprehend, any more than they were able to understand the meaning of the inexplicable objects hidden beneath their wind-whipped tarpaulins by the shores of Ennadai.

Within a few days after the departure of the tractors, most of the Ihalmiut men had followed the double line of tracks to the site of the new station and they had marveled at the immense quantity of cases, the piles of lumber, and the great steel sections of the aerial towers. They had marveled too that such wealth should be left unattended. The absence of a white man, and the inscrutable nature of the material, was to remain a mystery to them for months to come — but it was destined to be eclipsed within a few short weeks by a darker mystery which would bring terror to the camps, and which would fully justify the warnings given by Pommela's familiar spirits.

The story of the evil which came to the Barrens in the early months of 1949 began at Churchill the previous autumn when an Innuit from Eskimo Point visited the settlement. He was a young man and he had heard much of the wonders of the place, so that it was natural that he should wish to see them for himself. And the wonders of Churchill surpassed his expectations a thousandfold. Of all the fascinations that it held for him, none could approach the Army camp, with its great airport, its swarming vehicles of every size and shape, and the generosity of the many United States and Canadian soldiers. These men were equally fascinated by the young Eskimo, and they made much of him. They gave him many gifts, including one of which neither the giver nor the recipient was aware.

In October the young man started north, his sled laden with presents, and his mind overladen with stories to tell his people. A week after his departure one of the soldiers who had befriended him was hurriedly evacuated to a hospital in Winnipeg.

On his way north the Eskimo traveler could not resist the temptation to stop at every camp and talk about the things that he had seen. He stopped first at Nonalla, then at Thlewiaza River, and then at McConnel River, before finally reaching Eskimo Point. It was the Christmas season when he came home, and everyone for many miles about was gathered at the tiny settlement. There were even a number of Padliermiut from the interior, as well as some from the Maguse and Wilson Rivers. For many days these people visited their friends, whom they would not see again for perhaps a year, and they attended the hot and crowded religious services in the Catholic and Anglican missions. It was well into the new year before the gathering broke up and the people dispersed to their many distant homes, each of them carrying within him a part of the young man's gift.

The unsuspected gift from Churchill had traveled widely, but it had not yet reached the end of its journeying. In January, a week or so before the first cat-train reached Ennadai, Pommela had driven his dogs overland to Padlei Post to beg or borrow some tea and tobacco. At Padlei he had met and stayed with men who had attended the Christmas festivities at Eskimo Point. He brought back more than tea and tobacco to the Little Hills; and the unseen gift which traveled with him must have been present at the crowded séance occasioned by Yaha's first sight of the cat-train.

Meanwhile, that gift — the name of which was poliomyelitis — had begun to display itself in the coastal settlements. In camp after camp men, women and children were suddenly seized by raging fevers and by agonizing pains in their muscles which presaged paralysis. Many of the victims died within a day of the first symptoms of disease. So savage and universal was the epidemic that by mid-March an area encompassing a hundred thousand square miles was given over to it. The efforts of the single doctor provided by the government to care for the health of the entire population of Keewatin District could do little to halt or to control it, even though in desperation he placed more than half of the huge district under quarantine. The combination of winter weather, lack of transportation, and the general oppression of his work prevented him from being of effective service to any of the stricken people except those in the immediate vicinity of his hospital at Chesterfield Inlet. In this one locality — the sole locality which had a doctor and medical facilities, and where adequate records could be kept — fourteen people died and there were 78 cases of permanent paralysis among 275 Eskimos.

Pommela's spirits had spoken truly.

At Padlei there was no record of how many died, but seventeen people were permanently crippled. They received no assistance until the epidemic had run its course, and even then only three of the crippled people ever received medical attention.

Nor was there a doctor at the Little Lakes when, one black February night, Ootek's wife Howmik woke her husband and her child with her fevered ravings. Ootek did everything he could to help his woman, but though he donned his amulet belt and sang the sacred sickness songs known only to himself, which had been passed down to him through uncounted generations, they had no effect upon this alien invader. By morning both of Howmik's legs and both her arms hung limp and useless.

Halo, whose tent stood next to Ootek's, had risen in the night to help his friend, for Howmik's cries had awakened the whole camp. In the morning Halo stood with Ootek and looked at the wreckage of the woman Howmik, and his usually placid face was deeply furrowed. He glanced at Ootek seeking some reassurance or at least some explanation of the nature of this evil, but Ootek could tell him nothing.

They knew fear in that camp. And their fear bore fruit the following day when from Miki's shelter there came the wailing of a mourning woman, where Kahutsuak cradled the body of her youngest child.

The fear built to a crescendo as first one and then another of the People in Owliktuk's camp was striken. There was a weird and terrifying capriciousness about the disease, for it struck some a mortal blow, others it crippled horribly, and others it touched with a gentle hand, and left unharmed. There was no pattern and no reason in it — there was nothing that a man could understand.

For a few days Pommela's camp escaped the plague, and the old man believed that this was the work of his guardian spirits; but in the event even they proved unequal to the struggle. Ikok, Pommela's youngest wife and perhaps the only human being for whom he felt affection, fell sick one morning and within two days she lay dead, contorted into shocking ugliness.

Death was the least of the horrors of those weeks. Worse than death was the paralysis, which marked men's minds even more heavily than it marked their flesh. They knew too well the sure and bitter fate of the hunter who cannot walk or hold his weapons, and of the woman who cannot cook and sew or nurse her child. And by early March it seemed assured that half the People would be crippled for their brief remaining days.

Even Hekwaw, the old bear, was crippled from the waist down. His grown son Ohotuk, a strong giant of a youth, lay almost totally paralyzed, and doomed. In Hekwaw's tent the one untouched survivor, Belikari, labored to be hunter and wife too.

Halo's wife Kikik was stricken while she was in Ootek's shelter caring for Howmik, but though Kikik was looked upon as already dead by those who saw her, within ten days she had completely recovered from the disease, except for a slight limp which vanished in the months ahead. It was as well that she was spared, for a few days later Halo himself became insensible and raved the long night down. When he came to himself he had lost the use of his right arm.

Alekahaw was amongst those who were maimed for life, for he never recovered the full use of his right leg. But Pommela, who had again brought a plague upon the People as he had done once before in his youth, remained personally unscathed as always.

The many-pronged assault upon the People of the Little Hills, which had sunk into quiescence through the fall and early winter, had now been viciously renewed. The too brief armistice with fate was at an end. In the dark days of February, when the gales make no pause, and when the cold strikes into the very rocks until they split asunder; when the ice upon the lakes grows ten feet thick and contorts in the frost's grip until it cracks and thunders like a mighty cannonade, the crumbled fortress of the People was beleaguered once again, and men's hearts shrank within them. The fear of a known enemy can make men brave, but the fear of the unknown enemy is a succubus to drain the manhood from them. And there was no knowing this present enemy who thrust and cut into the fragile fabric of the People's lives.

This was the way of things when, in mid-March, men lifted their heads and listened to an unfamiliar sound — the roar of an aircraft coming to the Little Lakes. The plane landed on the ice of Halo Lake, and it disgorged two fur-clad members of the R.C.M.P. who had been dispatched from Churchill to discover if the epidemic had penetrated so far into the inland plains. The policemen saw at a glance that the disease had been before them, but they did not remove any of the stricken People from the camps. It was not their business. They left within the hour, but before they left they told the People that a doctor would soon come amongst them.

Two months passed before the doctor came, and even then he was only able to visit half the People. He had room in his air-craft for only two patients amongst the many in the camps, and he chose Ohotuk and Howmik. These two he flew to the hospital at Chesterfield, from which place Howmik was returned to her husband late in the summer, still partially crippled in both legs and arms, but able to be at least a semblance of a wife. Ohotuk did not return, but died in a foreign place.

So for the fourth successive year the Ihalmiut felt the scourge of hardship, and again they had no more than token help. They grew very hungry as the year advanced, for there had been no new supply of ammunition, and the deer were scarce. Never-theless they survived the abrupt days of the spring transition when the snow melts like fat in a fire, and the rivers break out of their ice bonds almost overnight and go roaring to the distant sea. With the coming of the warmer weather they even made progress against the paralysis which still lay heavily upon so many of them, and day by day men and women began to recover some of their lost strength — though there were many amongst them who would never have the full use of all their limbs again.

In midsummer my biologist companion of the previous year returned to spend a month at Windy Cabin in order to complete his studies of the deer. The People came to him and told him the story of the spring, and once more he was able to provide them with a little ammunition. He was again amazed at the incredible resiliency with which they recovered from their adversities. They came to Windy Cabin in the gay and cheerful manner we had known the previous autumn; even the cripples came, though for them the sixty-mile walk from the Little Lakes must have been a grave ordeal. Once more the tea parties and the drum dances lasted into the dawn, and there was laughter.

But beneath the laughter there was a residue of fear and a great uncertainty. The People wanted one thing only, as they said, to make them content with their hard lot, and that was the permanent presence of a white man in their lands. Over the long years since the first white men had come to the plains, the People had been weaned away from their old ways into a vital dependency on such a presence, so that the supplies which they could obtain from the traders had become their shield, and now they knew no other. During the past decade that shield had rusted through and so they looked to the future with apprehensive eyes.

Ootek had expressed this ever-present concern to me in the summer of 1948 when he had said:

"Many strange things have come into our land that only the white men understand. If there was a white man here to whom we could take fox pelts, and who could tell us what to do when there was trouble of a kind that our own spirits cannot fight against, then we could keep ourselves safe and see our children live."

Ootek spoke for all the People, and I do not think they asked too much. Yet for many years their hopes had gone unrealized. It was not until the summer of 1949 that these hopes seemed about to be fulfilled.

In July, with the lifting of the poliomyelitis quarantine, a big amphibious aircraft of the Royal Canadian Air Force descended heavily upon the green waters of Ennadai Lake. The plane brought many white men, and as July passed into August that lonely place in a lonely land saw the slow transformation of the piles of materials left by the cat-trains into modern buildings and high steel towers. These made a curious and startling contrast with the dun-colored tundra that rolled away on every side, unbroken by any work of man's. When the day comes that we construct refuges on the face of the moon, we will only be enlarging upon such ventures as the one at Ennadai, for they also will be outposts of a familiar world upon an unfamiliar one. The radio establishment at Ennadai bore no relation to the earlier attempts of white men to establish themselves in the land, for the white trappers and traders had been in some degree a part of the new world they had invaded, and were at least partially dependent on it for food and fuel and shelter. The new intruders were dependent on it for nothing, and were no part of it. They brought their own world with them, and within its small circumference, shielded and protected from the unfamiliar, and therefore hostile, elements without, they lived almost exactly as they would have done in the homes that waited for them in the distant south. They were true aliens, and their thoughts and habits, and understanding, were alien too — and this is a vital fact, and one that must be kept in mind when their relations with the People are considered.

It was on the 20th of August that the Ihalmiut came to see the miracle that had been worked upon their land.

There were six men of Owliktuk's group led by Ohoto, and they had stolen a march on Pommela, who had not yet learned of the arrival of the strangers. They came with some trepidation, and not even that brash man Ohoto was immune to awe as they breasted a ridge and looked down upon the strange buildings, the mighty towers, the great piles of oil barrels, and the raw scars upon the tundra where a bulldozer snorted and bellowed like a wounded muskox bull.

It was a subdued and timid file that followed Ohoto down the slope and walked uncertainly toward the place where half a dozen white men had suspended work to stare in open curiosity at these grotesque visitors who seemed to have sprung directly from the bleak tundra which had given no previous indication that it had ever known men before.

If both sides were at a loss what to do next, Ohoto at least knew the form. Leaving his contingent grouped disconsolately some distance off, he ambled forward, seized the hand of a startled Signals sergeant, and shook it with such gusto that the man pulled away in frank alarm. Ohoto followed, grinning broadly, and after unlimbering his few words of English he formally presented a grubby letter of introduction written for him by my biologist friend at Windy Cabin.

The ice was broken, and now the visitors were royally received, for soldiers have the happy faculty of making friends wherever they can find them. It may be that in this little band of fur-clad, quiet people they saw some chance of an alleviation of the colossal weight of loneliness which the inland plains had laid upon them. There was, at any rate, a titillating sense of novelty about the meeting for, as one of the soldiers wrote, "We felt a bit like Columbus when he laid eyes on the first Indians. Only two of our gang had ever seen an Eskimo before, and they sure were a curious bunch."

Amongst the stores provided by a thoughtful quartermaster's department for the Ennadai post had been an English-Eskimo dictionary, and this was now hurriedly unearthed. All work on the site ceased, and the soldiers gathered about Owliktuk, Miki, Yaha, Ootek, Halo and Ohoto, and in a few minutes there was mutual laughter and much good fellowship. Cigarettes were freely proffered and gratefully accepted. The cook, happy to have guests, concocted a magnificent dinner, which few of the Eskimos could stomach, but which they gamely ate rather than offend their generous hosts.

On that first visit the Ihalmiut only stayed for a few hours, perhaps because they were uncomfortably confused by the multifarious impressions and by the astounding plethora of previously unknown and therefore inexplicable things they saw. Owliktuk in particular needed time to take it in, to think about it, and it was he who led the visitors away as night came down. They did not go empty-handed, for every man was laden with tins of fruit and other foods, with cigarettes and candy bars.

For the Ihalmiut it had been a momentous meeting, far more momentous than they knew. As they discussed the visitation amongst themselves during the succeeding days, they were unable to comprehend its real import. The barriers imposed by language and by the unbridgeable divergence in experience which gaped between the whites and the Eskimos made understanding totally impossible. The Ihalmiut could only interpret what they had seen in the light of their own very limited awareness of our activities and interests, and they could come to no firm conclusions. These things alone seemed certain: that the new white men intended to remain permanently in the land; that they were friendly, sympathetic and generous, and that they were incredibly endowed with material wealth. Perhaps because they wished so greatly to believe it, most of the People convinced themselves that the soldiers were in fact traders, and they took great comfort from this belief, seeing in it a protection against the years which lay ahead.

Only Pommela suspected that, whatever the real interest of these strangers might be, it was not trade. Once, during the war, he had accompanied Charles to Duck Lake where the United States Army had operated a meteorological outpost for a year or two. Pommela had fond memories of that visit. He particularly remembered the unparalleled generosity, or the stupidity, of those white men who had been willing to give away whole cartons of cigarettes and cases of tinned meat in exchange for such trivial things as a pair of skin boots, or the worthless pelt of an arctic hare, which no trader would have allowed to cross his counter. Pommela, alone of all the People, guessed something of what the arrival of the outlanders at Ennadai might really mean; but he kept his thoughts to himself so that he alone might profit by them.

If the Eskimos could not begin to conceive of what lay behind the white wooden walls of the station, then the soldiers were even less able to comprehend the life led by the Ihalmiut. They saw the People as a species of friendly local denizens whose every aspect was curiously outlandish. They had no idea how such people managed to survive, nor did they think about it much. They were busy men, and when a visiting party of Eskimos disappeared over the visual horizon they also disappeared beyond the horizon of the soldiers' thoughts.

In the autumn, after the snow had come and it was permissible once again for the women to sew new clothing, many of the Ihalmiut returned to the station carrying gifts which were a return for those they had earlier received. They brought fine caribou-skin mitts, boots, and several complete outfits of double parkas and fur trousers. The soldiers were impressed and touched. One of them wrote:

"They seemed to take a proprietary interest in us and our welfare, regarding us evidently as a pretty feckless bunch who needed looking after. They pretty well outfitted us with winter clothes and showed us where the best fishing places were and offered to bring in meat when we needed any. They were a gay bunch, but they sure smelled high when they got inside the buildings . . ."

As winter drew on, the air of camaraderie which had been present at the earlier meetings between the white men and the Eskimos began to fade. Pommela contributed something to this, for he had made frequent visits to the station, and had attempted to establish the same sort of covert influence over the strangers that he had once held over Charles. His failure baffled him; but his attempts annoyed the soldiers, who came to look upon him as a confirmed scrounger, and one, moreover, who was not averse to theft.

Then, too, the general novelty of having these "stone age men" constantly about the place had begun to pall. As one of the soldiers pointed out, the Eskimos did not make ideal house guests, for they did not belong to the centrally heated living quarters amongst the easy chairs, the electric phonographs, and the general amenities of a different world. It was inevitable that barriers should begin to grow, and that the first happy contact should begin to solidify into something far less happy.

To the Ihalmiut, the change was inexplicable. They had done everything they knew to be as friends and brothers to the strangers, and their efforts had first been welcomed; but now were not. Pommela, and to a lesser extent Ohoto, who had seen the station as a port of entry into the white man's world, grew angry at the rebuffs which now became more frequent, but the most serious cause of perturbation amongst all the Ihalmiut was the gradual realization that the strangers were not traders, and had no real interest either in the land or in its inhabitants.

In describing that period, after the lapse of many years, Owliktuk gave some indication of the bafflement of his people.

"In the fall we started to come there to get things we would need and we asked for shells. Sometimes they would give us a few shells, but sometimes not. And there was never enough for what we needed. After that, when we began to catch foxes, we began bringing the pelts but the white men would laugh and say they did not want pelts; that other white men would not let them keep them. Sometimes they would give us some tea and tins of food, but what we needed was shells for our guns. They said they were not traders but they gave us some things even though they did not want our foxes."

The soldiers remained friendly, but in an offhand and guarded fashion which was inexplicable to the Ihalmiut. There seemed to be no way to make the white strangers understand how much depended on their help, and how much the People were prepared to offer in exchange. It was a deadly impasse.

That autumn, when the Ihalmiut waited the coming of the deer, they were almost out of ammunition, so that they had to trust to obtaining the requisite supplies of meat at the river crossings by the use of kayaks and spears. Unfortunately they had not expected to need kayaks after the arrival of the "traders" at Ennadai, and so they were not adequately prepared to make the sudden change back to the old hunting methods. Furthermore, the deer were very scarce that fall. The result was that the People began the winter with far too little meat put by in the caches, a situation which was made worse by the fact that more than a dozen of them still suffered from the paralytic effects of polio, and would be largely helpless and dependent on others for assistance during the months ahead.

Meanwhile, the soldiers remained unaware of the problems which beset the Ihalmiut. Had they known, they would undoubtedly have tried to help, for they were goodhearted men, as they demonstrated at Christmas time.

As the festival approached they decided that it would be worthwhile to have a party for the Eskimos. They thought in terms of a big meal; of presents for the children, and of offering the Ihalmiut a brief surcease from their world of bitter wind and endless snow—a world which appalled the soldiers as they gazed upon it through the double-windows of their living quarters.

They took a great deal of trouble with that party, for they meant well. The Eskimos came to it in response to a summons carried to all the camps by Ohoto. It was not easy for some of them to come, for already there were people who were weak from hunger, and it was not easy to bring the crippled, for there were still too few dogs to haul all the sleds. Yet they came, not knowing what awaited them, but hoping that the summons might presage an end to the terrible misunderstandings that had prevented them from obtaining what they needed to survive. Despite the earlier rejection of fox pelts, many of the men had continued to trap as best they could, not yet convinced that the soldiers had meant what they had said. Now they brought the pelts and when they presented them to the white men they were overjoyed to find that at last they were accepted. The People of the Deer knew nothing of the white man's habit of exchanging gifts at Christmas time.

The party was held in the basement of the main building and to the soldiers it appeared to be a considerable success. There was much singing and laughter and impromptu dancing, both to the old music of the drum and to the surprising new music of a phonograph. There was much food too, though it was all eaten on the spot. And every Eskimo received a gift.

The soldiers were not aware of the undercurrent of strain amongst their guests. They did not know the Eskimo, and they had no reason to look beneath the placid surface, and so the fact escaped them that the smiling guests at that happy party were in reality desperately worried and, in some cases, starving people.

There was a bitter irony in that situation. It was as if an impervious yet partially translucent wall separated the Ihalmiut from the soldiers, but only the Eskimos were aware of its presence, and they had tried to break through it — but they had failed.

6 *The Empires of the North*

ON the day after Christmas the Ihalmiut returned to their
camps, having completely failed to make the soldiers comprehend their plight. There was now nothing more that they
could do to help themselves. They could only wait beneath a
growing apathy for what must come. They had no meat left,
and again they were reduced to scavenging under the hard snow
for bones and offal cast aside the previous fall. Their clothing
was in pitiful condition, for they had managed to take only a
few good hides during the preceding autumn, and most of these
had been used to make the gift clothing for the soldiers. Scanty
and dilapidated as it was, the clothing that they did possess was
soon being taxed to provide food for their empty bellies. The
dogs, whose numbers had only just begun to recover from the
distemper epidemic, began to die of hunger. Some were eaten;
but the tough, acrid flesh of an animal which has died from
starvation is more poisonous than beneficial, and many of the

People who ate the dog meat could not keep it down. Once more the men found themselves without the strength, without the warm clothing, without the ammunition, and without the dogs, all of which were vital if they were to help themselves. It was an old story to the Ihalmiut now. They sat silent in their frigid tents and waited.

Some of them knew a brief respite in mid-January when a cat-train arrived at the Signals station, and those of the Eskimos who had the strength for it were hired to act as stevedores. These men (there were only five of them) were well fed during the three or four days of their employment, and when they returned to their tents they carried gifts of canned goods and flour. For the members of their immediate families the inevitable was delayed a little while.

During the first week in February, 1950, the first death occurred.

In Yaha's snow-block shelter the old woman Kooyuk, who was Yaha's mother, came to the decision which only she could make. One night while the rest of the family lay uneasily asleep upon the ledge, she dragged her bony limbs from under the worn and almost hairless robes, stripped off her few remaining clothes, and crawled out through the entrance tunnel into the whining darkness of the night.

She was an old woman, and she had not long to live in any case, nor was life dear to her. For many days she had refused her own minute portion of the family food so that her grandchildren might have a little more; and it may be that she no longer cared to think of the warm spring days which might still lie ahead of her, for beyond them she must have seen the winters which were yet to come.

So she crawled, naked, out of the shelter and walked in the white wind until she could walk no farther. In a little while she sank to her knees and the snows rose over her. There was one less mouth to feed in Yaha's house.

A few days later death came to Pameo, who was the four-year-old daughter of Pommela's dead wife Ikok. While her mother lived, Pameo could live, but with her mother gone she had no hope of life, for she bore none of Pommela's blood, and she was a woman-child and worthless to him. He starved her systematically until her huddled little body no longer shivered underneath its ragged skins. This man who could sire no children of his own had scant love for the children sired by other men. He fed no useless mouths.

It was a strange irony that Pameo's death should bring the gift of life to the rest of the Ihalmiut, but this was what happened, for when Pommela — who had camped close to the station — visited the soldiers one day to beg for handouts, he casually mentioned that Pameo had died. When the soldiers wished to know how she had died, he sucked in his stomach and his cheeks in a gesture that needed no words to make it understandable.

The soldiers were immensely shocked. They had had no suspicion of the true nature of the crisis in the Ihalmiut camps, and the discovery that a child had starved to death almost within sight of their warm and comfortable oasis came as a dreadful disclosure. Their immediate reaction was to break out emergency supplies from their own stocks and to distribute these to the people within reach of the station. At the same time they radioed an urgent message to their headquarters at Churchill to the effect that the local Eskimos were dying of starvation and required instant help.

In due course of time this message was "processed" at Ottawa and orders were issued to the resident doctor at Chesterfield Inlet to charter a plane and make a flight to Ennadai to investigate the report.

The flight was made on February 26. The doctor examined some of the People and confirmed that they were indeed suffering from hunger. Unfortunately this was a disease about which he could do little, for he had not been authorized to bring in relief supplies, the issuing of which was controlled by the R.C.M.P.

It was food, not medicines, that the People needed.

There were a good many people in the inland plains who needed food that winter.

Throughout the whole of interior Keewatin the autumnal caribou hunt of 1949 had been a failure, and by February there were many starving Eskimos, not only at Ennadai, but at Padlei, Baker Lake and Garry Lake as well.

That all of the resident white men, the traders, missionaries and policemen in the country could have remained in ignorance of the seriousness of the situation does not seem credible. Nevertheless the first message concerning the famine to reach the outside world was the one dispatched by the soldiers at Ennadai. It was confirmed early in March when Richard Harrington, a freelance photographer, traveled to Padlei by dogteam and subsequently gave the Canadian newspapers a horrifying account of the conditions which he had encountered there.

Although he was well equipped when he left Eskimo Point for the interior, and was accompanied by a competent Eskimo guide, Harrington soon found himself in dire straits. He lost four of his own dogs to starvation, and the drain on his supplies to feed the dying people whom he encountered in the Padliermiut camps was such that he came close to starvation himself. In his subsequent reports to the press he gave it as his opinion that some of the Padliermiut would indubitably perish, and that all of them might die if they should miss the spring migration of the deer, or if the deer should return too late. In the event, the deer did return in time, and in sufficient numbers to prevent a total catastrophe, but there were six known deaths from starvation amongst the Padliermiut that winter, and it is probable that many others died about whom no white man ever heard.

At Baker Lake conditions were not quite so severe, for those Eskimos who could reach the trading post received enough assistance from the local manager, a benevolent old Scot named Sandy Lunnan, to survive. Nevertheless there were eleven known deaths from starvation amongst the Akilingmiut on the Thelon River and amongst the Harvaktormiut on the lower Kazan.

Amongst the Hanningaiormiut at Garry Lake there was an unknown number of deaths. No official report of these was made, for Father Bulliard, an Oblate missionary who had recently gone amongst these people, was extremely anxious to protect them from contacts with any white man save himself, and he appears to have believed that his attempts at proselytizing might be prejudiced if he were to rouse too much interest in the plight of his self-chosen charges.

Bulliard need not have worried, for there was little likelihood that the responsible authorities would, in any case, have bothered themselves about the fate of such a remote group of people.

The government authorities were not particularly concerned about the plight of any of Canada's Eskimos, and the principal reason for their lack of interest is to be found in the nature of the unique situation which had resulted in the arctic from the continuing existence there of three white empires which exercised *de facto* sovereignty over the entire land and its native peoples.

The senior of the three empires was the Hudson's Bay Company which, until late in the nineteenth century, had legally possessed almost the whole of the Canadian arctic. In 1869, at the conclusion of a memorable struggle, the Company yielded up its exclusive charter, and its domains became a part of Canada. The transfer was almost purely nominal, however, for the Company continued to operate much as it had always done, and was not in the least hampered by the loss of paper sovereignty over its vast arctic holdings.

It was a good company, as trading companies go, though it was owned largely in England and had no particular allegiance to Canada or to Canadians. It was relatively benevolent as far as the Canadian native population was concerned. Most of its employees in the field were Orkneymen or Scots Highlanders, whose passionate loyalty to the Company almost transcended their own national loyalties, for to these men the fact that the Company was an empire in its own right seemed incontestable.

The Company's profits in the north were derived almost solely from the fur trade, which is to say, from the fur trapping activities of the Eskimos and northern Indians, and the policy of the Company toward these invaluable assets was therefore a practical one. As an historian of the H.B.C. wrote in 1932: "Common sense dictated the just treatment of an inferior people. Given fair treatment, and no opportunity to be dishonest, the native becomes a rather likeable chap. His very childishness is appealing and arouses a paternal instinct. The Hudson's Bay Company took an extreme care to select the protective type of post manager, and from that policy grew a relationship between the white race and an inferior people which for sheer beauty has not been equalled elsewhere on this earth."

The sheer beauty of that relationship, which bore marked resemblances to feudalism in medieval Europe, may be open to question, but there can be no doubt that many of the post managers sincerely tried to be good friends to the Eskimos, and that they often had what they conceived to be the best interests of the Eskimos at heart — though these interests had always, of necessity, to remain secondary to the purely financial interests of the Company itself.

It is not entirely fair to condemn the Company for its exploitation of the Eskimos, since it was, after all, a commercial firm, and it existed for the sole purpose of making money. It can hardly be castigated for making the most of its opportunities, for it never pretended to be a welfare agency. So long as Canada allowed it carte blanche to do what it pleased in the north, it was only to be expected that the H.B.C. would take full advantage of an effective monopoly.

From the point of view of the Company policy the Eskimo existed primarily as a source of marketable furs and it was therefore clearly to the Company's advantage to keep him in his aboriginal state and to discourage any attempts which might be made to enlighten him as to his rights and status as a human being of the twentieth century. It was equally to the Company's advantage to treat him moderately well, and to attempt to see that he did not starve to death as long as he was serving the

Company interests — for a dead hunter traps no furs. Beyond this, the obligations of the H.B.C. did not extend.

Nor did the obligations of the second empire exceed those of the H.B.C. This second power consisted of two disparate elements — the Roman Catholic Oblate missions, and the missions of the Church of England. The great majority of the representatives of both were not Canadians, and they took their direction and instructions from Europe, not from Canada. While relations between the two organizations were by no means harmonious, they did subscribe to a common objective. The primary concern of both was the acquisition of Eskimo adherents to their respective faiths, and the Oblates at least were quite frank in their opinion that the physical welfare of the hoped-for converts was not of much importance, for it was the soul which was the priceless jewel. As an American-born Oblate priest succinctly put it in a magazine article published as late as 1957: "We figure the missionary goes before the doctor, first things first. It's more important [for the Eskimo] to get into heaven than to be cured of tuberculosis."

Yet the religious empire of the arctic was by no means built entirely upon things of the spirit. Physical possessions entered very largely into it, for there were scores of missions, and even a few schools and hospitals, not to mention a number of trading posts operated by the Oblate order. The schools and hospitals were heavily subsidized by the federal government and were, in fact, the only such institutions available to the Eskimos until the mid-1950's. The hospitals were completely (if it had not been such a tragic situation, one might have said farcically) inadequate. The schools were devoted almost entirely to religious instruction and they were of great assistance in implementing the general mission policy (which was identical in this regard with that of the Hudson's Bay Company) that the Eskimos ought to remain primitives, in enforced isolation from the outer world, and beholden in all important aspects to their guardians and mentors of the two empires. As for the larger aims of education these were, with rare exceptions, not considered to be of value to the Eskimos and were eschewed, with the result that in

1951 — after some fifty years of mission control of arctic education — less than 3 per cent of Canadian Eskimos could speak,
read or write English, or were in any real sense literate, despite
the existence of a cumbersome syllabic script.

Despite the limitations imposed by mission policy, there were
individual missionaries who were imbued with the honest desire
to serve the Innuit. These were men of the best intentions, even
though, it must be admitted, they were sometimes men of inferior understanding. Their sincerity is not open to question, although the ultimate results of mission activity in the arctic cannot argue for an equal immunity for mission policy.

The last of the three empires belonged to that renowned and
prideful organization, the Royal Canadian Mounted Police. Initially the police had been sent to the arctic to show the flag and
thereby to establish Canada's political suzerainty over the vast
northern wastes. They remained, and prospered in the north,
until the day came when they too possessed an arctic domain,
complete with its own air force and nautical command, and a
glowing legend, all of which were most gratifying to an empire-
building higher echelon. Although their apparent role was that
of law enforcement, there was remarkably little demand for their
services in this capacity. So they became (perhaps partially to
justify their own existence, and partially because there was no
one else to do the job) a corps of colonial administrators — in so
far as any real administration was ever undertaken.

The police established a reasonably amiable entente with the
missions and the traders, and did not interfere with their activities. Indeed most members of the force wholeheartedly supported the view of the other empires that the "natives" (to this
day the term is used by the police) should be protected as far as
possible from contamination by our society — except for those
particular benefits which could be brought into the Eskimo's life
by these three chosen instruments of commerce, religion, and the
white man's law.

It would be unjust to blame the police too severely for what
happened to the Innuit in consequence of this attitude, for they
were not fitted either by temperament or training to assist the

Eskimos. They were, in theory at least, no more than the agents of the administration of the Northwest Territories, the Commissioner of which had been responsible for Eskimo affairs since Canada took her first official interest in the Innuit in the year 1927. Within the narrow limits of their ability and understanding, some individual policemen proved — as was the case both with the missionaries and the traders — to be wholehearted partisans of the Eskimos; while at the same time they subscribed to the general belief that *Inuk* would be best served by being kept isolated in his arctic limbo.

The Northwest Territories administration was a most intriguing body. In 1950 its Council consisted of the Commissioner (who was also the Minister of the Federal Department of Resources and Development), supported by the Deputy Commissioner (who was coincidentally the Deputy Minister of the Department of Resources and Development), and five appointed members, one of whom was the R.C.M.P. Commissioner. Nor were the rest of them all entirely devoid of special interest in the other empires of the north.

To guide the Council in matters pertaining to the Eskimos there was an advisory body, which came to consist of the Commissioner of the R.C.M.P., the Fur Trade Commissioner or the General Manager of the Hudson's Bay Company, the Anglican Bishop of the Arctic, and one, or sometimes more, Roman Catholic priests of the Oblate order.

The actual administrative machinery for dealing with Eskimo affairs consisted, according to a government memorandum dated 1950, of two officers and a stenographer employed by the Department of Resources and Development. This memorandum further stated that it was considered unnecessary to increase the size of the Eskimo administration section at that time since the commercial and religious organizations in the arctic, together with the R.C.M.P., were competent and willing to continue as executors for Eskimo affairs.

A somewhat cynical observer of this situation might have suspected that the federal government of Canada was happy to wash its hands of any real responsibilities for the Eskimos because, in the first place, it was cheaper and more politic to allow private organizations to deal with the Eskimos as they saw fit, and secondly, because the government and people of Canada felt themselves under no particular obligations toward the Innuit.

Nor would this have been such a gross canard against a modern and virtuously democratic nation as it might have seemed. While the fate of the Eskimos remained, to all intents and purposes, in the hands of the three empires, Canada's voice was often heard championing the cause of the world's underprivileged peoples. We Canadians looked askance at the South African exponents of *apartheid*, at the segregationists in the southern United States; and we gazed with holy horror upon the inhumanities which we were told were being perpetrated on primitive peoples under the rule of Communism. Indeed we looked virtuously in all directions; except northward into our own land.

For most of us, this was not conscious hypocrisy. Through many generations we had been carefully conditioned to accept a myth in place of the real Eskimo. The myth had become stereotyped into the figure of a happy, skin-clad little fellow, living in a white and shining igloo, carefree and contented; not quite human perhaps, but lovable for all of that; and asking no more of us than that we leave him to his prehistoric pleasures and his outlandish pastimes. Some of us even envied him his atavistic freedom from the complexities of modern life.

Believing that this was the real man, we felt conscience-free to leave him under the aegis of the three empires, which were themselves a vital element in the northern myth. We had long since acquired strong mental images of the dogged, persevering Mountie driving his dogs through howling blizzards, that justice might be done, and that his Eskimo brother might be served; of the paternal fur trader who treated the Eskimo with the kindly forbearance of a good father toward a rather feckless child; of the self-sacrificing missionaries who gave themselves up to searing frost and cruel hardships so that the immortal soul of the poor pagan might come safe to Heaven when he died.

Men believe that which they wish to believe, and most of them prefer to believe that which gives solace to their consciences. Who is to blame us if we chose the myth?

Even had we so desired, it would have been extremely difficult to ascertain the true reality, for this had been so carefully and thoroughly obscured that it was almost totally lost to the public view. The Hudson's Bay Company and the missions kept a close tongue in their heads. The R.C.M.P., a notoriously close-mouthed organization at best, reported secretly to the Minister of Justice (if indeed it reported to anyone save God) and its records were never profaned by public scrutiny.

As late as 1954 it was virtually impossible to uncover sufficient information with which to assess accurately the situation in the north. It was not until 1958 that the terrible nature of the reality began to be fully apparent. In 1958 it became known, for instance, that one out of every eight surviving Eskimos had a history of tuberculosis. It became known that the life expectancy of an Eskimo was only slightly more than twenty-four years. It became known that the infant mortality rate stood at more than 260 deaths for every 1000 births and was still rising. It became known that more than three-quarters of all Canadian Eskimos suffered from chronic malnutrition. By 1958 the carefully constructed myth was at last becoming threadbare; but in 1950 it still remained intact. Indeed in those not-so-far-distant days the government, and the R.C.M.P., did not even know how many Eskimos were under their protection — the figure was thought to be about 8,000 though it was probably much nearer to 12,000. But honest facts were unimportant in 1950, for the myth still flourished.

All of this must be kept in mind in order to provide some understanding of how little the brutal disclosures which Harrington made to the press were able to accomplish.

His charges were, of course, officially denied but, what was worse, they were slurred over by the appointed guardians of the old order who in their posture as the expert authorities on Eskimo affairs had, and held, the public ear. By the end of March the accounts of famine amongst the Padliermiut had been forgotten in the south, where men fed well and slept warmly through the winter nights.

Apart from the visit of the doctor, no further action was taken to assist the Ihalmiut until mid-April. Meanwhile, they survived as best they could.

On April 6, Ohoto arrived at the Signals station in a state of near-panic to report that some kind of disease had smitten all the children. The sergeant in charge was aware of what sickness might do to the emaciated and weakened youngsters, and he immediately radioed Churchill with a request for a doctor — but this time no doctor was forthcoming. Instead the authorities referred the problem back to Ennadai.

The soldiers thereupon resolved to organize an expedition to the sickness camps. They had no means of transportation other than their caterpillar tractor, which was unreliable at any time; and the Ihalmiut only possessed three dogs amongst them, so that any relief expedition had to be made on foot. Considering the unfamiliarity of these white men with the land, the journey which they contemplated called for courage, and vividly demonstrated the reality of their concern for the Eskimos.

The sergeant and one other soldier set out, with Ohoto as a guide, and after trudging twelve miles to the nearest camp — it was Alekahaw's — they were exhausted. They were also frustrated by the discovery that the sickness camps lay thirty miles farther off at the Little Lakes, a distance which might as well have been three hundred miles. Nevertheless there was work for them in Alekahaw's snow shelter, for his wife Kaluk was suffering from a paralysis of her right leg which was slowly spreading to include her whole right side. Her condition was obviously serious, though neither she nor her husband had made any complaint nor had they asked for aid.

The soldiers returned to their base and again radioed Churchill. They were instructed to have the woman at the station by April

11, when a military inspection party was scheduled to arrive at Ennadai by air. Getting her to the station was no light task — in the end it was accomplished by cranking up the recalcitrant tractor and making a harrowing journey to Alekahaw's and back, bringing Kaluk in upon a makeshift sled.

The aircraft arrived on the 11th, carrying as an extra passenger an R.C.M.P. sergeant from Churchill, together with some emergency food for the Eskimos. The policeman did not visit the outlying camps from which the sickness had been reported, but he agreed to take Kaluk back with him to the military hospital at Churchill.

For Kaluk and for Alekahaw this posed an anguishing dilemma. Their youngest daughter, Ookala, was only two years old and was still being breast-fed in the usual Eskimo fashion. There was no other woman at Alekahaw's camp with whom she could be left and, deprived of her mother, it did not seem unlikely to the Eskimos that she would die. Alekahaw and his wife pleaded that the child might be allowed to accompany Kaluk to Churchill; but the request was refused on the grounds that the child was not ill. It is possible that the sergeant did not understand the situation.

So Kaluk vanished from the land where, in the distant camps, the disease continued to run its course.

The policeman's visit to Ennadai does not appear to have been concerned with the present plight of the Eskimos, but was primarily intended to apprise the station personnel of a plan to move the Ihalmiut to a new location "nearer a trading post." The police sergeant asked the soldiers to have the Eskimos assembled at the station in readiness for the move as soon as possible. He gave few further details.

It could not have been that he did not have these details, for the police detachment at Churchill had been intimately concerned in the development of a most remarkable scheme.

Its genesis went back to 1948 when plans for the establishment of the Ennadai station were first made public in Churchill. News of the project aroused considerable interest amongst some of the local businessmen. They wasted no time in preparing a useful-looking scheme, and by late in 1948 they had already put the wheels in motion by submitting elements of their plan to the Department of Resources and Development for approval.

According to their submission, what they envisaged was a commercial fishery at Nueltin Lake, whose produce would be sold to the military establishment at Churchill. This operation — so they said — would be able to offer wage employment at $150 a month to the men of the Ihalmiut band who, "as everyone was aware," were having a hard time of it at Ennadai. Furthermore, the Eskimos would be provided with nets and the rest of the requisite fishing gear at no cost to themselves. Since the fisheries would not occupy all their time, they would be able to hunt caribou as of old and, conceivably, do considerable fox trapping as well. All that was required to realize this utopia for the Ihalmiut was to have the authorities consent to moving the Eskimos from their present home to the proposed fisheries site at Nueltin.

To clinch their case the fish company enthusiasts pointed out that the otherwise prohibitive cost of flying the fish three hundred miles to Churchill would be offset by the use of aircraft belonging to Arctic Wings (a small airline in which, incidentally, the fisheries entrepreneurs shared an interest with the Oblate order). Arctic Wings, so the planners claimed, firmly expected to receive a contract from the Army to make regular supply flights to the new Signals station at Ennadai. On the return flights the aircraft could stop at Nueltin, take on a load of fish, and proceed to Churchill.

The Department of Resources and Development received the plan with unalloyed enthusiasm, but with a naïveté which was astonishing even amongst the bureaucrats. No one seems to have bothered to examine the details with any care, for if they had done so they would have wondered why it was necessary to go three hundred miles from Churchill to catch fish which were more easily obtainable at half that distance. And they would have discovered, had they investigated, that the Army had no intention of chartering civilian aircraft to service Ennadai, since the bulk of the annual supplies were to be taken in during the winter by cat-train, while any summer flights which might become necessary would be made by service aircraft of the R.C.A.F. These oddities in the proposal were not immediately apparent, and the authorities were too enamored by the prospect of the Ihalmiut becoming not only self-supporting, but positively rich, to be particularly critical.

The R.C.M.P. who, as the administrative representatives in the field, should have been more closely in touch with reality, were consulted, and they gave the plan their full approval. After the lifting of the polio quarantine in the late summer of 1949 the requisite permits were therefore issued to the fisheries company, even though it was *known* by then that they would not have any contract with the Army, and would therefore have to cover the entire freight costs on the fish themselves.

The permits were issued, even though a fisheries biologist employed by the federal government had visited Nueltin and had reported that, while there were indeed fish in the lake, his studies had convinced him that transportation costs made commercial fishing at a profit, under any existing circumstances, a most unlikely possibility.

Neither did anyone pay any attention to the confirmatory evidence of a professional fisherman who explored Nueltin's possibilities during the early winter of 1949–1950, and who reported that, without the payment of heavy transportation subsidies, the operation would never be commercially feasible. This man's report contained other information, of an even more revealing nature, for he pointed out that — by himself — he had been able to catch up to a ton of fish a week, and that the catch of two or three fishermen would be enough to swamp the limited market available in Churchill. It was his considered opinion that the employment of numbers of native fishermen at Nueltin would be economic nonsense, even assuming that any way could be found around the transportation difficulties.

For that matter, no one paid any heed to the known fact that the Ihalmiut had never been fishermen, did not like fishing, and had always avoided it, having discovered in antiquity that fish was a starvation diet in a land where only meat and fat could adequately sustain human life.

The most generous view which can be taken of the authorities' refusal to face these facts is that they must have believed the fisheries company was quite prepared to lose formidable sums of money while engaging in a charitable enterprise on behalf of the Eskimos and Indians — for the Chipewyan Indians had been brought into the scheme too.

When the operation got under way in November of 1949, the fishery company persuaded a considerable number of Chipewyans from the Brochet area to come north and share in the good thing. It was intended to add the Ihalmiut to this labor force in early spring of 1950, by which time there would be enough Eskimo and Indian fishermen on hand to supply a market the size of Winnipeg — if such a market had been accessible.

It was no doubt mere coincidence that the owners of the fishery company also operated trading posts in Keewatin in competition with the Hudson's Bay Company, and had in fact run the post at Otter Lake near which five of the Ihalmiut had starved to death in the spring of 1947. It may have been quite coincidental that the Ihalmiut were not, after 1948, working for any trader, and that they were eligible to receive Family Allowance payments (as were the Chipewyan Indians). Certainly it was a fact that these payments, which would total a considerable sum every year, would have to be spent somewhere.

It may also have been coincidence that the new company closed down its trading post at Otter Lake and brought the manager to Nueltin to take charge of the new project.

The rest was inevitable. During the winter of 1949–1950 a trading post appeared in conjunction with the fishery, and its operations soon bid fair to eclipse the fishery itself.

All of this was, of course, known to the R.C.M.P. at Churchill, but had no effect upon the decision which had been already confirmed, to give the Ihalmiut into the control of the fishery company.

The move itself was conducted in secrecy as far as the Ihalmiut were concerned. They were given no indication of what the future held in store for them other than the statement of the R.C.M.P. sergeant that "they were to be moved nearer to a trading post." They were *not* told in advance that they were to be employed as fishermen. They were *not*, of course, permitted to make their own decisions as to whether they should move or not. Perhaps the police realized that the Ihalmiut might refuse if they were given such an opportunity.

Ohoto was the first to hear of the impending move, when he arrived at the station on April 12, to inquire whether the white men had forgotten about the sick children in the camps by the Little Lakes.

In telling Ohoto of the R.C.M.P. plan, the soldiers did their best to soften what even they realized would be a stunning blow, and they are to be forgiven for intimating that the chosen land for which the Ihalmiut were bound was a place where the deer were always numerous, where no man ever went hungry, and where the Eskimos would receive nothing but benevolence at the hands of the white men they encountered. Yet they must have felt some compunction, for one of them wrote:

"The Eskimos are primed to go to a land of plenty. Heaven help us if any of them ever find their way back here . . . !"

This, at least, was an honest comment on a situation about which there seems to have been all too little honesty.

At first Ohoto reacted to the news with bewilderment which rapidly became stubborn resistance. He refused to act as a messenger to persuade the rest of the People to gather at the station preparatory to the move. But in the end the visions of personal propinquity with white men seduced him, and he went out to gather the Ihalmiut. They were instructed to abandon all their belongings, except what they could carry on their backs, for there would be no room in the aircraft for anything but human freight.

At those camps where hopelessness was greatest, Ohoto had little trouble; but at Owliktuk's camps he ran into resistance. Owliktuk staunchly refused to obey the summons until several

days had been spent in discussion, and until his wife had reminded him that two of their children were still sick (the six-
month-old son of Yaha and Ateshu had already died), and that
there might be help for the surviving children at the Signals
station. Subjected to these pressures, Owliktuk eventually agreed
to the move, but only because he had convinced himself and the
others that the "trading post" referred to by the soldiers must
mean Padlei — a place many of the Ihalmiut had visited and
where they had relatives. The People were not adverse to being
taken there, for they knew that if they did not like it, they
could walk home again; and in the meantime they would be
able to visit friends, and perhaps obtain ammunition and supplies
"on debt" against next winter's furs, from the Hudson's Bay
post manager.

On April 19, 1950, the first of the deportees began, in the
words of one of the soldiers, "to straggle in; and a more tattered
and discouraged rabble it would be hard to imagine. All were in
poor shape, no food, no dogs, and precious few belongings.
When asked what they had been eating they replied that they
had kept going by boiling and eating old caribou robes and
parkas."

It was April 22 before Ohoto arrived with Owliktuk's group,
but he had not yet located Pommela nor Hekwaw and so after
a night's rest he was sent off again.

There were now thirty Eskimos at the station and they were
ordered to build snow shelters for themselves while rations were
being prepared. In order to ease the administrative problems, the soldiers began by distributing three days' rations at one
time; but they soon realized that this procedure would not serve,
for the entire amount was wolfed down by the starving people in
a single meal.

On the 24th, a military aircraft carrying an Army doctor
from Churchill arrived at Ennadai. The doctor had been instructed to examine the people preparatory to the move —
rather, one suspects, as cattle are vetted before being sold to a
new owner. However, this particular doctor was an Army man,

and he cared nothing for political expediency. He was horrified by the condition of the Eskimos, and when he returned to Churchill he issued a statement to the Canadian Press news service to the effect that the Ihalmiut were on the verge of starvation. He added that, lacking any authority or facilities himself, he could do no more for them than to send in drugs and medicine.

His visit had not been wasted, for he had quickly diagnosed the sickness amongst the children as influenza, and he had provided sufficient drugs to stamp it out.

Pommela was one of the last of the Ihalmiut to reach the station and he came in alone. His dependents, so he explained, were so weak from hunger that they could not travel. On the strength of this he was issued with a considerable supply of food to take to them but, being Pommela, he did not make any attempt to rejoin his family. Instead he camped a mile or so away, and ate the food himself.

His wife Onikok (who was dying of cancer, though no one knew it then) and three of his remaining adopted children staggered in two days later, in the last stages of exhaustion. Onekwaw, who went to help them, was the first to realize that the ten-year-old boy Alektaiuwa, the son of Pommela's dead brother Kakut, was missing. Word of this spread quickly amongst the other Eskimos, but such was the fear in which the old man was held that no one dared to question him about the disappearance of the boy. It was not until Ohoto nerved himself to tell the soldiers, who thereupon demanded an explanation of Alektaiuwa's absence, that Pommela deigned to speak. The boy, he said, had simply lagged behind the rest and would arrive within a few more hours — Onikok had assured him that this was so, and there was really no need for anyone to worry.

This explanation was sufficient for the soldiers, but not for Onekwaw, who knew Pommela far too well. Quietly and unobserved, Onekwaw took the back trail, though he was himself so weak that he could hardly travel.

He found the boy early the next morning, some ten miles

from the station, where he had collapsed in a drift and lay unconscious. Onekwaw endeavored to carry him to safety, but he had not the strength. He covered the child with snow and then dragged himself back to the station where he told his story to Ohoto, who promptly told the soldiers. A rescue party was organized, and by late that night Alektaiuwa lay on a bed in the basement of the station.

He appeared to be quite dead, but when he had been stripped of his frozen garments and covered with heated blankets the soldiers were able to detect a pulse. One of them wrote later that "the sight of that poor undressed body took my breath away for he had been starved to the point where we despaired of saving him." Nevertheless they worked all night to save him, and by morning they had succeeded in restoring him to consciousness.

As Alektaiuwa began to recover from his ordeal the outrage which the soldiers felt on his behalf was vented on Pommela. They searched the shaman's travel sled and when they discovered a hindquarter of caribou meat (though there was not a scrap of meat in the rest of the encampment) their anger knew no bounds. With Ohoto's help they then interrogated Onikok and she told them, hesitantly, that Alektaiuwa had been systematically starved for weeks on Pommela's orders, and that neither she nor the children had been allowed even to share their own meager rations with him.

Some of the soldiers were in favor of beating Pommela up physically, but they did not dare to go so far, so they beat him instead with angry and contemptuous words. They did this in full view of all of the Ihalmiut, and Pommela, who had never been bested by any living man, was forced to endure the assault without recourse. He who had terrorized his people for so many decades was stripped of his armor and mercilessly castigated as if he had been an erring child. He was shamed, and proven helpless in his shame, before the people. He, the great *angeokok,* was chastised with impunity, and not all his magic or his fearsome spirits could aid him or protect him. Pommela had brought tragedy to many people in his time, but the fate which overtook him in this hour was almost commensurate to any he had meted out to others. For an Eskimo there could have been no crueler punishment. It was a deserved punishment; but it is a measure of how little the men of the one world understood those of the other that the soldiers were bitter in the belief that Pommela had escaped unpunished for his treatment of Alektaiuwa.

7 *Journey into Fear*

As April, 1950, drew near its close the soldiers at Ennadai found themselves harassed to distraction by this mass descent of the Ihalmiut. They had neither the knowledge nor the time to cope with the situation which had been thrust upon them. When they were able, on April 29, to notify the R.C.M.P. that the collection was complete, they were heartily delighted at the prospect of ridding themselves of their unwanted dependents.

"It was not," one of them wrote, "that we did not have any affection for them; but the work details, the ration details, the sick calls and the courts of human relations simply snowed us under."

An Arctic Wings Norseman arrived on the morning of May 1, carrying the policeman who was in charge of the move. This man spoke no Eskimo, and had no interpreter with him. He was unable, had he so desired, to explain to the assembled people what was in store for them; and he was in a considerable hurry. Stripped of all their possessions except the small bundles which they could carry on their backs, the first batch of Eskimos was ordered into the plane and it immediately took off into a clear spring sky, circled once and then headed, not northeast for Padlei, but almost due south.

The rest of the People, clustered forlornly on the shore, watched it go with increasing bewilderment — and when it had vanished into the southern horizon they looked at each other with a mounting apprehension.

The plane flew a long way south, passing over the tenuous edge of the forests and penetrating deep into the black spruce and jack-pine scrub. There were sixteen Eskimos jammed so tightly into the cramped cargo space of the small single-engined aircraft that only one or two could crane their necks to see where they were going. They saw nothing which they recognized; instead they saw the forests thickening beneath them. The sight was terrifying. Below the plane was a foreign and forbidding world — the world of trees which had belonged through all time to their ancestral enemies, the Idthen Eldeli Indians.

Eventually the aircraft landed on the ice of south Nueltin Lake. The policeman swung open the door and the Ihalmiut looked out upon their promised land.

They saw the trees, marching almost to the shore, but what held their vision — filled it — was a row of waiting Indians, their faces lean and unfriendly in the hard spring sun.

The sixteen deportees were unceremoniously herded up the beach and turned over to the fishery manager, while the aircraft swung up the lake to fetch another load.

The next group did not enter the aircraft quite so resignedly. Some of the women wept. Owliktuk was with this group, and he hesitated briefly until a shouted order which he did not understand decided him. He could not resist the inscrutable design of the police. With a blank face he clambered into the cramped space.

It required three trips to carry the forty-seven Ihalmiut to their new home — two on May 1, and the third the following day. And then the land was empty. The People had gone; had abandoned their camps, most of their possessions, the graves of their dead, and the places of their memories. They had been taken from the one place in all the world where, even in the most tragic times, bedeviled by hunger and disease, they had at least been solaced by the familiarity of remembered things.

It may be felt that this is laboring the emotional and physical effects of this upheaval in the People's lives but, on the contrary, it would be impossible for a white man to do full justice to it. This was an unbelievably harsh uprooting of a people who possessed a most limited understanding and experience of anything beyond their own immediate frontiers; it was literally an expulsion — and none too gentle a one at that — from their known world into one that not only was peopled by men whom they still thought of as their blood enemies, but which was also the domain of hostile spirits over which the Eskimos could exert no control, and against which there was no defense. It was, for the Ihalmiut, a virtual hell on earth.

It was also — by decree — their new home. And this is what they found. They found themselves camped on an island where, when the thaws came, they would be cut off and unable to escape. They found themselves in the midst of a band of Idthen Eldeli Indians who wasted no time in making the Eskimos understand that they were not wanted, and that it would be better for them if they departed quickly to their own country. They found that they were not even wanted by the white man in charge of the fishery.

They were issued with some nets, tents, and a little flour and lard (for all of which the government was later billed), and told to get busy and fish — not for the company, but to support themselves. The fantasy of a commercial fishery had already vanished and, since it was now almost spring, and there would be no fur trapping again till fall, the Eskimos were in fact a useless encumbrance — or would have been had it not been for the fact that they had Family Allowance credits (which were a complete mystery to them) that could be spent at the company store.

Since they had not been told of the $150 a month salary they were to have received, they did not note its absence. But they did miss, and desperately too, the land from which they had been taken.

Not many details of that time of exile are known with certainty. The records are very scanty. But in June an itinerant American gospel preacher arrived at the camp in his small airplane and spent some days with the Ihalmiut. He was distressed at their pagan state, though their physical condition does not seem to have concerned him overmuch. He attempted to evangelize them, but elicited no response, for the Ihalmiut were in no receptive mood toward white men.

It is also known that, in this period, there were several deaths. Katelo, that lonely man, was one who died; and another was Kielok (Kala) who was Hekwaw's wife. The death of these two is shrouded in mystery. According to the official records the first died on July 1, and the second on August 1 of "old age and pneumonia." They were fifty-one and fifty-two years old respectively, and when they were examined by the doctor in April they had both been in good condition. Their bodies were not examined by a medical man nor by the police, who made out the death reports some time later. It is unlikely that the true causes of death will now be known, for the surviving Ihalmiut do not speak freely on this matter. Nevertheless there is reason to believe that these two died primarily because they no longer wished to live. They had no reason to desire life in exile.

There is much which will not now be known of that black interlude in the history of the Ihalmiut, and this may be as well, for what *is* known cannot sit easily upon the consciences of those white men who were involved.

On May 25, just twenty-three days after the transportation had been completed, the soldiers at Ennadai were amazed to see an Eskimo accompanied by three starving dogs come walking slowly up the shore toward the station. They recognized him from a distance. It was Pommela.

Mindful of his past history the soldiers questioned him as closely as they could, and with particular reference to his family.

Pommela told them that his people were still at Nueltin and that he would go back for them when he had established some summer meat caches on the land — but the old man lied, for he no longer had a family.

His wife Onikok had been ill for many months and when she was examined by the doctor in April he suspected what the trouble was and requested that she be evacuated to Churchill when the Nueltin move was completed. At Churchill the doctor confirmed his early diagnosis. Onikok had cancer. She died a few months later, and never saw the inland plains again.

During the first few days at Nueltin, with no woman in his tent, Pommela's family disintegrated rapidly. Alektaiuwa had never returned to him but, after his recovery from the ordeal in the snows, had gone to live with Yaha. Now the three remaining children abandoned the old man whom they had come to hate and fear, and placed themselves under the protection of other families of the Ihalmiut.

Even his former followers, Onekwaw, Alekahaw and Katelo, avoided the shaman, for his defeat at the hands of the soldiers was fresh in memory. Pommela was quite alone, and this, together with his growing resentment of all whites, decided him that he at least would no longer submit to the arbitrary orders and actions of the police.

Old and discredited as he might be, Pommela was still a man. One night he stole three dogs from the Indians, fled in darkness across the lake ice, and vanished into the thin forests beyond. The wooded lands did not hold the same terrors for him that they did for the rest of the People, for he had traded south to Brochet through this country in the old days. Nevertheless he did not linger under the shadows of the trees, but drove the three dogs north, each with a small pack upon its back, until the plains were reached. It was a long journey and it took him two weeks to walk to Ennadai.

In reply to the questions of the soldiers Pommela stated that the new place was no good, that the deer could not be hunted there because of the thickness of the forests, that the white men were no good, that the Indians had threatened the People, and that he — for one — had had enough of it. He planned to stay at Ennadai just long enough to build a kayak, before proceeding down the Kazan to an area where he could intercept the migratory deer herds, and make a summer kill.

With the old man's departure ten days later (it took him just eight days to build a kayak out of scraps of lumber and the skins of some deer he had killed on the way north), the soldiers saw no other Eskimos until November. They assumed that the rest of the People had remained at south Nueltin Lake — but they were wrong.

For some time after the arrival at the fishing camp the majority of the People were too dispirited and too disoriented to contemplate any attempt at escape. They were afraid of so many things: of the white man into whose charge they had been given; of the police who had brought them here; of the forests which surrounded them, and, not least, of the Indians. Left to shift for themselves, they clustered close together forming a little enclave of despair. They fished a little — for they had to do so in order to exist — while the Indians became bolder and more overt in their dislike of this invasion by their ancient enemies into the Indian lands. The Ihalmiut found that their nets were being interfered with and that their possessions were being stolen, and, in the eyes of the Eskimos, the Idthen Eldeli began to assume a dangerously menacing stature. Fear of the Indians began to approach panic, and this fear eventually overcame the other fears and became the key with which the People liberated themselves from servitude.

Things came to a head on June 17, when a nine-year-old girl called Ahto, who had been one of Pommela's adopted daughters, was shot and killed. No details of this affair have ever been made public. The R.C.M.P. have refused to elaborate upon the brief report which they subsequently made to the administrative officials, and which simply stated that Ahto died "accidentally from gunshot wounds." It is probable that they are unable to enlarge upon the affair for, if an investigation was ever made, it could not have been undertaken before mid-December when the police again patrolled to the interior, and by that time it would have been most difficult to discover the truth, since all those who were concerned were by then scattered far and wide.

If the Ihalmiut themselves are to be believed, the killing was no accident, and the Idthen Eldeli were involved in it.

In any event, the shock of Ahto's death released some of the People from the bonds which had held them prisoners, and a few days later — while the melting ice would still carry human traffic — Owliktuk, and those who chose to follow him, vanished from the fishing camp.

Once begun, the exodus continued through the summer until everyone had abandoned the moribund fishing enterprise, including even the white man who had been in charge of it. He appears to have moved his supplies to the old cabin at Windy River and there he retained some of the Eskimos — notably the families of Alekahaw and Onekwaw — by virtue of the fact that he was able to dispense rations to them against their Family Allowance credits.

The rest of the People had already fled the district. They went slowly, on foot, and they did not go near Ennadai, for they believed that if the police found them they would once more be herded south to the place of terror from which they were so desperately anxious to escape.

Yaha, Ohoto and Hekwaw, with their families, bypassed Ennadai and the Little Lakes and continued north until they reached the northwest bay of Hicks Lake, where for the moment they felt themselves secure against discovery. They had a little ammunition, and they were able to kill a few deer from the late-summer herds; but these herds were very much dispersed and small in size, so that they were unable to lay up sufficient meat to see them through the winter. Nevertheless they did not dare to visit the Army station until mid-November, when hunger broke down their resolution to remain in hiding and brought them to the station to plead for food.

Pommela seems to have wandered widely and alone during the summer, but not even a man of his tough and independent character could withstand the isolation of the land for long, and in late fall he appeared briefly at Ennadai to claim the three dogs which he had left there. Using these as pack beasts, he traveled south to Windy Cabin where he joined his old adherents, and slowly began to re-exert his influence over them, even to the extent of reclaiming one of his remaining adopted children, a boy eight years of age called Angataiuk.

The fragile fabric of the Ihalmiut society, which had been so overstrained for many years, had now given way completely. The events of the spring and summer had rent it into fragments and the People had fled as fugitives to the far corners of the inland plains. They could no longer even face their common fate as one, nor draw upon the essential strength of the community — that strength which is the very essence of Eskimo existence. Each small fragment of the band was now alone and isolated from the rest, harried by the fears and uncertainties which had arisen from the shattering experiences at Nueltin, and bludgeoned by the hard blows of famine against which there was no real defense left to them.

With this disintegration of their social structure there came an inevitable withering of the spirit within each human being. The weakest of the People succumbed first. These were the ones who had remained at Windy River and who now gave up all pretense of struggle and became no more than beggars, utterly dependent on the charity of Family Allowance, while Pommela preyed upon them with a restored and strengthened arrogance.

The small group at Hicks Lake was made of sterner stuff and held out longer, but in the end the frightful oppression of a land wherein they lived divorced from all other living men, combined with the effects of famine, proved too much to bear. So they struggled back to Ennadai, where they remained until early in the spring, becoming increasingly dependent on the bounty of the white men.

Only in Owliktuk's band did a semblance of the vital unity and strength of purpose which had marked the People in the past remain alive. This group had shrunk until it consisted only of the families of Owliktuk, Halo, Ootek and Miki. Nevertheless, it remained a unit, for the inner fortitude of Owliktuk was still proof against the forces of dissolution. There was a quality of basalt in his spirit.

He was deliberate, and courageous too. When he led his little band away from the nightmare of Nueltin, he chose a path that none of his people had ever walked before. It was a difficult route, but purposely chosen to avoid any contact with those who had banished his people to the fishery camp. The route avoided the known lands of the Ihalmiut, even the Little Lakes beside which the People had pitched their camps for generations. Owliktuk knew that the airplane is a mighty seeker, and that there was no safety in the old familiar places.

So he and his followers walked to the northeast, passing over the interminable rock ridges which lie like titanic slag heaps to the west of Nueltin, and which even the deer avoid, for they have a quality of lunar desolation about them that is unrelieved by any living thing save the gray moss and the black and blood-red lichens that cling to the shattered rocks. They walked very slowly, for the sharp stones cut their skin boots to shreds and the children could only maintain the slowest of paces. Although they had almost no ammunition, Owliktuk had thoughtfully taken some of the fishing gear from Nueltin and, though the People might frown on fish, he made them understand that in this time of danger and of flight, they must eat fish or die.

They were more than a month en route, and it was not until late in the summer that Owliktuk called a halt. The little travel tents of canvas which they had made from the wall tents issued to them at Nueltin were finally pitched beside the shores of Otter Lake about twelve miles to the south of the now abandoned trading post. There were no white men nearer than Padlei, as far as Owliktuk knew, and here he felt his people would be safe.

The omens for the approaching winter were very dark. The little band of exiles had seen few caribou during the long walk, and Owliktuk guessed that for the second year in succession the deer would not come through the land in any numbers. It did not matter much, for the men possessed only about two dozen rounds of ammunition for their four rifles. Owliktuk therefore prepared to meet the winter in a manner completely foreign to his people's past.

Under his direction two nets were set, and for the first time in their history the Ihalmiut became fishermen in earnest. Until the ice formed they caught fish enough to eat in the nearby rivers though, since they had no kayaks or canoes, they were forced to set the nets by wading shoulder deep in the frigid waters. When the ice became firm enough to bear, they moved the nets out to the lake, setting them through holes in the ice. At all hours of the shortening days, when there was no other work to do, Owliktuk set the children, and even some of the women, jigging for more fish with hand lines.

They made good catches, for this lake had not been fished for many years, if indeed it had ever been fished before. The drying fish hung from crude scaffolds, swaying in the autumn winds; and as winter came hard and white, the piles of frozen fish began to mount like cordwood beside the little tents.

Yet food was not everything. Despite hard hunting by Halo and Owliktuk, less than a dozen deer were obtained before the last caribou vanished to the south. There were not nearly enough hides to provide warm clothing for all the people. Consequently most of them faced the approaching winter wearing only torn and ragged summer garments which did not suffice to keep the wearers warm even in the early days of autumn.

The omens were dark enough for the four families by Otter Lake — but they were much darker for the Padliermiut, who were their nearest neighbors. The Padliermiut hunters had rifles, and an adequate supply of shells, and so they had relied entirely upon the deer. But the depleted caribou herds did not come to the Padlei country in the fall of 1950.

It was an ironic turn of fortune that Owliktuk's fugitive band should have survived that winter because they had so little ammunition, while their cousins, who had plenty of shells, were doomed to starve. Owliktuk had not been able to place a dependence on the deer, and so he had turned to fish. But when the Padliermiut understood that the deer would not be coming to them, it was already too late for them to seek a substitute.

The Padliermiut, who then numbered about one hundred and seventy people, and whose camps were scattered within a hundred-mile radius of Padlei Post, had begun to starve before November ended. Their dogs died quickly — those that had survived the preceding winter — and the men began to come in to Padlei on foot seeking food to keep the women and the children in the distant camps alive. The post manager radioed to the police at Eskimo Point, explained the gravity of the situation, and asked permission to begin issuing relief rations. Permission was granted, but he was instructed not to allow the Padliermiut to come in off the land or to congregate about the post.

The constable in charge of the R.C.M.P. detachment at the coast firmly believed that the tough official policy of making the Eskimo scratch their own living from the land was the only sal- vation for the "natives"; and he was a rigid man who — like most policemen — would choose to adhere to policy in the face of any eventuality. In normal times this particular policy was not entirely a bad one — but these were not normal times.

Only one white man in the area seems to have sensed the true magnitude of the approaching disaster. He was the Hudson's Bay post manager at Eskimo Point, a man who had spent thirty years amongst the Innuit and who both knew and loved them, but who could never have been accused of "spoiling" the Eskimos by accustoming them to dole, for it had always been his business to show a profit on his yearly outfit, and there is no profit in Eskimos who sit around the post.

Nevertheless, when he smelled death in the offing near the end of November, he acted in a manner directly contrary to the policy which the policeman was determined to implement. He dispatched messengers to the camps of all the People who traded to Eskimo Point, and the gist of his message was simple and direct: abandon your camps, load your families on your sleds, and come in to the post at once.

They knew him, and they obeyed without hesitation. Within a short time nearly two hundred Eskimos had converged on Es- kimo Point, and their igloos stretched in a solid line along the shore for half a mile. When they arrived some of them were already too weak to walk and had to be carried by their relatives and friends. Hunger had already eaten savagely into the strength of almost every one of them.

The policeman at Eskimo Point seems to have been outraged by the trader's action. He ordered the People to return immediately to their starvation camps; but for once they would not heed the voice of authority. They were deaf to him, and listened instead to the trader who told them, quietly enough, that they were to remain where they were until the famine ended. Perhaps irritated by this defiance, the policeman not only refused to authorize the payment of relief vouchers, but he also held back the Family Allowance credits (monies which belonged to the Eskimos by right of law) until the People would agree to leave the post and go back to the land — to the hungry, empty land.

The People did without their Family Allowance until after Christmas had come and gone. They were fed for three full months out of the Hudson's Bay warehouse, and not one of those who had come to the trader for assistance died.

But at Padlei, twenty-two men, women and children died directly or indirectly of starvation.

They died almost entirely because they were not allowed to bring their families to the post and to remain there until the crisis had passed. Only the men were allowed to come, and on each visit they were issued two weeks' relief supplies of flour and lard and baking powder, and sent away again. Some of these men had taken a week to reach the post, and needed a week to regain their camps — by which time the rations which they carried on their backs (they had no usable dogs remaining after November) were sadly depleted. The inevitable came to pass. After three or four such journeys the men either became too weak to face another journey, or they put it off until it was too late.

The deaths of these people were almost solely due to the inflexibility of the policy which the police, in their capacity as administrators, had determined was the right and proper one. It was no doubt the same policy which prompted the Commissioner of the R.C.M.P. to make this statement before the Northwest

Territories Council in January of 1958: "I feel it is just as bad for an Eskimo hunter to become a scavenger and a beggar as it is for him to starve or freeze to death."

Owliktuk's people all survived that winter, but it was no pleasant life they lived. In their small tents, walled around with snow blocks, they huddled in abject misery. They were never warm, for they had no suitable clothing and there was no deer fat with which to stoke their bodies' furnaces. They were always hungry, for the human stomach cannot contain sufficient frozen fish to satisfy it when the thermometer plunges to 40 degrees below zero, and the gales thunder down from the far distant arctic ice whirling the sharp snows before them until the particles cut like driven sand.

Once, in January, Owliktuk accompanied by Ootek and Halo walked north to try and obtain some deer fat from their cousins of the Padliermiut. They visited two camps in which men and women were already dead or dying; and they returned hurriedly and gratefully to their own daily diet of lean fish.

It was about this time that their sanctuary at Otter Lake was invaded. Two white men appeared and reoccupied the empty cabin. One of these was the ex-manager of the fishery at Nueltin Lake who had later run the trading post at Windy River. This latter post had now been finally abandoned, and the manager had left the service of the trading and fishing company to revert to his original profession as an independent trapper. He and his companion brought no trade goods to Otter Lake, but they did bring a woman of the Ihalmiut, called Ootnuyuk, who had borne three children to one of the white men.

Despite Ootnuyuk's presence and her assurance that the white men meant no harm, Owliktuk was deeply disturbed by these intruders. While he preserved courteous relations with them, he kept his group at a distance. He soon concluded that his people must abandon Otter Lake and find a safer sanctuary as soon as travel conditions and food resources made this possible.

In March, Owliktuk and Halo made a trip to Padlei Post bringing with them a number of fox furs which they traded for ammunition. This visit involved a calculated risk, for Owliktuk realized that it would undoubtedly result in news of his presence in the area reaching the police. Nevertheless, it was vital that he and his people have ammunition before they set out to the west, for he envisaged a period of many months during which there would be no further contact with the whites and no way to obtain supplies from them.

Convinced as he now was that the only hope of survival lay in isolating himself from the activities of the white men, he was confronted by an insoluble dilemma, for he knew that the Ihalmiut could no longer exist without access to certain of the white man's goods.

He did what he could to balance these two conflicting factors. As soon as he returned from Padlei, his people struck their camps and vanished toward the west.

Through the April days when the sun began to melt the snows a little in daytime, and the frosts hardened them again at night, Owliktuk's people walked westward into the great plains in search of a place where they could be at peace. Their journey took them near the Little Lakes and here they encountered Yaha who had walked to the Little Lakes to pick up a cache of equipment which he had abandoned there before the transportation to Nueltin.

Yaha was delighted to find his friends, for neither he nor they had known if the others had survived. He told Owliktuk of the Hicks Lake site, and Owliktuk concluded that this would be at least as safe a sanctuary as any other, and so he led his group northward, to be followed a few days later by Ohoto and Yaha.

Meanwhile, the abysmal failure of the Nueltin fishery plan had not gone entirely unnoticed in the outside world. As early as November of 1950 rumors that all was not well seem to have reached official ears, and on December 11, a chartered plane was dispatched to fly to the interior from Churchill and investigate. It carried a policeman, a federal government official, and one of the directors of the now defunct fishing company. The plane visited Windy Cabin and Ennadai, where the official heard that other Eskimos were living to the north somewhere near Hicks Lake. No one knew, apparently, that almost a third of the band was then far to the east at Otter Lake.

The report submitted by the official was, in general, a cheerful one. He reported that the people had lots of fish, and that they seemed perfectly happy and contented. He also had something to say about the failure of the fishery plan, but he was careful to ensure that no shadow of blame should be cast on any of those who had been responsible for it.

By spring of 1951 the shattered fragments of the Ihalmiut had drawn together once again within the boundaries of their remembered lands. To the north, at Hicks Lake, Owliktuk's group had been reunited and now embraced the families of Miki, Yaha, Ohoto, Ootek and Halo. Near Ennadai, Pommela's reconstituted group was living at the Little Lakes, for their fear of another transportation was outbalanced by their increasing dependency upon the radio station, which they visited at frequent intervals. Hekwaw was living at the station itself with Belikari, his remaining son; for the old hunter was very ill that spring and he could not travel even to join his friends to the northward.

Thus, to the superficial, and official, eye, it must have seemed that all was well again in the interior plains, and that the whole shameful episode of the Nueltin fiasco could now be safely buried and forgotten.

1 Spring is well advanced before the heavy ice begins to pull away from the shores of the tundra lakes.

II Portrait of Yaha who was one of the
very few Ihalmiut adults to survive
the disasters between 1947 and 1958.
This was taken at Windy Cabin in
the summer of 1947.

III Windy Cabin and storage sheds near
the mouth of Windy River on Nueltin
Lake. The ice in the river was just
breaking up although the date was
late in June.

IV Portrait of Pommela, the paramount
    shaman of the Ihalmiut, as he was
    in 1948.

V A summer camp on the tundra in the Ihalmiut country. Katelo is in the foreground. The others (from left to right) are: Mounik, Ohoto, Yaha and Miki.

VI Alektaiuwa, son of Kakut, as he
looked in 1948. He was the sole member of his family to survive the disasters of the next few years.

VII   A social evening on the Barrens near
Ennadai Lake. Ootek is drumming
while Yaha, Mounik and Halo sing
the cadence. Note the size of the trees
in this Land of Little Sticks.

VIII   A pair of young buck caribou (one resting, the other on watch) near Angikuni Lake. The time was early August when the antlers were still in velvet.

IX   Halo wearing a parka of caribou skin
with the hair turned in. Around his
neck he wears his *tapek*, or charm bag.

X   The Keewatin Barrens in midwinter.
     One of the rare oasis of stunted
     spruce lies off to the left of the picture.

XI This is one of the last winter camps
of the Ihalmiut in their own land. The
families of Owliktuk, Ootek and
Halo are preparing to move south to
Windy River.

XII   A starving survivor of the 1949 starvation winter, this Padlei woman
was visited and photographed by
Richard Harrington.

XIII   This portrait of Ootek was taken
during the summer of 1947 when he
believed that the hard times for the
Ihalmiut were over.

Ootek's widow, Howmik, and their daughter Kalak, at Rankin Inlet the summer after their rescue from the death camps at Henik Lake.

XV This photo of Ohoto was taken at Eskimo Point in 1967. He was by then stone-blind and living on welfare. The cap was given to him by a tourist on one of the Hudson's Bay Company boats.

XVI The "Rehabilitation" settlement at
Eskimo Point into which the survivors
of the People of the Deer were
moved in 1965.

8 The Rusting Rifles

B Y the spring of 1951 the R.C.M.P. had evidently begun to
feel that administration of the Ihalmiut was becoming too
great a burden. The Churchill detachment had its hands full
with local obligations, and the distance between Churchill and
Ennadai made it awkward to maintain even a semblance of
supervision of the inland Eskimos. The suggestion was therefore
made that the Army personnel at Ennadai should be given administrative charge over the Ihalmiut.

The Department of Resources and Development and the
Northwest Territories Council (they were really almost one and
the same thing) appear to have agreed to this proposal without
hesitation, for it suggested an easy and convenient way of dis-
posing of the minor problems of what to do with, and about, the
Ihalmiut.

In 1951 the Ihalmiut represented only a very small aspect of a
much greater problem, for as everyone connected with the north
was by then becoming uncomfortably, if belatedly, aware, the

entire economic basis for Eskimo existence throughout the Canadian arctic was disintegrating with frightening rapidity.

The second catastrophic collapse in fur prices, which had brought the average value of a white fox pelt down from about $40 to as low as $3.50, had seriously affected the trading companies — so much so that they were already preparing for the day when their arctic operations would no longer depend primarily upon the fur trade. Many of their posts in Eskimo territory were already running at a loss — a situation which no commercial organization could tolerate for long.

Meanwhile the government's expenditures for Eskimo relief were rising sharply, though the total amount involved still remained a bagatelle compared with other expenditures such as those involved in the caribou study, which had already cost more than a quarter of a million dollars. This survey had at least served to show that the caribou herds appeared to be inevitably headed for extinction — taking with them those Indians and Eskimos who depended on the deer for their survival.

Even the Commissioner of the R.C.M.P. seemed to have been aware of the general situation, for in his annual report for the year 1950 he wrote as follows:

"The necessity for relief of destitution amongst the Eskimos has been increasing in the past few years on account of the scarcity of game mammals in some districts, including sea mammals, and the scarcity of fur and low prices [for fur] . . . it is believed that the economic situation amongst the Eskimos is bound to deteriorate from year to year."

This was a masterful understatement. By 1951, Eskimos throughout the Canadian arctic were already dying of malnutrition and its attendant diseases at an unprecedented rate. In those few areas where the incidence of tuberculosis was known with any certainty, as many as 48 per cent of the population were afflicted. Outright starvation was known to have killed at least 120 Eskimos between January of 1950 and the middle of the following year. Except for some Eskimos in the Mackenzie delta who were able to trap muskrat, the average income of most Eskimo families had shrunk to a cash value of less than fifty dollars a year — a sum which had a purchasing power in northern trading posts equivalent to that of about twenty dollars in southern Canada.

This was a situation which we had deliberately created by our destruction of the aboriginal Eskimo way of life in favor of the white-fox trapping economy, and which we had intensified by discouraging the Eskimos from turning in any direction other than toward the trapping of foxes, in their search for a substitute way of life. We, and not the Eskimos, were responsible for the decimation of the food resources — the caribou, walrus and even the seals — for we had put the means for massive destruction into the hands of the Innuit, and far from attempting to show the people how to use their new killing power wisely, we had encouraged the wholesale slaughter of game animals.

There were no two ways about it. The hideous dilemma in which the Eskimos found themselves in 1951 was the direct result of the interference and intrusion of primarily selfish white interests into the arctic.

Despite this obvious fact, and despite the full knowledge of it possessed by the officials of the Northwest Territories administration, no steps were being taken in 1951 to enable the Eskimos to escape their obvious fate. It does not seem to have occurred to the men whom we had elected, hired, or appointed, to deal with Eskimo affairs, that the Innuit deserved any better fate at our hands than would semi-domesticated animals which had outlived their usefulness. There never had been any real policy directed at assisting the Eskimos to help themselves, and 1951 evidently did not seem to be a suitable time to formulate such a policy. Instead, the responsible authorities turned blind eyes upon the north and sought for an expedient way to avoid the entire problem.

They found it by a facile reversal of the principle which had been enunciated on their behalf by the police — that at all costs (even if it killed them) the Eskimos must be prevented from becoming dependent on handouts and relief.

The official solution to the problem of Eskimo survival now became the dole. Family Allowance payments and outright relief became the chosen instruments for the resuscitation of a stricken people.

On April 1, 1951, an R.C.M.P. patrol plane arrived at Ennadai carrying the sergeant in command of the Churchill detachment. The sergeant had not come to see the Ihalmiut. The purpose of his visit was to make arrangements with the soldiers to act as the distributors of Family Allowance and relief supplies and in effect to become the guardians and supervisors of the local Eskimos.

The soldiers were not pleased; but they had no choice in the matter, for arrangements had already been concluded between the Department of Resources and Development and military headquarters in Ottawa. Unwillingly the handful of Signallers now found themselves the arbiters of the Ihalmiuts' fate.

Their discontent did not stem from any lack of desire to assist the Eskimos, but from the honest realization that they were completely untrained and unprepared for such a job. As one of them wrote: "Most of us were signals technicians hailing from all over Canada. We would get moved from station to station at frequent intervals, and wherever we happened to be our main job was *inside* the radio shack, so we never got to know much about conditions outside. Most of our fellows knew no more about Eskimos than what we could pick up from casual meetings when they drifted in to one of our stations. Sure, we would have liked to have been grand-daddies to them, because they were a likeable people and in a tough spot. But what did we know about their problems?"

That was a frank and fair appraisal. The good will was there, but good will alone could not provide the required insight into the problems the People faced — and with which the Eskimos themselves were unable to cope. The situation at Ennadai was doomed to become a case of the blind leading the blind, and the results were inevitable.

In the event, the soldiers had few duties in their new role that spring and summer. Until an R.C.M.P. flight brought in a load of Family Allowance supplies on July 30, they had nothing to give the Ihalmiut. Owliktuk's band, still wary, remained at

Hicks Lake where (with the help of the ammunition they had obtained at Padlei) they had been able to kill a few of the late-spring deer so that they had some meat on hand that summer.

Oddly enough, it was the small group which lingered near the white men that suffered most, for they had no ammunition, and there was none for them at the station. Eventually Onekwaw and Alekahaw were forced to take their families back to the Little Hills, where the fishing was better than at Ennadai.

When the policeman arrived on July 30, he saw only Hekwaw and Belikari. Hekwaw was being treated for his sickness by the soldiers, and Belikari was repaying the white men by assisting them in the general chores about the place. The policeman interviewed these two and then departed for Churchill where he reported that all was well with the Ihalmiut.

Two weeks later the land was visited by another white man, and what he saw and reported was in direct contradiction to the optimism of the policeman.

The stranger was M. J. P. Michea, an anthropologist from the Centre National de la Recherche Scientifique, in Paris. Michea had previously spent five seasons with various Eskimo groups and was a responsible and accurate observer. In 1951, when he determined to visit the Ihalmiut, he went first to Ottawa where the Northwest Territories administration told him that the people he sought were still at Windy River. In Churchill he was told the same thing by the R.C.M.P. Acting on this erroneous information he chartered an aircraft and flew to Windy Cabin.

It is hard to know why Michea should have been misdirected, for unless the authorities kept their records in a worse state of confusion than is normal even in government organizations, they could not have helped knowing that the Ihalmiut had not been near Windy River since January. Conceivably someone may have felt that it would be as well if Michea did not encounter the People at all.

In any event Michea was duly deposited at Windy Cabin and the chartered plane departed, with orders to return and pick him up in three weeks' time.

Michea found no Eskimos, and no one else, at Windy River.

Only a few tattered nets whitening on the nearby rocks remained as a last memorial to the ill-fated fishing enterprise, and it was clear to the visitor that there had been no Eskimos about for many months. However, he was not a man to be easily daunted. He had brought with him a collapsable kayak, and taking this upon his shoulders he set out to the northward across the plains, intent on finding Eskimos if there were any to be found.

Without a guide, without even a map, he walked sixty miles, ferrying himself across rivers and lakes as he encountered them, and eventually fate smiled upon his stubborn search. He came at last to the shores of Halo Lake and in the distance he saw the squat conical silhouettes of two small tents.

The tents belonged to Onekwaw and Alekahaw and their families, and according to Michea these people were living in a state bordering on starvation. They had no reserve food of any kind, and they had barely been able to survive upon the fish they had been able to catch, supplemented by birds and small mammals. Michea was distressed by the low morale of these two families, and by the dependence which they placed upon the issue of supplies from the radio station. Only the fact that the station had no supplies for them during July had forced them to return to an approximation of their old life, but they had done so most reluctantly, and with no real initiative.

They told the visitor a good deal about the fishing enterprise at Nueltin, and they were able to give him a list of the surviving people, including those who were living near Hicks Lake. The total came to forty-two: twelve women, eight men and twenty-two children of all ages.

Michea could not stay with them long, for he had insufficient food. Reluctantly he said good-by to this miserable little group of human beings who seemed so utterly alone and isolated in the vastness of the land, and retraced his steps to Windy River. In due course he reached Ottawa again, and there he submitted a report of what he had seen. In a letter written in November of

1951 he concluded his description of the Ihalmiut situation with the remark that he was very uneasy as to what would happen to the People during the winter of 1951–1952.

No other white man seems to have shared his unease; but the Ihalmiut did.

Shortly after Michea's departure the two families from Halo Lake returned to Ennadai, where Pommela joined them, and they all settled down to spend the winter within sight of the radio station. The cold months were approaching, the months of darkness and the months of hunger; and these three families had determined that they would never again attempt to face those months without the bounty of the white men at their backs.

At Hicks Lake there were also people who looked to the approaching winter with a deep foreboding, and who were prepared to abandon their freedom and to take their chances at the radio station. Owliktuk argued against this, pointing out that the Ennadai station was a poor place to intercept the migrating herds, and that any who went there to live would forfeit their chances to lay in enough meat to last till spring. He reminded the waverers of what had happened to them the previous spring, and he was able to balance their fear of a hungry winter against the possibility of another transportation. Eventually it was agreed that Halo and Ootek alone should travel south to the station and there attempt to obtain enough ammunition for all five families at Hicks Lake. Meanwhile, the rest of the men would make a hunt of the late-summer deer using kayaks and spears at the water crossings.

Halo and Ootek reached Ennadai in the first days of September. They found that the station had been stocked with goods intended for the Eskimos — with new tents, flour, lard, oatmeal and tea. But they also found that *no ammunition whatsoever* was available.

This was a tremendous blow. Halo and Ootek were unable to make up their minds what to do, but eventually they decided to wait at the station through two precious weeks in the hope that an aircraft might answer the urgent radio requests of the soldiers, and bring in the vitally needed ammunition. By mid-September, when the first migrating deer had begun to pass Ennadai bound southward, and no aircraft had appeared, Halo and Ootek realized that it was now too late to make a hunt at Hicks Lake, even if the shells arrived at once. Reluctantly they turned northward, empty-handed, and carrying with them only the assurance that the winter which was already almost upon them once again bore the shape of nemesis.

At Hicks Lake the last pathetic remnants of the true People of the Deer faced the approaching winter together, as their own masters still, but with empty rifles and with the knowledge that they were almost helpless to defend themselves against approaching famine.

They did what they could with two kayaks which they built, but these little boats had been covered with skins reclaimed from old sleeping robes (for it had been impossible to obtain any new late-summer hides). The reclaimed skins were thin and rotten, and the kayaks were dangerously unseaworthy. Nevertheless, they offered the sole hope of survival for the five families in Owliktuk's group.

With Ootek and Halo away, the onus for the spear hunting at the water crossings devolved on Owliktuk, Yaha and Miki. They were assisted by the elder boys, although none of these had ever previously taken part in the ancient spear hunts of their ancestors. Two of these boys, Mounik — who was now seventeen and a man to all intents and purposes — and sixteen-year-old Iktoluka, the orphaned son of Katelo, took to the kayak hunts with enthusiasm. Iktoluka in particular was passionately enamored of the business, and whenever a kayak was not in use he would claim it and paddle away on a hunt of his own.

During the last days of August and the early weeks of September these hunts were distressingly unproductive. There did not seem to be any large herds passing south, and the small groups of deer which were to be seen here and there were wary and elusive. Had they been armed with rifles, the hunters could probably have procured a fair number of these scattered animals, but the whole technique of successful kayak spearing demands heavy concentrations of the deer so that, when they take to the water, their own numbers will prevent them from dispersing and escaping from the attacking kayaks. There had been no such concentrations up to the day in mid-month when Iktoluka took one of the cranky craft and paddled six miles westward to a narrows between two small lakes which lay athwart the traditional caribou migration routes.

What follows is a reconstruction of the probable events of this fateful voyage.

It was a brilliant September day, with the rolling plains flamboyantly beautiful under the orange flames of the dwarf willow leaves which had already been frost-turned to their autumnal colors. Immeasurably high in the pallid sunshine a raven or two hung like flecks of wind-swirled soot — and the presence of the great black birds was a good omen, for Iktoluka knew that the ravens are the outriders of the migrating herds of deer.

When the boy reached the narrows, he carefully drew his leaking kayak to the shore under the concealing loom of a mass of frost-riven rocks. Gingerly he squeezed out of the tiny cockpit and, climbing the black rocks, he found a sunny niche where he could squat and watch the white horizon to the north.

All that day he waited, and he saw nothing living except the ravens and flocks of summer birds that drifted past him to the south. Then, as dusk came near, and the sun filled the western sky with a great gout of color, his quick eyes saw at last what they had been seeking all that day. Atop a distant ridge, Iktoluka beheld the branching forest of a myriad antlers, and he knew that a great herd was bearing down upon him.

In an instant he regained the kayak. He drew the spear from its skin scabbard on the deck, and tested the edge of the polished steel point against his lips. And then he waited, frozen into tense immobility, until the herds should suddenly appear upon the farther shore.

It must have been a marvelously exciting moment when the

wind brought a faint clatter of hoofs on rocks to his aching ears, and when suddenly the ridge upon the other shore grew horns, then vanished under the flood of beasts that topped it and swept down toward the water's edge.

This was a truly great herd, of a kind that was not often seen in the years when Iktoluka approached his manhood. The deer were almost all fat bucks. There was meat enough within the hunter's reach to feed not only the family of Yaha — his adopted father — but all of the People in the Hicks Lake camp for many months. Iktoluka must have felt his heart swell with the knowledge that he, a boy in years, an orphan and alone, was to have this chance to do so much — to prove so much — to be a man in truth.

He waited as the leaders of the herd came to the shore and milled irresolutely, until the pressure of the beasts behind became irresistible, and they were forced into the cold, clear water.

He waited motionless until half the herd had plunged into the narrows; each great beast floating high with its antlered head thrown back, and striking strongly for the opposite shore.

Then Iktoluka came to life. His double-paddle dipped and flashed and the kayak shot out upon the broken surface of the water with the speed and lightness of a waterfowl.

The stream of caribou did not break as the kayak struck against its flank. There was no room for the individual animals to swing away, and in the instant that the fragile craft spun broadside to the herd Iktoluka's spear arm rose and fell. He felt the iron bite into the back of a fat buck. A quick twist, and a withdrawal, and then his arm ran red with blood as it was raised to thrust again, and yet again. Maneuvering his kayak with his left hand, he sent it twisting and turning amongst the now panic-stricken beasts while his spear glittered dully in the setting sun.

Exalted beyond any conscious thoughts, or beyond any experience that he had ever known, the boy had become one with his forebears.

It was Yaha who found the kayak two days later, where it had drifted up against the shore. One of the old skins with which it had been covered had burst like a wet paper bag, and it had filled and overturned. Yaha searched all of one day, but Iktoluka was never seen again.

Yaha and Miki recovered more than a score of deer which the boy had killed, and these they carefully preserved beneath rock piles near the shore. Iktoluka's had been the most successful hunt that the Ihalmiut were destined to make that fall, for in the succeeding weeks the best efforts of the men, using the remaining kayak, only accounted for a few more caribou. There were far too few to form a barricade against the winter famine which would come.

With the return of Halo and Ootek to Hicks Lake it became obvious to all that they could not remain in the present camps and still hope to see the spring again. Yet such was the respect in which Owliktuk was held, and such was the general distrust of the white men, that no one chose to leave the group and travel south until the time came when there would be no other choice.

Meanwhile, all through September and the first half of October, the soldiers who had become the official guardians of the Ihalmiut had been sending increasingly urgent radiograms to Churchill asking for ammunition. But the R.C.M.P. aircraft must have been very busy on other duties, for no time could be spared for a flight to Ennadai. It was not until October 14, when a Dakota aircraft of the R.C.A.F. was dispatched to air-drop a side of beef to the soldiers, that an opportunity was found to deliver some ammunition for the Eskimos. The delivery came far too late. By mid-October most of the deer had vanished from the land.

In November, as the lakes froze deep and the snow wraiths danced on the wind-swept ridges, a small two-seater aircraft on skis came to Ennadai with something for the Eskimos. It brought the promise of salvation and of eternal life to fill men's stomachs and to warm their flesh. The plane was piloted by the American evangelist who had visited the people at Nueltin the previous summer. The new arrival was coldly received at the Army station, but undeterred he flew off to visit the camps at Hicks Lake. To his chagrin he found that the already hungry members of Owliktuk's band did not seem overly interested in his proffered gifts. They were, in those bleak November days, more practically concerned with the salvation of their own flesh than with obtaining the approbation of the blood-and-thunder God of the evangelist. The little plane departed somewhat hurriedly for the more cheerful climes from which it had made its sally into the winter plains.

At Hicks Lake the cold grew more and more intense. Very soon Iktoluka's deer were eaten, and the deer which had been killed by the men were eaten too. Before the end of the month Owliktuk acknowledged that he was beaten. He and his little band gave up the hopeless struggle. They abandoned their last free camps, and began to straggle south toward the radio station.

It was no easy journey, for they had only a few dogs left, and both they and the dogs were already weakened by the hungry weeks. Men and women hauled the sleds, while the younger children rode, and the older children followed in the narrow tracks. It was a slow and miserable progress, made bitter for Owliktuk by the knowledge that, after all, there was no escape for him or for his people; that, in the end, they were still ensnared as certainly as if they had remained in exile at Nueltin Lake. For a year and a half he had struggled mightily to regain a measure of the freedom that had once belonged to the Ihalmiut, and it had been a useless struggle. Now he traveled, with the others, to beg for food from the hands of the white men, the *kablunait* — without whose help neither he nor any of his people could continue to survive.

It was a long, sad march, and there was tragedy near the end of it. They were only a day out from Ennadai when a full blizzard struck the attenuated line of people and sleds, enveloping them suddenly in swirling vortices of snow. The ground drift lifted higher than their heads and each of the fugitives became isolated in his own white universe. They did not halt, for they were afraid to stop in the open without shelter, and they were already so hungry that they did not have the strength to pitch a proper camp in the teeth of the storm. They plodded on, barely moving now, and each alone.

Halo's eight-year-old son Noahak was following his father's sled — the last in line — when the blizzard struck. He was not missed for a long time. When at last Halo understood that the boy had vanished, he turned back and fought his way into the maelstrom of wind and snow until his legs buckled under him; but he never found his son. Noahak had gone down before the weight of wind, and his own weakness, and the snows had buried him.

Noahak's death was to be the last overt sacrifice to the land which had once nurtured its People, and which had now become their nemesis. It was to be the last such death for many years; for from this time until almost the end of their tale the Ihalmiut ceased to be a part of their land, ceased to be the People of the Deer, and became, in common with so many thousands of Eskimos scattered across all of the Canadian arctic, the People of the Dole.

The last of the Ihalmiut reached Ennadai on the 27th day of November; the soldiers saw that they were starving and at once issued them with food. The five families built their shelters within sight of the station, and close to those of Onekwaw, Alekahaw, Hekwaw and Pommela, so that for the first time in many months the People were again united. They were united all that winter: united in passive and indifferent acceptance of the weekly dole which kept them living — barely. One and all they had at last become part of the same pattern.

This was no longer emergency relief they were receiving, this was the beginning of a continuing charity — a stone-cold and bitter charity, which was the easy solution to the problem of what to do with a race of men who had been deprived of their way of life, and who could find no other.

It was during the long winter of 1951–1952 that something

of the true nature of their situation began to be borne in upon the minds of men like Ootek, Owliktuk, Yaha and Halo. They began to understand that the old pattern established by the traders had now been permanently supplanted by another. The deer were gone now, and the fox no longer mattered. All that men could do to save themselves was to pitch their camps in the shadows of the white men's houses, and hold out their hands for food.

Ayoranamut! There was no help for it.

There was no other choice: yet no man of the Ihalmiut conceived of the magnitude of the price that he would have to pay in order to ensure a precarious handhold on a continuing existence.

There had been other men, in other times and other places, who could have told them what it costs to take the dole.

9 *People of the Dole*

THE ability to make capital out of the misfortunes of others had always been a major element in Pommela's character. As the fabric of the Ihalmiuts' lives grew more tenuous through the years, he himself had grown stronger, fattening on their tribulations, and expanding his domination over them as their increasing uncertainty weakened their ability to stand against him. When fate turned upon him in the matter of the abandoned boy Alektaiuwa, and in the death of his wife Ikok, this was a double blow which would perhaps have permanently shattered the pretensions, and stilled the strivings, of a lesser man; but Pommela seemed able to throw off the effects of this dual disaster with an energy and resilience which belied his age, and which must have been almost unique amongst his People.

Even before the winter of 1951 began he had recouped much

of his lost power and prestige. When, in the autumn of that year, the Signals staff was changed and a new group of white men, who did not know him or his reputation, took over the Ennadai station, Pommela made the most of the opportunity and ingratiated himself with the newcomers to such good effect that they soon came to accept him as the "chief" of the local Eskimos, and to work through him in their dealings with the People. Even before this event, he had re-established his hold over his one-time sycophants Alekahaw and Onekwaw, and to this little group under his personal control he was able to add Hekwaw and Belikari, for the old hunter now no longer cared what happened to him, and was content to sit in silence in his tent and dream of the days when he had been a man amongst men.

When Owliktuk's band came straggling into Ennadai in November, starving, and subservient in their need for help, Pommela thrust himself into the position of intermediary between them and the soldiers, and thus, for a time, he was able to exercise effective authority over the whole of the surviving People. This was a temporary suzerainty, which only lasted until Owliktuk's people had recovered their strength, and their desire and ability to resist the shaman. Nevertheless, it must have seemed to Pommela that, with luck and cunning, he could at long last hope to achieve the total domination over the Ihalmiut for which he had hungered all his life.

That it would be a hollow victory to become the overlord of a people who had been reduced to an ineffectual handful of despairing individuals seems to have had but little bearing on the strange and contorted design which had long been the most important motivation for Pommela's whole existence. Yet, from our viewpoint, there is a terrible pathos in this striving of an aged man to direct his final years to the achievement of a goal whose very substance had now become nearly as ephemeral as the snow ghosts which danced upon the wind-swept plains.

Although the summer of 1951 had seen his grip upon the Ihalmiut partially restored, Pommela still lacked one vital adjunct before he could hope for full success in his design. He lacked a family of his own. For almost two years there had been no woman in his tent, and consequently he had been forced into a humiliating dependency upon the wives of Onekwaw and Alekahaw for the essential services which a man cannot provide for himself without much loss of face. This, in itself, was intolerable to him; but there was still another consideration, for no Eskimo achieves, or can maintain, full stature in the eyes of his fellows unless he heads a family, and preferably a large and vigorous one. A man's dignity requires such a circle of intimate dependents, since the ability to provide for many mouths has always been a major yardstick against which an Eskimo hunter's worth is measured.

Pommela was fully aware of these things, but there was no woman for him in the Ihalmiut band. He pondered long upon this problem, until in December of that year he took the only course open to him and set out to find a wife elsewhere.

He was then sixty-six years of age, and ancient by the standards of that land. Yet such was his resolution and his compulsion that he set out alone, in midwinter, with almost no dog feed on his sled, to travel the two-hundred-mile route to Padlei.

He reached Padlei Post just before Christmas time, gaunt and hungry, but still vigorous. Having traded a few fox skins for food and tobacco, he then spent two weeks visiting the outlying Padliermiut camps, talking little, but looking hard. And eventually he found what he was after, in the person of the woman named Ootnuyuk.

At thirty, Ootnuyuk still retained something of the beauty which had once made her famous, and which — in combination with her competency — had brought her a strange and complex history. The daughter of that famous man Igluguarduak, she had been born a Padliermio, at Hicoliguak. In her childhood she had come south with her father to join the Ihalmiut near Ennadai, and there she reached womanhood. She remained there when her father journeyed north to die in solitude in his ancestral lands, and since she was a woman she became the ward and responsibility of her elder brother, Alekahaw.

When she was sixteen Alekahaw married her to a Padliermio

hunter, and she went to live with her husband near Ameto Lake. It was a short-lived marriage, for a white trapper saw her, desired her, and took her for himself.

She lived with the white man for several years and bore him three daughters, but in the spring of 1951 this man left the country and sent Ootnuyuk back to rejoin the Padliermiut. There she met Oolie, an Ihalmio widower who had taken part in the starvation trek to Otter Lake in 1947, and who had later emigrated to Padlei.

Oolie was in need of a wife, for women were scarce in the Padliermiut country too. He talked to Ootnuyuk, who was anxious to obtain a father for her children. She was agreeable to marriage, so Oolie sent a message to her brother Alekahaw, to the effect that he would give a new rifle, six dogs, and some tobacco in bride payment. This message was carried to Ennadai by Ootek who visited Padlei with Owliktuk in the early spring of 1951.

But 1951 was no year for an inland Eskimo to pay his debts. The foxes were scarce and the famine which swept the country made it almost impossible for Oolie to keep his new family alive, let alone pay off a bride price. These were facts of which Pommela was fully aware when he returned alone to Ennadai in January of 1952. He had said nothing of his intention to Ootnyuk, nor to anyone at Padlei; but now he called Alekahaw to him, reminded the younger man that his sister's bride price had not been paid, and demanded that Ootnuyuk be given to him. Whether Alekahaw had any right to do so did not matter — he agreed.

Meanwhile, Owliktuk and the families who followed him were finding that life at Ennadai was becoming more and more unpalatable. Although they were receiving enough food to keep them living — mainly flour and lard — they were being treated with a restraint which made it obvious that the soldiers considered the extra tasks of administering relief and Family Allowance to be a considerable nuisance. The Eskimos were reaping first fruits from their attachment to the dole, for no matter how sympathetic the giver of charity may be initially, he eventually comes to feel a growing contempt for the recipient. It was so at

Ennadai, and Owliktuk was quick to sense the change in mood and it served only to make him more bitterly aware of his own helplessness. Now it was he and his People, and not the intruding white men, who were the incompetents, unable to survive without assistance. The knowledge burned within him.

Things were made no easier by Pommela's assumption of the role of intermediary, and by the fact that much of the relief supplies which were distributed with his assistance inevitably stuck to his hands and got no farther.

By late January the situation had become intolerable and so one day Owliktuk struck his camp and moved away. The remainder of his group was torn between a desire to follow him and the fear that, if they did, they would only starve the sooner. Eventually Ootek took up Owliktuk's trail and prevailed upon his friend to pitch his tent near the Little Lakes, where the rest of the People would join him, and where they would still be close enough to the station to be able to obtain their ration issues.

The departure of Owliktuk's band took some of the savor out of Pommela's life, and after a few weeks he ordered his followers to pack up and move with him to the Little Lakes. Pommela had decided to dispatch Alekahaw to Padlei in early March to fetch Ootnuyuk, and he intended that the arrival of his new wife should be witnessed by all of the Ihalmiut.

Alekahaw duly did as he was bidden, and drove Pommela's team to Padlei, ostensibly to visit his sister and her husband. It could not have been a pleasant meeting for any of them. Ootnuyuk was happy with Oolie, and he with her; but the influence and reputation of Pommela was widely known and feared even amongst the Padliermiut, and when Alekahaw reluctantly explained why he had come, Oolie was unable to muster even a show of resistance. He knew that he was in the wrong about the bride price, and he also knew that Pommela was believed to have killed many men, even from a great distance, by his spirit power. So, in the end, Ootnuyuk and her three daughters joined Alekahaw on the long road back to the Little Lakes.

The effect of their arrival on Pommela's ego can hardly be

overestimated. At one stroke he had not only acquired a new, young and desirable wife who had slept with a white man for many years and knew all the *kablunait's* intimate secrets, but he had acquired a family as well. It was a tremendous coup, and one made even more effective when Pommela bluntly demanded that his adopted sons Kaiyai and Alektaiuwa, who had taken refuge with Yaha during and after the Nueltin debacle, be returned to him. Yaha dared not refuse this demand and so by the early spring of 1952 Pommela was the master of a wife, three daughters, and of the three boys Alektaiuwa, Angataiuk and Kaiyai.

So it came to pass that once again the Ihalmiut lived at their old camp sites by the Little Lakes. They remained here for the rest of the winter; but it was hardly an improvement over Ennadai. There was literally nothing to do but sit in their snow-banked tents and wait for the release of spring. Most of the men had no dogs, or too few to enable them to engage in any serious attempt at trapping, even had there been any incentive — and there was none. Once every week or so the men would walk to Ennadai to receive their handouts; but they were not welcomed any more, except on those rare occasions when their services were required. Twice during April they were ordered to the station to serve as stevedores in the unloading of aircraft; once for the soldiers, and once for a party of government geologists who intended to use Ennadai as a base for an aerial survey of the mineral resources of the inland plains. The Ihalmiut men were employed briefly to do the heavy cargo-handling for this project, which was designed to open up their ancestral land and its potential riches for exploitation by the intruders.

In humping freight the Eskimos were presumably fulfilling the intentions of a spokesman of the Northwest Territories Council who had just announced to the Canadian public that "Wherever possible the Eskimos will be made full sharing partners in the development of the arctic, and will benefit fully from the development of our natural resources."

For the rest, 1952 was a year of deepening apathy for the

Ihalmiut. They remained at the Little Lakes, and at intervals the men appeared at the radio station to receive their Family Allowance issues. A deadly stupor seemed to have settled over most of them. They did not live any more, they simply waited out the endless days.

The children too were at a loss. Imitative by nature, and by training, they found little enough to imitate about these lethargic camps. They had no incentive to imitate the hunters and become hunters themselves, for the hunt was ceasing to have much meaning. Even their games were being metamorphosed into queer combinations of the new and imperfectly understood experiences of the present and the half-forgotten memories of the past. The boys made crude models of aircraft instead of model dog sleds, but having made these toys they could not give them any meaning in terms of their own lives.

Even the women were no longer dedicated to their special tasks — the feeding and clothing of their families. The casual and listless hunting expeditions of the men yielded little meat and very few good hides for clothing; and in any event there seemed to be an inexhaustible supply of castoff white men's clothing to be had for the asking at the Army station. Now the people who only a few years earlier had dressed in well-cut, neatly turned out *attigi, holiktuk,* and other deerskin clothing, wore ragged and filthy denim trousers, raveled sweaters, and tattered jacket coats.

The pilot of an aircraft which visited Ennadai late in the summer of 1952 described the Eskimos he saw as "a sleazy, stinking bunch of bums, wandering about like so many lost curs." He was not an unfeeling man, and at heart he was sorry for the people. His problem was that he could not repress the very human urge to disassociate himself, and the way of living which he represented, from a group of beings who were a frightful reproach to him and all of us.

This disintegration did not of course all come about within a single year — but it was in 1952 that the Ihalmiut as a group reached the next-to-bottom level of the abyss that we had dug for them.

The wellsprings of desire were drying up. There was no reason any more to seek accomplishment.

Yet there were still men amongst the People who blindly strove to find an avenue of hope, and of escape.

There was Ohoto, who still believed with a kind of insensate stubbornness that he might yet become a white man and enter a new world. He was impervious to the inevitable and constant rebuffs that his attempts to cross the barrier elicited from the whites with whom he came in contact. He simply would not face the knowledge that there would be no acceptance of him in his new guise by those he sought to emulate. To them he remained a rather pathetic, but at the same time rather obnoxious, native, who clearly did not know his place. When his importunities became too much to bear, they suppressed his pitiful endeavors with a brutality of which they were totally unconscious.

And there was Ootek who, as the years passed, seemed to become less a tangible human entity, and more of a thin ghost. His great eyes stared into places that no other man could penetrate, as he searched the lonely darkness where unknown spirits dwelt, for understanding of the inexplicable design of which he was a part. For hours, and sometimes for days, he spoke to no one, not even to the patient cripple, Howmik, who was his wife; but sat in silence, lost in time — tormented by his inability to bring some comprehension out of the groping chaos of his thoughts.

There was Owliktuk, too. His was perhaps the greatest struggle, for he alone of all the People seems to have had the ability to see clearly the certain shape of the future which awaited himself and them. He seems to have known, even then, that there was no way out for him; but he also seems to have been supported and impelled to struggle by a belief that his sons and daughters need not share the parents' fate. He and his wife Nutaralik, almost alone of the People, were resolute in their determination to preserve some of the substance of their pride. Owliktuk still hunted, and hunted hard. He sometimes refused the Family Allowance issues, or gave them away. He provided his wife with meat and skins, and she in turn provided food and clothing for her children. Between the two of them they preserved at least an outward semblance of a life which was not yet utterly bereft of meaning. And this they did for their children's sake. Owliktuk believed that someday there would be a bridge across the gulf which separated the Innuit from the white men, but, unlike Ohoto, he knew that the bridge was not yet built.

What would Owliktuk's thought have been had he known that, in this year when the Ihalmiut had almost ceased to be, some twenty thousand Eskimos in a nearby land had crossed the bridge and had entered into a new world?

It was in 1952 that the Danes announced the penultimate step in the development of an Eskimo nation in Greenland. After long years of careful guidance, the Greenland Eskimos were taking over their own internal government and were almost ready to emerge as full-fledged citizens of the modern world. But Owliktuk knew nothing of this, nor did any other Canadian Eskimos. There were few Canadians of any race who gave much attention to the announcement from Denmark, although the event did not go entirely unremarked in Canada, for in July an editorial appeared in a Toronto newspaper, which said in part:

"What should strike thoughtful Canadians most forcefully is Denmark's determination to give a native population every possible political, social and economic advantage. . . . Canada has no such policy . . . are we to see a prosperous and advancing segment of Eskimo population flourishing just across our northern frontier while on our side we continue a policy of sentimental paternalism?"

No one rose to give an answer to that question.

The gentlemen of the Northwest Territories Council might have answered had they chosen — though their reply would have had to be an unqualified affirmative. Within the Council, the R.C.M.P. Commissioner was easily able to convince his hearers that the police were doing a magnificent job, and needed no assistance; while Mr. Louis Audette, who had been an appointed Council member since 1947, and who held the Oblate missionary order (which had given him much of his education) in high esteem, was equally convincing with his contention that the missionaries had the situation well in hand.

The old order still stood firm. In speech after speech, and statement after statement, the members of the Northwest Territories Council extolled the kindly virtues of the missionaries, the police and the traders, and appeared to evade any suggestion that the Eskimos of Canada were not living the best of lives in the best of all possible worlds.

Fortunately for all our consciences, it was still possible for us to ignore the realities of Eskimo existence; for no compilations of facts and statistics yet existed which could prove the Council wrong — there were only the jovial, if vague, assurances of the constituted authorities in the arctic that all was well. As for the Eskimos themselves — they had no voice.

What was happening at Ennadai in 1952 was happening also throughout the rest of the Canadian arctic. In the igloos and tents of most of Canada's eleven or twelve thousand Eskimos there was slow starvation, and a slow death of hope.

Meanwhile, across the Davis Strait things were not the same. Denmark, a small country, with only a fraction of Canada's wealth to work with — but with a standard of moral rectitude which Canada did not appear to possess — had poured its efforts and its money selflessly into a land from which it could never hope to draw a commensurate financial return; and it had done this because it felt a duty and an obligation toward a native race.

As far back as 1860 the Danes had eliminated illiteracy in Greenland, whereas in 1952 only a few score Canadian Eskimos were in any sense literate.

As far back as 1900 Denmark had begun to give a measure of self-government — a voice — to the Greenland peoples, and had taught them how to use that voice in their own interests. In 1952 the Canadian Eskimo still had no voice, but was restricted to the status of a mute dependent who was expected to give unquestioning obedience to the traders, the missionaries, and the police.

In the early days of Danish interest in Greenland, laws had been passed which effectively curbed purely selfish commercial penetration by white men, and the only trading posts which were allowed to operate were run by the government.— often at a loss to the Danes, but with much gain to the Eskimos. Only one religious denomination had been allowed to proselytize (also under state control), so that there had been none of the internecine strife between opposing faiths which stigmatizes the history of Christianity in the Canadian arctic.

Indeed things had been done differently in Greenland, and it was now a far greater distance from the little villages on Greenland's coasts to the tent camps of the Ihalmiut than could be measured in mere miles. It was, in fact, the distance between a morally insensible, and apparently calculated, indifference towards the Eskimos on the part of one civilized nation, and the deliberate acceptance of full moral obligations with all their consequent and costly physical involvements, on the part of another such civilized nation.

In the summer of 1952, an unbiased observer was able to write as follows in a Canadian newspaper: " The Danes have pursued a policy to which those who object to the exploitation of native populations must extend endorsement. What they have done to date for Greenland has been almost exclusively on behalf of the Eskimo population, which has doubled in numbers within a generation and whose income per capita has also doubled."

In the spring of that same year the Canadian press recorded the results of a two-day conference on Eskimo affairs called by the Commissioner of the Northwest Territories, and attended by the Anglican Bishop of the Arctic, the Roman Catholic Bishop of Mackenzie District, the Commissioner of the R.C.M.P., the General Manager of the Hudson's Bay Company, and sundry civil servants.

" The conference was told that Eskimo relief had risen from

$11,000 in 1945 to $115,000 in 1951 . . . knowing that there is always Government aid to fall back on, the Eskimo in some parts of the north has lost a certain amount of his interest in hunting and fishing for a living . . . reports indicated that the spread of tuberculosis was increasing seriously . . . the conference was generally agreed that the present measures for the care and advancement of the Eskimos are sound [and] that the Eskimo should be encouraged to live off the land and follow his traditional way of life."

In the country of the Little Hills and in a hundred other places throughout the Canadian arctic, the Eskimos were to be encouraged to live off the land and to follow their traditional way of life. The incontrovertible facts that the land was rapidly becoming a land of death, and that the traditional Eskimo way of life was already dust and ashes, were not acceptable to the missionaries, the police, the traders and the administrators, for they were convinced that the present measures for the care and advancement of the Eskimos were sound. Nor can they be accused of dishonesty in this. They believed what they said; though as to why they chose to believe these things — they alone must answer.

When the summer of 1952 ended and the plains once more burned with an orange flame as the frosts swept over them, only a few of the Ihalmiut men went out to meet the south-bound deer. There were several reasons why they did not go. For one thing Pommela, whose lust for domination had by now become insatiable, seized the ammunition which had been issued both to the men of his group and to Yaha and Ohoto as well. He apparently had also hoped to intercept the share due to Owliktuk's band, but in this he had been frustrated for Owliktuk and Halo had gone early to the radio station, and had quietly but resolutely refused to leave until they obtained their quotas.

Perhaps Pommela had intended (once he had cornered all the shells) to dole them out again to those who came as supplicants — but having failed in his intention he seems to have determined to revenge himself at least upon those whom he controlled. At any rate he steadfastly refused to give away any of the ammunition he had amassed.

In the event it did not matter much. Apart from Halo and Owliktuk, no one was very anxious to go hunting anyway. In order to stand a chance of finding enough deer to ensure a decent hunt, the men knew they would have to travel to crossing places on the Kazan, two days' journey from Ennadai, and that they would perhaps have to stay away a month. This would mean missing at least one ration issue from the station — and they had become so habituated by this time to the regularity of the dole that few of them were anxious to leave a certain security for an extremely uncertain opportunity of killing caribou.

Thus it was that only two men visited the old killing places that autumn. They were Owliktuk and Halo, whose wives had given birth to the only two children born in the Ihalmiut camps that year. Both these men knew that a nursing mother cannot make good milk on a diet of flour and lard. So they went hunting, and they succeeded in killing enough deer between them to last their two families through the first part of the winter.

They might have saved themselves the trouble. When, in December, the ration issue from the station was considerably reduced, the Ihalmiut turned — as they had always done in ancient times — to the hunters who had meat. Owliktuk and Halo gave freely of their stocks, for it would have been unthinkable for either of them to refuse. In this respect, at least, things had not changed in the Ihalmiut way of living; for the automatic generosity of the successful hunter toward his less successful neighbors was too deeply ingrained to be easily destroyed.

The reduction in the Family Allowance issue had not been caused by a shortage of supplies at Ennadai, but seems to have resulted from a new ukase of the police to the effect that the Ihalmiut were now to be persuaded to take up active trapping once again. The plan envisaged by the authorities was that the Eskimos would trap, then turn the pelts over to the soldiers, who would in turn ship them out to the R.C.M.P. detachment at Churchill as opportunity allowed. The R.C.M.P. would subsequently sell the pelts and purchase those supplies which they felt were best for the Ihalmiut. Meanwhile, the police were authorized to hold back Family Allowance and relief in order to force the Eskimos to trap.

Apart from its flavor of coercion — something which was by no means unusual in the dealings of the arctic authorities with the Eskimos — the plan had merit. But like so many plans formulated by unthinking men at a distance from the problem it would not work in practice. In the first place the Ihalmiut had no dog feed and therefore could not trap far afield. In the second place, the very existence of a relief and allowance issue had ensured that they would all cluster close to the radio station, and therefore would all be forced to trap over much the same ground. Finally, men who lived day in day out on the flour pancakes known as bannocks had barely enough energy to stay alive, let alone walk great distances afield in winter weather in pursuit of foxes.

The outbreak of a distemper epidemic in late December and the consequent loss of most of the dogs ensured that the trapping efforts of the Ihalmiut would lead to no more than token results. Once more the People huddled in their shelters and hoped only to outwait the winter, and to be alive to see the return of spring.

By this time the soldiers were becoming alarmed by the lethargic depths into which most of the People had descended, and they notified the police that the Eskimos appeared to be increasingly unwilling to do anything to help themselves. The police responded by ordering that all the Ihalmiut should be gathered at the station on January 12, at which time a patrol would visit them and, presumably, breathe new vigor into them.

Docile, and dull-eyed, the people duly gathered at the station, but, though they waited a week, the patrol did not come. They were sent back to their camps, only to be recalled on February 2; but again the aircraft did not come, and once more they drifted apathetically back to their cold and hungry camps.

By this time they were obviously starving, and the soldiers

arbitrarily increased the ration issue and again radioed to the police. It was not until the second week in March, however, that the patrol at last arrived. The aircraft carried additional relief rations; but the policemen were not able to stay long enough to see the Eskimos.

In May the cumulative effects of a winter of severe malnutrition made themselves felt, when an epidemic of pneumonia swept the camps. Within two weeks more than three-quarters of the people, of all ages, had been stricken. Had it not been for the prompt and vigorous action of the soldiers there would undoubtedly have been many deaths; but the new sergeant in charge acted with decision. He radioed military headquarters, and an R.C.A.F. Norseman flew in at once bringing sulfa drugs. Ten days later, in the middle of breakup, the plane returned, and, though unable to land, it air-dropped further drugs to the hard-working sergeant and his men. By the end of June the epidemic was at an end and there had been no deaths. It was a considerable personal victory for the Signals sergeant, but it was in reality only one more delaying action in a battle which was already lost.

During the summer, all of the people remained within easy reach of the Army station. They fished a little, but primarily so that they could barter fresh fish to the soldiers for tea and tobacco. Then one day they were all summoned to the station where a rather apologetic sergeant informed them that, on orders from Ottawa, they were to begin earning their keep by carving pipe bowls out of soapstone.

In Ottawa, at the same time, a spokesman for the administration had released a statement to the press to the effect that "A new program of economic endeavour for the Eskimos has recently been implemented and there are considerable hopes that within a very short time all the Eskimos will be gainfully employed."

There is a photograph extant which shows the beginnings of that new economic endeavor at Ennadai.

One bright September day, when the ravens hung high to mark the approach of the deer herds, Pommela, Hekwaw, Alekahaw and Onekwaw sat in a row upon the ground outside the radio shack. Each man had a knife and a piece of soapstone in his hands, and they were busily engaged in carving pipes.

They knew how to do it, for through innumerable generations they had made pipe bowls from soapstone after an oriental fashion which is still popular in Siberia. But the pipes they had once made had been for their own use and were a part of their lives. Now, most mysteriously, the white men had ordered them to manufacture pipes en masse. Who for and what for? No one knew. It did not matter. So they sat in the pale sunlight and worked slowly at their tasks, while beyond the most distant hills *tuktu*, the deer — the heart and spirit of the land — pursued their own inscrutable destiny unhindered.

10 *Madness and Denial*

WHILE the struggles of the Ihalmiut against their common fate became progressively weaker and less effective, the personal struggle between Owliktuk and Pommela mounted in intensity. The conflict between these two had become almost the only emotional reality left in the People's lives, and they watched its development with a sick fascination.

Although he was now completely obsessed by, and engrossed in, what was to be his climactic effort to dominate the People, Pommela had still been unable to make any real impress upon the stubborn resistance of Owliktuk; and until Owliktuk was overwhelmed, those who followed him remained beyond Pommela's reach. For his part, Owliktuk could not completely free himself or his followers from the old shaman's influence, for he lacked Pommela's magical abilities and therefore could not meet his enemy on equal terms. Although he had Ootek's support, this was not enough to enable him either to give battle or to break clean away.

It was an uneasy impasse, and from Pommela's point of view

an insufferable one. But during the early months of 1953 the old man apparently devised a means of ending the stalemate.

In early April a frightening rumor began to spread amongst the People. It was said that the troubles of the Ihalmiut, and the miseries from which they suffered, stemmed from the presence in their midst of a particularly inimical devil hiding within a human body. The rumor gained strength with each passing day, for those who heard it were in no condition to resist the terrors of the supernatural, nor to look for rational explanations of their own pitiful condition.

Although the rumor undoubtedly originated with Pommela, there is some possibility that it may not have been entirely contrived. Perhaps it was so at first, but as it grew and took on form, Pommela may have come to believe in it himself. In any event he gave ample substance to it, as far as the rest of the Ihalmiut were concerned, by pronouncing that his guardian spirits had confirmed the presence of a devil in the camps. He waited a few days for this to do its work, and then he announced that he would hold a séance to unmask the evil one.

On a night in late April the entire adult population gathered, unwilling and yet directly driven, in Pommela's snow-block and canvas shelter. Most of the women, and many of the men, were in a state of near-hysteria before they arrived, and the mouthings and wild gesticulations of the shaman as he entered his trance did nothing to pacify their leaping fear. As silent as the rocks without, the people squatted in a compact mass that stank of panic while, by the dim flicker of a single candle, Pommela worked himself into a frenzy; to fall at last upon the snow floor where he lay writhing like a wounded beast, his eyes rolled up until only the discolored whites showed beneath his flickering lids.

His familiars began to come to him, and one by one they muttered and screamed unintelligible noises through the shaman's twisted lips. The tension mounted until the watchers, even Owliktuk among them, began to know the palsy of outright terror.

For more than an hour the unseen spirits yammered and muttered in that confined space and when at last Pommela lay silent and to all appearances unconscious, there was not one of his audience who retained a grip upon reality.

Pommela recovered slowly from his trance, dragging out the long minutes while the people waited in intolerable suspense to know the verdict of his guardian spirits. But Pommela did not immediately give them what they waited for; instead he turned upon Ootek — the competing shaman in the enemy camp — and roughly demanded that the younger man interpret what the spirits had said.

It was a totally unexpected, and remarkably astute, move, and one with which Ootek was incapable of coping. How could *he* understand the words spoken by another man's guardian spirits? It was an unheard-of suggestion, yet in their present mood the people who waited rigidly for the evil in their midst to be identified would not consider this. Ootek must have realized that he was trapped in an impossible position and, had he been less honest, or less of a true priest, he might have given rein to his imagination and mumbled something which would offer an escape. But Ootek spoke no word. He sat in silence while Pommela turned to the others and incontinently derided his opponent. Then, while the impression of Ootek's failure remained strong, Pommela told the People what the spirit voices had said.

They had spoken grim words; words that appalled the listeners and filled them with a cold apprehension. For if Pommela was to be believed, his spirits had told him that the evil entity dwelt in one of his own adopted children, Ootnuyuk's daughter who was called Akagalik. Furthermore the spirits had also said that only the death of the little girl would banish the devil from her body, and its influence from the Ihalmiut camps.

Akagalik was then seven years of age. She was half white, for her father had been the trapper who abandoned Ootnuyuk and her children in the spring of 1951; but the only link which she now bore with her father's people was the nickname he had given her — he had called her Rosie. Rosie had been born clubfooted, and it was this deformity which had enabled Pommela's spirits to identify her as the repository of a devil.

There followed two nightmare weeks in the camps by the shores of the Little Lakes. Pommela insisted that the child must die and, furthermore, that it was the will of his familiars that she die by Ootek's hand. There was no overt resistance to his dicta, since reason had all but vanished from that unhappy place. Only a few individuals, with Owliktuk paramount amongst them, had kept a grip on sanity. The temporary effect of the séance upon Owliktuk had been abruptly dissipated by Pommela's shocking announcement that a child must die. Yet not even Owliktuk dared openly resist Pommela in this matter, for the fear which the shaman had generated throughout the camp had by now become so real that it was almost tangible.

Ootek was shattered by events. The one sure thing to which he had clung desperately through the tragic years — his steadfast belief in the immutable infallibility of the unseen being who ruled his world — was now being strained to the breaking point; and if it broke, Ootek would perish. He knew that Pommela had tricked him, and he must therefore have guessed that there had been a falseness to the whole séance. Yet he had always believed that Pommela was a true mouthpiece of the spirits. He did not dare accept the possibility that the whole affair had been a travesty; but there was at least one thing of which he was quite certain — it would not be his hand which struck down Akagalik. And so one night in early May he vanished from the camps beside the Little Lakes.

With Ootek's flight, Pommela had achieved a partial victory, for the younger shaman was now completely discredited. Nevertheless, Ootek's disappearance posed a difficult problem. Pommela had said that the child must die, preferably at Ootek's hands, and he could not easily commute the sentence without grave risk of weakening the hold he had established on the People. He may also have been counting upon some kind of moral blackmail against Owliktuk's group if he had been able to force

Ootek to commit murder. He was certainly wise enough to know that the child's death might be avenged by the police, and Pommela had no desire to taste the white man's vengeance. For a time after Ootek fled he seems to have tried to persuade Aleka-haw to shoot the girl, but Alekahaw had no stomach for this kind of thing.

The execution could not be indefinitely postponed or Pom-mela's hegemony of fear would disintegrate. The old man was at last forced to compromise. He announced that, during a second visit from the spirits, he had been told that it would be enough to amputate the child's clubfoot, wherein the devil dwelt.

But Pommela had already delayed too long. Ootnuyuk had managed to free herself of the web of terror put upon her by her husband, and one day she took her three daughters and fled to Owliktuk's tent, where she sought sanctuary.

With Pommela's long-dreamed-of victory almost in his grasp, the flight of Ootnuyuk now bade fair to undo all that he had accomplished and to leave Owliktuk stronger than before. The old man's rage at the new turn of events became so ominous that even Alekahaw began to avoid him, and passed a warning to Halo that Pommela was contemplating the murder of Owlik-tuk and all within his tent. This may only have been intended as a threat to force Owliktuk to send Ootnuyuk and the children back. Pommela could not openly demand their return, for this would have betrayed a weakness, and would have cost him much prestige. Or perhaps he really had become almost berserk enough to murder his opponent; and it may only have been the knowl-edge that his finger might not be the first to squeeze a trigger which deterred him.

He waited, closeted in his tent, and after three days Owliktuk still had not sent the woman and her children back to him. Pom-mela must have been aware by then that the frenetic passions he had fired were now rapidly cooling, and that more and more people were drifting back to sanity, and to Owliktuk's side.

Nevertheless he stayed sequestered in his tent and spoke to no one until a week had passed. By then the people of the camp had recovered from their frenzy, and life had begun again to move in its accustomed ways.

Then Pommela emerged. He came out at dusk one evening, and ordered poor, dull-witted Onekwaw to follow him. Behind a ridge which backed against Owliktuk's camp, he found Rosie Akagalik playing with some of Miki's children and he called her to him. Still with Onekwaw's uncomprehending help, he took the girl to a valley some three or four miles distant, and there he hacked her foot off with his knife.

It was an act of madness.

A wild-eyed and gibbering Onekwaw brought the news into the camps, and Yaha, Miki and Owliktuk accompanied him back to that place of blood and madness. They found the child mercifully unconscious, and they brought her home. Shocked, and uncertain what to do, they attempted to deal with her wound themselves, but when it began to fester they carried her to the Army station. An urgent radio message to Churchill soon brought a Norseman roaring to the scene, and a few hours later the mutilated girl was in hospital.

Although many of the details of the incident were recorded by the soldiers at Ennadai, it does not seem to have been investigated by the police or, if it was, no action seems to have resulted. Pommela went unscathed as far as our justice was concerned.

But there was justice for him in his own land. The shaman himself was never seen again, for he had vanished, leaving in his place only the restless hulk of an old man who was despised by all, and feared by none. Pommela, the man who had displayed the tenacity and the strength of twenty men in his fateful and ruthless pursuit of a useless and unattainable ambition, had ceased to be. Yet, because this was an Eskimo society, the living image of the vanished man was tolerated in its decay, and no one took outright vengeance on him.

While the conflict between Owliktuk and Pommela drew to its conclusion, the Ihalmiut were unwittingly involved in still another conflict. But this new struggle was being waged far from the Land of the Little Hills. It had its origins in 1952, when I published my book *People of the Deer*, dealing with the Ihalmiut and their plight as I had seen it in 1947 and 1948.

It was a heated book, and it had its share of faults and frailties, for it was written with too much subjectivism, and with too few statistics. Vilhjalmur Stefansson had these prophetic words to say of it in a review published in the *Dartmouth Quarterly*:

"Like many another book written at white heat, this one is vulnerable in that it has errors which are readily detected and handily useful towards discrediting the whole on the basis of ' lets see how right it is on a few points we can check' following with the conclusion that since a, b, and c are demonstrably wrong, we are justified in dismissing the whole as a tissue of misinformation and wrong conclusions . . . this reviewer wants to plead against that attitude toward ' People of the Deer.' "

Stefansson's plea went unheeded, at least by the Hudson's Bay Company, the Oblate missions, the Northwest Territories Council, and the Department of Resources and Northern Affairs (as the former Department of Resources and Development was now called). All of these organizations displayed markedly hostile reactions toward the book; and the editor of *The Beaver*, a magazine published by the Hudson's Bay Company, made space available to Dr. A. E. Porsild, a long-time employee of the Department of Resources and Northern Affairs, to speak out on behalf of the indignant empires of the north.

Dr. Porsild's contribution duly appeared in *The Beaver*, as a book review, and quite the longest one *The Beaver* has ever run. Despite its length, however, no space was wasted on literary matters, for Dr. Porsild's forthright and declared objective was to discredit me personally, and thereby discredit what I had said about the Eskimos and their unhappy fate. With rather awesome thoroughness the Doctor ran the gamut from accusations of illegal trading and flagrant and malicious prevarication to the suggestion that I had probably never even been to the interior Barrens anyway. From the pinnacle of his authority as a senior government official, he further stated that the Ihalmiut had never exceeded more than a few score in numbers, and rather surprisingly he went on to claim that there were no more than 5,600 Canadian Eskimos extant — a piddling number of people about which to raise such a hue and cry, even assuming that there was a grain of truth in what I had written. But, as Dr. Porsild vehemently assured his readers, there was *no* truth in the book anyway, and precious little in Farley Mowat either. The review concluded with the bestowal of a pseudo-Eskimo title upon me: that of *Sagdlutorssuaq* — Great Teller of Tall Tales.

Publication of the review was only a preliminary step. Copies of it were mailed to all the major Canadian newspapers, together with a covering letter suggesting that I had perpetrated a hoax upon the Canadian public. Some libraries were even asked to withdraw the book from circulation, and *The Beaver* very nearly gave me apoplexy by consistently refusing to publish my rebuttal of Dr. Porsild's charges, or even to reply to my impassioned letters on the subject.

The storm eventually blew itself out in the House of Parliament in Ottawa, where a brief but revealing rear-guard action was fought on January 19, 1954.

The exchange which took place that day on the floor of the House between the Hon. Jean Lesage, Minister of Resources and Northern Affairs (aided at one point by Mr. Adamson), and an opposition member, Mr. Knight, has its revealing overtones.

MR. KNIGHT: I do not know whether the Minister will remember the last time this subject [Eskimos] was under discussion I brought to his attention certain allegations that had been made in "People of the Deer" by Farley Mowat. I think that at that time the Minister said he would look into the subject and see what he could tell me about it . . . If the allegations in the book are true it is a terrible indictment of neglect upon the part of somebody and I do not know anybody better to blame than the Department of the Dominion Government that handles these affairs.

It is true that some of Mr. Mowat's allegations were denied publicly and to that denial he has replied in terms which I see no reason to disbelieve. His allegations were that a certain tribe of Eskimos have been allowed, through various circumstances, to disintegrate and that in fact their numbers were decreased and depleted through starvation. The theme of the book is that the natural way these people live is through the use of their natural food, the caribou . . . Now the allegation is that these people were separated from their ordinary means of livelihood. I should like to know if the Minister has anything to tell us about it. It is a rather serious business. It involves the lives of people. It involves their extermination by starvation . . .

I made some inquiries of the Minister in the last Parliament. I have to say that the answers I received were not adequate. I would not like to call them evasive, but they certainly were not satisfactory. I am informed now that this tribe is subsisting largely on the charity of the members of some military expedition in that north country . . . What are the comments of the Minister upon the whole situation, and the allegation that this particular tribe was allowed to be starved and separated from their natural means of livelihood?

MR. LESAGE: I said, and I do not believe I can say anything more, it [the book] is false, the allegations are false. If the Hon. Member wishes to have a detailed criticism of that book [Dr. Porsild's review] indicating the extent to which the information upon which the book is based is false, I am sure that my officers and especially my Deputy, would be delighted to send it to the Hon. Member . . . there is nothing more false than that part of the book which says that a certain tribe was allowed to perish by starvation. There is no grounds at all for that allegation. . . . As I said, I do not have in my mind all the facts concerning the allegations in this book, but I shall be delighted to have an officer give the Hon. Member all the information he requires in order that his soul, as a Member of this Parliament, may be at peace, and that he will not believe he has been at fault in allowing starvation to occur in this country without any measures being taken against it.

MR. KNIGHT: Since the Minister has said categorically that these things are false, I should like to say that I, too, have information from what I consider to be a fairly competent authority stating that such allegations are largely true. . . .

MR. LESAGE: At the time the book was written and the events occurred to which my Hon. Friend has referred, I was not very well versed in either northern affairs or Eskimo affairs. However, I am now informed by responsible officers in my Department that the information in the book is false, and that the statement just made by the Hon. Member would not be exactly correct. My officers are in a position to satisfy him that there was no delay by the proper officers in doing what was necessary to cope with an emergency.

MR. KNIGHT: I think it would be wise if the information which the Minister asserts his officers can give, were to be given publicly to the whole country.

MR. ADAMSON [for the government]: Would it be possible to have Dr. Porsild's monograph on the subject given to those Members who may be interested in it?

MR. LESAGE: I thank the Hon. Member for his suggestion . . . and I will see to it that Dr. Porsild's monograph is mimeographed and distributed to them. This would be one of the best answers to the allegations in the book "People of the Deer."

MR. KNIGHT: Let me suggest that in all fairness . . . if Dr. Porsild's statement is to be made public [here] then the reply by Mr. Mowat should be made public so that Hon. Members can come to their own conclusions . . . If the government is going to mimeograph Dr. Porsild's reply at public expense, then I suggest that it should mimeograph the other at the same time. Does not the Minister consider that this would be the fair way to handle the matter?

MR. LESAGE: I do not want to enter into this controversy and I can see no reason at all why we should perpetuate it. And, under the circumstances, since the Hon. Member objects, nothing will be mimeographed.

So this struggle, too, came to its conclusion; but not before Dr. Porsild had fired one conclusive shot to mark the end. Late in 1953 an award was made to *People of the Deer* for its "contribution to better human understanding." When the news reached Dr. Porsild, he wrote a letter in his capacity as an official of the Department of Resources and Northern Affairs, addressed to the chairman of the awards committee. "I am sure," wrote Dr. Porsild, "Farley Mowat is pleased with the award and perhaps a little amused too — for he has a keen sense of humour — that his 'plea for the understanding help without which these people will vanish from the earth' has been heard. What worries me is that the Ihalmiut people never did exist except in Mowat's imagination."

11 *A Dawn Extinguished*

THE distance from Ottawa to Keewatin remained immeasurably great. Almost at the same time that Mr. Lesage was denying the fact of starvation in the arctic, a band of Eskimos at Perry River, including three Hanningaiormiut families who had been forced to abandon their inland homes at Garry Lake due to hunger, were being driven to eat their dogs to keep alive. In early February the R.C.A.F. made a mercy flight to Perry River with a supply of meat; and if this meat was unfit for normal human consumption, it was at least adequate for Eskimos, and the Perry River people survived into the spring.

Those of the Hanningaiormiut who had remained at Garry Lake, where Father Bulliard had now established a minute church-state, were not so lucky. Four starved to death that spring, and one more died of what was euphemistically called "exposure." The rest barely endured until the starvation season ended and the priest returned again to minister to them.

Things were not quite so desperate amongst the Ihalmiut, for no one died directly of starvation that winter. But at the end of February, Ohoto's wife Nanuk, who was big with child, became so ill that the soldiers demanded and obtained a rescue flight, and she was flown to Churchill. Ohoto had hoped and dreamed that the child would be a boy, for he had never had a son and this was a part of his personal tragedy. This child was indeed a son; but it was stillborn, and the reason given by the doctors was a state of advanced toxemia in the mother, brought about by severe malnutrition.

The caribou migration came late to Ennadai in 1954, and when it came there were no hunters to meet it and to take their toll of it. Almost every adult Eskimo was sick, stricken by a virulent form of influenza which was then raging throughout most of Keewatin. In the interior it went unchecked, except at Ennadai where, once again, the soldiers became doctors and nurses. They labored to such advantage that there was only one death amongst the twenty-two adults who contracted the disease. But at Baker Lake and Garry Lake a reported total of eighteen Eskimos died during this epidemic, and no one will ever know how many actually succumbed.

By early June, largely as a result of their failure to make a kill of caribou, the Ihalmiut were again starving since the stocks of relief supplies at Ennadai had early been exhausted. Despite the dispatch of a whole sequence of urgent radio requests for emergency help, no assistance was to be had from Churchill. The Signals sergeant *was* authorized to issue flour from his own stock but, as he was unhappily aware, the small amount of flour, lard and baking powder which he could spare was no more than a gesture to a people starved by a long winter, exhausted by sickness, and starved again throughout the spring.

During May, June and most of July, the diet of the Ihalmiut was limited to an inadequate ration of flour, lard and tea. By this time the people had become so physically debilitated that none of them, not even Owliktuk, had the strength or the ambition to venture more than a mile or so away from the relative safety

of the radio station. They did not even have sufficient initiative
to fish successfully. Throughout July there was a constant sequence of sickness, which the soldiers attributed in their reports:
"Mainly to poor diet."

In early August an epidemic of mumps swept through the
camps and two of the children who contracted the disease became so ill that a military aircraft had to be summoned to evacu-
ate them to Churchill.

By this time the soldiers had become frantic. They were dispatching almost daily messages to their own headquarters, to the
police, to the civilian authorities, asking for new supplies of food.
But no food came, despite the fact that there were five tons of
foodstuffs in storage at Churchill destined for the Ihalmiut. This
huge stock of food had been purchased with the Eskimos' own
Family Allowance credits and with money from the sale of the
few furs they had been able to trap during the two preceding
winters; but the R.C.M.P. aircraft was too involved in other
tasks to deliver these supplies to Ennadai.

On August 18, Mr. Lesage's officers at last took action, and on
that date a plane load of buffalo meat arrived from Fort Smith.
It elicited the following message from Ennadai:

> ONE AIRCRAFT LOAD OF BUFFALO MEAT SENT HERE BY
> DEPT. RESOURCES AND NORTHERN DEVELOPMENT FOR
> STARVING ESKIMOS STOP THIS IS THE FIRST MEAT TRIBE HAS
> TASTED FOR MONTHS STOP CONDITION OF PEOPLE PAR-
> TICULARLY CHILDREN IS PITIFUL MAIN DIET FLOUR AND A
> FEW FISH STOP DOGS ARE JUST BAGS OF BONES AND HAIR
> AND HAVE BEEN TURNED LOOSE TO FEND FOR THEM-
> SELVES STOP ALL OLD BONES AND CARIBOU HOOVES IN
> AREA HAVE BEEN GATHERED BY ESKIMOS TO MAKE SOUP
> STOP THE GENERAL HEALTH IS POOR AND THEY ARE CATCH-
> ING ALL SORTS OF DISEASE STOP TO DATE TWELVE ESKIMOS
> EVACUATED TO CHURCHILL FOR HOSPITALIZATION.

The entire course of events through the spring and summer of
1954 seemed to indicate that the Departmental officials were in
full agreement with their chosen spokesman, Dr. Porsild, that
indeed the Ihalmiut did not exist at all. And had it not been for

the efforts of the handful of soldiers at the radio station, there is considerable likelihood that Dr. Porsild's contention would have become truth indeed.

It had been no happy time for the soldiers, who were humane men, and it was with relief that they heard the news that the radio station was to pass from military control to the control of the Federal Department of Transport, in the early autumn of 1954.

The soldiers may have been glad to leave, but their departure was a severe misfortune for the Ihalmiut. Through the terrible years since 1949 the soldiers had done their best, within the limits of their own experience and authority, to assist the people. To them, and to them alone, must go the credit for the physical survival of the last remnants of the Ihalmiut; nor can they be blamed in any way for the spiritual disintegration which took place during those years. They were good men all, and they did the best they could at a time when no other Canadians appear to have been more than academically concerned with the fate of the People of the Deer.

If 1954 brought little or no improvement in the fortunes of the Ihalmiut it did at least see the beginnings of what appeared to have the makings of a revolution in Ottawa. During this year the department responsible for Eskimo affairs again changed its name, becoming the Department of Northern Affairs and National Resources and, for the first time in Canada's history, a government agency began to display a nascent sense of responsibility towards the Eskimos.

On October 21, Mr. Lesage, still Minister of the Department, gave the outline of a new Eskimo program to the press. He explained that, for the first time, the civil authority would have its own men in the field in the shape of six Northern Service Officers who had been chosen to go to the Eskimos, to live with them, and to lead them to a new and better way of life. These six were to be responsible for "approximately 9,500 Eskimos" (no accurate census of their numbers yet existed), scattered over an area equal in size to that occupied by about two-thirds of the United States.

"This is a work with a rare kind of challenge," said Mr. Lesage with tactful understatement. "Canada is now turning in earnest to the development of its northland. The Northern Service Officer will have a great responsibility for the lands and the people who live there."

Those Canadians who were startled by the government's suddenly awakened interest in the Eskimos did not have far to seek for an explanation. They noted the order of precedence in the words "the lands and the people who live there" and they must be pardoned if they accepted Mr. Lesage's protestations of concern about the Eskimo with a degree of skepticism.

The fact was that Canada was indeed turning in earnest to the development of its northland and of *all its potential resources* there. Since 1950 Canadians, most of whom had traditionally considered the arctic to be a useless and sterile waste, had been undergoing a change of heart. It was becoming increasingly obvious that the arctic held a good many economic opportunities, particularly in the field of mineral exploitation. Furthermore, the rapid development of military activity throughout the Canadian north, most of it under the direct aegis of the United States, had aroused some belated anxiety amongst Canadians that, if they did not take it on themselves to possess the broad northlands in full reality, they might find that they no longer possessed them even in name.

So Canada was looking north; and in 1954 she began to recognize the existence of the Eskimos in the context of her own ambitions and desires. She did not see them as a minority that had been callously disregarded for half a century. She saw them instead as a potential asset which could be of service in the fulfillment of her own ambitions and economic hopes. The words of Mr. Lesage's press release made this quite clear:

As the tempo of activity steps up in Canada's far north there will be an increasing demand for skilled and semi-skilled labour. The supply of qualified white men who can endure life in the bleak and cold arctic wastes is, however, extremely small. To the Eskimos, on the other hand, the hardships of the north form a part of everyday life. In addition it is the opinion of many who have worked among them that they can be trained to meet the need for labour that is bound to arise. It is a common misconception [and, the release did not add, one that had been assiduously fostered as long as it suited us] that the Eskimo has the mentality of a child, but to those who know better he is a highly intelligent person who possesses many capabilities, most particularly an aptitude for all things mechanical. These natives of the north know no greater joy than driving a truck, running a boat, or caring for a machine. . . .

Here, then, was the crux of the matter. Nevertheless, whatever Mr. Lesage's — and the government's — real motives may have been, some of the changes which his release portended seemed, at first glance, to be to the Eskimos' advantage.

The concept of employing Northern Service Officers would indubitably have been a good one if it had meant a change from the haphazard and incompetent administration of Eskimo problems under the R.C.M.P., the traders and the missions, to a vital and intelligent approach under the direction of well-trained and competent field men who were free of the pressure which could be exerted by the old empires of church, police and trader. But with the announcement of the actual appointment of the first six N.S.O.'s, it became tragically obvious that no real change was intended. One of the new N.S.O.'s was a serving R.C.M.P. officer seconded from his force for temporary duty. Another was an ex-R.C.M.P. officer. Two had served for many years in the arctic as traders. Furthermore, it was apparent almost from the start that these men were not to be encouraged to interfere with the existing patterns of white domination of the Eskimo.

The tasks of the N.S.O.'s, as defined by Mr. Lesage, fell into two categories, the flagrantly impossible and the deliberately nebulous. The first were perhaps designed to impress the general public; the second were probably intended to quiet any anxiety which the old empires might feel at this intrusion into their preserves. In the actual words of the Department officials as these were recorded in the press release of October 21:

"The Department is approaching the new undertaking with extreme caution. When the N.S.O.'s are first dispatched to their posts, for example, they will be under strict instruction to tell no one why they are there, or what their jobs involve. If asked, they have been told to say they don't know why they have been sent or what they are supposed to do, one official explained . . . this attitude illustrates the healthy respect the Department has for the dangers which lie in tampering with the ancient habits and customs of primitive peoples."

The release could not add that the new emissaries to the Eskimos had also been instructed that under no conditions were they to interfere with R.C.M.P. activities amongst the Eskimos, and that they were *not* to consider that they had any authority to effect changes contrary to the desire of the traders, missions, or police in their areas.

Without putting too fine an interpretation upon the N.S.O. scheme, it was inevitable that some observers should jump to the conclusion that these new government employees were intended to serve primarily as labor recruiters; and that in fact the government had not suffered any real change of heart about the Eskimos at all.

Those who believed that this was the case were not slow to make their opinions known, and five days later Mr. Lesage made a new speech, in which he said very little about the role of the Eskimo as a truck driver, but soared instead to heights of oratory in an endeavor to show how disinterested and altruistic the government's program really was.

It was the government's sincere hope, said the Minister, to see Eskimo settlements across the north governed by councils of their own people and, before many years had passed, it was hoped to see, not only self-governing Eskimo settlements, but Eskimo men and women trained and serving as teachers, nurses, craftsmen and, in fact, in every activity in the Canadian northlands.

He continued, "We hope to see such Eskimos as are interested in doing so, enter into the life of Canada as workers in fields of their choice — in public service, the professions, in business."

But even while he was propounding this magnificent fantasy,

Mr. Lesage could not wholly refrain from returning to more practical matters, for he concluded:

"It is the task of the Government at once to protect the aboriginal Eskimos from the ill-effects of civilisation and on the other hand to create the conditions which will enable them to take their places in the expanding economy of Canada with particular reference to the fact that they are already dwellers in the arctic, not only used to the country and competent to live there, but loving their country as men the world over love the land they live in."

It is an unhappy truth, as Mr. Lesage soon became aware, that compromise decisions seldom please anyone. Even before the N.S.O.'s went north to take up their appointments, there were undercurrents of suspicion from the old empires. No amount of assurances from the Department could entirely quell the fears of the missions that the days of church domination, particularly in the educational field, might be threatened.

Nor were the police particularly happy about the change. Although they retained their hegemony intact, and although they were actively represented amongst the N.S.O.'s, they were, nevertheless, disturbed for the future; and the attitude of their staffs in the field toward the interlopers was, to put it rather mildly, uncooperative.

The traders alone seem to have had the intelligence to realize that things were changing. Although the Hudson's Bay Company can have hardly welcomed the new intrusion into its traditional domains, it made no overt resistance; and in fact it was by then very busy reorienting its entire approach to the arctic. It had accepted the obvious conclusion that the day of the fur trade, as a major industry, was done; and it had formulated and was implementing a new policy which was intended to turn its network of trading posts into retail merchandising stores which could take advantage of the economic exploitation of the arctic which was now about to start.

Despite Mr. Lesage's anxious and sincere desire to allay the fears and suspicions of the police and the missions, there were in fact some grounds for the unease of the old orders. Even at this early stage there were a few men of integrity and humanity in Canada who were deeply concerned about the future of the Eskimos and who had concluded that their only hope of accomplishing anything was to associate themselves with the Department of Northern Affairs. One or two of these men had become N.S.O.'s and several others had obtained positions within the Department at Ottawa, where they could eventually hope to assist in shaping a new official attitude which would result in real and enduring benefits to the Eskimos. These few were to know frustrations and defeats, at the hands of the old orders, which must have been well-nigh unendurable. Still they persevered, though it was to be a long time before their efforts came to anything.

The People of the Little Hills meanwhile remained insensible to the brave new world which Mr. Lesage envisaged for them, and through the winter of 1954–1955 they existed much as they had done for many years. The only external change apparent to them was in the attitude of the new white men who now manned the radio station. These were civilians and, for the most part, they were highly trained specialists in communications, whose lives were bounded by the confines of their jobs. At first they were mildly interested in the Eskimos as curiosities, but when it became apparent that they were expected to concern themselves with the problems of these primitives, their interest rapidly waned. They seem to have felt, and with justification, that Eskimo administration was no affair of theirs, and they appear to have harbored some resentment of the fact that they were ordered to carry out duties which clearly lay within the province of another government department.

Consequently their contacts with the Ihalmiut were largely limited to those things which they could not avoid — the issuing of Family Allowance supplies, relief rations, and the receiving of such furs as the Eskimo hunters might manage to obtain. The result was that no bond of human intercourse or understanding

could be established between the new white men and the Ihalmiut, and the contacts which did exist were unpalatable to both
parties.

This change was momentarily to the benefit of the people.
Those who still retained some pride of race and person reacted to
the atmosphere of barely concealed hostility and disdain by
withdrawing as far as possible from contact with the whites.
Owliktuk's group, which had regained a considerable amount
of its cohesion as a result of Pommela's downfall, returned to the
Little Lakes where it became more self-sufficient and vital than
it had been for two long years. The older men, Halo, Ootek,
Owliktuk, Miki and Yaha, together with the younger men,
Kaiyai, Anoteelik and Mounik, even managed to make something of a deer hunt during the late autumn of 1954, and were
consequently able to do some trapping.

It was indicative of their relations with the radio station personnel, and of a nascent resurgence of independence and pride,
that they chose to take most of the furs to the distant post at
Padlei, rather than to the station where, in due course, the pelts
would have been picked up by the R.C.M.P., sold in Churchill,
and their value returned to Ennadai in the form of supplies arbitrarily chosen by the police.

In January of 1955, Ootek, Halo and Owliktuk made the long
journey to Padlei, and Owliktuk remembered that trip as being
one of the happiest of his life. They had barely sufficient dogs to
haul their sleds, but they had lots of meat for men and dogs.
They traveled well and hard, knowing the satisfaction of being
free men in harmony with their own land once more. As they
neared Padlei they encountered outlying camps of their cousins
of the Padliermiut who had also made a good autumn hunt and
so had lots of meat. The visitors were welcomed in the all-but-
forgotten fashion with drum dances and song-feasts that lasted
the long night through, while the women kept the meat trays
and the soup pots full.

At Padlei Post the travelers traded their furs for the things *they* wished to buy — tea, tobacco, ammunition, thread and duffle cloth for the women, and oddments of equipment needed in the hunt. They bought little food, for they *had* food — the kind of food they needed.

Nor did they have food for the stomach alone. The relative abundance of the deer in the autumn had provided food for men's spirits too. For the first time in many years the herds had seemed almost as numerous as in the good days of the past; and the presence of the deer had revitalized both the land and the men of the land. At Ennadai, at Padlei, on the Thelon and at Garry Lake, the inland Eskimos had witnessed the return of *tuktu* with an upsurge of hope, and they had taken it as a sign that the hard years were done.

They could not know that what they had beheld was an illusion; that accident alone had directed almost the entire surviving Keewatin herds along a narrow path leading past the Eskimo camps. They could not know what the more enlightened biologists or the Dominion Wildlife Service already knew — that the caribou were doomed.

This winter of 1954–1955 was to be the last winter when the the Ihalmiut, the Padliermiut, the Akilingmiut and the Hanningaiormiut would know a degree of certainty; when they would eat to repletion and could forget the evils of the preceding years.

There was light in the long nights that winter.

When Owliktuk and his friends returned from Padlei in early February they were met by cheerful women, and by contented children; and there was a great round of tea-drinking parties while the travelers recounted the Padlei gossip to the stay-at-homes.

There was hope in the dark months when hope is hard to hold.

In February, Arlow, Owliktuk's fifteen-year-old son, was formally betrothed to Miki's daughter Kugiak, and the two youngsters slept together from this time on, alternating their nights between the tents of Miki and Owliktuk. Furthermore, one of Owliktuk's daughters, Akjar (who had married the youth Anoteelik a year earlier), was now expecting her second child. Since their marriage, Akjar and Anoteelik had lived with Owliktuk but now the time seemed ripe for them to become an independent family. All the men contributed fall-killed deer-hides, and the women went to work in concert to cut and sew until, in the early days of March, a new tent stood by the shores of Halo Lake. It was a stirring sight. For the first time in a decade the number of the Ihalmiut tents had increased — instead of shrinking year by year.

Nor was this all. In mid-March Owliktuk's oldest son Mounik, married Yaha's daughter Ookanak, who had just turned fourteen, but who was a woman in all ways. There was hope now that before another spring, new tents for Mounik and Ookanak, and for Arlow and Kugiak, would join that of Anoteelik and Akjar. There was hope that from these three new families would come many children so that the Ihalmiut could turn their faces away from the narrowing angle of their declining years and look forward into the widening perspective of a new futurity.

Indeed it was a time of hope. The men awaited the return of the deer that spring with a new enthusiasm and with an excitement that fired the blood as it had not been fired for a full decade. They believed that the days ahead would lead them to the life that they had lost.

* * *

During the last month of winter the deer began to move north from timber to seek the open plains; but where once they had surged out of the forests from Hudson Bay to Great Slave Lake, treading a hundred highways to the north — now they came by only half a dozen roads. The shrunken river of life which still flowed up from the famous wintering grounds near Reindeer Lake was no longer supported, nor channeled north, by the pressure of other rivers on its flanks. It flowed into an empty land and it had hardly cleared the edge of timber when it faltered and began to bend toward the west as if frightened by its own loneliness and bent on seeking union with the great tides of the past which had been wont to inundate the entire Barrens in one contiguous sea of life. Farther and farther to the westward the meager river swung, and still it was alone. It became seized with an inexplicable and feverish compulsion, nor did it cease to flow until it had reached the Dismal Lakes, hard on the arctic coast beyond the Coppermine — and nearly six hundred miles to the northwest of Ennadai.

It was an almost incredible and inexplicable migration, and to this day the biologists can offer no concrete explanation of why it happened. But it did happen, and the result was that the Keewatin plains from Ennadai to the Back River saw almost no deer that spring.

It was an occurrence which should have underlined the findings and the prophecies of the caribou survey biologists with such dramatic emphasis that no one, not even a government official, should have been able to avoid the conclusion that the deer were done for. But that was a truth which the authorities, and which the old arctic hands too, were unable, or unwilling, to assimilate. Although the scientists had presented their findings, and were in no doubt about the accuracy of them, they were ignored.

They had proven to the satisfaction of any thinking man that the deer were doomed by a combination of the destruction brought about by rifles and unlimited ammunition, and by the wanton and gigantic wastage of the forests to the south by fire, and the consequent destruction of the lichens and mosses which alone enabled the great herds to survive upon the winter range. The biologists had shown that it takes seventy-five to a hundred years for the spruce-lichen forests to renew themselves after a fire; and they had shown that as much as fifty per cent of the winter grazing grounds of the deer had *already* been destroyed by fires set, for the most part, by prospectors, anxious to expose the naked rocks, or by settlers anxious to clear land, or simply as a result of the kind of casual carelessness with which white men treat their heritage — and the heritage of others.

The biologists had demonstrated that it was starvation which was now primarily responsible for the decimation of the deer; even as it was starvation, either outright or by degrees, which was destroying the peoples of the deer — the inland Eskimos and the northern taiga Indians. But those who had the power and the authority to use this knowledge for the salvation of men and beasts alike chose rather to deny the evidence, and thereby to ensure that men and deer should perish.

The year 1955 failed to bring the deer back to the Ihalmiut, but it did bring a remarkable influx of white men, all of whom were more or less concerned with their welfare. In a sense, this year marked the real discovery of the Ihalmiut, and their recognition as a segment of humanity.

The invasion began with the first visit of the N.S.O. who was responsible for the Keewatin Eskimos. This man, an ex-R.C.M.P. constable, had been given the charge of about two thousand Eskimos spread over an area of more than 150,000 square miles. He had no means of transportation at his own disposal, and was almost wholly dependent upon the R.C.M.P. to carry him about in police aircraft. He was stationed at Churchill, where his primary task was the establishment of an Eskimo community comprised of exiles from Ungava Bay, who were to be taught to work for the Army establishments at Churchill. In his spare time he was expected to look after the needs of all the inland peoples, as well as those of the Eskimos along the whole west coast of Hudson Bay.

He made his first trip to Ennadai in January, accompanying an R.C.M.P. patrol, and he was shocked by the condition of the people, though they were then doing very well as compared to previous years. He was, however, helpless to do any more for them than was already being done by the police and the Department of Transport staff. He therefore confirmed the existing arrangements and returned to Churchill. His report on the Ihalmiut eventually reached Ottawa, where it seems to have caused considerable surprise, and even some incredulity.

An unofficial visitor who followed the N.S.O. to Ennadai was a member of the Northern Evangelical Mission to the Eskimos, a businesslike young American who flew to the camps of Owlik-tuk's group in July and was able to remove three of the children from the camp and carry them off to attend a three-week revival meeting.

The next visitors had a legitimate reason for coming to Ennadai, for they were members of the first medical inspection team ever to visit the inland peoples. Until 1955 all medical inspections of the Eskimos had been carried out by parties aboard either the Hudson's Bay Company vessels, or the new Canadian government arctic supply ship, *C. D. Howe*. Until 1955 no more than 40 per cent of the total *known* Eskimo population of Canada had ever been medically examined in any given year; but in 1955 the addition of air-borne teams was expected to extend the coverage to about 80 per cent.

The team which visited Ennadai found that tuberculosis was present, but not widespread (during the preceding four years sixteen of the Ihalmiut had been evacuated at one time or another as a result of tuberculosis), and that apart from the usual disabilities and diseases associated with malnutrition, the people were fairly healthy.

The medical team had barely departed when another official visitor arrived. This one was a rare bird indeed. He was a young Dutchman who had, for some inscrutable reason, perhaps associated with his strong partisanship for the Oblate missions, been employed by one of the branches of the Department of Northern Affairs to investigate the legal structure of the Ihalmiut society. Though his investigations were somewhat hampered by the fact that he did not speak Eskimo and had no interpreter, he was nevertheless able to prepare a long and learned account of law concepts amongst the Ihalmiut, together with some concrete suggestions as to their future.

The Dutchman was still present when, on August 13, the Ihalmiut were at last properly discovered — by a party from *Life* which had flown to Ennadai to do a picture-story on Stone Age Man.

If the activities of the Dutchman puzzled the Ihalmiut, the

activities of this new group baffled them completely. Nevertheless they were, as always, hospitable in the extreme; and they courteously obliged the strangers, even when the cameraman insisted on moving tents about, and in generally upsetting the tenor of the camps.

These minor inconveniences resulted in Anoteelik and Akjar, together with their baby son Igyaka, eventually appearing in full color on the cover of *Life* above an illuminating title which read: "Stone Age Survivors." It was a distinction (the appearance, not the comment) which many white men would have envied — but it was of little concrete value to the People.

By August 29, the autumnal deer had not yet appeared and a serious food shortage was already developing. In early September, when a few stragglers from the vanished herds began to pass through the land, the Ihalmiut were unable to hunt, for they had no ammunition. It was not until September 15 that the R.C.M.P. flew in the season's supply of shells, but by then there were almost no deer remaining in the Ennadai area.

On September 23, when the young Dutchman departed, he noted that the people had not been able to get enough meat to last them for more than a few weeks. Clearly the Ihalmiut were again in difficulties; but the expert on Eskimo law had a solution to their continuing problem, a solution which he included in his official report.

"No experiments," he wrote, "should be made with the few hundred Eskimos of the inland. Only a close teaching of the gospel, after my opinion, will save their small communities and offer some perspective for the future. It needs no elucidation that the conditions for their personal happiness can be assured by this."

It was a sincere, if somewhat incredible, statement, but it was dictated directly by the Oblate policy which was frankly one of holding the Eskimos in their present and primitive conditions despite all odds, and in resisting the first hesitant efforts of the few thoughtful men in Ottawa who foresaw that eventual survival for the Eskimos could only be ensured by bridging the gap between their culture and ours, and by admitting them to full

equality in our society. The Oblate resistance to this as yet nebulous trend was being effectively demonstrated at Garry Lake
where the majority of the Hanningaiormiut were now firmly
under the control of Father Bulliard, who was using every
method at his disposal to prevent them from establishing relations with the outer world, and to ensure that they remained
"unspoiled."

Before coming to Ennadai the young Dutchman had arranged
to be joined there by Father Ducharme, an Oblate priest from
Eskimo Point who could have introduced the "conditions for
the personal happiness" of the Ihalmiut, as these were presently
being enjoyed by the Hanningaiormiut at Garry Lake. Fortunately the R.C.M.P., who had volunteered to fly the priest to
Ennadai, were unable to do so due to an accident to their aircraft,
and so these plans went unrealized.

"The caribou hunt at Ennadai in the fall of 1955 was just
short of a total failure," to quote the words of the N.S.O. In
fact the people obtained only enough meat to last them until
November, and when it was eaten they were back where they
had been two years earlier — on the dole once more.

The N.S.O. was not able to visit them until January when he
again accompanied the R.C.M.P. patrol. His time at Ennadai was
too short to allow a visit to the rest of the camps at the Little
Lakes, but the N.S.O. authorized the Department of Transport
staff to issue some frozen buffalo meat which had been in storage
at the station since the starvation summer of 1954, and which
was now perishing. With one notable exception this was to be the
only meat the Ihalmiut would see until the spring.

The police and the N.S.O. paid a second visit in February,
bringing supplies of flour, lard and oatmeal, and the N.S.O. subsequently reported to Ottawa that he had found almost no fur
waiting to be taken out, and that the people appeared to be completely shiftless. He recommended that a competent person be
employed to supervise and direct their activities on the spot. Unfortunately no such person was available.

So things continued as before. Most of the people clustered as close to the station as the Transport men would allow, and huddled in their snow-banked tents, there to outwait the winter in the kind of physical misery which had become second nature to them. But this year they were totally without hope, and abjectly resigned to an acceptance of their lot. Their very will to live seemed to have been stifled by this renewed descent into despair after the previous winter's brief journey into hope. There seemed to be no room in their minds now for anything except an all-embracing apathy.

apathy

12 *The Promised Land*

B Y early March of 1956 the Ihalmiut were as close to physical and spiritual extinction as people can come, and still survive. The relief supplies had been exhausted and the Department of Transport staff had been forced to issue flour from their own stocks, supplemented by three hundred pounds of ham that had gone bad and been condemned. Some of this foul meat was fed to the handful of surviving dogs, and when they did not die of it the rest was issued to the Eskimos who "ate it with relish."

Such was their condition when, on March 19, they received an epochal visit. On that day the Eastern Arctic Patrol, consisting of a party of officials of the Department of Northern Affairs and the Department of Health and Welfare flew to Ennadai to make a firsthand assessment of the problem of the Ihalmiut.

Within the Department of Northern Affairs the persistent struggles of the handful of dedicated men were now beginning to have some small effect, and this visit was the first concrete evidence that their efforts might eventually amount to something. In March of 1956 a senior official looked for the first time upon the remnants of the Ihalmiut, and he was deeply disturbed by what he saw.

Later, he described the conditions under which the people were existing as intolerable. He visited some of their tent shelters and discovered that they lacked everything a human being needed to survive in that hard land, including bedding. He noted that the people were suffering so severely from hunger that they were quite unable to fend for themselves; and that their morale was so low that they were incapable of making any sustained effort on their own behalf. He reported that of the seventy-five dogs which the people had possessed at the beginning of the winter, only five skeletal survivors remained.

The visit of the Eastern Arctic Patrol was brief, but it had an immediate effect. During the next two weeks the N.S.O. and the R.C.M.P. flew in several plane loads of supplies to Ennadai, and outright starvation was temporarily halted. The visit also established, beyond any further possibility of evasion, that, unless the pattern of life amongst the Ihalmiut was radically altered to prevent a continuing repetition of the events of the past years, the last of the Ihalmiut would soon vanish from the land, and from humanity.

But even before the visit of the official party to Ennadai, other agencies had been at work preparing a plan for the salvation of the Ihalmiut, a plan which was certainly radical, not to say drastic. This plan seems to have originated with two men, the Hudson's Bay Company manager at Padlei and the R.C.M.P. corporal in charge of the Eskimo Point detachment.

The corporal was a man of parts. During his stay at Eskimo Point he had shown that he possessed vigorous ideas as to how the "natives" should be handled, and most of the other whites in the tiny settlement — it consisted of the trading post, an Oblate mission and the police detachment — seem to have agreed that his methods were at least efficacious. The Eskimos of the area, however, were not inclined to agree with their betters. They were, in fact, terrified of the policeman, for the corporal was a very forceful man.

In December of 1955 he suggested in a memorandum that the

only hope for the Ihalmiut lay in their transportation to his area, where they would come under his control and would be subject to his "no-nonsense" policy of native administration. The N.S.O. was not in favor of this plan at first, for he still hoped that a competent supervisor might be found who could go and live with the Ihalmiut in their own country and gradually lead them out of the morass in which they were immersed. However, he was persuaded to change his mind by the combined arguments of the corporal and of the Padlei Post manager.

The trader at Padlei, who was himself of Eskimo extraction, had always been a good friend to the Padliermiut. He had lived with them for fifteen years and knew no other home; but since 1951 he had witnessed an abrupt decline in the numbers of his hunters — a decline due primarily to death by starvation and disease, which was rapidly depopulating the Padlei area and thereby threatening the continued existence of the post itself.

Awareness of this danger may have contributed to the post manager's anxiety to see the Ihalmiut brought to Padlei; yet he believed, in all sincerity, that such a move would be to their advantage. He believed that proximity to a trading post would act as a stimulus to help them regain something of their independence. He was personally convinced that the caribou were not really threatened with extinction, or even with a serious decline in numbers. It was his belief that, under his guidance, the Ihalmiut would soon shake off the apathy engendered by years of dole, and would be able to live adequately, if not well, on the meat and fish the Padlei district could provide.

Essentially his hopes were reasonable; but they were founded on a false premise — that the deer could still remain the mainstay of the inland people's lives.

The recommendations of the R.C.M.P. corporal, backed by those of the trader, made the decision inevitable; for the old orders still spoke in loud and imperative tones. The report of the Eastern Arctic Patrol clinched matters. Something obviously had to be done, and done at once. The decision was made to move the Ihalmiut eastward to the Padlei district.

Although this decision became final in June, it was not until

August that the N.S.O., accompanied by the corporal from Eskimo Point and by the Padlei Post manager, could fly to the interior in search of a suitable location for the people. Their choice finally fell on Offedal Lake, which is an inlet on the western shores of North Henik Lake. It was unoccupied territory, being south and west of the area which the Padliermiut themselves still held.

The surrounding country consisted of high ridges and bald rock hills, in whose sheltered valleys stood stunted stands of black spruce trees. It was good white fox country and, while the value of fur had remained high, it had been a favorite trapping ground for numerous white trappers. It was not, however, and had not been in living memory, a good place for caribou.

The last Eskimos who had attempted to live on the land near the two Henik Lakes had been the Taherwealmiut, a people of the Ihalmiut stock who had moved eastward from the Kazan before the turn of the century. They had found that the Henik area was not good caribou country and so they gradually moved down the Th'Anne River toward the coast, where a small remnant of them still exists.

During the late 1920's and the early 1930's a few Padliermiut tried to live at Henik, but by the late '30's the entire western regions near this lake had been abandoned to the white trappers who were not so dependent on the land for food.

These were indubitable facts, and they must have been known to those who proposed that the Ihalmiut be settled at Henik Lake. But if they were known, their implications were totally ignored. Indeed the N.S.O. gave, as one of his main reasons for the choice, that the "Ennadai Eskimos" were intimate with the new area, and considered it to be a good place for deer. The Ihalmiut, when they were officially interrogated about this in March of 1958, denied that they had ever said these things, and they were vehement in their statements that Henik had always been a notoriously bad place for caribou. As for their familiarity with Henik Lake, the only contact they had ever had with the area was when they traveled through it en route to Padlei, together with the two despairing journeys they had made to the vicinity of Otter Lake in 1947 and in 1951.

It is also known that when the projected move was first broached to them they were unenthusiastic. Not only were they aware that Henik was poor caribou country, but they had other cogent reasons for disliking it as a place to live. For countless generations they had avoided broken hill country of the type which characterizes the western shores of Henik, knowing such areas to be the domains of particularly unpleasant spirits. The sincerity of their belief in these hill trolls is amply documented by Knud Rasmussen in his *Intellectual Culture of the Caribou Eskimos* and, as far as the Ihalmiut were concerned, this was an extremely potent reason for giving Henik as wide a berth as possible.

Nor were they favorably impressed by the argument put forward by the N.S.O. that Henik was a good fish lake and that, in the unlikely event that deer might happen to be temporarily scarce, the people could live handsomely on fish.

The idea that Eskimos could survive on fish as their primary article of diet had by now become one of the most widespread, and fatal, misconceptions in the arctic. Almost certainly the idea originated amongst those who wished to keep the Eskimos on the land at all costs, even though the meat mammals were to vanish utterly, and it had been so strongly advocated by these people that men who should have known better had come to believe it too. The Eskimos never believed it. They were fully aware that fish, and particularly fresh-water fish, can provide no more than a starvation diet for those who must cope with the inimical physical environment of the arctic. They knew that fish might suffice to keep a man alive if there was nothing else to eat, but only at a fearful cost in the slow wastage of his body. The inland Eskimos, who had been masters of the land for centuries, had learned *not* to rely on fish. Indeed they thought so little of it as a source of sustenance that they had never devised any fishing techniques beyond the use of the spear. A whole body of tabus and restrictions had grown up about the use of fish and, as any student of primitive society knows, most native food tabus have a solid basis in reality. Amongst the inland peoples these restrictions had no doubt been intended to ensure that men did not come to rely on fish (which were often more easily obtainable than meat) and so court self-destruction.

The presence of these tabus amongst the Ihalmiut was well known, and had been described with exasperation by the N.S.O. and the R.C.M.P. who had often railed at the people for their stubborn refusal to accept the advice of their mentors and turn to fish.

Whether the many arguments against moving the Ihalmiut to Henik Lake were even considered must remain an academic question. For whatever unexplained reasons, the decision had been taken and nothing was to be allowed to alter it.

While the plans were maturing, things had not been going well at Ennadai. The deer again failed to appear in any numbers during the spring migration. Two animals, killed on May 12, appear to have represented the grand total for that month, and they were eaten in a single day. A report from that period has this to say:

"The natives continue to spend their time hanging about the D.O.T. station begging food, and they seem to be almost utterly dependent on what is being supplied to them. It is believed they could catch fish, but they do not seem to want to. However, good nets have been purchased for them on Family Allowance credits and they will not have any excuse for not keeping themselves well supplied . . ."

In Ottawa the plans for the move were being passed from department to department, and at the headquarters of the R.C.M.P. they elicited some sensible advice from one of the senior officers. This man insisted that the move should not be made at all unless the Ihalmiut could be accompanied by a trained and competent white man who spoke the language and who would remain with the people at the new location until they had become permanently established there. He was emphatic in his opinion that there was a definite risk of failure if the Eskimos were left to their own resources within a month or two of their arrival at Henik Lake.

In August, after the reconnaissance of Offedal Lake was completed, the N.S.O. and the R.C.M.P. corporal, again accompanied by the Padlei Post manager, flew on to Ennadai to inform the Ihalmiut of what was in store for them. Through the medium of the trader the people were told that they would be given transportation to Henik Lake as a gesture of good will on the part of the government, but that if they attempted to leave that place in order to return to Ennadai, they would get no further assistance. They were then asked if they wished to move and, since they clearly had no alternative (or at least thought that they had none), they agreed to do as the white men wished.

It had been intended to move them by R.C.M.P. Otter aircraft, sometime in August; but at the last minute the police plane was called away on other duties, and arrangements had to be hurriedly concluded with the R.C.A.F. for the use of a Canso amphibian. The usual snarl of red tape delayed matters so that it was not until September 16 that this aircraft could reach Ennadai where the people had been patiently waiting since August 2, prepared to leave on a moment's notice. Now it was decided that the season was too far advanced, and that the move could not be made in 1956.

The Ihalmiut did not display any marked unhappiness at the postponement. During early September they had killed a few caribou, and Owliktuk's group had recovered enough incentive to trek back to the Little Lakes in the hope of being able to survive the winter there. Owliktuk was having second thoughts about the move in any case. He remembered all too vividly the events which had followed upon the previous transportation of his people.

The supply of autumn deer lasted Owliktuk's band until the end of January, when they were once again forced to return to the station and to the flour and baking powder diet. Yet the Ihalmiut were luckier than most of the inland Eskimos that winter. To the north, at Baker and Garry Lakes, influenza again swept through the camps of people who were attempting to survive on fish, and twenty-one individuals, most of them children, are known to have died from the disease. At Padlei the annual epidemic was measles; but it killed only four people. It was a normal year amongst the inland Eskimos.

In early April the Ihalmiut received an unpremeditated visit from Canon Sperry of the Church of England, who was forced down at Ennadai while en route from Churchill to Yellowknife. His account of what he saw is worth recording:

> There was a group of about fifty Eskimos nearby and the sound of the plane brought them to the landing strip to see what was going on. They presented a picture of such abject misery and such indescribable filth that I found it hard to believe they were Eskimos at all. They stood huddled together in old skins; were gaunt and dirty and had faces hollowed out with malnutrition. Between the fifty of them they had one dog, if it could be described as such.
>
> I visited their hovels, circular walls of snow with old skins forming a roof. An old fuel can in the centre formed a stove for twigs and willows. That morning, they said, they had breakfasted on pieces of caribou skin — boiled. This meagre starvation diet was supplemented by the leavings of the radio men at the nearby station. Indeed they formed a pitiable spectacle. . . .

The good canon was so appalled, and so distressed, that he was unable to resist some disparaging comparisons between these miserable and apathetic starvelings and other Eskimos he had known in happier times and better places. Probably he would have found it hard to believe that not much more than a decade earlier these had been a proud, vigorous, and happy people. He was glad enough when his aircraft was able to pursue its journey on the following day.

In late April some caribou miraculously appeared, but the hunters were unable to make more than a token kill due to the fact that the D.O.T. staff had been instructed by the police to issue only ten rounds of ammunition at a time. This necessitated a long and laborious trek back to the station after each sally to the hunting places. Considering the scarcity and dispersion of the deer, and the consequent tendency of the hunters to begin shooting from excessive ranges, a man was lucky if he got one animal with his ten shots. The result of this rationing of shells was effectively to prevent a successful hunt — which may have been the intention, since the restriction of ammunition was apparently imposed by the R.C.M.P. on the recommendation of the Wildlife Branch of the Department of Northern Affairs in order "to prevent the natives from slaughtering the already depleted caribou herds."

In the event, the failure of the hunt was unimportant for on May 6 a radio message reached Ennadai with instructions that all the Eskimos were to be gathered at the station prepared to fly to their new home at Henik Lake.

On the morning of May 10, 1957, the distant mumbling of an approaching aircraft engine reached the people who had gathered about the radio station at Ennadai. Men, women and children came from their tents to stand uncertainly, staring into the northeast. They did not talk amongst themselves. All of them knew what the sound portended, and there was nothing to talk about. Once more the time had come when the People of the Little Hills must leave their land and, submitting to the will of others, must go to a new destiny.

The big R.C.M.P. Otter aircraft circled once and came in heavily upon the ice. Two policemen and the N.S.O. climbed down and walked toward the land where the D.O.T. men waited impatiently — waited with relief writ large upon their faces; for the plane's arrival meant the end of a long and weary period during which the Eskimos had represented an increasing burden.

It was a fine morning. The sun stood high, and was already hot with the distant promise of spring. There was a sharp aseptic glare from the snow on the nearby ridges, and in the distance to the northeast the Little Hills loomed dimly like the backs of primordial and gigantic beasts emerging from a glacial sleep. It was the time of the year when men were used to climb those hills so that they might stare southward in anticipation of the moment when the horizon would begin to shift and shimmer with the oncoming tide of *tuktu*. But there were no living men on the Little Hills that day. There were only the stone *inukok*, the "semblances of men"; and they had no eyes with which to watch the last of the people of that land being herded out upon the ice, to disappear into the bowels of the aircraft.

The Ihalmiut made their farewells to their land in silence. They obeyed the instructions of the whites, and did so quietly. One by one they carried their bundles to the plane.

It took five flights to move the fifty-seven people and the five dogs which the N.S.O. had purchased for them at Churchill. They were allowed no baggage, except what they could carry in their hands and on their backs. Their traps remained upon the land. Their sleds and kayaks, and two canoes, their tents and most of the rest of the heavier gear which was vital to existence on the plains, were left behind. During the preceding few days Owliktuk and Ohoto had even been refused permission to visit the Little Lakes in order to pick up caches which included Ohoto's rifle. Perhaps someone may have feared that they would not return to Ennadai to join the exodus.

On their arrival at Offedal the people were issued with canvas tents and they were given some extra canvas with which to patch their tattered clothes. According to the official reports they were also given a month's supply of flour and other food, paid for out of their Family Allowance credits.

It was felt by the N.S.O., the trader and the policeman that these supplies would be quite adequate to tide the people over a transition period, "for the caribou were expected in a week or two, and in any case it was believed that there were ptarmigan in the hills and fish in Offedal Lake."

Originally it had been intended that the advice of the senior R.C.M.P. officer in Ottawa should have been followed; and an excellent man named Louis Voisie was to have been left with the Ihalmiut until they settled in. In the event Voisie's services were dispensed with. It was the opinion of the three men who conducted the move that he would not be needed.

The transportation of the Ihalmiut was completed on May 11. The people were told that they were now on their own resources — that they were again hunters and men — and should behave accordingly. With a final injunction to remember that they were

not to return to Ennadai, the three white men climbed aboard
the Otter and it soon vanished eastward over the ice of Henik
Lake.

Without enough dogs to make sled travel possible while the ice
remained, and with no canoes to provide transportation during
the season of open water, the Ihalmiut were virtually cut off
from Padlei, though it lay only forty-eight air miles away. Their
isolation was intentional. They were to be subjected to a cure for
their lethargy, their indolence, and their passive acceptance of
the dole. It was, to be sure, a somewhat drastic cure; but those
who devised it must have had confidence that it would work.

When I talked to Owliktuk about those early days at Offedal
he told me a remarkable story. To preserve the flavor of it I re-
peat it here in the first person, translated into free English from
the original tape recording.

We were surprised when the white men told us this was a good
place for caribou, for we knew it was a hungry country. All the
same it was the right time for the deer to come north and we
needed meat. The food that had been left for us only lasted a
few days. Our people were hungry and they ate a lot.

The white men had made us pitch the tents under a big hill.
We knew this to be an evil place but we let the tents stay there
for a while and took our rifles and went looking for deer trails
and crossing places. We found no trails. We knew there had not
been any deer in this place for a long time because there were no
old trails. After a while we came back to the tents and we decided
to move because we were afraid of the hill spirits.

We knew we could not go back to our own country, but we
thought if we went a little way to the west we might find level
ground where the deer might pass. Some of the people would not
move, because they said it was no use. So they stayed at the camp
the white men had chosen for us. They were Pommela, Alekahaw
and Onekwaw. All the rest of us walked for a day to the southwest until we had crossed the big hills and reached some little
lakes where we could see flat country to the west. Here we set up
our camps. There was lots of wood here, and we had fires, but
we had no food. There were some ptarmigan but not enough
to be much use. We tried to fish in the lakes, but the ice was

very thick [it would then have been from six to eight feet in thickness], and when we had cut through it we did not catch any fish by jigging. I do not think there were any fish in those lakes.

It was on the second day after we had come to Henik that we moved to the new place. While we were making the new camp we heard some airplanes flying to the southwest and Anoteelik thought they were landing. So he and Mounik and another walked that way. They found some white men with a big camp, and with a tractor, and one of the white men gave them some food.

The next day all of the men walked to that camp and they gave us food again, but they did not have very much to give us.

One day Alekahaw arrived at our camp and said that Pommela had died and that he had starved to death. He said there was nothing to eat at the first camp and so he had come to see if there was food where we were. We did not have any food, for no deer had come at all and we could not get any fish.

Some thought we ought to walk back to our own country but it was too far when the children were hungry, and anyway the white men had told us we had to stay where we were.

One day a white man from the camp came to visit us with Anoteelik. He slept with us and went back the next day. He said he would send a message that we were hungry and that some food would be brought in. Nothing happened for a long time. We were all hungry, but the white men at the camp could not give us much food. Mostly we stayed in the tents and some people wished they had run away and hidden when the plane came to Ennadai to take us away.

It was by an unlikely coincidence that, on the day before the Ihalmiut were moved from Ennadai, an advance party for a large mining corporation should have established a base for their summer prospecting operations at Bray Lake, only fifteen miles southwest of Offedal. This camp was established with considerable secrecy, and it appears that the police corporal at Eskimo Point was not aware of its existence. If he had known about it, there is a strong possibility that the Ihalmiut would have been settled elsewhere — and that would have been unlucky for the people. Had it not been for the accidental propinquity of the mining camp it is probable that most of the remaining Ihalmiut would have died that spring.

The Bray Lake operation was a large one. While the four white men in the advance party erected buildings and hauled supplies to the site with a caterpillar tractor, a big Canso aircraft from Churchill brought in load after load of supplies, landing with them on the lake ice. It was this Canso which Anoteelik heard, and on May 12 he walked south to try and find its landing place. What follows is from the personal record of Mr. P. Lynn, who was one of the party at Bray Lake:

One day shortly after a Canso had landed and taken off I was sitting in my tent when the flap was thrust open and a figure stepped in. He was a grotesque looking fellow and I was momentarily startled. He introduced himself as Anoteelik. I offered him tea and food which he readily accepted. He asked if I had seen any caribou and I said I had not. I asked where his village was and he said it was some hours off to the northeast and that there were many of his people there. I kept offering him food and he ate in such a famished way that I thought he had not eaten in some time. Later I discovered that this was the case, not only for him, but for his whole tribe. Later more Eskimos came and I offered them food, but they were eating so much that I became apprehensive about our fresh meat supply which was limited.

In the evening I explained to the foreman that these Eskimos wanted to work for us and would accept food in lieu of wages. He said that this was not possible, and the Eskimos went away.

The following day the Eskimos returned and brought some of their fellow hunters. They seemed to be in desperate need of food and accepted every opportunity to take it. [There are photographs extant of this visit which show Anoteelik and Yaha grubbing through the camp garbage pile.] Unfortunately we were not fully aware of their dire circumstances and had to save our meat for ourselves, so we did not offer them too much.

In the afternoon Anoteelik brought another Eskimo named Uhoto [Ohoto]. I learned from Uhoto, who could speak a few words of English, that the little group was in need of food for they were starving and already one of their elder tribesman had died of starvation.

The next day a Trans Air Norseman arrived and the pilot listened to Uhoto tell of the conditions of his people. He said he would mention this to the authorities when he returned to Churchill. Uhoto then asked if he had seen any caribou. The pilot told him that he had seen thin trails to the south and that they should be here in a few days. Uhoto seemed to feel better about this. Later the pilot told me that the caribou were few and were slanting off to the north and west and the chances were they would pass a number of miles to the west of us.

A few days later an old Eskimo woman with two children came to the tent. [This appears, from the photographs, to have been Nanuk, Ohoto's wife, who was then forty-one years old.] I gave them a sack of flour, thirty pounds, which they eagerly accepted. I noticed that the old woman's eyes were in poor shape; red-rimmed and almost completely swollen shut. I gave her a pair of sun-glasses for I thought she was going snow-blind.

After the Eskimos had been dropping in for about a week I made up my mind to visit their village. I asked Anoteelik if he would take me and he agreed. We started on May 17th. The journey took about six hours. At four in the afternoon we arrived at the shores of a small lake and I could see eight or nine tents in a huddle near a grove of stunted spruce trees some of which had been cut down. As we approached, the whole village turned out to greet us. I noticed that bark had been stripped away from some of the trees. I questioned Anoteelik about this. He said some of the people had taken this bark and boiled it for a long time and then drank the liquid and ate the bark. I resolved to try it. Anoteelik's wife seemed surprised and asked if I was starving too. I gulped some of the liquid. Immediately I retched up this bitter and most distasteful substance.

In my inspection of the camp I saw no food whatsoever except the sack of flour I had given to the old woman some days earlier. Most of the women were making a kind of biscuit out of this. They gave it to the children and to the men who were able to go out hunting. The men seemed to be very demoralized and confused and they looked to me as if expecting that I could do something for them.

In the morning I gave what food I had with me to Anoteelik's wife and returned to my own camp.

That afternoon we had a visitor. A well-dressed and healthy looking Eskimo arrived with a fine set of huskies and a sturdy *komatik* [sled]. [This man was Karyook, the post manager's servant from Padlei.] I was very much interested in this man for he was in direct contrast to the other Eskimos who were in poor shape. At length the stranger asked for a piece of paper and a pencil. Without hesitation he quickly wrote a note which he gave to me. [It was written in syllabic script.] Uhoto told me the stranger wished me to give this note to the R.C.M.P. — it was an explanation of the circumstances in which Uhoto's people found themselves. Some days later when the plane returned I gave this note to the pilot and he said he would give it to the R.C.M.P.

Near the end of June our job was finished and we prepared to leave. All the perishable food-stuffs we had left — it wasn't much — we gave to the Eskimos. All canned and boxed food-stuffs were piled in one of the aluminum-clad huts. This food was to be used by the exploration crews who would come in after break-up.

Uhoto, seeing we were about to leave, tried again to impress on us the seriousness of the situation that he and his fellows found themselves in. He said to me: "What shall we do? We starve, and in there (pointing to the building containing the food) there is food. If we starve we will have to take the food in the hut."

Even before this I felt that the Eskimos might be forced to do this as a last resort. I mentioned it to the foreman, but while he sympathized with the Eskimos, he could not accept the responsibility of giving the Company food to the Eskimos. I thought that once we got to Churchill everything would be all right, for the R.C.M.P. would immediately handle the situation once they were aware of it. I told Anoteelik and Uhoto that I would inform the R.C.M.P.

On June 1, we arrived at Churchill and the following day I went to the R.C.M.P. headquarters. I explained everything about the circumstances of the Henik Lake Eskimos. I mentioned that one of the elders [Pommela] had starved to death and the strong possibility that the Eskimos would break into our food cache unless help got to them soon. I even showed the place where the Eskimos were encamped, on the map in the office. The Constable seemed bored with the details, and curtly informed me that the R.C.M.P. were quite aware of the location and the circumstances of these people, for they sent in an aircraft periodically to check on these people. There was nothing to worry about and these people were being looked after.

Despite the lack of concern displayed by the R.C.M.P. constable at Churchill, a report that the Ihalmiut had not been able to kill any caribou did reach the N.S.O. He radioed Padlei to ask about the deer, and he was told that the caribou *were* returning to the district. Nevertheless he seems to have been uneasy, and on June 5, after flying to Eskimo Point with a number of Eskimos who had been released from tuberculosis sanatoria, he continued inland to Offedal Lake.

Only four tents still stood at the original site. The people who were living in them told the N.S.O. that the majority of the Ihalmiut were somewhere to the southwest. From another source, presumably the R.C.M.P. in Churchill, the N.S.O. had already heard that these people were in touch with the prospectors' camp and "had been trading fish for tea and tobacco." When the Offedal families told him that the rest of the people were also very hungry, the N.S.O. was therefore not inclined to believe them. He suspected that Owliktuk's group was not really hungry, but had deliberately spread a famine story in order to keep the prospectors' bounty for themselves, and to discourage the Offedal families from joining them.

Convinced that there was nothing to be gained by visiting the outlying camp, the N.S.O. unloaded some relief supplies and departed. He assumed that Owliktuk's group would hear his plane (the airline distance between the two camps was about eight miles, and there was a high intervening range of hills), and come to Offedal to share in the supplies if they had need of them. Although he recognized that the deer were alarmingly late, he felt that the Ihalmiut now had sufficient relief supplies, together with what ptarmigan and fish they could obtain, to see them through. In point of fact the relief supplies were insufficient even for the people at Offedal, and they were completely consumed within a few days.

There is no doubt but that the N.S.O. was a conscientious man — if a harried one — and it can be assumed that the reason he failed to comprehend and investigate the situation fully was because the R.C.M.P. either failed to place much reliance upon the report submitted by Lynn, or did not see fit to relay it in its entirety to the N.S.O. In any event it is known that the corporal at Eskimo Point, within whose jurisdiction the Ihalmiut now lived, had assured the N.S.O. that conditions at Henik Lake gave no cause for concern.

Meanwhile, the nine families at Owliktuk's camp were striving desperately to stay alive. Owliktuk built a kayak which he covered with part of his tent, in order to ensure the killing of some deer when the migration came. The migration never came.

With the advance of spring, the only food available was the occasional hare or ground squirrel, a few ptarmigan, a very few fish and the bark of the spruce trees. By mid-June the situation had become desperate.

The people starved, though all the time they knew that ample food existed within easy reach. The mystery is not why the mining company's cache was eventually broken into, but why it was not raided earlier. Yet this is not so great a mystery in reality, for though the beliefs which had governed the lives of the Ihalmiut for centuries were now in decay, they still retained some power over men's minds; and foremost among those old beliefs was the conviction that to steal food was to commit a crime almost as heinous as murder.

It was Ohoto who eventually brought the matter into the open when he suggested to several of the men that they would have to enter the cache. Owliktuk stood firm against the idea, and in doing so he found himself in direct conflict with his son Mounik. Mounik was young, he had a baby son to worry about, and he had grown up during the dissolution of the Ihalmiut society so that he had known much bitterness against the whites. Not only did he side with Ohoto, but he now took the lead in demanding that food be taken from the cache. In thus going counter to his father's will, Mounik created an intolerable situation, for it is one of the great tenets of Eskimo belief that a son must defer to his father in all things. Not knowing how to deal with Mounik's rebellion, Owliktuk withdrew into silence, but in that famine camp the tension between father and son mounted steadily toward an open rift.

At this juncture the camp received a visitor. He was a

Padliermio called Iootna, who was a distant relative of Miki's. Iootna had come hunting far afield, for the caribou migration had largely bypassed Padlei too. He had also heard of the arrival of the Ihalmiut in the land and he decided to visit their camps to see if they had managed to kill any deer.

Iootna was immediately drawn into the struggle of wills regarding the cache. Although he was a professing Christian, he had also had a fairly wide experience of the flexibility of white men's moral and ethical codes. Consequently he did not hesitate to throw his weight on Ohoto's and Mounik's side. One day the three of them visited the storage cabin, broke down the door, and stole what food they needed.

After the deed was done the rest of the people shared in the results; but they were uneasy and upset by what had happened. Iootna hurried home with his part of the loot, and word of the affair soon spread through the Padliermiut camps.

In early July, when the inland lakes were free of ice, the mining company's field parties flew in to Bray Lake, to find that their food stocks had been rifled. This was a serious matter, since it involved dispatching their aircraft to Churchill for more supplies, and thus losing several valuable days which could have been devoted to exploratory surveys. They were discussing the problem when a figure appeared over a nearby ridge and came slowly down to join them.

It was Ohoto, come in all good faith to explain what he had done, and why it had been necessary.

His reception was hardly what he had expected. His friend Lynn was not present, and the prospectors were so enraged at the damage done to their supplies — and to their plans — that they were not of a mind to listen to someone else's tale of woe. They dealt with Ohoto as if he had been a sneak thief and a wanton vandal. Their words struck him with the effect of physical blows, and after a little while he turned from them and walked back toward the hills — toward the empty hills.

The plane returned to Churchill where a representative of the mining company visited the N.S.O. and reported what had happened. The N.S.O. recommended that the information be passed on to the R.C.M.P., and toward the end of the month a complaint was laid before the corporal at Eskimo Point.

If the police had been slow to react to the reports of starvation from Bray Lake, they made up for it by the celerity they displayed now that there was a question of lawbreaking involved. The corporal at Eskimo Point seems to have been properly outraged that Eskimos under his jurisdiction should have dared to steal — and particularly from white men. On August 2, therefore, he and the N.S.O. flew into the interior determined to arrest the perpetrators of the crime and bring them out for trial.

At Padlei, Iootna's part in the affair was easily uncovered, and he was arrested and loaded aboard the plane which then flew on to Offedal. The main Ihalmiut camp was eventually located, but it proved impossible to arrest Mounik and Ohoto, since the aircraft could not approach the shore because of rocks; while the two Eskimos could not get out to the plane unless they swam — a skill which they did not possess. It was a stalemate, and the aircraft had to return to Eskimo Point with a fuming corporal, to try again some other time.

Five days later these policemen of the modern era managed to establish dry-land contact with their quarry, and the two Eskimos were arrested and flown to the coast. Their wives and children remained behind, unattended and without assistance, and dependent for existence on what little help the remaining people in the camp could offer.

The N.S.O., perhaps reverting to his own years as a policeman, concurred with the corporal that "the ring-leaders of the gang should be fully prosecuted as an example to the other Eskimos."

The punishment of the three men began soon after they arrived at Eskimo Point, and almost two months before their trial. There is, in the Northwest Territories and Yukon Prison Regulations, a useful statute which permits prisoners to be given employment while awaiting trial, *if they so desire*. In the light of what follows, it must be assumed that Mounik, Ohoto and Iootna "desired" to be employed — with sledgehammers, breaking stones on a rock pile. At any rate this was what they were soon doing.

The idea of pre-trial punishment was not, however, unfamiliar to the corporal. On one occasion in 1951 he had kept a Padliermio named Okalik in chains while under custody awaiting trial. When questioned about this event a few years later, the constable stated that, in his opinion, "seeing Okalik in chains did more to prevent crime [amongst the other Eskimos] than the entire subsequent sentence."

Whether Ohoto and his companions did in fact ask to be allowed to break stones probably cannot be established now. Ohoto himself denies that he ever made such a request. His story is that he was *put* to work upon the direct orders of the policemen. The corporal, on the other hand — backed by the Commissioner of the R.C.M.P. himself — insists that he was only obliging Ohoto.

Whatever the truth of that may be, the fact remains that while Ohoto was breaking stones, a chip flew up and ruptured his right eye. He was eventually evacuated to Churchill after, as Commissioner Nicholson has said, "aggravating the injury by rubbing it." The doctors at Churchill hospital found that the damage was too severe for them to deal with, and Ohoto was sent on to a hospital near Winnipeg.

Ohoto missed the trial, which was held at Eskimo Point on September 20. The defense of Mounik and Iootna, that they had broken into the cache only because they were starving, could not offset the evidence of the chief witness for the prosecution, the R.C.M.P. corporal, who testified that relief rations had been delivered to their camp and that, with great care, they would have had enough food without stealing from the cache. Mounik and Iootna were found guilty and sentenced to three months imprisonment.

Ohoto missed that trial — but the law has a long arm. In August of 1958, between two bouts in hospital, he too was brought before the judge, was tried, and was found guilty. He was sentenced to the time that he had already spent in custody.

With the approach of autumn, the problem of what to do with, or about, the Ihalmiut again began to grow acute. The police corporal strongly recommended that they be brought to the coast in the spring and placed under his direct control so that he could be in a position to curb their lawless propensities more easily. The N.S.O. thought that the people should be taken entirely away from their old land, and their old ways, and placed in the newly established rehabilitation settlement at Churchill, where they could come to an adjustment with our way of life, where their children could attend schools, and where they would have no need to fear starvation; but his was too daring a suggestion. The old orders looked askance at it, for both the police and the missions were now making a public outcry against the increasingly determined efforts of the new men in Northern Affairs to lead the Eskimos out of their despair and into a world where there was hope for their survival. This battle was being fought on the highest levels, where policy is made, and where politicians balance precariously between contending forces. But as yet the old orders held the edge of power, and in the end it was their will which prevailed.

It was agreed, therefore, that in the spring the Ihalmiut should be transported once again; this time to a desolate spit of rock called Term Point which juts out into Hudson Bay between Rankin Inlet and Eskimo Point. There they would learn to become seal hunters while, in the words of the police, "They would be removed from the temptation to commit theft . . . [for they] are not suited to live without supervision, and as yet are not ready for adaptation to life in or near a settlement."

Meanwhile the winter months had still to run their course before this new plan could be implemented.

On August 28, young Louis Voisie was at last permitted to go to the Ihalmiut. He was instructed to remain amongst them for as long as they had need of him, and to assist them to make a sufficient kill of caribou to last until the spring.

When he arrived at Offedal Lake, Louis found the People widely dispersed. The events of the spring and summer had shattered even the tenuous bonds of unity which Owliktuk had managed to maintain for so many years, in spite of Pommela and all his works. Fear of the police; a state of chronic unease arising from the theft and its aftereffects; and finally the crumbling of the last remaining tower of strength amongst them — Owliktuk — had turned the gradual dissolution of the People into a climactic and almost total disintegration. Strangers in a strange land, haunted by fears of many kinds, they no longer had even the comfort of propinquity. The individual families had drifted away from one another like the isolated bits of human flotsam which they had now become.

Now that Pommela was dead, the way might have been clear for unopposed leadership; but Owliktuk, the only possible leader, had suffered a blow more severe than any the old shaman had ever dealt him. He had never recovered from the turmoil of the spring days when Mounik had rebelled against him. He had been unable to resolve the difference between himself and this well-loved son before the police took Mounik away. Owliktuk seems to have believed he would never see the boy again, and this, together with the draining of his last reserves of hope and purpose, had left him a beaten, silent, and empty man.

Alekahaw, who had quietly made the best of evil during the days of Pommela's power, one day struck his tent and vanished. He did not go back toward Ennadai but made his way to Padlei where he had many relatives. He had never been a true member of the Ennadai Ihalmiut in any case, and now he abandoned the doomed remnant of that people in order to save himself and his own family.

The wives and children of Pommela, Ohoto and Mounik were without men to help them through the winter which lay ahead, and they drifted from tent to tent, looking for the strength which had now vanished from the People. Two years earlier Kaiyai, the eldest of Pommela's adopted sons, had married Alekashaw, who was the adopted daughter of Onekwaw; now he did what he could for his stepmother Ootnuyuk and her two remaining children — but he could do little enough, for he had two babies of his own to keep alive. The boy Angataiuk, who had been orphaned for a second time by Pommela's death, attached himself to Onekwaw, that poor dull-witted fellow who had only managed to survive down through the years because he had been useful to Pommela.

Miki and Yaha still clung uncertainly to Owliktuk; but they got no comfort from his presence, for Owliktuk gave them no leadership and no direction.

Almost alone of all the men, Halo seemed to have retained something of his old indomitable assurance. He and Ootek remained inseparable, and in their camp there was still some semblance of vitality, though it was but a pallid shadow of what once had been.

Louis Voisie's presence provided a nucleus for this broken people and they gathered to him. He spoke their language as one of them, for he *was* one of them in part at least. Owliktuk said of him:

"He knew our minds. While he was with us we were happy. We did not worry. We hoped that he would stay for a long time. But after a little while he went away."

Louis was permitted to remain with the Ihalmiut only until September 20. During this time (which should have seen the mass migration of the deer pass through the land), he and the other hunters killed only eighteen caribou. An attempt to establish a fall fishery came to nothing, for few fish ran up the streams from Henik Lake that fall. By mid-September both Voisie and the Eskimos could recognize the sure shape of the future which awaited the Ihalmiut.

Voisie walked overland to the prospectors' camp and sent a radio message to Churchill to the effect that the People were *already* hungry and that he and they had failed to obtain a winter supply of meat or fish.

On the 20th of the month an aircraft arrived at the camps bearing 1400 pounds of relief supplies — consisting, as usual, mainly of flour. The plane also brought instructions for Voisie to return at once to Churchill.

He left unwillingly. On his arrival at Churchill he reported that the People would not be able to survive the winter without considerable help, and he offered to return to Henik Lake; but

Ottawa had other plans for Louis Voisie. His services were more urgently needed to serve the deer than to serve the People of the Deer. He was instructed to spend the winter killing wolves.

Ottawa was notified of Voisie's opinion as to the prospects for the Ihalmiut, and the Department of Northern Affairs at least made an effort to do something about it. The R.C.M.P. were asked to take whatever action was required; and the police replied that the matter was well in hand. The corporal from Eskimo Point said that he intended to make an air patrol to the Ihalmiut early in December, to be followed by a full-scale dog patrol a little later, at which time he would spend a week or two at the Henik camps.

Ottawa accepted this, and let the matter rest.

There is some confusion as to what actually did happen to these projected patrols. The Commissioner of the R.C.M.P. has since claimed that, to use his own words, "There was a police patrol at an Eskimo camp on Henik Lake on December 8, 1957." On the other hand, the surviving Ihalmiut claim that they saw no white man at their camps after Voisie departed on September 20. If a flight was indeed made on December 8, to an Eskimo camp, it would appear that it must either have been to a Padliermiut camp or to the camp of one of the Ihalmiut families which did not survive. In any event, it is admitted by the police that the dog patrol was never made at all.

The Ihalmiut began that winter with 1400 pounds of food for forty-eight people — a little less than thirty pounds for each man, woman and child. They had no meat after the middle of October, and almost no fish. Some of the men were able to make a trip to Padlei for relief supplies in November; but they had no dogs after that month ended, and they could not carry back enough food on their backs to make further trips worthwhile. In the first weeks of December the Ihalmiut were starving; and if they *were* visited by a police plane at that time, its passengers must have been blind men.

As the snows grew deeper the dispersed camps (for the People had again separated into their component elements after Voisie left) seemed to diminish and to be absorbed into the winter plains. The People themselves seemed to be physically diminished, as they fought their way through the snow wraiths to sit for hours jigging through the ice for fish which seldom took the hook. They lost form and substance, until they began to be as unreal, as disembodied, as the very spirits of their ancient land.

The days grew shorter, and the nights colder. The fish grew scarcer — and no one came to Henik Lake. January dragged its weight slowly across the buried lakes and hills, while the winter darkness became a winding cloth.

13   *The Ordeals of Kikik*

ON the morning of April 14, 1958, the Territorial Court of
the Northwest Territories convened in the beer-parlor-
cum recreation hall of the North Rankin Nickel Mine which
squats upon the western shore of Hudson Bay a hundred and
fifty miles north of Eskimo Point. Ceremoniously the judge took
his place behind a deal table while on his right six jurors shifted
their bottoms uncomfortably upon a wooden bench. In front of
the judge (and awkwardly aware of the needs of propriety), an
audience consisting mainly of off-shift miners' wives tried not
to drown out the proceedings in the clatter of folding chairs.
Outside the doubly insulated building a husky nuzzled at a garbage can as the sun beat down upon the white immobility of a
frozen world.

The prisoner sat at the right hand of the judge. She smiled
steadily at the assembled court, but in her eyes there was the
blankness of total bewilderment, of such an absence of comprehension that she might have been no more than a wax man-
nequin. Yet perhaps, since there was the flush of life under the
brown shadows of her skin, she more nearly resembled a denizen

of some other world who had become inexplicably trapped in ours. It is not too far-fetched a simile, for this woman had indeed been plucked out of another time and space in order that she might be brought to this alien place to answer to the charges laid against her.

Those to whom she would have to answer had also come great distances in space. The judge and the crown attorney had flown eastward from Yellowknife, some 700 miles away. Another plane had brought a learned doctor, together with the young attorney for the defense, from Winnipeg which lay 900 miles to the southward. From Ottawa, more than 1400 miles distant, representatives of the Department of Northern Affairs had come to serve as friends to the accused. Through many days, aircraft had been converging from across half a continent upon the transient cluster of drab buildings which huddled under the gaunt headframe of this arctic mine. Between them they had spanned vast distances; yet none had come a fraction of the distance that this woman had traversed in order that she might stand before this court and listen while a white man spoke incomprehensible words to her.

"You, Kikik, of Henik Lake, stand charged before his Lordship in that you, Kikik, No. E 1–472, did murder Ootek . . . How say you to this charge?"

During the long night of February 7, the great wind from off the congealed white desert of the arctic sea came seeking south across five hundred miles of tundra plains, to strip the unresisting snows from the black cliffs at Henik Lake and to send the snow-devils dancing like dervishes across the ice. The driven snow scoured the darkness like a blast of sand until no living thing could face it. Nothing ran, nor crawled, nor flew over the broken ridges, the frozen muskegs and the faceless, hidden lakes.

Yet there was life unseen beneath the wind. On the shores of a narrow bay in North Henik Lake two snow houses crouched against the implacable violence of the gale and, within their dark confines, people listened to the wind's voice. Its muted roar changed pitch as the night hours advanced, until before the dawn it had become a high-throated wail that sank into the mind like needles into naked flesh.

In the smaller of the two houses — it was in reality no more than a snow-block barricade roofed with a piece of canvas — there were four people. One of these, the year-old boy Igyaka, lay rigidly inert, and did not hear the wind. His small body was shrunken into a macabre travesty of human form by the long hunger which, two days earlier, had given him over to the frost to kill.

Beside him on the sleeping ledge of hard-packed snow his two sisters lay. There was Kalak who had been born deaf and dumb out of a starvation winter ten years earlier, and there was little Kooyak who was seven years of age. They lay in each other's arms under the single remaining deerskin robe — and they were naked except for cotton shifts grown black and ragged through the months. There were no more robes to lay across their bloated bellies and their pipestem limbs, and none to hide the frozen horror of the boy who lay beside them — for the other robes which the family had possessed when winter came had long ago been eaten, as had the children's clothes; for all of these had of necessity been sacrificed to hunger.

Oddly contorted from the paralysis which had stricken her in 1949, the mother of the children crouched over a handful of white ashes by the sleeping ledge. These ashes had been cold through the three days of the blizzard, for the willow twigs which were the only fuel available had long since passed in evanescent flame. Howmik crouched motionless; and in that meager shelter the darkness was so absolute that she could not see her husband, Ootek, who lay against the farther wall and stared with wide open eyes that saw through darkness, and which could see death as vividly before him as other men might see the sun.

In the second of the two shelters, a hundred yards away, were Kikik, her husband Halo, and their five children. Hunger had laid its mark upon all of these, but death had as yet been unable to take any of them; its long assault upon this family had not yet overmastered the indomitable resistance of a man who could not comprehend defeat. Through all his years Halo had never known defeat, nor had he even recognized its shadow, for always he had looked no farther than the hour in which he lived. He had not looked back into the dark days of the past, nor yet had he stared forward into the obscurity of the future which awaited him and all his race. He had been free to live within the confines of the moment — to live with a kind of frenzied vigor which made each day give life to him and his. And he owed this special freedom to his song-cousin and lifelong companion Ootek, who had been the visionary and the unraveler of timeless questions for the two of them.

They complemented each other so completely, these two, that they were almost a single man. Slightly built, and with no great reserves of physical stamina, Ootek had never been more than a mediocre hunter, relying often enough on Halo's help to keep his family fed. Yet Halo had always relied upon Ootek to shoulder and resolve those nebulous problems of the mind and spirit which have confronted man since he *was* man. In a true sense they were the two archetypes of Man: the one, who sought to limit and assuage the hostility of fate with his mind's weapons — the other, with the weapons of his hands.

These two families were the people whom the wind had found, and they were almost alone in the wind's world on that February day; alone in a particular hell that had not been of their own contriving, but which we had contrived for them. They were almost alone, because eight of the nine other Ihalmiut families had seen their doom approaching and had made desperate efforts to escape it by attempting to trek, on foot, to Padlei Post.

Owliktuk, he who had tried to stand against acceptance of the soul-destroying dependence on the whites for so many years, had been amongst the first to flee the Henik country and to beg for food at Padlei. With his defection, there was no strength left in the People, and the rest began to follow after. Not all of them survived that savage journey to the sanctuary which they sought.

Onekwaw and his wife Tabluk, with the orphaned boy Angataiuk, made their attempt to escape inevitable death during the last week in January. As with the rest of the Ihalmiut, they had almost no caribou skin clothes, and were dressed largely in castoff cloth garments given them by the white men. They might almost as well have gone naked into the white winds. The boy survived five foodless, fireless days and nights; but on the last day of the passage of the ice of Henik Lake, he died.

Onekwaw only lived a few days longer. He died a mile or two beyond the lake, and many measureless miles from Padlei Post. Thus, of that little group of doomed and driven people, only Tabluk survived; and she did so only because she was discovered by a Padliermio hunter with a dog team, who brought her safely to the post.

Ootnuyuk and her two children had left Henik early in December, for she knew the land, and knew what winter portended there. When she reached Padlei she reported that the young man Kaiyai lay helpless in his snow house. He had frozen his leg, she said, and it had thawed and then been frozen a second time, and thawed again so that now it had swelled like a great dead fish in summertime, and stank like one.

The post manager radioed Eskimo Point and asked that the police plane fly a rescue mission to Henik Lake at once to bring Kaiyai to hospital — for he had recognized the description of gangrene. But the short days and the long nights passed, and the plane did not come, and Kaiyai could wait no longer. His wife Alekashaw placed him on a small hand-sled, and with her two baby sons upon her back, she set out to haul her husband to the post. She had fifty miles to go. She hauled that sled for eight days — and then there was no need to haul it any farther, for Kaiyai was dead. Alekashaw with her two children eventually reached Padlei — but her feet were frozen marble white and hard, and she spent many months in hospital.

*　　*　　*

This was the pattern of that winter flight. By the time the belated dawn was staining the storm with the opaqueness of a blind man's eye on February 8, the flight was almost over. Yaha's family was still en route, and only Halo and Ootek and their families remained in the promised land to which they had been led by the white men.

For these families, too, the time had come when they must flee, or meet a certain death within their wind-swept camps.

Ootek was aware of this, but he was also aware of a harder truth — it was too late for him to go. He and his family had stayed too long. Having now eaten most of the skin clothing and robes with which they had begun the winter, they could no longer escape from the snow-shelter which had become Igyaka's coffin. Ootek knew this beyond any doubt, and yet in the morning he spoke to Howmik saying:

"I shall go to the trading place; and in a little time I will return with food for all." *

Howmik looked slowly up into her husband's face but she made no reply. She knew that he could not reach the post alive. But Kooyak, who knew only that she was bitter cold and that her bowels were twisted in agony by the glut of caribou hair and crushed bones which filled them, moaned — and cried aloud.

That cry must have been an intolerable reproach, and Ootek, who had never before raised his hand against any man, least of all against a child, stumbled toward the sleeping ledge, his smooth and gentle face contorted into a sudden savagery. He raised his hand so that it hung trembling over the girl. "I *shall* bring food!" he cried — and struck his daughter on her shrunken lips . . .

Indeed it was too late for Ootek, but it was not yet too late for Halo and his family to flee, for they still had the means. As Halo took his ice-chisel and fought his way against the gale to-

---

* The events and conversations in this chapter are taken from the detailed police interrogations, the transcripts of the trial and from independent interrogations of survivors.

ward the lake, there to chip laboriously through two feet of new-made ice which covered his fishing hole, he knew that the time had come when he must try to reach Padlei. He thought about the implications of his decision as he squatted, back to the whining wind, keeping his jigging line in motion. Two hours later he caught a small fish. He took it back to the snow house and the family shared it — and when they had finished they were starving still.

Meanwhile, Ootek had crept out of his own place and had turned to face the north. His eyes were blind as he took half a dozen faltering steps toward the goal that he would never reach. The gale scourged him until he staggered and fell to his knees — and he sobbed deep within his emaciated chest, and turned away defeated and went stumbling across that lesser distance to the house of his companion and his friend. He came into Halo's house and crouched exhausted and blank-eyed against the inner wall.

So they sat, these two who had been closer than brothers. Halo offered Ootek the tail of the fish, and Ootek wolfed it. When it was gone he asked for the few remaining bones of the fish to take home to his family, and these were given to him; but still he sat against the wall and waited. Perhaps he sensed what Halo would say even before the words were framed. Yet it was a long time before Halo could bring himself to speak.

"There is nothing left in this place," Halo said at last. "And so, when the storm weakens, I must take my family and go somewhere. There are few fish in this lake. If we stay we will all be as Igyaka is."

Thus it was done. With those few words Halo dissolved the bonds which had held these two men through the many years. He cut them ruthlessly, for he had no other choice. But he did not look again at Ootek as he picked up his line and went out once again to take up his vigil at the fishing hole.

Ootek made no protest even though sentence of death had been passed on him and on his family. He knew that he no longer had the strength to travel, nor to endure at the fishing hole, nor even to scrabble under the snows for willow twigs. He knew all this, yet he did not protest. He sat silently for a long time watching Kikik, who was his half-sister for, though these two had been born of different fathers, their common mother had been Epeetna who had starved to death in the spring of 1947.

At last Ootek rose, smiled strangely at his sister, and said quietly, "Now I will go to Padlei. Only first I will shoot some ptarmigan with Halo's rifle so my children can eat when I am gone." So saying he picked up Halo's .30.30 and left the igloo.

He had not far to go — and he had sufficient strength to carry him on that final journey. Perhaps he no longer even felt the cold, or knew the agony within him. He went before the storm, directly driven toward the one thing in all the world which could sustain him.

Unseen, unheard, shrouded by the snow and wind, he did not pause until he stood a single pace behind the crouching figure of his other self. Perhaps he stood there for an eternity, knowing what he would do, yet hesitating until the wind, blowing through the torn cloth parka, warned him that he must finish quickly. For indeed this *was* the finish — not only of the broken life that Ootek had led through the long years but, so he believed, the finish of the interminable struggles of the people who called themselves Ihalmiut.

When such an ending comes, it is not good to go alone. Ootek intended that the few survivors by the shores of Henik Lake should be together at the end — and so he raised the rifle and, without passion, blew in the back of Halo's head.

The wind swallowed the thunder of the shot as the sea swallows a stone. Soundless still, Ootek climbed the slope to Halo's house. He leaned the rifle in the snow outside the tunnel and crawled inside.

He came as nemesis — but he was a weak and tragic emissary of the fates for he was so chilled that he could not even raise his arms until Kikik used some of her few remaining twigs to brew him a cup of tepid water. The warmth revived a little of the purpose in his sad design and he attempted to persuade the children to leave the igloo on some absurd pretext. When they would not go, and when he began to be aware that his sister was disturbed by his strange behavior, he could think of nothing else to do but turn and leave the place himself. He was so easily defeated; as he had been defeated all his life by the necessity of doing. He was the dreamer, and the doer no longer lived; and Ootek was no longer whole.

Standing irresolute, and hopelessly confused, in the arms of the storm again, he picked up the rifle and aimlessly began to brush the snow away from the metal parts. He was still there a quarter of an hour later when Kikik emerged from the igloo tunnel.

Kikik had become seriously uneasy. Not only was she surprised that Ootek had borrowed Halo's rifle and had not brought it back, but she was perturbed by his odd actions. Yet when she scrambled to her feet and looked into Ootek's eyes, she lost all other emotions in a surge of fear.

"Give me the rifle," she said quickly.

Ootek made no answer, and his hand continued to stray over the steel, brushing away the snow. Kikik stepped forward sharply and grasped the gun, but Ootek would not release it and so brother and sister began to struggle with one another in the whirling center of the storm. Kikik slipped and stumbled and when she recovered herself it was to see Ootek slowly bringing the rifle to his shoulder. But his movements were painfully slow and she had time to step in and push the muzzle to one side so that the bullet rushed harmlessly away into the wind.

Now the woman, better fed and stronger, and driven by a fierce anxiety for her five children, easily overpowered the man. He fell, exhausted, and she fell on him and her slight weight was sufficient to pin him, helpless, in the snow. Ootek struggled faintly as Kikik shouted to her eldest daughter Ailouak, telling the child to fetch Halo from the jigging hole.

Ailouak came from the igloo, glanced in terror at the struggling pair, and then went racing toward the lake. She was not gone long. Sobbing wildly she emerged from the enveloping ground drift. "My father cannot come, for he is dead!" she cried.

What followed has the quality of nightmare. Sprawling astride the feebly resisting body of her husband's killer, who was her own half-brother, Kikik began to question him with the quiet and detached voice of someone speaking in an empty room. There was no rancor and no passion in her voice, nor in the steadfast, half-whispered replies of the man. There was only a terrible remoteness as these two emaciated travesties of human beings, whose hold on life was almost equally tenuous, engaged each other in dead words while the wind roared darkly over them and the quick snow drifted up against their bodies.

They talked so — but even as they talked Kikik was coming to the realization of what she must do next. In Ootek's mind the certainty of their common fate might be inevitable; but Kikik would not accept this truth. She was well fitted to be Halo's wife for she too was of adamantine stuff. Therefore she did not think, she *knew*, her children would survive — and of the many obstacles which lay between her and their survival, the first was Ootek.

She called Ailouak again who, horrified and frightened, had retreated to the igloo.

"Daughter! Bring me a knife!" Kikik demanded.

Ailouak crawled out, close followed by her younger brother Karlak — and both children had knives clutched in their hands . . .

"*I took the larger knife from Ailouak and I stabbed once near Ootek's right breast but the knife was dull and would not go in. Then Ootek grasped the knife and took it from me, but as we struggled for it it struck his forehead and the blood began to flow. Karlak was standing near and so I took the small knife which he handed me and stabbed in the same place near the right breast. This time the knife went in and I held it there until Ootek was dead. . . .*"

The killing might have been easier for Kikik had there been passion in it — but there was none. She acted out of intellect, not out of emotion, and she knew exactly what she did. She knew too what lay ahead of her. She had no illusions. She was fully aware of the almost insupportable burden which Halo's death had laid upon her. There would be no more food of any kind. There would be no man's strength to haul the sled if she moved camp. The inevitable doom which Ootek had envisaged was in reality only a step away. Yet stubbornly, and with a singleness of purpose which will be her epitaph when she is gone, Kikik engaged her fate in battle. As Ootek died she ceased to be a woman and became instead an unfaltering machine. The humane passions left her. Love, pity, sorrow and regret were past. With terrible efficiency she stripped away these things so that nothing might weaken her indomitable resolve.

After Ootek was dead she placed the two knives upright in the snow beside his head and went at once into her snow house. She found the children hunched together under the skins upon the sleeping ledge, staring at her out of black, depthless eyes. Brusquely she ordered Ailouak to follow after, and together they went out into the unabated storm, dragging Halo's heavy sled down to the jigging hole. Together they raised the already frozen body of the husband and the father, laid him on the sled, and brought him home to lie beneath the snow beside the door. The effort exhausted both of them and they crawled back into the igloo to lie panting on the ledge.

"We will sleep now," Kikik told her children, and there was a quality in her voice that belonged to the north wind itself. "And in the morning we will go to Padlei where we will find food."

That night, in Ootek's snow house, his children and the crippled woman huddled close to one another so that no part of their ephemeral body warmth would be wasted. Kooyak still whimpered in her agony, and Howmik gave her water, for there was no food. Even water was only obtainable at a fearful cost, for there was no fire, and Howmik was forced to melt handfuls of snow in a skin bag warmed by her slim reserves of body heat.

Howmik herself slept little that night, for with Ootek's failure to return to the igloo she could only assume he had meant what he had said, in which case death would have soon overtaken him amongst the drifts along the route to Padlei. She believed that she was now alone except for Halo and his family, and she knew that they could give her no assistance.

Before dawn on February 9, the wind fell light; the sky broke clear and the temperature plummeted to forty-five degrees below zero. Kikik, who had also slept little enough that night, roused her children, gave them each a cup of warm water in which some scraps of deerskin had been softened, and bade them prepare to travel. They went about their tasks readily, for there was no gainsaying the inexorable resolution in their mother's face. Within an hour the few possessions which were essential for the journey had been placed aboard the long sled; then Kikik tore down the canvas ceiling of the igloo and cut it into halves. One piece she placed over her husband's grave. With the other she made a bed for her younger daughters, Nesha and Annacatha, upon the sled. These children were too young to stagger through the snow and, in any case, they had no skin clothing left. Their clothes had long ago been sacrificed as food for Halo and the elder children so that they could hunt, and gather fuel.

It was at this juncture that Howmik emerged from her snow-shelter and came hobbling across toward the others. She stopped beside the sled, shivering uncontrollably, for her own clothing had been reduced to tattered remnants. She did not need to ask what was afoot, for she could see and understand the implications of the loaded sled. She knew too, as Ootek had known, that there was no point in protesting; and so she contented herself with asking Kikik if she knew where Ootek had gone.

Kikik was evasive. She denied any knowledge of her brother, except to intimate that he had probably gone towards Padlei in which direction, so she said, Halo had already gone to break a trail for Kikik and the children. This was a very thin explanation for Halo's absence from the scene, but Howmik did not question it. Her mind was filled with thoughts of Ootek, and with the certainty of his fate.

"If he has gone for Padlei, he is dead by now," she said, half to herself.

Kikik made no comment. Imperturbably she continued with

her preparations. She had been Howmik's best friend, and had helped the other woman with domestic tasks for fifteen years; but as of this moment that was past and dead. She could do nothing more for Howmik, nor for Howmik's children and, since this was so, she dared not even allow herself the luxury of pity.

And this was the second of the bitter things that Kikik was forced to steel herself to do — to deny her friend, and to leave her by the shores of Henik Lake to die.

Howmik understood. As unemotionally as if she had just concluded a casual morning visit, she said, "Well, I am pretty chilly now. Perhaps I will go home till Ootek comes."

And Kikik, straightening from her task, watched as the cripple limped away across the snows.

So Kikik left the camp by Henik Lake. With the hauling straps biting into her shoulders she dragged the awkward sled upon which Nesha and Annacatha crouched beneath two deerskin robes. Her youngest child, the eighteen-month-old boy Noahak, rode upon her back in the capacious pocket of her parka. Karlak and Ailouak trudged stolidly along behind.

For a time the going was good. The gale had packed the snow, and the route lay over the level surface of the lake. Seldom pausing to rest, Kikik forced the pace to the limit of the children's endurance. When the pace began to tell upon Karlak, she ordered him to climb upon the sled, and she toiled on. By late afternoon she had gone ten miles; and then something occurred which must have made Kikik believe she had outdistanced the hounds of fate.

A mile ahead, near the tip of a great rock point, she saw a centipede of human movement on the ice. She came erect, stared for a long moment, and then her voice rang out through the crystal air — and the distant movement slowed and ceased.

In a little while Kikik was talking to four of her own people.

The four were Yaha (who was Howmik's brother), his wife Ateshu and their six-year-old son Atkla, together with the last survivor of Pommela's adopted children, the young man Alektaiuwa. They too were making for Padlei, but Ateshu's lung sickness (it was tuberculosis), and the fact that both of Alektaiuwa's feet were frozen, had slowed their progress to a fatal crawl. They were in desperate straits, and they could offer no island of hope and strength to which Kikik could drag herself and her own children.

Kikik's sick disappointment when she discovered that Yaha's family had barely enough resources to enable them to survive for a day or two longer, let alone a surplus to share with others, must have been a crushing blow. Yet she could bear that too. She told her tale and Yaha heard that his own sister and her children lay abandoned only ten miles distant — and he knew he could do absolutely nothing for them. He was carrying on his back the last food that his family owned — two or three pounds of caribou entrails dug from underneath the snows where it had been discarded in the fall. Yaha had no sled, and his pace was therefore that of the sick woman and the injured boy. He was by no means hopeful that his family would ever get to Padlei alive, and he knew that to turn back for Howmik would only mean certain death for all. He made his inevitable decision, as he listened to Kikik's story, and when she was done he said no word, but turned again toward the northeast. Into the darkness of that frigid evening the little group crawled slowly forward. When they could no longer see their way, they made camp in a tiny travel igloo which Yaha built, and here exhaustion held them till the dawn.

That night *Kaila*, the unpredictable and heartless goddess of the weather, struck again. Before dawn the wind was back in all its frenetic fury; but the ten people who fled could not hide from it. They dared not stay in their minute igloo and hide. So they went on.

The agonies of that day, facing a growing blizzard, freezing, and pitifully weakened by the long starvation, were such that the younger children who took part in it have lost its memory — to them it is now no more than a blank white space in time. But the older ones, and the adults remember. . . .

As the long hours passed and the straggling column slowed even more (for Kikik, with her load, could not keep up), Yaha knew that they would find no sanctuary except beneath the snows. When dusk came he and his family, with Karlak and Ailouak, had left Kikik a mile behind. Such was the exhaustion of these people that Kikik could not close the gap to the travel igloo Yaha built, nor did any of those at the igloo have the strength to go back for her. Kikik crouched in the snow all that roaring night with her three youngest children huddled underneath her body.

In the morning Kikik threw off the snows that all but covered her and faced north. She saw the little igloo and struggled to it. Yaha's wife gave her warm water and a fragment of caribou gut, and when she had drunk and eaten, Yaha spoke to her. His speech was gentle, for he was a gentle and a childlike man.

"You must stay in the snowhouse," he told Kikik. "If I take your sled to pull my wife, we may go fast enough to reach Padlei before we starve. Then we will send help. Perhaps the airplane will come. If it does not, then the trader will send his dog team. But you and your children must remain here and wait."

Kikik, recognizing the truth of this, made no demur. Yaha and his family left soon afterwards and she remained with her five children inside the frail snow shelter, and strained her hearing to catch the rustle of receding footsteps against the whine of the wind.

Kikik and her children remained in that travel igloo through five full days.

During that timeless interval they ate nothing — for there was nothing to eat; but Kikik gathered some dead spruce branches and she made a tiny fire so that they at least had water. More than that, she was even able to squeeze a few drops of bluish liquid from her shrunken breasts for the child Noahak.

For five interminable days the children and their mother huddled together under their two robes and the fragment of canvas, and simply waited — with no certainty. They did not talk much, for even words require strength to utter them. They waited while the storm waxed and waned, and waxed again; and while the keening of the wind heralded the sure approach of the malevolent pursuit.

But Yaha's promise had not been made in vain. On February 13, three days after leaving Kikik, he and his family reached the shelter of Padlei Post, where the trader fed them first, then listened to their tale. With Yaha's arrival all but two of the Ihalmiut families had been accounted for, and now the trader knew what had happened to the rest.

He was appalled. He had earlier radioed his concern about the people to the police at Eskimo Point and now he sent a message which brooked of no delay. In the outer world the slow and almost toothless gears of bureaucracy meshed suddenly. The R.C.M.P. patrol plane which had been so fatally delayed in Kaiyai's case came thundering out from Churchill and on February 14 it reached Padlei. With the trader aboard as a guide, it took off again for Henik Lake, landing on the wind-swept ice of that place shortly before noon.

The policemen went ashore toward the two almost buried igloos and at Howmik's house they found the crippled woman and two children miraculously still alive. They, and the body of Igyaka, were carried to the plane — light burdens all, for the living too had been reduced to skeletal caricatures of human beings. Then the police found Halo's grave, and after a little time they stumbled on the snow-covered body of Ootek. These two were also taken to the plane, and so Halo and Ootek, those enduring friends, came together for the last time, lying stiffly contorted at the feet of Howmik and of her two surviving children.

What followed must constitute the most inexplicable aspect of this whole dark tale. The police aircraft left Henik Lake for Padlei and though it flew directly over the area where Kikik and her children were known to be waiting in the travel igloo, no real attempt was made to find them. Nor can the entire weight and majesty of the police prevail against this truth. The events which followed provide corroboration which cannot be assailed.

The patrol aircraft returned to Padlei. But despite the suggestion of the trader that it remain overnight in order to have the advantage of the precious extra hours of daylight to search for

Kikik the next day, the police decided to fly on to Eskimo Point, bearing three dead bodies out of the land, and leaving six who might be alive to wait a little longer. In making this decision the police sacrificed the advantages of having two more hours of daylight for a search on February 14 — assuming that they had indeed intended to make such a search.

In the event, however, the patrol aircraft did not return to the interior at all the following day.

It was not prevented from doing so by bad weather, or by any other physical cause. It was not sent back simply because it was considered to be more important to send the aircraft north to Rankin Inlet in order to fly the coroner down to Eskimo Point to conduct an inquest into the cause of death of the three bodies which were already on hand.

Had the trader at Padlei known that the police had no intention of returning, he would undoubtedly have sent his post servant Karyook by dog team to search for Kikik; and Karyook would easily have been able to reach her on that day. But in the belief that the police plane would arrive at any minute, the trader did not send Karyook out.

Thus for two additional days and nights, Kikik and her children remained abandoned.

Sitting in Yaha's travel igloo Kikik heard the double passage of the plane on February 14, and when that day drew to a close and no help had come, she was convinced that none would ever come.

This should have been her moment of ultimate despair — but no fiber of her being would acknowledge it. There was no more hope — but what of that? On the morning of February 15, while the police plane was winging its way north to Rankin Inlet on official business, Kikik wrapped Annacatha and Nesha in the skin robes and used the piece of canvas to make a crude toboggan on which to haul them. Then these six, who had eaten no food for seven days, and little enough in the preceding months, set out for Padlei.

It was a blind, almost insensate, effort. Staggering like demented things, they moved a yard or two, then paused as Karlak or Ailouak collapsed on the hard snow. Blackened by frost, and as gaunt as any starving dog, Kikik would rest beside them for a moment and then remorselessly would goad them to their feet — and they went on another yard or two.

Kikik drove the children with a savage, almost lunatic obsession. She drove herself, hauling what had become a gargantuan weight behind her, and bowed beneath the incubus of the child Noahak upon her back. She had become a vessel filled with a kind of stark brutality — filled with it to the point where there was room for nothing else.

In six hours they moved two miles closer to their goal — which still lay twenty-seven miles ahead.

It was dark by then, but Kikik had no strength to build a shelter. The best that she could manage was to scoop a shallow hole in the snow using a frying pan as a shovel. Into this depression the six of them huddled for the night — the long and bitter night, while the ice on nearby Ameto Lake cracked and boomed in the destroying frost.

That shallow hollow should have become a common grave for all of them. They had no right to live to see the slow dawn's coming. Yet when the gray light broke in the east, Kikik lifted her head and looked toward the unseen Padlei Post. Still she would not give her hand to death.

And now she came to the most frightful moment of her years; for Kikik knew that they could not all go on. She could no longer think to save them all; and so in the dark half-light of morning she came to the most terrible of all decisions.

Quietly she roused Karlak and Ailouak from their mindless sleep, and firmly forced them to their feet. Then she drew a caribou hide softly across the faces of the two little girls who still slept on. While the elder children watched, wordless and mercifully uncomprehending, she laid sticks across the hole and piled snow blocks on top.

Early on the morning of February 16, three figures moved like drunken automata on the white face of a dead land . . . and behind them, two children slept.

In the morning of February 16, the R.C.M.P. plane came back.

It did not reach Padlei until the day was well advanced and then it landed to pick up the trader once again. It was noon before the search began.

On his arrival at Padlei, Yaha had given the trader explicit instructions as to how to find the travel igloo, and this time the aircraft went directly to it, experiencing no difficulty in locating it — as there would have been no difficulty two days earlier. But by now the igloo was empty.

Airborne again the plane lumbered uneasily through the frigid edge of dusk while the men aboard strained their vision for a sight of motion on the snows below. They saw nothing. Dusk was rushing into the land as they turned back for Padlei — but then, on a last suggestion from the trader, the plane deviated slightly to pass over an abandoned trapper's cabin. There, by the door, the searchers saw a human figure, its arms upraised in the immemorial and universal gesture of a supplicant.

As for Kikik — as she watched the plane circle for a landing — that indomitable structure which she had created so ruthlessly out of her own flesh and spirit began to crumble into senseless ruin. She could sustain it no longer, for there was no longer need of it. As the plane came to a halt and policemen began to run toward her, she faced them with nothing left in her but dust, and the apathy of nothingness.

They asked many, and urgent, questions, for it was almost dark, and they were very anxious to get away. Where were her children? Three of them were in the shack. Where were the other two? What had she done with them? Coherence left her and she could explain nothing, for out of the emptiness an old emotion had quickened into life within her. She who had known no fear through the eons of her travels now remembered fear. She answered out of fear of those who were her rescuers. She lied. Believing that Nesha and Annacatha must now be dead, she told the police that they had died and she had buried them.

The police were not so anxious this time to recover bodies, and so they flew Kikik and her remaining children out of the land to Eskimo Point, after leaving a constable behind at Padlei with orders to collect the dead children by dog team the next day.

The constable followed his instructions and late on February 17 he reached the unobtrusive hummock in the snow where Nesha and Annacatha lay. The Eskimo guide who had accompanied him stopped in terror as they approached the grave, for he had heard a voice — a muffled, childlike voice. The constable tore away the snow blocks and the twigs, and there he found the children. Insulated from the killing cold by the snow crypt, Annacatha was alive — but Nesha had not lived.

So the ordeal of the winter ended for all of the Ihalmiut — except for Kikik, and her ordeal had only just begun.

The flight to Eskimo Point bridged the final chasm between her time and ours in one gigantic and immutable step. Within the day she ceased to be the woman she had been, for now she sat under arrest in a small igloo beside the police barracks, a woman of *our* times destined to live or die according to our laws. The transcendent fortitude she had displayed; the agony that she had voluntarily embraced when she left Nesha and Annacatha to their long sleep; the magnificence of her denial of death itself — all came to this: Kikik had killed a man — Kikik had willfully abandoned two children in the snow — Kikik must answer for her crimes.

Through interminable weeks she remained at Eskimo Point, her children taken from her and she herself subjected to endless interrogations. She was not even told that Annacatha had survived until it suited the needs of the police to confront her with this information in a successful attempt to force her into the admission that she had lied. She endured two preliminary hearings before a justice of the peace at Eskimo Point and she was searchingly examined by a very competent crown attorney who was flown from Yellowknife for the occasion. There was no defense attorney present at either hearing. The verdict of the justice was that she must stand trial on both charges.

She knew nothing of the shape of what awaited her; she only knew that her life remained in jeopardy. She endured. She who had already endured so much could still endure.

In the middle of April they flew her to Rankin Inlet and there the whole mighty paraphernalia of our justice closed about her, and she was tried.

But here, if anywhere in this chronicle, there emerges some denial of the apparent fact that man's inhumanity to man is second nature to him. Kikik was tried before a judge who understood something of the nature of the abyss which separated Kikik from us, and who was aware that justice can sometimes be savagely unjust. In his charges to the jury, Judge Sissons virtually instructed them to bring in a verdict of acquittal. And be it to the everlasting credit of the handful of miners who held the woman's life in their hard hands, they did acquit her, not only of the murder of Ootek, but also of the crime of "unlawfully, by criminal negligence, causing the death of her daughter Nesha."

Thus, on the sixteenth day of April in the year of our civilization 1958, Kikik's ordeal ended. At 9 P.M. under the glaring lights of the improvised courtroom the judge looked at the woman who sat, still smiling blankly, still uncomprehending, and he spoke gently:

"You are not guilty, Kikik. Do you understand?"

But Kikik did not understand, as she had understood so little through the days since she had come to Eskimo Point, except that a threat she could not comprehend, and one more fearful, therefore, than any she had met and mastered in the months and years behind, lay over her.

At length a white man who is almost an Eskimo in his feeling for the people came forward and led her, unresisting, from the room. He took her into the adjoining camp kitchen, sat her down, and gave her a mug of tea. Then, standing over her and looking down into her eyes, he spoke in her own tongue.

"Kikik," he said softly. "Listen. It is all finished now — it is all done."

And then at last that fixed smile faltered — and the black eyes looked away from him toward the darkened window, and past it, and into the void beyond.

14 *For Us to Say*

URING the morning of August 19, 1958, the Beaver aircraft
in which I was a passenger swung northward up the coast
of Hudson Bay. To the west the Barrenlands rolled inward from
the sea: a muddied palette sponged into weird designs, flecked
with innumerable lakes, and shattered by the quicksilver cracks
of many rivers.

The sky was the Barrens sky — pale with unlimned distances
and hard as winter ice. The plane drifted through it and after a
time the minute white excrescences which were the buildings at
Eskimo Point slipped into view over the horizon. There was a
trail of smoke hanging pendent above the anchorage to mark the
Rupertsland, the Hudson's Bay Company supply ship for the
Eastern arctic, which was making its annual visit to the settlement. The Beaver took the water close beside the ship, and taxied
toward shore.

Forty or fifty coastal Eskimos in their best clothes crowded the landing place, while still others piloted their big seagoing canoes across the anchorage, drawing frivolous patterns in the calm waters around the ship. Watching them from the vessel's rail were the government agents, a medical party, R.C.M.P. constables resplendent in their crimson jackets, and even a few tourists with glittering cameras slung aggressively about their craning necks.

They were engrossed in the spectacle provided by the boisterous and jovial welcome being given to the ship by the Eskimos; they were enjoying the atmosphere of this gala day which comes to most arctic outposts only once in every year.

Ship-time is the best of times to see the Eskimo, for then he wears his happiest and most carefree guise. Then he is indeed the living embodiment of the myth we have so painstakingly created in his image.

After a while some of the *Rupertsland's* passengers came ashore, and one of them stopped to talk to me. He waved his hand toward the gay throng on the beach and said:

"God! What I wouldn't give to stay right here and be an Eskimo. No problems. Lots of meat, and hunting, and nothing to worry about. Do you guess they *know* how lucky they are?"

A smart young Mountie who was also a passenger on the ship overheard the remark and added:

"It's a pretty good life they lead. The way they are, they're about the most contented people in the world."

As for me, I turned away from the most contented people in the world and walked toward another people whom the young policeman, and the tourists, did not know existed.

Beyond the trim red-and-white buildings of the trading store, beyond the neat rectangle of the R.C.M.P. barracks, I walked over the frost-shattered rocks toward six tents that clustered grayly in the distance. I went to meet again, after an absence of ten years, the men, women and children who call themselves Ihalmiut.

I had a companion on my walk, an Eskimo special constable of the R.C.M.P. He was a little dubious about my visit to the distant tents, and he tried to prepare me for what I would find there. He told me — and it was not pride of race, but pride of his association with the white police which put the edge on his voice — that the people in the six tents were a shiftless and hopeless crowd with whom nothing could be done. He was still echoing the opinions of his superiors when we came to a halt outside the first of the dirty canvas shelters. The constable called out a peremptory command. There was a stir within and a man crawled out and rose slowly to his feet, blinking against the brilliant sun. I recognized him, though that was not an easy thing to do, across the years which he had lived since last I saw him. His name was Yaha.

I spoke to him and after a time he replied — but he did not look at me. Neither did he look toward the beach where the happy Eskimos were gathered, nor toward the harbor where the great ship — such a one as he had never seen nor yet imagined — lay to her anchors. Yaha looked inland; away from the sea, into the yellowing distance of the tundra plains. He spoke when he was spoken to; but for the rest he stood as immobile as an *inukok* — those men of stone who stand upon the far ridges in the land towards which Yaha's hazed eyes stared.

We left him standing there and went on to Ohoto's tent. When Ohoto failed to obey the constable's summons, I stepped inside, past the hanging flap which shut the world away.

Ohoto sat in the center of the floor space, his legs extended straight before him and his eyes cast down. He wore an ancient woolen sweater-coat, caked with dirt and unraveled at the sleeves and hem. He gave no sign that he was aware of my presence, even when I squatted by his side and spoke his name.

The constable, who had thrust his head and shoulders into the noisome space, said loudly:

"He is a little crazy. He got hurt once. You got to yell at him."

I did not yell — instead I touched his arm; and as I did so his fingers twitched so that my gaze was drawn to them and I saw that he was clutching the weathered tine of a caribou antler, gripping it so hard that the knuckles shone almost as white as the deer bone. I looked away, and my eyes met those of his wife Nanuk, who sat, grim and corroded, staring back at me with dead black eyes.

Suddenly Ohoto raised his head. For a long moment his one living eye searched my face, and then he smiled, and in a voice unchanged from that which I had known, he spoke in English.

"Ello, Skibby."

It was the name the People had called me by a decade earlier, and his use of it helped dissipate the horror which had come upon me. I burst into talk and Ohoto listened with his head bent to one side and a half-smile on his broad lips, while I strove to recall and to restore the times that now were gone.

But he only seemed to listen; for his gaze dropped slowly until he was again staring blankly at the piece of bone in his right hand.

The constable was sympathetic with me in my distress.

"You see," he explained. "His mind gone bad. Nothing to do. We go look some other tent."

Nanuk had not spoken, nor had she relaxed a muscle of her harsh rigidity.

We went to all six tents. In some there were living people — the very young — but for the rest there was only a pallid animation that had no reality. Howmik crouched speechless with her crippled arm about her daughter's waist. Old Hekwaw mumbled amiably and pointed to a great herd of nonexistent caribou. Miki came reluctantly from his tent and looked at me for a moment — not with recognition, but with a blind, insensate hatred — and turned his back upon us.

Of them all, only Owliktuk still seemed to be aware. He asked me to enter his tent, but I could not face that. It was not dirt or stench which held me back — it was the knowledge that, once inside, I would be shut off from the world of neat white buildings, ships and airplanes, and laughing people.

So we sat outside, on the gray rocks, and Owliktuk talked. His voice was low and listless, but he could still remember things. He talked of the events of the preceding winter and of the death of men and women I had known. He ignored the presence of the special constable and it may be that he also ignored the reality of my presence, for he spoke with a steady and monotonous insistence that was proof against the interjections of the constable or against my own hesitant questions. His face was in repose, but it was the repose of total apathy.

I did not remain long during that first visit, for the plane was waiting. And it was with a sense of relief, of which I am ashamed, that I said good-by to Owliktuk. I stopped once, on the ridge beside the barracks, and I looked back at the six tents. There was not a living being to be seen. The People had vanished into the shadows of their canvas caves. Having no part in the bright world around them, they had returned into darkness to wait, as they had been waiting through the months since they had been brought to this place.

On the 27th day of February in the spring of 1958, the surviving Ihalmiut were loaded into a police aircraft at Padlei and flown to Eskimo Point, where they came under the direct aegis of the R.C.M.P. They were ordered to build igloos behind the barracks, out of direct contact with the local Eskimos. After the thaw, they were given tents; but they were still in effective isolation. They were no asset to the settlement. The ordeal which they had just passed through had left them in a condition bordering on coma.

They were fed an average of fourteen pounds of flour per family each week. Under the eye of the police they were made to work for this ration, first by shoveling snow for an airstrip on the ice, and later by carrying rocks from one part of the settlement to another — and then back again.

Late in March they were visited by two officers of the Department of Northern Affairs. The visitors found them, quite literally, starving. They were told that this was the Ihalmiuts' own fault because they were too lazy and shiftless to catch fish. Unhappily, as the visitors soon discovered, there *were* no fish available locally, but this did not alter the general judgment of the whites that the hunger of the Ihalmiut was their own fault, for they were too lazy to even try to fish.

Unimpressed, the senior official took it on himself to order a planeload of meat from the south, together with a full issue of warm clothing — for the people had nothing but rags to cover their starving bodies. This action drew much adverse criticism from the local whites, some of whom were still complaining in August that such generosity was wasted on "those arctic Irishmen" and had tended to "spoil the good natives" of the area.

The visitors further alienated the good will of the whites by insisting on investigating the Ihalmiut story firsthand, and by recording in detail the account given by each individual Eskimo. Their obvious sympathy for the Eskimo point of view irritated many of the local whites, for as one of the most important of these said:

"These inland Eskimos are unfeeling and without emotion, and they live like dogs."

This was by no means an entirely inaccurate assessment. Certainly the Ihalmiut had but few remaining outlets for emotions, and those which they still possessed were not encouraged. When some of them made a pathetic attempt to draw together in the unity evoked by a drum-dance, the tent was invaded by the police, the drum — presumed symbol of abhorrent paganism — was smashed; and they were denied even this meager anodyne in future.

The official visitors departed — but the Ihalmiut remained at Eskimo Point. The local priest, the Rev. Lionel Ducharme of the Oblate order, was sure that no one needed to feel disturbed about their fate, for he was convinced that the Ihalmiut were contented with their lot, and, as he expressed it later in a letter to a newspaper, they were both grateful and full of respect toward the R.C.M.P.

Some members of the Department of Northern Affairs did

not share his convictions and they were anxious to implement their own plans to "save" the remaining Ihalmiut. However, a combination of limited personnel and funds, together with the reluctance of government to reach a policy decision about what might be done for the Eskimos, delayed any action until the impact of another and even grimmer arctic tragedy was felt.

The Ihalmiut had not been alone in their ordeal that spring. At Garry Lake the attempt to establish a church-state among the last of the true inland Eskimos had collapsed in an atmosphere of unadulterated horror, when nineteen of the fifty-eight remaining Hanningaiormiut starved to death during February and March.

The magnitude of the disasters which had overwhelmed the Keewatin Eskimos that spring was such that it could not be adequately concealed, nor glossed over, as innumerable similar tragedies of the past had been concealed or ignored. Finally, and one suspects reluctantly, the government of Canada felt compelled to attempt some positive action to prevent the utter dissolution of the inland people. For the first time since Canada assumed the wardship of the Innuit, *laissez faire* was abandoned and a policy for Eskimo affairs was devised. It was decided that the Eskimos could only survive if they became fully assimilated into our culture, totally abandoning their own.

The rationale was succinctly expressed by a senior official when he said, "It is amply demonstrated that Eskimos cannot go on living in a state of nature. Death and disease is all they can expect under such circumstances. It is therefore imperative, and it is the desire of this government, that they be brought fully into the twentieth century as soon as possible."

At the time there appeared to be no immediate alternative to the solution proposed by the government, so it drew considerable support from concerned southerners, myself included. I supported the new policy because I was convinced that, without it, many of Canada's Eskimo peoples would simply vanish. In 1958, when the new policy was promulgated, infant mortality among the Innuit was more than 30 per cent in the first year; tuberculosis was so widespread that nearly 80 per cent of the Eskimos contracted it at some point during their all-too-short lives; the average life span of an Eskimo was under fifty years; and chronic malnutrition was the handmaiden of almost every individual from birth until the grave.

In early September of 1958 I returned to Eskimo Point just in time to see the first unfolding of the brave new policy. A rehabilitation center was to be established by the Department of Northern Affairs at Term Point on the coast of Hudson Bay not far from Rankin Inlet. It was to contain not only the Ihalmiut survivors but all the broken remnants of Eskimo groups from the whole of the Keewatin area. Here, these shattered fragments of humanity were to begin their transformation from "stone-age men" into machine-age men.

Term Point was an omen, for it was an unmitigated disaster. Autumnal gales burst over Hudson Bay while the materials and equipment for the enterprise were being off-loaded from a freighter standing-to on a dangerous lee shore. Much of the material was lost or ruined; much of what was saved was unsuitable to the land and the climate. The whole affair was a defeat for technology. As for the Eskimos, the defeat meant that they spent that winter in a make-shift camp, in a state of complete disorganization, and without the vaguest idea of what the future might portend for them.

This was something they would have to learn to live with.

In 1959 Term Point was abandoned. Some of its inmates were shipped back to Eskimo Point where they again came under the aegis of the Mission, the R.C.M.P., and the trader. The rest were moved to Rankin Inlet where another great experiment in rescuing the Eskimos was already in progress.

Under the management of a remarkable man named Andrew Easton, a small nickel mine had been opened at Rankin. Easton was an Eskimophile and a man of good intentions who prided himself on being a practical sort of fellow. He was convinced that the answer to the problem of Eskimo survival was to make use of the Innuit in the new and burgeoning exploitation of the north. To this end he prevailed upon the federal government to let him train Eskimos for mine jobs. He was given carte blanche and at first his approach seemed phenomenally successful. By midsummer of 1959 more than three-quarters of the mine employees were Eskimos, and some of them were earning wages that ran as high as $800 a month. It appeared that the Innuit were capable of making a rapid adjustment to our way of life, for they were now living in wooden houses, buying and using electrical appliances, shopping at the new Hudson's Bay Company supermarket, and even learning how to obtain credit from a newly established bank.

This apparent adaptation was so impressive that most observers, again including myself, were deluded into believing that this must indeed be the way to salvation for the Eskimos. In an article which I wrote at that time for a national magazine, I said:

"It is true, of course, that most of these things represent material benefits, and there has been a cry raised by the exponents of the old orders that the Rankin Inlet Eskimos are being changed into mere carbon copies of ourselves and are losing their age-old cultural heritage. There is but one answer to these criticisms. The Eskimo of today has only one choice open to him. He can eschew some elements of his ancient culture, become an equal citizen in our common land, and so survive; or he can remain an anachronism whose own aboriginal culture has now disintegrated to near the vanishing point — and die. Rankin Inlet has proved beyond any possibility of doubt which course the Eskimo himself prefers to follow. . . ."

Men believe what they wish to believe. I believed those words when they were written. I believed the visions that I saw . . . and was blind to the fact that they were little more than the creations of wishful thinking.

For I was wrong . . . dead wrong!

Early in the 1960's the Rankin Inlet mine closed down. The ore reserves had been small, but high grade, and the company had made a satisfactory profit. The nearly one hundred Eskimos who had been employed by the mine, and who were no longer capable of reverting to their earlier mode of life, had no choice but to go on the dole with their families. A very few of them were later shipped to distant mining towns such as Yellowknife, but they did not stay long. Yellowknife was a white man's community, and the Eskimos soon learned what the local Indians already knew so well — that their acceptance was conditional on their being content with second- or third-rate human status.

Meanwhile other Eskimos, particularly from the western arctic, had been sent south for special training courses in mining, heavy machinery handling and other technical trades. Suddenly, large sums of government money had become available to aid the Eskimos in making the transition; whereas in the past almost no funds had ever been available to help them survive in their own way of life. There were cynics, even in 1959, who equated the government's sudden and generous interest in the Eskimos with a spate of grandiose plans for the exploitation on a massive scale of the oil and mineral resources of the arctic regions, and the anticipated need for a large and highly trained local labor force.

In the event the Eskimos demonstrated that they could easily master the machine skills of our technology yet, with rare exceptions, they did not make their white employers happy. They were labeled as unreliable because they would not accept the vital necessity of being slaves to a time schedule. When an Eskimo, who had become a first-rate mechanic, decided it was time to take a week off and go seal hunting, he went seal hunting — and his employer fumed, and finally fired him. The Eskimo was required to make great accommodations to our culture, and he did so — but we were not prepared to make any meaningful accommodations either to his culture or to his nature. The results were inevitable.

By the late 1960's the great experiment in total assimilation had collapsed into chaos although then, as now, this fact was not officially admitted. Because it has never been admitted there has never been any official explanation for the failure. Yet the explanation is a simple one. In 1966 it was explained to me by one of the Hudson Bay Eskimos who had been sent to work in a gold mine at Yellowknife:

"What's the matter? I'll tell you . . . the government fellows, they came to us like white men always came to us, and they said, 'This is what you have to do.' Sometimes they said it like, 'This is what you ought to do — what is *good* for you to do.'

"Eskimo people was used to doing what white men told them. They just thought, 'Well, that's what they *say* we got to do, that's what we *got* to do.' What was wrong was nobody ever asked our people what *we* wanted to do. And if some of us tried to say, white people never listened. Just turn away, and get mad at us.

"I tell you something else. Not so many of our people believed you wanted us to work in the mine, drive the bulldozer and stuff like that to make *us* happy . . . make us rich. We know what you want anyway . . . just some Innuit to work for you up in the north so people down south get rich from our land.

"And having all that stuff — the TVs and all that stuff — it don't make our people so happy. Maybe it makes you happy, but you don't act so happy.

"Our young people now, they're different from us. They don't want to listen to white men tell them what to do anymore . . . they see how much we lose from listening to white people.

"Now they going to say, 'Why don't you listen to *us*, white man? You better start listen to us for a change!' "

In 1966 I flew the length and breadth of the Canadian arctic, stopping at almost every inhabited Eskimo settlement. They were all nearly identical in appearance: rows of shoddy pre-fabricated shanties laid out like company towns . . . or like high-grade concentration camps. The new white administrators, the teachers, nurses and police lived in elite enclaves a safe distance from the people they were supposed to be serving.

Very few of the Eskimos were employed, or even occupied. Most of them sat in their bleak shanties simply waiting. Almost all of them survived on welfare. They were already a dispossessed people — *dispossessed in their own land*.

On this journey I learned to listen. I listened to and recorded the feelings and opinions of more than a hundred Eskimos and northern Indians. One of them was Ohoto.

By then he had gone stone-blind. He was living in squalor in a plywood shack supplied by the government, at Eskimo Point. Nanuk was dead, and he was alone, totally dependent on the dole.

". . . Twenty years ago when we first met, Skibby, I told you I wanted to be *kablunak* — a white man. In my head I thought it was the best way to go on staying alive. I wanted to be like you so I could go on living . . . I tried to be like you, and now I am not living. That was foolish, eh? All of us who tried that, all dead now. Maybe you are dead too? I can touch you, but maybe you are dead too? . . . Goodby, Skibby."

Ohoto never understood . . . had never understood. . . . But in the spring of 1973 I listened to an Eskimo at Frobisher Bay, that pretentious administrative capital and showpiece of the eastern arctic where a high-rise apartment, complete with indoor swimming pool, symbolizes all that we are, and all that we have done for, and to, the people of the north. This man was young, and tough, and he knew us. He had gone to one of our universities, and had lived in our world in order to be sure that he knew us.

"I read that book you wrote — *The Desperate People*. When you stuck to the story of what happened you wrote close to the truth about us. But when you got talking about what we needed and wanted you talked bullshit! You and pretty near every other white man I ever heard. I'll tell you what we want!

"We want you whites to leave us make our own decisions. *We'll* decide how much of your phony world we have to have to stay alive. I heard so much crap about freedom when I was down south I could stuff an elephant with it! What the hell do *you* know about freedom? You *take* freedom away from people!

You used us as long as you could get any good out of it; the traders, the missionaries, the government empire-builders, the hot-shot exploiters. Now we don't go for that shit anymore.

"There's no big difference between you people and any other colonial sons-of-bitches. You don't give a frigging hell that it's *our* country — always *was* our country . . . You and your democracy! You can sure take your democracy and shove it . . . all the way!

"Just give us back the chance to live in our own country the way *we* figure out we want to live. A place to live in . . . that's what we want! Our *own* place to live in."

This is the true, the authentic, voice of the Desperate People of the Canadian north. But will we listen? And will we attempt to make amends?

It is for us to say.

Epilogue

ACROSS the northern reaches of this continent there lies a mighty wedge of treeless plain, scarred by the primordial ice, inundated beneath a myriad of lakes, cross-checked by innumerable rivers, and riven by the rock bones of an elder earth.

It is a land uncircumscribed, for it has no limits that the eye can find. It seems to reach beyond the finite boundaries of this planet. Brooding, immutable, given over to its own essential mood of desolation, it showed so bleak a face to the white men who came upon its verges that they named it, in awe and fear, the Barrengrounds.

Yet of all the things that it may be, it is not barren.

In the brief summer it is a place where curlews circle above the calling wildfowl on the ice-clear lakes. It is a place where gaudy ground squirrels whistle from the sandy casts of vanished glacial rivers; where the dun summer foxes den, and lemmings dawdle fatly in the thin sedges of the bogs. It is a place where minute flowers blaze in a microcosmic revelry, and where the thrumming of insect wings assails the greater beasts, and sends them fleeing to the bald ridge tops in search of a wind to drive the unseen enemy away. And, not long since, it was a place where the caribou

in their unnumbered hordes could inundate the land in one hot
flow of life that rose below one far horizon, and reached unbroken past the opposite one.

In all its harsh hostility it is not barren; nor has it been since
the first crawling lichens spread like a multicolored stain over
the ice-scoured rocks. And in the cold millennia since the lichens
came, life in ten thousand forms has prospered on the plains,
where the caribou became a living pulse fleshed by the other
beasts, and waiting for the day when man brought sentience into
a new world.

That world is sentient no more.

The living pulse which was the caribou flutters with the almost
imperceptible beat that speaks of dissolution.

And the great plains roll to the white horizons under the un-
seeing eyes of the stone *inukok* — the semblances of men — who
have inherited an empty land.

Appendix

THE IHALMIUT FROM 1946 TO 1958

THIS list includes all the Ihalmiut who were alive in the spring of 1946 and who were born thereafter until September 1958, divided into family groups.

As explained in the foreword, all names are the actual names of individuals, replacing the occasional pseudonyms used in *People of the Deer*. Children who later married appear twice, but the number beside their names refers back to the original family group from which they came.

Certain children are listed as "nameless." Ihalmiut children are not named until about ten days after birth; thus a child who dies in the first ten days dies without a name. Only a portion of the nameless children born in the twelve-year period are here included, for a nameless child is soon put out of memory by its parents.

The dates of birth for people born before 1946 are only approximate, since the Ihalmiut themselves keep no accurate record of the years.

One or two complete families which emigrated from the Ihalmiut area to Padlei in 1946 are not shown in this list. Individuals who remained behind when their family groups emigrated are, however, listed.

The spelling used in the list is arbitrary. Since no fixed system of writing Eskimo names exists, and since as many as ten or fifteen variants of a single name have been recorded by an equal number of whites, it is impossible to produce a standard version.

Repetition of the same name, within the same family, and applying to people of both sexes, is common practice amongst all Eskimos.

Surviving individuals, as of May 1959, are indicated by the use of italic type.

THE IHALMIUT 1946–1958

1. *Alekahaw* (b. 1932)	Living at Rankin Inlet.
2. *Kaluk* (wife, b. 1928)	Living at Rankin Inlet.
3. *Keluharut* (son, b. 1938)	Living at Rankin Inlet (an adopted son).
4. *Kowtuk* (son, b. 1942)	Living at Rankin Inlet.
5. *Ookala* (daughter, b. 1948)	Living at Rankin Inlet.
6. Nameless child (b. 1950)	Died at birth, or soon after.
7. *Oolipa* (son, b. 1954)	Living at Rankin Inlet.
8. Anarow (b. 1910)	Died of diphtheria, 1946.
9. Jatu (wife, b. ?)	Died of diphtheria, 1946.
10. Emyekuna (child, b. 1925)	Emigrated to Padlei, fate unknown.
11. Angak (b. ?)	Died, 1946, cause unknown.
12. Kahutna (daughter, b. ?)	Died of diphtheria, 1946.
13. Angleyalak (b. 1900)	Died of starvation, 1947 (2 children starved in 1944).
14. Itkuk (wife, b. ?)	Died of starvation, 1947.
15. Tiktuk (daughter, b. ?)	Married a Padliermio, fate unknown.
16. Pama (daughter, b. 1932)	Died of starvation, 1947.
17. *Anoteelik* (son, b. 1934)	Living at Rankin Inlet (see below).
18. *Kunee* (Rita) (daughter, b. 1942)	Taken to Churchill by trader, now married to Arlow, at Rankin Inlet.
19. Angolia (b. 1916)	Died of diphtheria, 1946.
20. *Tabluk* (wife, b. 1918)	Remarried Onekwaw, 1946, remarried at Eskimo Point, 1958 (see below).
21. *Alekashaw* (daughter, b. 1938)	Married Kaiyai (see below), living at Rankin Inlet.
17. *Anoteelik* (b. 1934)	Living at Rankin Inlet (see above).

22. *Aiyai* (Akjar) (wife, b. 1938)

23. *Owliktuk* (son, b. 1953) — Living at Rankin Inlet.

24. *Igyaka* (son, b. 1955) — Living at Rankin Inlet.

25. Atunga (b. 1915) — Died of diphtheria, 1946 (3 children died prior to 1946).

26. Kekwaw (mother, b. ?) — Died of diphtheria, 1946.

27. *Nanuk* (wife, b. 1916) — Married Ohoto (see below), widowed at Rankin Inlet.

28. Aljut (son, b. 1944) — Died of starvation, 1947.

29. Elaitutna (son, b. 1946) — Died of starvation, 1947.

30. Aveaduk (b. 1890) — Died of diphtheria, 1946 (wife and 3 children died prior to 1946).

31. Onikok (daughter, b. 1912) — Married Pommela, died of cancer, 1951 (see below).

32. Elaitutna (b. 1900) — Died of starvation, 1947 (2 children died prior to 1946).

33. Epeetna (wife, b. ?) — Died of starvation, 1947.

34. *Ohoto* (son, b. 1920) — Living at Rankin Inlet (see below).

35. *Kikik* (daughter, b. 1918) — Married Halo, remarried at Padlei (see below).

36. Ootek (son, b. 1923) — Killed at Henik Lake, 1958 (son of Epeetna, but adopted son of Elaitutna) (see below).

37. Halo (b. 1914) — Killed at Henik Lake, 1958 (see below) (1 child died prior to 1946).

35. *Kikik* (wife, b. 1918) — Remarried a Padliermio, living at Padlei.

38. Noahak (son, b. 1943) — Died of exposure and starvation, 1951.

39. *Belikari* (Ailouak) (daughter, b. 1946) — Living with mother at Padlei.

40. *Karlak* (son, b. 1948) — Hospitalized with tuberculosis.

41. *Annacatha* (daughter, b. 1952) — Living with mother at Padlei.

42. Nesha (daughter, b. 1954)

Died of exposure and starvation, 1958.

43. Aklaya (daughter, b. 1955)

Died of unknown cause, 1955.

44. *Noahak* (daughter, b. 1956)

Living with mother at Padlei.

45. *Hekwaw* (b. 1897)

Living at Rankin Inlet (6 children died prior to 1946).

46. Kala (wife, b. 1898)

Died of "old age" and/or pneumonia, 1950.

47. Eepuk (wife, b. ?)

Died of starvation, 1947.

48. Ohotuk (son, b. 1926)

Died of poliomyelitis, 1949.

49. *Belikari* (son, b. 1928)

Living at Rankin Inlet.

20. *Tabluk* (daughter, b. 1918)

Living at Eskimo Point (see above).

50. Pama (daughter, b. 1933)

Died of diphtheria, 1946 (adopted).

51. Homogulik (b. 1908)

Died of diphtheria, 1946 (wife and 2 children died of starvation, 1944).

52. Petow (son, b. 1924)

Died of diphtheria, 1946.

53. Kaiyai (b. 1939)

Died of gangrene and exposure, 1958.

21. *Alekashaw* (wife, b. 1938)

Widowed at Rankin Inlet.

54. *Pommela* (son, b. 1956)

Living with mother at Rankin Inlet.

55. *Boonlak* (son, b. ?)

Living with mother at Rankin Inlet.

56. Kakut (b. 1885)

Died of diphtheria, 1946 (3 or more wives and 7 children died prior to 1946).

57. Okinuk (wife, b. ?)

Remarried Katelo, died of starvation, 1947.

58. *Nanuk* (daughter, b. 1916)

Married Ohoto, living at Rankin Inlet (see below).

59. *Alektaiuwa* (son, b. 1939)

Living at Rankin Inlet with Yaha.

60. Katelo (b. 1899)   Died of starvation and/or disease, 1950 (2 wives and 7 children died prior to 1946).

    61. Oquinuk (wife, b. ?)   Died of starvation, 1947.

    62. Onekwaw (son, b. 1918)   Died of starvation and exhaustion, 1958 (see below).

    63. Kowtuk (daughter, b. 1926)   Married a Padliermio, fate unknown.

    64. Iktoluka (son, b. 1935)   Drowned in 1951.

65. Kokea (widow of Kudjuk, b. ?)   Died of diphtheria, 1946.

66. *Miki* (b. 1918)   Living at Rankin Inlet (1 child died of starvation, 1944).

    67. *Kahutsuak* (wife, b. 1920)   Living at Rankin Inlet.

    68. *Kokeeuk* (Kugiak) (daughter, b. 1940)   Living at Rankin Inlet.

    69. *Ilyungyaiuk* (son, b. 1945)   Living at Rankin Inlet.

    70. Nameless child (b. 1949)   Died, probably of poliomyelitis, 1949.

    71. *Hekwaw* (daughter, b. 1952)   Living at Rankin Inlet.

72. *Mounik* (b. 1934)   Living at Rankin Inlet.

    73. *Ookanak* (wife, b. 1940)   Living at Rankin Inlet.

    74. *Tabluk* (daughter, b. 1956)   Living at Rankin Inlet.

34. *Ohoto* (b. 1920)   Living at Rankin Inlet, blind in one eye (2 children died prior to 1946).

    75. Kekwaw (wife, b. ?)   Died of diphtheria, 1946.

    58. *Nanuk* (wife, b. 1916)   Living at Rankin Inlet.

    76. *Ilupalee* (daughter, b. 1946)   Living with parents at Rankin Inlet.

    77. Nameless child (b. 1953)   Died at birth or soon after.

78. *Kirkut* (daughter, b. 1957/58)

Living with parents at Rankin Inlet.

62. Onekwaw (b. 1918)

Died of starvation and exhaustion, 1958.

20. *Tabluk* (wife, b. 1918)

Remarried and living at Eskimo Point.

21. *Alekashaw* (daughter, b. 1938)

Daughter of Angolia-Tabluk, married Kaiyai (see above), living at Rankin Inlet.

79. *Oolie* (b. 1917)

Believed alive at Padlei (wife and 2 children died prior to 1946, later married Ootnuyuk).

36. Ootek (b. 1923)

Killed at Henik Lake, 1958 (3 children died prior to 1946).

80. *Howmik* (wife, b. 1920)

Widowed, at Rankin Inlet.

81. *Kalak* (daughter, b. 1947

Born deaf and dumb, now in institute in Winnipeg.

82. *Kooyak* (daughter, b. 1950)

Living with mother at Rankin Inlet.

83. Nameless child (b. 1952/53)

Died at birth or soon after.

84. Igyaka (son, b. 1956)

Died of starvation, 1958.

85. *Owliktuk* (b. 1912)

Living at Rankin Inlet.

86. *Nutaralik* (wife, b. 1914)

Living at Rankin Inlet.

72. *Mounik* (son, b. 1934)

Living at Rankin Inlet (see above).

22. *Aiyai* (Akjar) daughter, b. 1938)

Living at Rankin Inlet (see above).

87. *Arlow* (son, b. 1942)

Living at Rankin Inlet, married Kunee, 1959.

88. *Katelo* (son, b. 1945)

Living at Rankin Inlet.

89. Uktilohik (son, b. 1946)

Died of starvation, 1947.

90. *Tanugeak* (son, b. 1948)

Living at Rankin Inlet.

91. *Neebalnik* (son, b. 1952)

Living at Rankin Inlet.

52. Petow (b. 1924)

Died of diphtheria, 1946.

92. Kena (wife, b. ?)

Remarried to a Padliermio, fate unknown.

93. Ota (child, b. ?)   Accompanied mother, fate un-
                                          known.
94. Takwa (child, b. ?)   Died, probably of disease, 1946.
95. Homoguluk (son, b.
    1937)   Died of starvation, 1947.

96. Pommela (b. 1885)   Died, probably of starvation and
                                          old age, 1958 (note: all his chil-
                                          dren fathered by other men).
    31. Onikok (wife, b. 1912)   Died of cancer, 1951.
    97. Ikok (Itkuk) (wife, b.
        1915)   Died of poliomyelitis, 1949.
    98. Inoyuk (wife, b. ?)   Died about 1946, cause unknown.
    99. Ootnuyuk (wife, b.
        1922)   Widowed at Rankin Inlet.
    53. Kaiyai (son of Inoyuk, b.   Died of gangrene and exposure,
        1939)   1958 (see above).
    100. Angataiuk (son of Ikok,   Died of starvation and exposure,
         b. 1943)   1958.
    101. Ahto (daughter of Ikok,
         b. 1941)   Killed at Nueltin Lake, 1950.
    102. Pameo (daughter of Ikok,
         b. 1946)   Died of starvation, 1950.
    59. Alektaiuwa (son of
        Kakut, b. 1939)   Living at Rankin Inlet with Yaha.
    103. Rosie Akagalik (daugh-   Ootnuyuk's daughter, leg ampu-
         ter, b. 1945)   tated, now in foster care in
                                            Winnipeg.
    104. Rosie Enitnak (daughter,   Ootnuyuk's daughter, at Rankin
         b. ?)   Inlet.
    105. Aksak (child, b. ?)   Ootnuyuk's child, in foster care
                                            at Churchill.

106. Yaha (b. 1907)   Living at Rankin Inlet.
     107. Kooyuk (mother, b. ?)   Died of starvation, 1950.
     108. Ateshu (wife, b. 1919)   Living at Rankin Inlet.
     73. Ookanak (daughter, b.   Married at Rankin Inlet (see
         1940)   above).
     109. Itkilik (son, b. 1942)   Drowned in 1954.
     110. Nameless child (b. 1949)   Died at birth or soon after.
     111. Atkla (son, b. 1951)   Living at Rankin Inlet.

About the Author

Farley Mowat was born in Belleville, Ontario, in 1921, and grew up in Belleville, Trenton, Windsor, Saskatoon, Toronto and Richmond Hill, following his librarian father Angus Mowat's peregrinations around the country. He served in World War II from 1940 until 1945, entering the army as a private and emerging with the rank of captain. He began writing for his living in 1949 after spending two years in the Arctic. Since 1949 he has lived in or visited almost every part of Canada and many other lands including the distant regions of Siberia. He remains an inveterate traveller with a passion for remote places and peoples. He has twenty-two books to his name, which have been published in translations in over twenty languages in more than forty countries. They include such internationally known works as *People of the Deer, The Dog Who Wouldn't Be, Never Cry Wolf, Westviking, The Boat Who Wouldn't Float, Sibir* and *A Whale for the Killing.* His short stories and articles have appeared in the *Saturday Evening Post, Maclean's, Atlantic Monthly* and other magazines.